T0235591

Lecture Notes in Computer Science　　12040

More information about this series at http://www.springer.com/series/7408

Holger Hermanns (Ed.)

Measurement, Modelling and Evaluation of Computing Systems

20th International GI/ITG Conference, MMB 2020
Saarbrücken, Germany, March 16–18, 2020
Proceedings

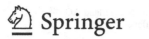 Springer

Editor
Holger Hermanns 🆔
Saarland University
Saarbrücken, Germany

Institute of Intelligent Software Guangzhou
Guangzhou, China

ISSN 0302-9743   ISSN 1611-3349   (electronic)
Lecture Notes in Computer Science
ISBN 978-3-030-43023-8   ISBN 978-3-030-43024-5   (eBook)
https://doi.org/10.1007/978-3-030-43024-5

LNCS Sublibrary: SL2 – Programming and Software Engineering

This Springer imprint is published by the registered company Springer Nature Switzerland AG
The registered company address is: Gewerbestrasse 11, 6330 Cham, Switzerland

Preface

This volume contains the proceedings of the 20th International GI/ITG Conference on Measurement, Modelling and Evaluation of Computing Systems (MMB 2020), which was held during March 16–18, 2020, at Saarland Informatics Campus in Saarbrücken, Germany, hosted by Universität des Saarlandes.

The biennial MMB conference is the major German forum covering all scientific aspects of measurement, modeling, and evaluation of computing systems. It started in the early 1980s to address quantitative system aspects. Over the decades, this topic has gained dramatically in importance and has embraced technology areas including computer architectures, communication networks, distributed systems and software, autonomous systems, workflow systems, cyber-physical systems and networks, Internet of Things, as well as highly dependable, highly performant, and highly secure systems.

This year we received 32 submissions. The technical program was composed by the Program Committee in a thorough single-blind reviewing procedure involving at least three reviewers, after intensive discussion and a careful selection process. All in all, 16 papers were selected representing the broad spectrum of methodological and applied work very well. The program was framed by three distinguished invited keynotes, providing insights into striking foundational advances, latest technological trends, and major application fields:

- "Interference Networks" by François Baccelli, Simons Chair in Mathematics and ECE at The University of Texas at Austin, USA
- "Safety Certification of Deep Learning" by Xioawei Huang, Department of Computer Science at The University of Liverpool, UK
- "Predictable Latency in Softwarized Networks" by Wolfgang Kellerer, Chair of Communication Networks at Technische Universität München, Germany

The technical program additionally offered five sessions of regular papers, covering Learning and Optimization, Networks, Performance Analytics, Markov Modelling, and Model-based Analysis, as well as a PhD presentation session. As in previous MMB conferences, two satellite workshops were organized covering highly relevant research topics:

- 5th Workshop on Network Calculus (WoNeCa5) organized by Steffen Bonndorf, Universität Bochum, Germany, and Amr Rizk, Universität Ulm, Germany
- 2020 ROCKS Workshop on Rigorous Dependability Analysis using Model Checking Techniques for Stochastic Systems, organized by Erika Ábrahám, RWTH Aachen, Germany, and Arnd Hartmanns, Universiteit Twente, The Netherlands

At the beginning of the conference, three invited tutorials were presented to the audience:

- "Modelling and Analysing Dependability with BDMP and KB3" by Marc Bouissou, Électricité de France, France
- "Clusters of Exceedances of Stochastic Processes and Their Application to Traffic Modeling and Identification Problems" by Natalia M. Markovich, Russian Academy of Sciences, Russia
- "Spreading Dynamics in Complex Networks" by Verena Wolf and Gerrit Großmann, Universität des Saarlandes, Germany

The conference was organized by the Center for Perspicuous Computing (CPEC) TRR 248, a Transregional Collaborative Research Centre of the Deutsche Forschungsgemeinschaft (grant 389792660).

As program chair and general chair, we would like to express our gratitude to all members of the Program Committee and all external reviewers for their dedicated service, for the timely provision of their valuable reviews, for maintaining the quality objectives of the conference, and for the intensive and constructive discussion. We express our sincere appreciation to Universität des Saarlandes as the conference host, to CPEC as the conference organizer, and to all members of the Local Organizing Committee of MMB 2020 for their great efforts devoted to the success of the conference. This pertains in particular to Felix Freiberger, Sabine Nermerich, Kristina Scherbaum, and Florian Schießl. We thank all the authors for their submitted contributions, all the speakers for their lively presentations, and all the participants for their contributions to interesting discussions. Finally, it is our hope that readers will enjoy these MMB 2020 proceedings and refer to them in their future research.

February 2020   Holger Hermanns
                                                                    Verena Wolf

Organization

MMB 2020 was a joint event of the German "Gesellschaft für Informatik" (GI) and the "Informationstechnische Gesellschaft im VDE" (ITG), Technical Committees MMB on Measurement, Modelling and Evaluation of Computing Systems. It was organized by CPEC, the Center for Perspicuous Computing TRR 248, a Transregional Collaborative Research Centre of the Deutsche Forschungsgemeinschaft (grant 389792660) at Saarland Informatics Campus in Saarbrücken, Germany, hosted by Universität des Saarlandes.

General Chair

Verena Wolf   Universität des Saarlandes, Germany

Program Chair

Holger Hermanns   Universität des Saarlandes, Germany, and Institute
                                     of Intelligent Software Guangzhou, China

Program Committee

Erika Abraham	RWTH Aachen University, Germany
Peter Buchholz	Technische Universität Dortmund, Germany
Hans Daduna	Universität Hamburg, Germany
Hermann de Meer	Universität Passau, Germany
Susanna Donatelli	Università di Torino, Italy
Rüdiger Ehlers	Technische Universität Clausthal, Germany
Markus Fidler	Leibniz Universität Hannover, Germany
Jean-Michel Fourneau	Université de Versailles, France
Reinhard German	Universität Erlangen, Germany
Gerhard Hasslinger	T-Systems ENPS Darmstadt, Germany
Boudewijn Haverkort	Tilburg University, The Netherlands
Thorsten Herfet	Universität des Saarlandes, Germany
Tobias Hossfeld	Universität Würzburg, Germany
William Knottenbelt	Imperial College London, UK
Samuel Kounev	Universität Würzburg, Germany
Udo Krieger	Otto-Friedrich Universität Bamberg, Germany
Wolfram Lautenschläger	Nokia Bell Labs Stuttgart, Germany
Rupak Majumdar	MPI for Software Systems, Germany
Natalia Markovich	Russian Academy of Sciences, Russia

Michael Menth	Eberhard Karls Universität Tübingen, Germany
Mohammadreza Mousavi	University of Leicester, UK
Antoine Rauzy	Norwegian University of Science and Technology, Norway
Peter Reichl	Universität Wien, Austria
Anne Remke	Westfälische Wilhelms-Universität Münster, Germany
Jens Schmitt	Technische Universität Kaiserslautern, Germany
Marielle Stoelinga	University of Twente and Radboud University, The Netherlands
Miklos Telek	Budapest University of Technology and Economics, Hungary
Dietmar Tutsch	Bergische Universität Wuppertal, Germany
Isabel Valera	MPI for Intelligent Systems, Germany
Oliver Waldhorst	Hochschule Karlsruhe – Technik und Wirtschaft, Germany
Sabine Wittevrongel	Universiteit Gent, Belgium
Katinka Wolter	Freie Universität Berlin, Germany
Lijun Zhang	Chinese Academy of Sciences, China

Award Committee Chair

Markus Siegle	Universität der Bundeswehr München, Germany

Workshop Chair

Udo Krieger	Otto-Friedrich Universität Bamberg, Germany

Local Organization

Felix Freiberger	Universität des Saarlandes, Germany
Sabine Nermerich	Universität des Saarlandes, Germany
Kristina Scherbaum	Universität des Saarlandes, Germany
Florian Schießl	Universität des Saarlandes, Germany

Additional Reviewers

Jörg Deutschmann

Juan Andres Fraire

Maciej Gazda

Fatemeh Ghassemi

Alexej Grigorjew

Johannes Grohmann

Florian Heimgärtner

Stefan Herrnleben

Jannik Hüls

David N. Jansen

Steffen Lindner

Waseem Mandarawi

Peter Osterholzer

Carina Pilch

Andreas Stockmayer

Thomas Stüber

Andrea Turrini

Florian Wamser

Abstracts of Invited Talks

Interference Networks

François Baccelli

The University of Texas at Austin, Austin, TX 78701 USA
francois.baccelli@austin.utexas.edu

Abstract. This invited talk features networks of coupled processor sharing queues in the Euclidean space, where customers arrive according to independent Poisson point processes at every queue, are served, and then leave the network. The coupling is through service rates. In any given queue, this rate is inversely proportional the interference seen by this queue, which is determined by the load in neighboring queues, attenuated by some distance-based path-loss function.

The model is a discrete version of a spatial birth and death process where customers arrive to the Euclidean space according to Poisson rain and leave it when they have transferred an exponential file, assuming that the instantaneous rate of each transfer is determined through information theory by the signal to interference and noise ratio experienced by the user.

The discrete and the continuous models will be discussed, both in finite and infinite domains. The stability condition is identified. The minimal stationary regime is built using coupling from the past techniques.

The mean queue size of this minimal stationary regime is determined in closed form using the rate conservation principle of Palm calculus. Some bounds on the tail of latency will be discussed.

In infinite domains, when the stability condition holds, for all bounded initial conditions, there is weak convergence to this minimal stationary regime; however, there exist initial conditions for which all queue sizes converge to infinity.

Joint work with Sergey Foss and Abishek Sankararaman.

Safety Certification of Deep Learning

Xiaowei Huang

University of Liverpool, UK
xiaowei.huang@liverpool.ac.uk

Abstract. Deep learning techniques have been shown successful in a number of tasks such as image classification, robotic control, and natural language processing, etc. This motivates their application to broader industrial sectors, including safety critical sectors – such as automotive sector, healthcare sector, and avionic sector, etc. – and business critical sectors – such as financial services sector. There is an urgent need to certify the safety of learning-enabled systems, i.e., systems with (deep) learning components, when such systems are increasingly deployed and interact with human operators. This talk will review some recent progresses on formal verification and coverage-guided testing, and discuss whether and how they can be utilised to support the certification of deep learning. Existing formal verification techniques – including layer-wise refinement, reduction to global optimisation, reduction to constraint-solving, etc. – are able to provide provable guarantees to the results, but may be subject to the scalability problem. Coverage-guided testing, on the other hand, is able to intensively test deep learning models with a large number of test cases generated under the guidance of coverage metrics. But research is needed to determine the relation between coverage metrics and the safety risks of deep learning. While both verification and testing can provide evidence to low-level claims, such as the robustness of a neural network for a given input, it is desirable to know how to utilise these low-level evidence to support high-level safety claims of deep learning such as the rate of failure within a number of new inputs.

Predictable Latency in Softwarized Networks

Wolfgang Kellerer◉

Chair of Communication Networks, Technical University
of Munich, Arcisstr. 21, 80333 Munich, Germany
wolfgang.kellerer@tum.de

Abstract. The trend towards softwarized networks provides ample opportunities and hence a high degree of flexibility in the way to plan and operate your communication networks [1]. Such flexibility supports the realization of novel applications with largely varying requirements. Many emerging applications pose stringent dependability requirements such as industrial communication, autonomous vehicles, telepresence and teleoperation in healthcare. In particular, ongoing research on 5G networks focuses on predictable low latency communication [2]. This raises the question to what extent softwarized networks also enable such more predictable networks. As network performance relies on the underlying switches, we have a closer look at Software-Defined Networking infrastructure and SDN switches, in particular, as enablers of softwarized networks. This work presents an empirical study of the predictability of SDN switches with a focus on latency and addresses the question of modeling of network latency with SDN switches based on Network Calculus. Therefore, we benchmark seven hardware OpenFlow switches in a first step [3]. Our measurement results reveal several unexpected and unpredictable behaviors and performance In particular, we observe unpredictable behaviors related to flow management and buffer management. We further uncover unexpected overhead introduced with conventional quality-of-service mechanisms such as priority queueing, which can lead to violations of latency guarantees. In a second step, we extend our empirical investigations to small networks with a comprehensive measurement campaign of low cost, low capacity SDN hardware switches [4]. We propose a novel measurement-based methodology that uses deterministic network calculus to derive a reliable performance model of a given switch. Our experiments with the Zodiac FX switch show that the derived models are accurate enough to actually provide deterministic end-to-end guarantees with low-cost softwarized network devices.

Keywords: Softwarized networks · Software-defined networking · SDN · Programmable switches · Measurements · Switch modeling · Latency · Predictability · Guarantees

References

1. Network Flexibility Homepage of the ERC Grant FlexNets Project. http://www.networkflexibility.org. Accessed 28 Jan 2020
2. 5G Research Hub Munich Homepage. http://www.5g-munich.de. Accessed 28 Jan 2020

3. Van Bemten, A., Deric, N., Varasteh, A., Blenk, A., Schmid, S., Kellerer, W.: Empirical predictability study of SDN switches. In: Proceedings of 15th ACM/IEEE Symposium on Architectures for Networking and Communications Systems (ANCS 2019) (2019)
4. Van Bemten, A., Deric, N., Zerwas, J., Blenk, A., Schmid, S., Kellerer, W.: Loko: predictable latency in small networks. In: Proceedings of 15th International Conference on emerging Networking EXperiments and Technologies (CoNEXT) (2019)

Contents

Performance Analytics of a Virtual Reality Streaming Model

Markus Fiedler[✉]

Department of Technology and Aesthetics, Blekinge Institute of Technology,
374 24 Karlshamn, Sweden
markus.fiedler@bth.se
https://www.bth.se/eng/staff/markus-fiedler-mfi/

Abstract. This work focuses on post-analysis of performance results by means of Performance Analytics. The results to be post-analysed are provided by a Stochastic Fluid Flow Model (SFFM) of Virtual Reality (VR) streaming. Performance Analytics implies using the Machine Learning (ML) algorithm M5P for constructing model trees, which we examine amongst others for asymptotic behaviours and parameter impacts in both uni- and multivariate settings. We gain valuable insights into key parameters and related thresholds of importance for good VR streaming performance.

Keywords: Machine Learning · M5P algorithm · Stochastic Fluid Flow Model · Asymptotic behaviour · Multivariate analysis

1 Introduction

Emerging real-time applications, such as Virtual Reality (VR) streaming, are putting high demands on network communication resources and solutions. Indeed, the chase for milliseconds demands for a good understanding of key dependencies between performance and underlying system parameters. Such dependencies might be obtained from measurements in real or simulated systems, or from analytical performance models. The latter are typically expressed by a set of equations, which have to be solved numerically. As an example, the Stochastic Fluid Flow Model (SFFM) or Anick-Mitra-Sondhi (AMS or A-M-S) Model [1] abstracts data flow and resource availability into (modulated) rate processes, thereby allowing to focus on the impact of the dynamics of the interaction between traffic demands and available resources on streaming performance. The latter is obtained from numerically solving partial differential equations that capture those dynamics. Although closed-form analytical solutions are available under specific conditions [1], performance results are typically available as numbers, the dependencies of which on system parameters are not immediately visible. Thus, *post-analysis* of such numerical performance results can identify and

---

This work was supported in part by the KK Foundation, Sweden, through the project "ViaTecH" under contract number 20170056.

H. Hermanns (Ed.): MMB 2020, LNCS 12040, pp. 1–18, 2020.
https://doi.org/10.1007/978-3-030-43024-5_1

in particular quantify fundamental dependencies on system parameters, such as asymptotic behaviours, sensitivities, relevant orders of magnitude, etc.

In this work, we are specifically interested in a potential model for Virtual Reality (VR) streaming [2], which to the best of our knowledge has not been addressed in literature so far. VR streaming should avoid buffering as much as possible in order to avoid synchronisation issues between user movements and the displayed 3D images in the VR headset. The question arises to which extent a disturbance may cause data loss, and how the intensity of the latter depends on a set of system parameters such as channel on/off-times. In particular, we explore to which extent is it possible to formulate approximate dependencies together with underlying parameter spaces, which amongst others might indicate asymptotic behaviour and scaling phenomena.

Above challenge can be tackled using the concept of *Performance Analytics* that was introduced in [3]. Performance Analytics implies the use of Machine Learning (ML) for post-analysis of (numerically obtained) *performance* results, where the notion *Analytics* suggests (semi-)automatic and robust procedures. Our specific interest lies in ML that *learns regression formulae* and the *corresponding parameter spaces* on which those regression formulae are built. To this aim, we use the *M5P* algorithm [4] that has its origins in [5]. It finds a set of *model trees*, containing regressions formulae and has so far shown to be *robust* [6] and able to outperform other ML algorithms for specific matching tasks [7]. A summary of potential benefits of Performance Analytics by M5P include:

1. Quantification of dependencies and impacts of parameters in the absence of straightforward-to-interpret closed-form formulae, and otherwise hard-to-describe and hard-to-capture behaviours (e.g. from numeric, measurement and simulation results) [6,7];
2. Identification of asymptotic behaviours [3,6];
3. Selection of parameters that are relevant to some specific behaviour (cf. Sect. 6 of this paper);
4. Delimitation of the parameter space to which a specific model applies (e.g. thresholds for asymptotic behaviours) [6].
5. Extension of the linear M5P to allow for different types of additive and multiplicative types of scaling [3].

We investigate above benefits in the context of VR streaming performance. They allow us to gain quantitative insights into the impact of key parameters of the dynamics of a wireless link onto the performance of a VR system, which exemplifies the usefulness of Performance Analytics for post-analysis of performance data. This work represents an extension of the work in [3] with specific application to VR and focus on multivariate studies.

The remainder of this paper is structured as follows. Section 2 addresses related work in the area of ML and performance evaluation. Section 3 describes the underlying Stochastic Fluid Flow Model used to generate the performance results to be analysed for asymptotic behaviours and key performance parameters, and Sect. 4 reviews the basic steps of the M5P-based Performance Analytics. We focus on such details that the underlying results can be re-generated, in order to allow the interested reader to verify the results and validate the findings. Performance Analytics of the model of the VR streaming system are performed both in a univariate and a multivariate scenario in Sects. 5 and 6, respectively. Section 7 concludes the paper.

2   Machine Learning and Performance Evaluation

Performance and its evaluation in the area of ML typically addresses high-performance and real-time analytics [8,9], focusing on the capabilities of the algorithms themselves. In the application area of network-related performance evaluation, ML algorithms have amongst others been used for data mining and classification [10–12], quality prediction and management [7,13,14] and tuning of performance models [15]. In the latter case, deep learning was used to develop a heuristic for the bounds for deterministic network calculus. Borchert et al. [13], for instance, compare several approaches for correlating QoE and technical parameters with focus on the classification performance. Torres and Liotta [14] discuss the feasibility of un-/supervised learning methods for cognitive no-reference video quality models.

References [6,7,16] show details of performance models that are *generated* by ML, which is of specific interest to us. We will first take a short glance at decision trees, and then a deeper look at model trees.

2.1   Decision Trees

Various kinds of *decision trees* that represent structured regression models that predict the value of a target based on one or several input variables, thereby implementing a tree of decisions. Leaves represent class labels, and nodes or branches represent conjunctions of features that lead to class labels. Though a commonly used tool in data mining, decision trees are widely used in ML for classification purposes [8]. Decision trees are learned during training phases and evaluated during test phases.

Random Forests (RF) denote a collection of decision trees, over which averaging is performed in order to reduce the risk of overfitting [17]. The corresponding algorithm has amongst other been applied successfully in the area of QoE modeling. The ITU-T Recommendation P.1203.3 [16] contains a machine-learned RF model in combination with a traditional parametric model.

2.2   Model Trees

Model trees are specific decision trees with linear regressions at the leaf nodes, instead of constant values as in *regression trees* [5]. The M5P algorithm [4] is an extended version based on the M5 algorithm that was originally developed by Quinlan [5]. They have shown to be able to handle large data sets with many dimensions and partially missing data, and have been applied successfully in a range of application domains.

The *decision rules* that span the model tree define a set of spaces (in the sense of multi-dimensional intervals) $\mathcal{X}_i$, stretching from an exclusive lower bound to an inclusive upper bound:

$$x_i^{\mathrm{lo}} = \inf\{x \in \mathcal{X}_i\}\,;\;\; x_i^{\mathrm{up}} = \max\{x \in \mathcal{X}_i\} \tag{1}$$

This notation implies the possibility for several variables, a.k.a. *features*, to change within the same *sub-space* $\mathcal{X}_i$ of the parameter or *feature space*, over which a set of *linear models* (LM) is constructed by the M5P algorithm:

$$\mathrm{LM}\,i : y_i(\boldsymbol{x}) = a_i + \boldsymbol{b}_i^{\mathbf{T}}\,\boldsymbol{x} = a_i + \sum_{j=1}^{n} b_{i,j}\,x_j \quad \forall \boldsymbol{x} = [x_1 \ldots x_k] \in \mathcal{X}_i \tag{2}$$

As input, the M5P algorithm requires a matrix with n columns containing the features x_j, and an additional column with the results y to be modeled. Before we review the necessary steps, we describe how those results y are obtained.

3   Stochastic Fluid Flow Model

Stochastic Fluid Flow Models (SFFM) have been designed for modeling streaming data, when single packet occurrences are less important to capture than the performance of the flow itself [1], which may be impeded by temporal capacity issues due to resource overbooking [1] and/or temporary unavailability [18]. In this work, we apply the SFFM to Virtual Reality (VR) streaming, with voluminous and regular data flows that might be affected by above disturbances.

3.1   Model Parameters

We assume a SFFM with a constant inflow and a variable channel rate, which is typical for wireless systems. Once the sender-side buffer fills up, data is lost and cannot be displayed at the receiver side, which in case of VR video implies freezing. Using Kendall-like notation, we describe the system as an **RP/ⅢRP/K** system:

1. Source with Constant-Rate **P**rocess[1], rate $R = r$
2. Channel with variable capacity $C = c > r$ during its on-phase, and $C = 0$ during its off phase(s). Its capacity dynamics are modelled by two independent/superposed **I**nterrupted **R**ate **P**rocesses (a.k.a. on-off processes [1]):
   (a) One slow *fading process* with exponential state durations [19], parameterised by average on time $\mathbf{E}T_{\mathrm{on},1}$ and average off time $\mathbf{E}T_{\mathrm{off},1}$. This process is a first-order approximation of the measured temporal interruption behaviour of a VR link, where a wireless headset (HTC Vive with TPCAST wireless link running at 60 GHz) was exposed to movements yielding reproducible disruptions [2].

---

[1] RP is a typical notion in the fluid context, and not to be confused with a deterministic discrete arrival process, denoted by D in Kendall notation.

(b) One fast *Automatic Repeat reQuest (ARQ) process* with exponential state durations [20], parameterised by average (ARQ) on time $\mathbf{E}T_{on,2}$ and average (ARQ) off time $\mathbf{E}T_{off,2}$. This process is assumed in anticipation of a future shared use of the so far exclusive wireless link [2], e.g. in a future 5G/6G scenario.

The rates of these server-side processes multiply ("Π") each other [21] in the way that only if both IRPs are in the corresponding on phase, the channel is available ($C = c$). As soon as one of the sub-IRPs is off, the channel becomes unavailable ($C = 0$), which entails buffering at the sender side.

3. Buffer of limited size K, entailing loss in case of overflow. Such a buffer may represent a deadline at the receiver end that has to be kept, otherwise the late data has to be discarded. Fortunately, the SFFM scales in both data and time units, which means that suitable units can be chosen. We henceforth use one millisecond (ms) as time unit, and scale the data unit such that $r = 1$ data unit/ms. Thus, we can specify the buffer size in time units:

$$k = K/r \qquad (3)$$

which relates it immediately to a corresponding deadline.

Two-state RP/IRP(/K) systems have been addressed before, a.o. in [18,22]. Here, we are extending the analysis towards two IRPs in the channel, yielding four states and allowing for the inclusion of different dynamics. In the forthcoming subsections, we shortly review the analysis of four-state RP/ΠIRP/K and of two-state RP/IRP/K systems, both providing numerical results for the loss probability P_L.

3.2 Fluid Flow Analysis of the Four-State System

For the resulting four-state system, we obtain a state space as follows:

$$S \in \begin{cases} s = 1 : \text{Channel on} \\ s = 2 : \text{Channel off (ARQ)} \\ s = 3 : \text{Channel off (Fading)} \\ s = 4 : \text{Channel off (ARQ and fading)} \end{cases} \qquad (4)$$

The corresponding drift values d_s represent the rates at which the buffer changes unless the buffer gets full (in case of a positive drift $d_s = r$ when the channel is off) or empty (in case of a negative drift $d_s = r - c$ when the channel is on). The drift values are arranged in the *drift matrix* as follows:

$$\mathbf{D} = \begin{bmatrix} r - c & 0 & 0 & 0 \\ 0 & r & 0 & 0 \\ 0 & 0 & r & 0 \\ 0 & 0 & 0 & r \end{bmatrix} \qquad (5)$$

With the transition rates $\lambda_i = 1/\mathbf{ET}_{\text{on},i}$ and $\mu_i = 1/\mathbf{ET}_{\text{off},i}$, the *generator matrix* is obtained as

$$\mathbf{M} = \begin{bmatrix} -\lambda_1 - \lambda_2 & \mu_2 & \mu_1 & 0 \\ \lambda_2 & -\lambda_1 - \mu_2 & 0 & \mu_1 \\ \lambda_1 & 0 & -\lambda_2 - \mu_1 & \mu_2 \\ 0 & \lambda_1 & \lambda_2 & -\mu_1 - \mu_2 \end{bmatrix} \tag{6}$$

The vector of the *compound probability distribution* $\mathbf{F}(x)$ of the buffer content X with components $F_s(x) = \Pr\{X \le x \land S = s\}$ is given by

$$\mathbf{F}(x) = \sum_{q=0}^{3} a_q \boldsymbol{\varphi}_q \exp(z_q x) \tag{7}$$

where the *Eigensystem* $\{z_q, \boldsymbol{\varphi}_q\}$ is obtained from

$$z_q \mathbf{D} \boldsymbol{\varphi}_q = \mathbf{M} \boldsymbol{\varphi}_q \tag{8}$$

At this point, we assume that there is no vanishing drift (i.e. $d_s \ne 0 \,\forall s$). The *coefficients* a_q are obtained from the boundary conditions that the buffer is never full when the channel is on and never empty when the channel is off, i.e.

$$F_1(K) = \Pr\{S = 1\} \tag{9}$$
$$F_s(0) = 0, \; s \in \{2, 3, 4\} \tag{10}$$

Finally, the *loss probability* is equivalent to the probability that the buffer is full (which implies loss at data rate r) and obtained as

$$P_{\text{L}} = \sum_{s=2}^{4} \left(\Pr\{S = s\} - \lim_{x \to K} F_s(x) \right) \tag{11}$$

Such result is generally available numerically, not in closed form.

3.3   Fluid Flow Analysis of the Two-State System

The two-state system only has one process that governs the rates of the channel; the state space is given by

$$S \in \left\{ \begin{matrix} s = 1 : \text{Channel on} \\ s = 2 : \text{Channel off} \end{matrix} \right\} \tag{12}$$

The drift matrix is obtained as

$$\mathbf{D} = \begin{bmatrix} r - c & 0 \\ 0 & r \end{bmatrix} \tag{13}$$

and the generator matrix as

$$\mathbf{M} = \begin{bmatrix} -\lambda & \mu \\ \lambda & -\mu \end{bmatrix} \tag{14}$$

The compound probability distribution $\boldsymbol{F}(x)$ is given by

$$\boldsymbol{F}(x) = \sum_{q=0}^{1} a_q \boldsymbol{\varphi}_q \exp(z_q x) \qquad (15)$$

with the Eigensystem $\{z_q, \boldsymbol{\varphi}_q\}$ according to (8). The non-vanishing Eigenvalue is a.k.a. the dominant Eigenvalue z_{dom}. Again, we assume that there is no vanishing drift (i.e. $d_s \neq 0 \,\forall s$). The coefficients a_q are obtained from the boundary conditions

$$F_1(K) = \Pr\{S = 1\} \qquad (16)$$
$$F_2(0) = 0 \qquad (17)$$

Finally, the loss probability is obtained as

$$P_{\text{L}} = \Pr\{S = 2\} - \lim_{x \to K} F_2(x) \qquad (18)$$

Although this result may be given in closed form, the corresponding terms are rather voluminous [22] and thus difficult to analyse. In the sequel, we will see how Performance Analytics simplifies such analysis, reducing the complexity of tedious terms to a set of simple linear equations, together with the corresponding feature subspaces on which those equations are defined.

4   Steps in Performance Analytics

4.1   Data Generation

For the different systems, we obtain loss probabilities P_{L} numerically from Eqs. (11) and (18). In other settings, such results could have been obtained from measurements in real or simulated systems. While in *univariate* scenarios, one feature will be varied at a time (usually the buffer size), the *multivariate* scenarios will address changes of several parameters (beyond the buffer size).

4.2   Data Preparation and Transformations

In order to capture different types of effects by parameter values or by their orders of magnitude, we can extend the M5P-supported linear approximations through transformations on abscissae (feature value/order of magnitude) and/or ordinate (resulting value/order of magnitude) as shown below. The following expressions apply to any base B. If post-analysis results are to be compared to analytical results, e.g. from [1], $B = e$ is a natural choice. On the other hand, if orders of magnitude are of interest, $B = 10$ may convey the most valuable messages.

– *Logarithmic* (order of magnitude w.r.t. base B on abscissa; additive relationship)

$$\text{LM}\,i : y_i(\boldsymbol{x}) = a_i + \sum_{j=1}^{k} b_{i,j} \, \log_B(b(x_j)) \tag{19}$$

– *Exponential* (order of magnitude w.r.t. base B on ordinate; multiplicative relationship)

$$\text{LM}\,i : \log_B(y_i(\boldsymbol{x})) = a_i + \sum_{j=1}^{k} b_{i,j} \, x_j \Rightarrow y_i(\boldsymbol{x}) = B^{a_i} \prod_{j=1}^{k} B^{b_{i,j}\,x_j} \tag{20}$$

– *Power* (order of magnitude w.r.t. base B on both abscissa and ordinate; multiplicative relationship)

$$\text{LM}\,i : \log_B(y_i(\boldsymbol{x})) = a_i + \sum_{j=1}^{k} b_{i,j} \, \log_B(x_j) \Rightarrow y_i(\boldsymbol{x}) = B^{a_i} \prod_{j=1}^{k} x_j^{\,b_{i,j}} \tag{21}$$

The in-data for M5P (features on the abscissa, results to be approximated on the ordinate) needs to be transformed, and the results from (2) to (21) need to be interpreted accordingly, which will be demonstrated in Sects. 5 to 6.

4.3 Implementation

We obtain our model trees from applying the Weka [23] M5P implementation, with the following settings:

– minimal number of instances per leaf = 1
– number of decimal places = 8
– batch size = 100
– all other options (useUnsmoothed, unpruned, saveInstances, doNotCheckCapabilities, debug, buildRegressionTree) = false

This M5P implementation uses the whole data set as training set for constructing the reported model tree, which is natural to the descriptive analytics problem at hand, for which overfitting is not an issue.

4.4 Validation

Besides the numbers of instances and rules, as well as the run time of the algorithm, Weka reports a set of statistics, of which we confine ourselves to *correlation coefficient R*, *root mean square error* (RMSE) and *root relative squared error* (RRSE). Above statistics depend on the selected *validation method*. As recommended by [4,5,7], 10-fold cross-validation has been applied. Indeed, reference [6] has revealed rather small differences between different validation methods for the matching task at hand.

5   Univariate Performance Analytics

5.1   Analytics of an RP/ΠIRP/K System

We analyse the behaviour of the loss probability w.r.t. one variable feature, the buffer size. We choose parameters as shown in Table 1, where the case of a vanishing buffer – a specific feature of the SFFM – has been included as far as possible.

Table 1. Feature and parameter list for the RP/ΠIRP/K system.

Feature	Parameter	Min.	Max.	Step	Note
x_1	$ET_{on,1}$		1 min		
x_2	$ET_{off,1}$		60 ms		Fading [2]
x_3	$ET_{on,2}$		1 ms		
x_4	$ET_{off,2}$		1 ms		ARQ
x_5	k	0 ms	100 ms	0.1 ms	1001 values (lin, exp)
		0.1 ms	100 ms	0.1 ms	1000 values (log, pow)
y	P_L		from (11)		

Naturally, the fading process acts on a much slower time scale than the ARQ process. We assume a capacity of $c = 10r$. Due to the chosen ARQ parameters – representing an artificial and a rather unfortunate case – the effective channel capacity is upper-bounded to $c_{eff} < 5r$. We use the four transformations described in Sect. 4.2, in order to highlight the switch from values to orders of magnitudes, and to investigate both additive and multiplicative relationships between parameters as shown in (2), (19), (20) and (21). This provides us with four datasets in total, to which we apply the M5P algorithm with the settings shown in Sect. 4.3. We first take a look at the overall matching performance, shown in Table 2.

Table 2. Application of M5P to the RP/ΠIRP/K system with different underlying transformations.

Type	x_i	y	Instances	Rules	R^2	RMSE	RRSE
linear	lin	lin	1001	11	0.9727	0.0126	33.7 %
exp.	lin	log	1001	18	0.9722	0.1158	9.6 %
log.	log	lin	1000	3	0.9873	0.0063	18.6 %
power	log	log	1000	21	0.9958	0.0480	9.3 %

All cases have a similar performance in terms of correlation in common, at the expense of rather large trees (with one exception in the logarithmic case), as compared to the more coarse example in [3]. Taking the structure of the solution (7) into account, we turn our attention towards the exponential case. Table 3 shows an excerpt of the model tree, for $B = e$, using the local approximations

$$LM\,i : \ln(P_{\mathrm{L}}(k)) = a_i + b_i k\,,\ \ k \in]k_i^{\mathrm{lo}}, k_i^{\mathrm{up}}] \tag{22}$$

Table 3. Model tree based on an exponential transformation (20) with $B = e$.

LM i	k_i^{lo}	k_i^{up}	a_i	b_i
LM 1	**0 ms**	**0.35 ms**	**-1.5064**	**-0.7366/ms**
LM 2	0.35 ms	0.85 ms	-1.5067	-0.7357/ms
:	:	:	:	:
LM 4	1.35 ms	1.85 ms	-1.5118	-0.7300/ms
LM 5	1.85 ms	2.25 ms	-1.5375	-0.7156/ms
:	:	:	:	:
LM 8	3.65 ms	4.15 ms	-1.5475	-0.7120/ms
LM 9	4.15 ms	4.65 ms	-1.8966	-0.6273/ms
:	:	:	:	:
LM 12	5.15 ms	5.65 ms	-1.9481	-0.6165/ms
LM 13	5.65 ms	6.15 ms	-2.3323	-0.5497/ms
LM 14	6.15 ms	6.65 ms	-2.3489	-0.5470/ms
LM 15	6.65 ms	7.65 ms	-2.4965	-0.5249/ms
LM 16	7.65 ms	11.15 ms	-5.7011	-0.1104/ms
LM 17	11.15 ms	20.05 ms	-6.5998	-0.0334/ms
LM 18	**20.05 ms**	**100 ms**	**-6.8711**	**-0.0169/ms**

5.2   Asymptotic Behaviours of RP/IRP/K Subsystems

In Table 3, we can clearly distinguish two asymptotic behaviours w.r.t. the buffer size, one for small buffer sizes towards the ordinate ($i \leq 4, k \leq 1.85$ ms), and the other one for large buffer sizes ($i = 18, k > 20.05$ ms).

ARQ Subsystem. We investigate a two-state RP/IRP/K system with the ARQ-related parameters $\mathbf{ET}_{\mathrm{on},2} = \mathbf{ET}_{\mathrm{off},2} = 1$ ms and $c = 10r$ as before. The dominant Eigenvalue (cf. Sect. 3.3) amounts to $z_{\mathrm{dom}} = -0.8889$/data unit, equivalent to -0.8889/ms w.r.t. normalisation (3). The same Eigenvalue appears in the original RP/ΠIRP/K system. On the other hand, the approximation is less steep, cf. $b_1 = -0.7366$/ms in Table 3, which might be improved by reducing the step size or using a fine-grained multiplicative scaling of k.

Fading Subsystem. We now take a look at a two-state RP/IRP/K system with the ARQ-related parameters $\mathbf{E}T_{\text{on},1} = 1\,\text{min}$, $\mathbf{E}T_{\text{off},1} = 60\,\text{ms}$ and $c = 10r$. The dominant Eigenvalue (cf. Sect. 3.3) amounts to $z_{\text{dom}} = -0.0167/\text{data unit}$, due to (3) equivalent to $-0.0167/\text{ms} = -1/\mathbf{E}T_{\text{off},1}$, i.e. the negative reciprocal average ARQ off time. This value is almost matched by $b_{18} = -0.0169/\text{ms}$ in Table 3, which means that the asymptotic behaviour is well-captured by the M5P.

6   Multivariate Performance Analytics

So far, we have been investigating the dependency of a single parameter, the buffer size k. In this subsection, we study cases in which several parameters are varied. We use the base $B = 10$, in order to facilitate insights into applicable orders of magnitude.

6.1   ARQ

As we are mostly interested in the loss behaviour for small buffer sizes in the RP/ΠIRP/K case, we confine ourselves to $k \leq 10\,\text{ms}$, and leave the fading-related parameters $\mathbf{E}T_{\text{on},1}$ and $\mathbf{E}T_{\text{off},1}$ untouched. Yet, the latter parameters impact the result towards larger buffer sizes, cf. Sect. 6.2.

Variation of Average ARQ On Time and Buffer Size. We vary the parameters as stated in Table 4. M5P produces a model tree with 30 nodes (not shown for sake of brevity) with $R^2 = 0.9956$, RMSE $\simeq 0.077$ and RRSE $\simeq 9.4\%$.

Table 4. Feature and parameter list for an RP/ΠIRP/K system with varied average ARQ on time and buffer size; $\mathbf{E}T_{\text{on},1} = 1\,\text{min}$, $\mathbf{E}T_{\text{off},1} = 60\,\text{ms}$.

Feature	Parameter	Min.	Max.	Factor	Note
x_1	$\mathbf{E}T_{\text{on}}$	1 ms	100 ms	$10^{0.1}$	21 values
x_2	$\mathbf{E}T_{\text{off}}$		1 ms		
x_3	k	0.1 ms	10 ms	$10^{0.1}$	21 values
y	$\log_{10}(P_{\text{L}})$		from (11)		441 values

We observe that the weights $b_{i,1}$ and $b_{i,3}$ are negative, correctly indicating a decrease of loss as the average ARQ on time and the buffer size grow. The absolute weights of the buffer are (much) larger than the corresponding absolute weights of the average on times: $|b_{i,3}| > |b_{i,1}|$. For instance, LM 1 is given by

$$\log_{10}(P_{\text{L}}) = -0.266 - 0.1264\,\mathbf{E}T_{\text{on},2}/\text{ms} - 0.4123\,k/\text{ms} \qquad (23)$$
$$k \leq 0.45\,\text{ms} \ \wedge \ \mathbf{E}T_{\text{on},2} \leq 1.79\,\text{ms}$$

That means that the contribution of each extra millisecond of buffer time to the order of magnitude of the loss probability is more than three times stronger than an extra millisecond in the average ARQ on time. As the latter grows, its impact becomes even smaller, cf. LM 13:

$$\log_{10}(P_L) = -1.037 - 0.0133\,ET_{on,2}/ms - 0.4003\,k/ms \tag{24}$$
$$k \le 0.45\,ms \;\wedge\; ET_{on,2} \le 28.37\,ms$$

Indeed, the weight $b_{13,3} = -0.0133/ms$ in (24) is only about $1/10$ of the weight $b_{1,3} = -0.1264/ms$ in (23). Furthermore, the weight of the buffer decreases as the buffer grows; while $|b_{1..18,3}| > 0.3/ms$ for $k \le 2.84\,ms$, we observe $|b_{26..30,3}| < 0.1/ms$ for $k > 5.66\,ms$.

Variation of Average ARQ Off Time and Buffer Size. We vary the parameters as stated in Table 5. M5P produces a model tree with 15 nodes (not shown for sake of brevity), $R^2 = 0.9845$, RMSE $\simeq 0.17$ and RRSE $\simeq 17.7\%$.

Table 5. Feature and parameter list for an RP/IIIRP/K system with varied average ARQ off time and buffer size; $ET_{on,1} = 1\,min$, $ET_{off,1} = 60\,ms$.

Feature	Parameter	Min.	Max.	Factor	Note
x_1	ET_{on}		1 ms		
x_2	ET_{off}	0.1 ms	1 ms	$10^{0.1}$	11 values
x_3	k	0.1 ms	10 ms	$10^{0.1}$	21 values
y	$\log_{10}(P_L)$		from (11)		231 values

We observe that the weights $b_{i,2}$ are now positive, correctly indicating a growth of loss as the average off time increases. The absolute weight of the average ARQ on time is larger than the corresponding weight buffer size: $|b_{i,2}| > |b_{i,3}|$. The most frequent case (45 of 231 instances) is that of LM 11, given as follows:

$$\log_{10}(P_L) = -2.8631 + 0.496\,ET_{off,2}/ms - 0.0512\,k/ms$$
$$k > 1.42\,ms \;\wedge\; ET_{off,2} \le 0.28\,ms \tag{25}$$

Here, the impact of the average ARQ off time on the order of magnitude of the loss probability is almost ten times as big as that of the buffer size ($b_{11,2} = 0.496/ms$ as compared to $b_{11,3} = -0.0512/ms$). In other words, a growth of the average ARQ off time by a small amount would need to be compensated by a ten-fold increase in the buffer size.

Variation of Average ARQ On Time, Off Time and Buffer Size. We vary the parameters as stated in Table 6. M5P produces a model tree with 25 nodes (not shown for sake of brevity), $R^2 = 0.9887$, RMSE $\simeq 0.13$ and RRSE $\simeq 15.2\%$.

Table 6. Feature and parameter list for an RP/ПIRP/K system with varied average ARQ on time, off time and buffer size; $\mathbf{ET}_{\text{on},1} = 1\,\text{min}$, $\mathbf{ET}_{\text{off},1} = 60\,\text{ms}$.

Feature	Parameter	Min.	Max.	Factor	Note
x_1	$\mathbf{ET}_{\text{on}}$	1 ms	10 ms	$10^{0.2}$	6 values
x_2	$\mathbf{ET}_{\text{off}}$	0.1 ms	1 ms	$10^{0.2}$	6 values
x_3	k	0.1 ms	10 ms	$10^{0.2}$	11 values
y	$\log_{10}(P_{\text{L}})$		from (11)		396 values

In most cases, we observe $|b_{i,2}| > |b_{i,3}| \gg |b_{i,1}|$, meaning that the average ARQ off time has the strongest impact, followed by the buffer size and the average ARQ on time. This is a.o. visible in the most frequent (96 of 396 instances) LM 21, given as:

$$\log_{10}(P_{\text{L}}) = -2.7709 - 0.0196\,\mathbf{ET}_{\text{on},2}/\text{ms} + 0.6347\,\mathbf{ET}_{\text{off},2}/\text{ms} - 0.0708\,k/\text{ms}$$
$$k > 2.05\,\text{ms} \wedge \mathbf{ET}_{\text{off},2} \leq 0.52\,\text{ms} \tag{26}$$

Thus, we can conclude that the average ARQ off time plays a crucial role for the order of magnitude of loss, difficult to compensate with a larger buffer.

6.2 Fading

As we are interested in the asymptotic impact of the fading, we confine ourselves to the RP/IRP/K subsystem. We also take advantage of the SFFM:s scaling options and choose a time unit (TU) related to the average off time, which gives immediate insight in the orders of magnitude relevant to the asymptotic behaviours.

Variation of Average On Time and Buffer Size. We vary the parameters and obtain the model tree as stated in Table 7, with $R^2 = 0.9281$, RMSE $\simeq 2.85$ and RRSE $\simeq 37.2\%$.

Let us take a closer look at that model tree, whose LMs are represented by the rows of the lower sub-table in Table 7, with corresponding intervals of features (spanning the relevant sub-spaces) in column 2 and 3, and parameters of the LMs in columns 4–6, respectively.

We observe that there is a certain dependency on the average on time until the buffer gets about one order of magnitude larger than the average off time. In case of an even larger buffer, the average on time looses its influences on both decision and approximation, i.e. the asymptotic behaviour is purely dominated by the buffer size, as seen from LM 3.

Variation of Average Off Time and Buffer Size. We assume a constant average on time of 100 TU and the remaining parameters as shown in Table 8. The application of the M5P results in a model tree with 19 rules, with $R^2 = 0.9767$, RMSE $\simeq 0.93$ and RRSE $\simeq 22.3\%$.

Table 7. Feature and parameter list for an RP/IRP/K system with varied average on time and buffer size, and obtained model tree based on the exponential transformation (20) with $B = 10$.

Feature	Parameter	Min.	Max.	Factor	Note
x_1	$\mathbf{E}T_{\mathrm{on}}$	1 TU	10000 TU	$10^{0.1}$	41 values
x_2	$\mathbf{E}T_{\mathrm{off}}$		1 TU		
x_3	k	0.01 TU	100 TU	$10^{0.1}$	41 values
y	$\log_{10}(P_{\mathrm{L}})$		from (18)		1681 values

LM i	Bounds for $\mathbf{E}T_{\mathrm{on}}$	Bounds for k	a_i	$b_{i,1}$	$b_{i,3}$
LM 1	≤ 112.95 TU	≤ 11.30 TU	-0.7221	-0.0168/TU	-0.4233/TU
LM 2	> 112.95 TU	≤ 11.30 TU	-2.5871	-0.0002/TU	-0.4326/TU
LM 3	any	> 11.30 TU	-6.2873	$\simeq 0$/TU	-0.2447/TU

Table 8. Feature and parameter list for an RP/IRP/K system with varied average off time and buffer size

Feature	Parameter	Min.	Max.	Factor	Note
x_1	$\mathbf{E}T_{\mathrm{on}}$		100 TU		
x_2	$\mathbf{E}T_{\mathrm{off}}$	1 TU	100 TU	$10^{0.1}$	21 values
x_3	k	1 TU	100 TU	$10^{0.1}$	21 values
y	$\log_{10}(P_{\mathrm{L}})$		from (18)		441 values

The model tree, which is omitted for sake of brevity, consists of approximation formulae and decision rules with both $\mathbf{E}T_{\mathrm{off}}$ and k involved, from which no regular behaviour can be seen.

Variation of Average On and Off Times. We assume a constant buffer size of 100 TU and the remaining parameters as shown in Table 9, and obtain a four-rule model tree shown in the same table with $R^2 = 0.9005$, RMSE $= 4.1$ and RRSE $= 43.5\%$. The decisions in the tree only depend on the average off time, while the average on time hardly contributes to the approximations. Thus, the performance is dominated by the average off time and its relation to the (constant) buffer size. The smaller the average off time, the more effect the buffer has, the less the loss and the steeper the decline becomes.

Variation of Average On, Off Time and Buffer Size Our final example addresses the variation of all three features, which is reported in Table 10, together with relevant parts of the obtained 74-rule model tree with $R^2 = 0.954$, RMSE $\simeq 1.7$ and RRSE $\simeq 30\%$.

Table 9. Feature and parameter list for an RP/IRP/K system with varied average on time and average off time, based on the exponential transformation (20) with $B = 10$ ($b_{i,3} = 0$).

Feature	Parameter	Min.	Max.	Factor	Note
x_1	$\mathbf{ET}_{\mathrm{on}}$	100 TU	10000 TU	$10^{0.1}$	21 values
x_2	$\mathbf{ET}_{\mathrm{off}}$	1 TU	100 TU	$10^{0.1}$	21 values
x_3	k		100 TU		
y	$\log_{10}(P_{\mathrm{L}})$		from (18)		441 values

LM i	Bounds for $\mathbf{ET}_{\mathrm{off}}$	a_i	$b_{i,1}$	$b_{i,2}$
LM 1	[1.00 TU, 7.13 TU]	-28.0964	0/TU	3.3202/TU
LM 2	]7.13 TU, 11.20 TU]	-10.6264	-0.0002/TU	0.4440/TU
LM 3	]11.30 TU, 22.54 TU]	-7.788	-0.0002/TU	0.1967/TU
LM 4	]22.54 TU, 100.00 TU]	-4.0067	-0.0002/TU	0.0361/TU

Table 10. Feature and parameter list for an RP/IRP/K system with varied average on time, off time and buffer size, based on the exponential transformation (20) with $B = 10$; a_i and $b_{i,1}$ not shown for sake of brevity.

Feature	Parameter	Min.	Max.	Factor	Note
x_1	$\mathbf{ET}_{\mathrm{on}}$	1 TU	100 TU	$10^{0.1}$	21 values
x_2	$\mathbf{ET}_{\mathrm{off}}$	1 TU	100 TU	$10^{0.1}$	21 values
x_3	k	10 TU	100 TU	$10^{0.1}$	11 values
y	$\log_{10}(P_{\mathrm{L}})$		from (18)		4851 values

LM i	Bounds for $\mathbf{ET}_{\mathrm{off}}$	Bounds for k	$b_{i,2}$	$b_{i,3}$
LM 3–6	[1.00 TU, 1.42 TU]	]14.22 TU, 17.90 TU]	3.0003/TU	-0.1337/TU
LM 9–12	[1.00 TU, 1.13 TU]	]17.90 TU, 28.37 TU]	3.3962/TU	-0.2561/TU
LM 13–16	]1.13 TU, 1.42 TU]	]17.90 TU, 28.37 TU]	3.3962/TU	-0.2374/TU
LM 17–20	[1.00 TU, 1.42 TU]	]28.37 TU, 35.72 TU]	5.5299/TU	-0.1337/TU
LM 21–24	]1.42 TU, 1.79 TU]	]17.90 TU, 28.37 TU]	1.8721/TU	-0.1793/TU
LM 27–30	]1.42 TU, 1.79 TU]	]28.37 TU, 35.72 TU]	2.7299/TU	-0.1033/TU
LM 52–57	]2.84 TU, 3.57 TU]	]71.26 TU, 100.0 TU]	1.1246/TU	-0.0762/TU

When investigating that model tree, it becomes obvious that a lot of neighbouring intervals share the same coefficients $b_{i,1}$ and $b_{i,2}$. This occurs when rather short average off times coincide with rather large buffer sizes, which is the typical asymptotic regime of this kind of system.

From the model trees of the multivariate cases, we observe that the average off time $\mathbf{E}T_{\text{off}}$ often appears in conjunction with the buffer size k, where $k/\mathbf{E}T_{\text{off}} \gg 1$ fosters asymptotic behaviour [1]. On the other hand, it also clarifies that the average on time $\mathbf{E}T_{\text{on}}$ plays a minor role in the corresponding decisions and approximation formulae; in many cases, that feature is simply suppressed from the corresponding formulae.

If fading were not present, similar observations would even hold for the ARQ subsystem, as it is of the same kind (RP/IRP/K) as the fading subsystem, just with different dynamics with a shorter TU.

7   Conclusions

In this work, we have shown how to apply Performance Analytics for investigating asymptotic behaviour and the impacts of key parameters in a Virtual Reality (VR) streaming scenario with both ARQ and fading impacts.

The M5P Machine Learning algorithm used for Performance Analytics provides us with straightforward-to-interpret model trees with linear models and related feature subspaces. These models help us to identify parameters of relevance and their quantitative impacts on (the order of magnitude of) the risk for data loss or deadline violation.

We observe that the ARQ dominates for small buffer sizes, while fading takes over control of the loss performance for larger buffer sizes. As the buffer size grows beyond the average off time, asymptotic scaling becomes obvious, with a decay rate of the reciprocal average off time, which is the key parameter. At the same time, impacts of other parameters, e.g. the average on time, vanish. This regime is not of very much interest for VR operations with its strict delay requirements. Yet, it is important to minimise the risk for fading, as once it happens, it becomes obvious that it can hardly be mitigated within a reasonable time horizon.

In the area of small buffer sizes or short deadlines, the average ARQ off time plays a major role – one more millisecond may increase the loss probability by almost one order of magnitude – and its impact is not easily mitigated by increasing the buffer size. Similar as in the fading case, the average ARQ on time has a minor impact on the loss performance. It is thus mandatory to keep outages due to resource competition as short as possible.

Encouraged by the quantitative insights to VR streaming provided by Performance Analytics that were presented in this paper, future work will include more in-depth studies using this powerful tool in various fields and for various applications.

References

1. Anick, D., Mitra, D., Sondhi, M.: Stochastic theory of a data-handling system with multiple sources. Bell Syst. Tech. J. **61**(8), 1871–1894 (1982)
2. Fiedler, M., Zepernick, H.-J., Kelkkanen, V.: Network-induced temporal disturbances in virtual reality applications. In: Proceedings 2019 11th International Conference on Quality of Multimedia Experience (QoMEX), Berlin, Germany, June 2019
3. Fiedler, M.: Performance analytics by means of the M5P machine learning algorithm. In: Proceedings 31st International Teletraffic Congress (ITC), Budapest, Hungary, August 2019
4. Wang, Y., Witten, I.H.: Induction of model trees for predicting continuous classes. In: Poster Papers of the 9th European Conference on Machine Learning (1997)
5. Quinlan, R.J.: Learning with continuous classes. In: Proceedings 5th Australian Joint Conference on Artificial Intelligence, Singapore, pp. 343–348 (1992)
6. Fiedler, M., Chapala, U., Peteti, S.: Modeling instantaneous Quality of Experience using machine learning of model trees. In: Proceedings 2019 11th International Conference on Quality of Multimedia Experience (QoMEX), Berlin, Germany, June 2019
7. Casas, P., Wassermann, S.: Improving QoE prediction in mobile video through machine learning. In: Proceedings 2017 8th International Conference on the Network of the Future (NOF), pp. 1–7 (2017)
8. Osman, A., El-Refaey, M., Elnaggar, A.: Towards real-time-analytics in the cloud. In: Proceedings 2013 IEEE Ninth World Congress on Services, Santa Clara, CA, June/July 2013
9. Maheshwar, R.C., Haritha, D.: Survey on high performance analytics of bigdata with apache spark. In: Proceedings 2016 International Conference on Advanced Communication Control and Computing Technologies (ICACCCT), pp 721–725 (2016)
10. Casas, P., Mazel, J., Owezarski, P.: MINETRAC: mining flows for unsupervised & semi-supervised classification. In: Proceedings 23rd International Teletraffic Congress (ITC), San Francisco, CA, pp. 87–94, September 2011
11. Morichetta, A., Bocchi, E., Metwalley, H., Mellia, M.: CLUE: clustering for mining web URLs. In: Proceedings 28th International Teletraffic Congress (ITC), Würzburg, Germany, pp. 286–294, September 2016
12. Montieri, A., Ciuonzo, D., Aceto, G., Pescapé, A.: Anonymity services Tor, I2P, JonDoym: classifying in the dark. In: Proceedings 29th International Teletraffic Congress (ITC), Genua, Italy, pp. 81–89, September 2017
13. Borchert, K., Hirth, M., Zinner, T., Constantin, D.: Correlating QoE and technical parameters of an SAP system in an enterprise environment. In: Proceedings 28th International Teletraffic Congress (ITC), Würzburg, Germany, pp. 34–36, September 2016
14. Torres Vega, M., Liotta, A.: Cognitive real-time QoE management in video streaming services. In: Proceedings 30th International Teletraffic Congress (ITC), Vienna, Austria, pp. 123–128, September 2018
15. Geyer, F., Carle, G.: The case for a Network Calculus heuristic: using insights from data for tighter bounds. In: Proceedings 30th International Teletraffic Congress (ITC), Vienna, Austria, pp. 43–48, September 2018

16. ITU-T Recommendation P.1203.3: Parametric bitstream-based quality assessment of progressive download and adaptive audiovisual streaming services over reliable transport - Quality integration module. International Telecommunication Union, January 2019. https://www.itu.int/rec/T-REC-P.1203.3/en. Accessed 3 Apr 2019
17. Ho, T.K.: Random decision forests. In: Proceedings 3rd International Conference on Document Analysis and Recognition, Montreal, QC, pp. 278–282, August 1995
18. Bosman, J.W., van der Mei, R.D., Nunez-Queija, R.: A fluid model analysis of streaming media in the presence of time-varying bandwidth. In: Proceedings 24th International Teletraffic Congress (ITC), Cracow, Poland, September 2012
19. Akin, S., Fidler, M.: Backlog and delay reasoning in HARQ system. In: Proceedings 27th International Teletraffic Congress (ITC), Ghent, Belgium, pp. 185–193, September 2015
20. Jain, I.K., Kumar, R., Pawar, S.: Driven by capacity or blockage? A millimeter wave blockage analysis. In: Proceedings 30th International Teletraffic Congress (ITC), Vienna, Austria, pp. 153–159, September 2018
21. Fiedler, M., Carlsson, P., Nilsson, A.: Voice and multi-fractal data in the Internet. In: Proceedings 26th Annual Conference on Local Computer Networks (LCN), Tampa, FL, November 2001
22. Fiedler, M., Popescu, A., Yao, Y.: QoE-aware sustainable throughput for energy-efficient video streaming. In: Proceedings 2016 IEEE International Conference on Sustainable Computing and Communications (SustainCom), Atlanta, GA, pp. 493–500, October 2016
23. Frank, E., Hall, M.A., Witten, I.H.: The WEKA Workbench. Online Appendix for "Data Mining: Practical Machine Learning Tools and Techniques", 4th edn. Morgan Kaufmann, Burlington (2016)

To Fail or Not to Fail: Predicting Hard Disk Drive Failure Time Windows

Marwin Züfle[(⊠)], Christian Krupitzer, Florian Erhard, Johannes Grohmann, and Samuel Kounev

Software Engineering Group, University of Würzburg, Würzburg, Germany
{marwin.zuefle,christian.krupitzer,johannes.grohmann,
samuel.kounev}@uni-wuerzburg.de, florian.martin.erhard@gmail.com,
https://descartes.tools

Abstract. Due to the increasing size of today's data centers as well as the expectation of 24/7 availability, the complexity in the administration of hardware continuously increases. Techniques as the Self-Monitoring, Analysis, and Reporting Technology (S.M.A.R.T.) support the monitoring of the hardware. However, those techniques often lack algorithms for intelligent data analytics. Especially, the integration of machine learning to identify potential failures in advance seems to be promising to reduce administration overhead. In this work, we present three machine learning approaches to (i) identify imminent failures, (ii) predict time windows for failures, as well as (iii) predict the exact time-to-failure. In a case study with real data from 369 hard disks, we achieve an F1-score of up to 98.0% and 97.6% for predicting potential failures with two or multiple time windows, respectively, and a hit rate of 84.9% (with a mean absolute error of 4.5 h) for predicting the time-to-failure.

Keywords: Failure prediction · S.M.A.R.T. · Machine learning · Labeling methods · Classification · Regression · Cloud Computing

1 Introduction

Large IT companies like Google, Amazon, Microsoft, and IBM have millions of servers worldwide. The administration of those servers is an expensive and time-consuming task. Especially unexpected crashes of servers, e.g., due to hard disk failures, can result in unavailable services and data loss. Hence, hardware is usually equipped with data collection mechanisms to observe the current state.

One such example is the Self-Monitoring, Analysis, and Reporting Technology (S.M.A.R.T.) [21]. This technology uses sensors to gather information about the current state of hard disk drives (HDDs) and solid-state drives (SSDs). S.M.A.R.T. also provides an overview of the current state of the drives including vendor-specific thresholds that indicate a current malfunction. However, it misses intelligent analysis and linking of the different parameters. Especially, predictive analytics would help to identify potential faults or crashes in advance,

© Springer Nature Switzerland AG 2020
H. Hermanns (Ed.): MMB 2020, LNCS 12040, pp. 19–36, 2020.
https://doi.org/10.1007/978-3-030-43024-5_2

can eliminate delays resulting from unexpected issues and, thus, increase reliability in Cloud Computing. Further, as it enables warning ahead of a failure, it can support administration, e.g., it offers the potential to guarantee the presence of a backup of the data and the availability of a substitute device.

In this paper, we provide three machine learning based approaches to predict disk failures in advance. Leveraging this method, data center providers can identify their disk drives with imminent failures at an early stage and replace them to avoid unexpected downtime and data loss. Our contributions are threefold:

- A comparison of data preparation steps for binary classification of disk failures in near future.
- A random forest approach for predicting the time window of a disk failure.
- A regression based approach for continuous time-to-failure prediction.

We show the applicability of those approaches in a case study with real data collected from 369 HDDs equipped with S.M.A.R.T. The results are promising: The application of oversampling improves the predictive quality of the binary classifier with an accuracy of 97.642%, the multi-class classification of time windows achieves a multi-class accuracy of 97.628% and downscaled to two classes an accuracy of even 98.885%, while the time-to-failure regression achieves an average hit rate of about 84.9% (with a mean absolute error of only 4.5 h).

The remainder of the paper is structured as follows: Next, Sect. 2 introduces the topics HDD monitoring (see Sect. 2.1) as well as machine learning based on random forest (see Sect. 2.2). Subsequently, Sect. 3 summarizes the current state-of-the-art in predicting disk failures and delineates our contribution. Section 4 presents our three approaches for disk drive failure prediction. Afterwards, Sect. 5 describes the results of the case study for evaluating the applicability of our approaches. Finally, Sect. 6 discusses the evaluation findings and concludes the paper with an outlook on future work.

2   Background

This section contains the necessary background information on hard disk drive monitoring and random forest, which is used in this paper.

2.1   Hard Disk Drive Monitoring

Failure Indicators. Monitoring internal HDD parameters to improve the reliability was first implemented in HDDs by IBM in 1992 [21]. IBM named this system Predictive Failure Analysis. Compaq, Seagate, Quantum, and Conner together integrated another monitoring system called IntelliSafe just a few years later [17]. In 1995, Seagate aimed to create a version that is compatible also with other hardware manufacturers. Therefore, IBM, Quantum, Western Digital, and Seagate cooperated to develop a novel HDD monitoring system based on IntelliSafe and Predictive Failure Analysis. The result of this collaboration was the Self-Monitoring, Analysis, and Reporting Technology (S.M.A.R.T.) [21].

This technology is used as a monitoring system in most HDDs and nowadays also SSDs. Here, several internal parameters and operations, e.g., head flying height, spin-up time, and drive calibration retry count, are stored during runtime. Today, most drive manufacturers include the S.M.A.R.T. system for drive monitoring. However, each drive manufacturer can define its own set of attributes to monitor and thresholds for these parameters that should not be exceeded. Yet, there is still a subset of S.M.A.R.T. attributes that most drive manufacturers monitor in common, e.g., spin-up time, read error rate, and start/stop count.

Types of Failures. Failures of HDDs can be separated into two types: (i) predictable and (ii) unpredictable failures. The predictable failures occur due to slow mechanical processes like wear. Since the S.M.A.R.T. technology only uses thresholds of individual parameters, it can only detect the slow degradation effects caused by predictable mechanical failures. According to Seagate [21], mechanical and thus mostly predictable failures make up about 60% of failures. Therefore, the detection rate based solely on S.M.A.R.T. thresholds is not sufficient. In contrast, unpredictable failures usually emerge rather spontaneously. The reasons for such unpredictable failures are typically of an electronic nature or abrupt physical failures. Although using only the manufacturer thresholds does not cover both types of failures, a study by Google [18] shows that some S.M.A.R.T. attributes, e.g., (offline) uncorrectable sector count and reallocation event count, are strongly correlated to HDD failures.

2.2 Random Forest Models

Random forest is a machine learning method which uses the concept of ensemble learning. It was first introduced by Breiman and Cutler [4] and builds up on a former version of Ho [12]. Ensemble learning methods use the concept of the "wisdom of the crowd". That is, these methods combine a large number n of uncorrelated models to derive a final outcome. Typically, ensemble learning methods create many weak learners[1] and fuse their outcomes to derive a model with high predictive power, i.e., a strong learner. The two most common ways of creating and combining such weak learners are boosting and bagging. While boosting aims at iterative improvement of the models by focusing on the instances that were wrongly classified in the previous iteration, bagging generates many individual models and provides a result that is derived by majority decision of the models' predictions [3]. Random forest belongs to the category of bagging ensemble learners. As weak learners, random forest creates decision trees based on the training data. Subsequently, random forest aggregates the individual predictions of the decision trees to produce a final prediction.

By applying the ensemble technique, random forest overcomes the main disadvantage of single decision trees, i.e., their tendency to overfit the training data and therefore generalize rather poorly [12]. However, to prevent overfitting,

---

[1] Weak learners are classification methods that correlate rather weakly with the true classification, while strong learners correlate very well with the true classification.

random forest has to ensure that the decision trees do not correlate with each other. An initial approach to reach this goal was introduced by Ho [12]. She proposed to use only randomly selected features for model learning of each decision tree. Breiman and Cutler [4] built up on this so-called random decision forest as they introduced the bagging approach. Using bagging, not only the features are selected randomly but also the training samples themselves. That is, for each of the n decision trees, a subset of all training data is sampled with replacement[2] and then the feature space of each sample is also sampled randomly.

Random forest can be parameterized to perform either classification (binary or multi-class) or regression. In terms of classification, the final prediction is the class with the most individual predictions of the decision trees. For regression, the individual predictions are combined using the arithmetic mean.

3   Related Work

The prediction of HDD failures is not only an important task for cloud providers, but also an interesting research area for the scientific community. This field of research arose especially due to the introduction of S.M.A.R.T., which simplified the data collection and thus formed the basis for approaches of statistical and machine learning as well as of artificial intelligence.

The most common approach found in literature is binary classification. The main focus of the papers following this approach is to determine whether an HDD will fail within a certain period of time or not. Botezatu et al. [2] propose such an approach based on informative downsampling, regularized greedy forests, and transfer learning. While Shen et al. [22] apply an approach based on part-voting random forest, Xiao et al. [25] present a mechanism for predicting HDD failures based on an online random forest so that the model can evolve as new data arrives. An algorithm to predict these failures using the multiple-instance learning framework combined with naive Bayesian classifier is introduced by Murray et al. [16]. Sun et al. [23] propose a CNN-based approach to predict HDD failures as well as memory failures. For this purpose, Sun et al. also designed a new loss function to handle the imbalanced training instances effectively. In contrast, Zhao et al. [28] treat the data as time series to construct Hidden Markov Models and Hidden Semi-Markov Models.

Hamerly and Elkan [11] model the failure prediction task as an anomaly detection approach. To this end, Hamerly and Elkan introduce two models. The first model is based on a mixture model of naive Bayes submodels with expectation-maximization and the second one applies a naive Bayes classifier to detect the anomalies. Wang et al. [24] also propose an approach based on anomaly detection and failure prediction. Therefore, Wang et al. apply Mahalanobis distance, Box-Cox transformation, and generalized likelihood ratio tests.

Pitakrat et al. [19] compare various machine learning methods with regard to their binary HDD failure classification performance. Aussel et al. [1] conduct a study assessing the performance of support vector machines, random forests,

---

[2] Sampling with replacement means that instances can be selected multiple times in the same sample.

and gradient boosted trees as well as the impact of feature selection. Similar to these works, dos Santos Lima *et al.* [20] evaluate the performance of several recurrent neural models with shallow and deep architectures.

To not only predict whether an HDD will fail or not, some researchers apply the binary classification repeatedly with different failure time windows to provide more information about the time horizon of the predicted failure [14,15,29]. Li *et al.* [14,15] propose a classification approach based on decision trees and an algorithm to estimate the health degree of the HDD using regression trees. Zhu *et al.* [29] present a backpropagation neural network approach and a support vector machine based model for the prediction of imminent failures.

While Chaves *et al.* [7] present an approach to estimating the time-to-failure as a continuous variable using a Bayesian network, Yang *et al.* [27] introduce an approach based on linear regression. An approach to predict the health status of HDDs using a recurrent neural network is proposed by Xu *et al.* [26].

In distinction to the existing work, we compare the performance of different data preparation steps, i.e., oversampling techniques, for the binary classification of upcoming failures. In addition and contrary to most of the approaches presented, we explicitly model the time-to-failure in time windows and predict it by applying multi-class classification using only a single model. Finally, we assess the impact of pre-filtering the training data for regression model learning.

4   Approaches for HDD Failure Level Prediction

This paper aims at three major failure prediction aspects based on S.M.A.R.T. measurements. First, we compare three binary classification alternatives with different preprocessing steps. Second, the time-to-failure is predicted using multi-class classification. Therefore, a new labeling strategy is applied to generate meaningful target values. In a third approach, regression is used to predict the time-to-failure as a continuous value.

4.1   Binary Classification of Failing HDDs

To perform a binary classification task, we create two distinct classes. Therefore, all instances with a time-to-failure of one week or less receive the class label 0. The remaining S.M.A.R.T. data instances get the class label 1. This labeling procedure was also performed by Pitakrat *et al.* [19]. Although Pitakrat *et al.* performed a broad comparison of different machine learning methods, they did not assess the impact of preprocessing techniques. For this purpose, we apply three different ways of training the machine learning model: (I) binary classification without further data preparation (Unmodified), (II) binary classification with Enhanced Structure Preserving Oversampling (ESPO) as oversampling technique, and (III) binary classification using Synthetic Minority Oversampling Technique (SMOTE) as oversampling mechanism. We apply random forest as machine learning method since it is typically comparatively fast for model learning and prediction, robust against overfitting, and can handle multiple classes efficiently[3]. In addition, random forest achieved very good and robust results in the comparison of machine learning methods in Pitakrat *et al.* [19].

Unmodified. In the binary classification approach without further preprocessing steps, we pass the S.M.A.R.T. measurement instances along with their label to random forest to learn a model that represents the training data. After model learning, we provide the learned model with unseen instances to predict whether the instance of the new HDD indicates a future failure or not.

ESPO. Dealing with imbalanced data is a non-trivial task for machine learning methods. In this context, imbalance means that the training data contains significantly more instances of one class (majority class) than of the other class (minority class). This often results in biased models that tend to overestimate towards the majority class. In our case, the number of instances of the class representing HDDs that fail within the next week is much smaller. There are two common ways to deal with such class imbalances: undersampling and oversampling. Undersampling discards instances of the majority class to reach a balance in the number of class instances. Oversampling, in contrast, creates new instances of the minority class based on existing instances. In our approach, we use oversampling instead of undersampling, since removing majority class instances would reduce the size of the training data set and typically decrease the quality of the model[4]. In this second alternative, we apply Enhanced Structure Preserving Oversampling (ESPO) for oversampling. ESPO synthetically generates new instances of the minority class on the basis of multivariate Gaussian distribution [6]. To this end, ESPO estimates the covariance structure of the minority class instances and regularizes the unreliable eigenspectrum [6]. Finally, ESPO extends the set of minority class instances by maintaining the main covariance structure and by generating protection deviations in the trivial eigendimensions [6]. After oversampling the minority class, we apply the same model learning procedure as in alternative (I). However, this alternative offers the machine learning method more training data and with regard to the two classes approximately equally distributed training data.

SMOTE. This alternative is similar to alternative (II), but it uses Synthetic Minority Oversampling Technique (SMOTE) instead of ESPO as oversampling technique. SMOTE creates new instances of the minority class by combining instances that lie close to each other in the feature space [8]. To this end, SMOTE determines the nearest neighbours of each instance of the minority class. Subsequently, it takes a random subset of these neighboring instances and computes

---

[3] The handling of multiple classes is not explicitly required for comparing data preparation for binary classification. However, it is necessary for multi-class classification in Sect. 4.2 and to maintain comparability between the approaches.

[4] This does not apply if the data set is sufficiently large to still be large enough after undersampling.

the differences between their features and the feature of the respective instance. The feature difference is weighted with a random number between 0 and 1. Finally, SMOTE adds the resulting weighted difference to the features of the considered instance and provides this as new instance of the minority class [8].

4.2   Classification of Multiple Failure Levels

Failure Level Labeling. To predict future failures in multiple levels, a new target variable needs to be defined. For this purpose, we changed the failure variable of the original data and used the new failure label as target variable. In the original data, the failure label is 0 if the HDD is running and only changes to 1 if the HDD stops due to a failure, i.e., the time-to-failure is zero. Since we want to predict multiple failure levels, other class labels are required. Therefore, we define a set of relevant classes, each representing a different failure level: 0, (0,1], (1,2], (2,5], (5,12], (12,24], (24,48], (48,72], (72,96], (96,120], (120,144], (144,168], (168,∞). Thus, each of these labels represents the interval of the time-to-failure in hours. The last class label (168,∞) indicates that no failure is expected within the next week. If, for example, the random forest model predicts label 48, the failure is expected after 24 h at the earliest (i.e. after the next smaller class label), but no later than 48 h. For the sake of simplicity and readability, in the following, we will refer to each of these classes only with its upper limit, e.g., we will refer to the label (24,48] as 48.

Model Learning. After calculating the new class labels based on the time-to-failure, we pass the S.M.A.R.T. attributes as features to random forest with the newly created labels as target variable. Thereby, the random forest model learns not only whether the HDD will soon fail or not, but also the time-to-failure in discretized form. This extends the binary classification (cf. Sect. 4.1) to a multi-class scenario where each class represents a specific time window in which the predicted failure is to be expected.

4.3   Regression for Time-to-Failure Prediction

Applying the binary classification of Sect. 4.1 only provides predictions on whether an HDD is likely to fail within the next week or not. The multi-class classification approach in Sect. 4.2 extends the provided information by delivering a time window, i.e., the predicted class, within the failure is expected to occur. However, all these predictions are only discretized.

To obtain continuous predictions about the time-to-failure, regression must be used instead of classification since classification can only predict a discrete output that must be included in a specified set of classes. In addition, the output class must also be present in the training set so that the model can learn the correlation between the features and the output class. Regression, in contrast, can predict any continuous value based on the input features. This allows regression models to predict values that are not included in the training set.

We implemented two alternatives of time-to-failure regression using random forest: (i) using all available data to learn the random forest regression model (Naive) and (ii) train the random forest regression model exclusively on the training instances where the failure occurs during the next 168 h (Pre-Filtering). Then, we apply the random forest regression models only on the measurements where a failure will occur within the next week. To retrieve this information, the approaches of Sect. 4.1 or Sect. 4.2 can be used, for example. The idea of pre-filtering the training set to HDDs that actually fail within the next week aims to focus the regression model on failing devices. For intact HDDs, a time-to-failure regression does not make sense, because if there is no indicator for an imminent failure yet, it cannot be distinguished whether the HDD will last another year or two years, for example. Therefore, the time-to-failure can only be guessed. By pre-filtering the data set, we explicitly focus our model on the relevant part of the data in order to achieve a more precise prediction.

5   Evaluation

We implemented the approaches in R using the libraries randomForest [5], OSTSC [10], and unbalanced [9]. First, this section describes the evaluation design. Then, the achieved predictive qualities of the binary and multi-class classification approaches are provided. Afterwards, the performances of the regression models are presented and, finally, the runtimes required for model training are compared for all approaches.

5.1   Evaluation Design

To assess the performance of our classification and regression models, we use a data set consisting of 369 HDDs[5]. This data set was first used by Murray et al. [16]. Although the data set encompasses 64 S.M.A.R.T. features for each instance, we only include 25 in our experiments. Many of the excluded parameters are constant during the entire measurement period and, thus, do not contain any information on the health status of the HDD. The time-to-failure is of course excluded for the classification tasks and used as target variable for the regression task. The remaining 25 features included in the remaining data set are FlyHeight5-12, GList1-3, PList, ReadError1-3, ReadError18-20, Servo1-3, Servo5, Servo7-8, and Servo10. The reduced feature set was also used by Pitakrat et al. for their comparison of machine learning methods. Of the 369 HDDs included in the data set, 178 did not fail during the measurement period, while 191 suffered a critical failure. This large number of failed HDDs is due to consumers sending in their failed HDDs containing the S.M.A.R.T. parameters of the past several weeks. Thereby, the number of defective and intact HDDs is fairly balanced in this data set. However, the data set contains continuous, i.e., approximately two-hourly, measurements of each HDD. This results in a total

---

[5] HDD data set: http://dsp.ucsd.edu/~jfmurray/software.htm.

amount of 68411 measurement instances. Since we do not only predict for each HDD whether it will fail some day in the future, we predict the time-to-failure for each measurement instance of the S.M.A.R.T. parameters. Yet, this procedure results in an unbalanced data set. Figure 1 shows a histogram of the distribution of the time-to-failure classes. For this purpose, the time-to-failure classes are shown on the horizontal axis and the number for each time-to-failure class on the vertical axis. The figure clearly shows the dominance of the last class, i.e., the class indicating that there will be no failure within the next 168 h. Furthermore, it can be seen that especially the classes 0 to 5 are very small with only 260 to 653 instances. For binary classification, the class indicating an imminent failure within the next 168 h comprises 23749 instances, while the class indicating no failure within the next 168 h consists of 44662 instances.

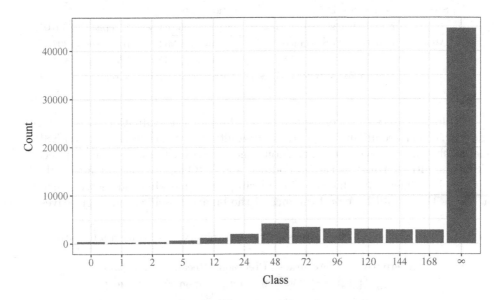

Fig. 1. Histogram of the distribution of failure classes.

In accordance with the literature, we use a split of approximately 80:20 for model training and model testing. That is, about 80% of all data is used to learn the model, while the model is evaluated on the remaining about 20% of the data. Since a single experiment alone is not significant, we perform the experiment 25 times to reduce the random distortion, as most of the techniques and methods applied are based on random numbers.

Although a comparison with existing approaches would be interesting, the reported metrics cannot be compared since the approaches were executed on different data sets (real world and synthetic) –without handling the class imbalance adequately– which affects the evaluation metrics significantly. In addition, the authors presented in Sect. 3 have not made their code publicly available, hence, it was not possible to reproduce their measurements in our setting.

5.2 Binary Failure Prediction

To ensure reproducibility, Table 1 summarizes the parametrization of the applied methods for the comparison of binary classification random forest models. We set the number of decision trees generated to 100 and the number of features that are randomly selected as candidates for each split to 5 for all three alternatives.

Table 1. Used libraries and methods along with the parametrization for the binary classification random forest models. Alternative (I) is without oversampling, (II) applies ESPO for oversampling, and (III) uses SMOTE to oversample the minority class.

Alternative	Library:Method	Parameters
(I) Unmodified	randomForest:randomForest()	ntree = 100, mtry = 5, replace = TRUE
(II) ESPO	OSTSC:OSTSC()	ratio = 1.0, r = 1.0
	randomForest:randomForest()	ntree = 100, mtry = 5, replace = TRUE
(III) SMOTE	unbalanced:ubBalance()	type = "ubSMOTE", percOver = 300, percUnder = 150, k = 5
	randomForest:randomForest()	ntree = 100, mtry = 5, replace = TRUE

Table 2 presents the average achieved values for the evaluation metrics accuracy, precision, recall, and F1-score. The results show that alternative (II) ESPO yields the highest accuracy, precision, and F1-score. Only in terms of recall, ESPO is outperformed by the unmodified and SMOTE approaches, although all approaches differ only slightly. Considering all four evaluation metrics, ESPO achieves the overall best performance of the binary classification alternatives.

Table 2. Average achieved values of the three binary classification alternatives.

Alternative	Accuracy	Precision	Recall	F1-Score
(I) Unmodified	97.472%	94.347%	96.993%	95.649%
(II) ESPO	**97.642%**	**94.913%**	96.970%	**95.928%**
(III) SMOTE	95.734%	89.086%	**96.995%**	92.869%

As Table 2 only shows the average values and not the variation within the 25 replications, Fig. 2 illustrates the performances using box plots. To this end, the horizontal axis presents the evaluation metrics, while the vertical axis depicts the achieved values. The orange, blue, and purple colored boxes describe the (I) approach without oversampling, the (II) ESPO oversampling approach, and the (III) SMOTE oversampling approach, respectively. Again, the figure shows that the unmodified and ESPO approaches clearly outperform SMOTE in all metrics besides recall. Regarding recall, all three approaches yield approximately the same value with only marginal variation within the replications. The highest variation can be seen for the metric precision. Here, the interquartile range, i.e., the difference between the third and first quartiles, shows the largest value.

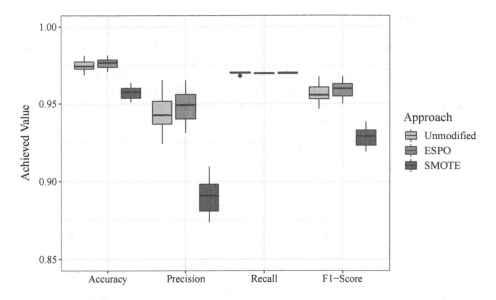

Fig. 2. Performance of the binary classification alternatives for each evaluation metric. (Color figure online)

5.3 Failure Level Classification

In contrast to binary classification, we set the number of classification trees to $n = 500$ because predicting multiple classes is more difficult than distinguishing between only two classes. Table 3 shows the average confusion matrix over all 25 runs. The confusion matrix clearly shows that most values are on the diagonal and therefore most instances are correctly predicted. In addition, for the failure classes, most false predictions are predicted in the neighboring classes. This means that the upcoming failure is detected, only the time windows are missed by a few hours up to one day. Thus, these wrongly predicted classes are uncritical in practice since the failure is nevertheless predicted with a relatively accurate time horizon. Moreover, it can be seen that the actual time-to-failure classes 1, 2, and 5 cannot be predicted as accurately as the others. This is due to the fact that there are only very few training instances for these classes and the temporal difference between these classes is very short. However, the rightmost column shows the number of cases in which the HDD failed in the respective time window, but our multi-class approach did not predict a failure within the next week. This column also contains some instances, which can be explained by the fact that the S.M.A.R.T. parameters cannot cover all aspects that can lead to an HDD failure [21], e.g., sudden electronic or physical impacts.

To summarize the quality of the random forest multi-class classification model, it achieves an average micro-F1-score of 97.628%. The micro-F1-score is the sum of instances on the diagonal (highlighted) divided by the total number of instances in the confusion matrix. It should be noted that for multi-class classification, the micro-F1-score is equal to the multi-class accuracy.

Table 3. The confusion matrix for the multi-class classification approach. The rows show the actually observed (Ob) time-to-failure classes, while the columns present the predicted (Pr) ones. The value in each cell illustrates the number of instances predicted for that particular set of observed and predicted class labels. The highlighted cells indicate the correctly predicted instances. The second cell from the left in the third row, for example, shows a single instance that is predicted as "a failure will occur within the next hour", while the failure actually occurred in the time window of one to two hours after the measurement.

Pr \\ Ob	0	1	2	5	12	24	48	72	96	120	144	168	∞
0	67	0	0	0	0	0	0	0	0	0	0	0	2
1	0	35	0	0	4	2	9	0	0	0	0	0	0
2	0	1	12	0	0	2	0	0	0	0	0	0	2
5	0	0	0	52	24	17	1	0	0	0	0	0	2
12	0	0	0	0	185	14	2	0	0	0	0	0	8
24	0	0	0	0	17	339	21	0	0	0	0	0	12
48	0	0	0	0	0	6	773	10	0	0	0	0	18
72	0	0	0	0	0	0	12	740	22	0	0	0	24
96	0	0	0	0	0	0	0	6	768	15	0	0	24
120	0	0	0	0	0	0	0	0	14	752	6	0	24
144	0	0	0	0	0	0	0	0	0	20	762	8	29
168	0	0	1	0	0	0	0	0	0	0	16	729	66
∞	0	0	1	1	0	1	0	1	1	0	1	5	14143

As the micro-F1-score of this multi-class approach cannot be directly compared with the F1-scores obtained in Sect. 5.2, we downscaled the multiple classes to the same two classes presented in Sect. 5.2. That is, we merge all classes except ∞ into one big class, i.e., the class that indicates an upcoming failure within the next 168 h. This way, the classes match those used in Sect. 5.2, which allows us to compare them. However, since ESPO achieved the best values, Fig. 3 shows the comparison of the ESPO approach with the downscaled multi-class approach in terms of box plots. Again, the evaluation metrics accuracy, precision, recall, and F1-score are depicted on the horizontal axis, while the achieved values of ESPO and downscaled multi-class approach are shown on the vertical axis. The blue and red boxes represent the ESPO and downscaled multi-class results, respectively. The figure shows that the downscaled multi-class approach yields even better results regarding accuracy (98.885% vs. 97.642%), precision (99.818% vs. 94.913%), and F1-score (98.019% vs. 95.928%). Yet, the binary classification with ESPO oversampling achieves a little higher recall (96.970% vs. 96.283%). This fact demonstrates that the ESPO approach, on the one hand, detects more failed HDDs. On the other hand, it shows that ESPO also predicts more good HDDs as failed, i.e., ESPO has a higher false positive rate. In numbers, our downscaled multi-class approach achieves a false positive rate of only 0.07% while ESPO shows a value of 2.09%. The false positive rates of the other two binary classification approaches are even higher. The detection of more defective HDDs with a higher false positive rate can be useful if the costs for false alarms are not relevant. However, in cases where false alarms lead to high costs, a more conservative model is advantageous since it detects almost as many failing HDDs and produces less costs for unnecessary HDD replacements.

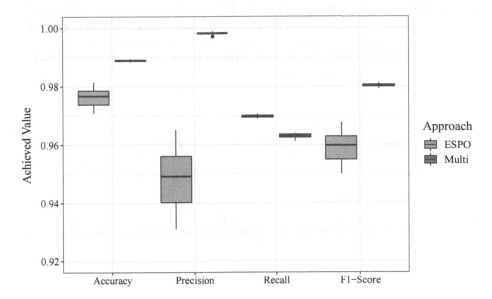

Fig. 3. Comparison of the best binary classification approach (ESPO) and the multi-class classification approach downscaled to two classes. (Color figure online)

5.4 Time-to-Failure Regression

Similar to the evaluation of the multi-class classification approach, we set the number of decision trees to $n = 500$. Figure 4 depicts the achieved hit rate, mean absolute error (MAE), and root mean square error (RMSE) for both regression approaches as box plots. The brown and green boxes represent the naive regression approach and our regression approach using pre-filtering, respectively. We define the hit rate as the ratio of correct time-to-failure regressions to the number of total regressions. Further, a time-to-failure regression is correct if the actual time-to-failure falls within an interval of the predicted time-to-failure $\pm 10\%$.

The left subfigure of Fig. 4 shows the achieved hit rates. It can be seen that our approach of applying pre-filtering before model learning yields a higher hit rate than the naive version. In numbers, our pre-filtering approach achieves an average hit rate of around 84.9% while the naive version only predicts a correct time-to-failure in about 80.2% of all tries. In contrast to the hit rate, a smaller value is better for MAE and RMSE. Regarding the MAE (middle subfigure of

Fig. 4), our pre-filtering approach results in an average MAE of about 4.5 h. The naive regression approach, instead, shows an average MAE of around 10.0 h. In addition, the interquartile ranges are very small for both approaches. The large difference between the MAEs and the small interquartile ranges imply that our pre-filtering approach predicts the time-to-failure much more accurate. The same conclusion can be drawn by taking a look at the RMSE (right subfigure of Fig. 4). Our pre-filtering approach shows an average RMSE of around 12.8 h while the RMSE of the naive approach reaches around 44.6 h. Again, the interquartile ranges are very small for both approaches.

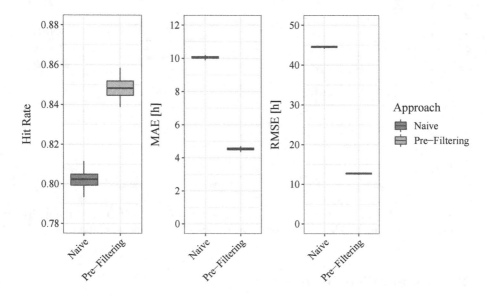

Fig. 4. Achieved values of the two regression alternatives for each evaluation metric. (Color figure online)

Taking all three measures into account, it can be concluded that our pre-filtering approach predicts the time-to-failure much more accurately than the naive version. With an average hit rate of nearly 85% and a mean absolute error of only 4.5 h, the time-to-failure regression is very precise.

5.5   Training Time Comparison

After assessing the quality of the predictions of all presented approaches, we also analyzed the runtimes for model training. The time needed for the prediction is negligible compared to the training time. We executed the experiments in our private cloud using Apache CloudStack and Kernel-based Virtual Machine (KVM). The virtual machine is deployed on a host with 32 cores each providing 2.6 GHz and 64 GB memory, having hyperthreading activated. The virtual machine runs Ubuntu 16.04 (64-bit) with 4 cores each with 2.6 GHz and 8 GB memory. We implemented the approach in R version 3.4.4.

Figure 5 illustrates the training times of all classification and regression approaches using box plots. To this end, the horizontal axis depicts the approaches, while the vertical axis presents the required training time. The boxes are colored according to the respective approach, whereby the coloring corresponds to the previous figures. With an average training time of about 27 s, the unmodified binary classification approach yields the shortest training time followed by our multi-class classification approach with about 174 s. Both of the binary classification with oversampling approaches require a much larger training time of on average around 420 s and 335 s for ESPO and SMOTE, respectively. Thus, our multi-class classification does not only achieve an overall better prediction performance but also a much shorter training time than the best binary classification approach, i.e., ESPO. Regarding the regression approaches, the naive procedure takes on average about 2175 s, while the approach that pre-filters the data only requires around 346 s. That is, our pre-filtering approach is more than 6 times faster than the naive version and even faster than the binary classification approach with ESPO oversampling, while significantly improving the hit rate, MAE, and RMSE.

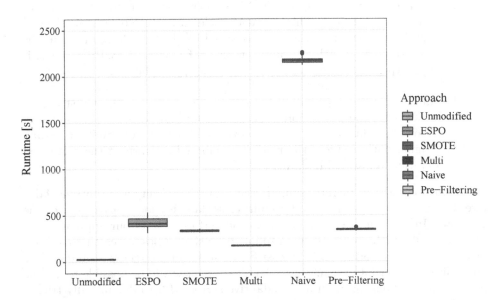

Fig. 5. The required training times for all of the presented approaches. (Color figure online)

6   Conclusion and Discussion

In this paper, we aim at the early prediction of HDD failures. For this purpose, we present three contributions: (i) a comparison of data preparation steps for binary classification of imminent HDD failures, (ii) the introduction of a random forest based approach for time-to-failure classification using multiple time-to-failure classes, and (iii) a pre-filtering and regression based approach to predict the time-to-failure as a continuous variable.

(i) For the first contribution, we compare different data preparation steps for binary classification of imminent failures. The results show that applying ESPO oversampling to balance the number of instances per class improves the prediction quality with an F1-score of 95.928% but also requires more runtime to build the model and perform predictions. In contrast, the application of SMOTE oversampling performed worse than the unmodified version.

(ii) Since the time horizon of upcoming failures is essential for cloud administrators to prevent downtimes and data losses, our second contribution focuses on predicting the time window of upcoming failures using multiple classes by grouping close times-to-failures into the same classes. Based on these classes and the respective S.M.A.R.T. features, we learned a random forest classification model. This approach yields a micro-F1-score of 97.628% for multi-class classification. If downscaled to the two classes used in the first contribution, it achieves an even higher F1-score of 98.019%. Thus, it clearly outperforms the binary classification approaches while maintaining a very low false positive rate of only 0.07%.

(iii) Finally, we present a pre-filtering prior to learning a random forest regression model for the prediction of the time-to-failure as a continuous value. We show that this pre-filtering improves the hit rate from 80.2% to 84.9% and significantly reduces the runtime compared to learning the regression model using all available data.

As future work, we plan to compare the predictive quality and runtime of different machine learning methods for multi-class classification of drive failure time windows. In addition, we want to assess the performance of our approaches on SSDs as well. Furthermore, we plan to integrate time series forecasting methods from our previous work [30] to forecast future states of the HDDs for integrating an additional facet into the analysis. Additionally, it would be possible to use the forecast in combination with a self-adaptive system [13] to dynamically trigger additional backups or other maintenance tasks for critical HDDs.

Acknowledgements. This work was co-funded by the German Research Foundation (DFG) under grant No. (KO 3445/11-1) and the IHK (Industrie- und Handelskammer) Würz-burg-Schweinfurt.

References

1. Aussel, N., Jaulin, S., Gandon, G., Petetin, Y., Fazli, E., Chabridon, S.: Predictive models of hard drive failures based on operational data. In: 2017 16th IEEE International Conference on Machine Learning and Applications (ICMLA), pp. 619–625. IEEE (2017)
2. Botezatu, M.M., Giurgiu, I., Bogojeska, J., Wiesmann, D.: Predicting disk replacement towards reliable data centers. In: Proceedings of the 22nd ACM SIGKDD International Conference on Knowledge Discovery and Data Mining, pp. 39–48. ACM (2016)
3. Breiman, L.: Bagging predictors. Mach. Learn. **24**(2), 123–140 (1996)
4. Breiman, L.: Random forests. Mach. Learn. **45**(1), 5–32 (2001)
5. Breiman, L., Cutler, A., Liaw, A., Wiener, M.: Breiman and Cutler's random forests for classification and regression (2018). https://cran.r-project.org/web/packages/randomForest/randomForest.pdf
6. Cao, H., Li, X.L., Woon, D.Y.K., Ng, S.K.: Integrated oversampling for imbalanced time series classification. IEEE Trans. Knowl. Data Eng. **25**(12), 2809–2822 (2013)
7. Chaves, I.C., de Paula, M.R.P., Leite, L.G., Gomes, J.P.P., Machado, J.C.: Hard disk drive failure prediction method based on a Bayesian network. In: 2018 International Joint Conference on Neural Networks (IJCNN), pp. 1–7. IEEE (2018)
8. Chawla, N.V., Bowyer, K.W., Hall, L.O., Kegelmeyer, W.P.: Smote: synthetic minority over-sampling technique. J. Artif. Intell. Res. **16**, 321–357 (2002)
9. Dal Pozzolo, A., Caelen, O., Bontempi, G.: Unbalanced (2015). https://cran.r-project.org/web/packages/unbalanced/unbalanced.pdf
10. Dixon, M., Klabjan, D., Wei, L.: OSTSC (2017). https://cran.r-project.org/web/packages/OSTSC/OSTSC.pdf
11. Hamerly, G., Elkan, C., et al.: Bayesian approaches to failure prediction for disk drives. In: ICML, vol. 1, pp. 202–209 (2001)
12. Ho, T.K.: Random decision forests. In: Proceedings of 3rd International Conference on Document Analysis and Recognition, vol. 1, pp. 278–282. IEEE (1995)
13. Krupitzer, C., Roth, F.M., VanSyckel, S., Schiele, G., Becker, C.: A survey on engineering approaches for self-adaptive systems. Pervasive Mob. Comput. J. **17**(Part B), 184–206 (2015)
14. Li, J., et al.: Hard drive failure prediction using classification and regression trees. In: 2014 44th Annual IEEE/IFIP International Conference on Dependable Systems and Networks, pp. 383–394. IEEE (2014)
15. Li, J., Stones, R.J., Wang, G., Liu, X., Li, Z., Xu, M.: Hard drive failure prediction using decision trees. Reliab. Eng. Syst. Saf. **164**, 55–65 (2017)
16. Murray, J.F., Hughes, G.F., Kreutz-Delgado, K.: Machine learning methods for predicting failures in hard drives: a multiple-instance application. J. Mach. Learn. Res. **6**(May), 783–816 (2005)
17. Ottem, E., Plummer, J.: Playing it smart: The emergence of reliability prediction technology. Technical report, Seagate Technology Paper (1995)
18. Pinheiro, E., Weber, W.D., Barroso, L.A.: Failure trends in a large disk drive population. In: 5th USENIX Conference on File and Storage Technologies (FAST 2007), pp. 17–29 (2007)
19. Pitakrat, T., Van Hoorn, A., Grunske, L.: A comparison of machine learning algorithms for proactive hard disk drive failure detection. In: Proceedings of the 4th International ACM SIGSOFT Symposium on Architecting Critical Systems, pp. 1–10. ACM (2013)

20. dos Santos Lima, F.D., Pereira, F.L.F., Chaves, I.C., Gomes, J.P.P., de Castro Machado, J.: Evaluation of recurrent neural networks for hard disk drives failure prediction. In: 2018 7th Brazilian Conference on Intelligent Systems (BRACIS), pp. 85–90. IEEE (2018)
21. Seagate Product Marketing: Get S.M.A.R.T. for reliability. Technical report, Seagate Technology Paper (1999)
22. Shen, J., Wan, J., Lim, S.J., Yu, L.: Random-forest-based failure prediction for hard disk drives. Int. J. Distrib. Sens. Netw. **14**(11), 1550147718806480 (2018)
23. Sun, X., et al.: System-level hardware failure prediction using deep learning. In: Proceedings of the 56th Annual Design Automation Conference 2019, p. 20. ACM (2019)
24. Wang, Y., Ma, E.W., Chow, T.W., Tsui, K.L.: A two-step parametric method for failure prediction in hard disk drives. IEEE Trans. Industr. Inf. **10**(1), 419–430 (2013)
25. Xiao, J., Xiong, Z., Wu, S., Yi, Y., Jin, H., Hu, K.: Disk failure prediction in data centers via online learning. In: Proceedings of the 47th International Conference on Parallel Processing, p. 35. ACM (2018)
26. Xu, C., Wang, G., Liu, X., Guo, D., Liu, T.Y.: Health status assessment and failure prediction for hard drives with recurrent neural networks. IEEE Trans. Comput. **65**(11), 3502–3508 (2016)
27. Yang, W., Hu, D., Liu, Y., Wang, S., Jiang, T.: Hard drive failure prediction using big data. In: 2015 IEEE 34th Symposium on Reliable Distributed Systems Workshop (SRDSW), pp. 13–18. IEEE (2015)
28. Zhao, Y., Liu, X., Gan, S., Zheng, W.: Predicting disk failures with HMM- and HSMM-based approaches. In: Perner, P. (ed.) ICDM 2010. LNCS (LNAI), vol. 6171, pp. 390–404. Springer, Heidelberg (2010). https://doi.org/10.1007/978-3-642-14400-4_30
29. Zhu, B., Wang, G., Liu, X., Hu, D., Lin, S., Ma, J.: Proactive drive failure prediction for large scale storage systems. In: 2013 IEEE 29th Symposium on Mass Storage Systems and Technologies (MSST), pp. 1–5. IEEE (2013)
30. Züfle, M., et al.: Autonomic forecasting method selection: examination and ways ahead. In: Proceedings of the 16th IEEE International Conference on Autonomic Computing (ICAC). IEEE (2019)

Concurrent MDPs with Finite Markovian Policies

Peter Buchholz[(✉)] and Dimitri Scheftelowitsch

Informatik IV, TU Dortmund, 44221 Dortmund, Germany
{peter.buchholz,dimitri.scheftelowitsch}@cs.tu-dortmund.de

Abstract. The recently defined class of *Concurrent Markov Decision Processes* (CMDPs) allows one to describe scenario based uncertainty in sequential decision problems like scheduling or admission problems. The resulting optimization problem of computing an optimal policy is NP-hard. This paper introduces a new class of policies for CMDPs on infinite horizons. A mixed integer linear program and an efficient approximation algorithm based on policy iteration are defined for the computation of optimal polices. The proposed approximation algorithm also improves the available approximate value iteration algorithm for the finite horizon case.

Keywords: Concurrent Markov Decision Processes · Optimal policies · Robust optimization · Integer linear programming · Local search heuristics

1 Introduction

Markov Decision Processes (MDPs) are an established model for optimizing the control of probabilistic state based systems [13] including queueing systems. Parameters of MDPs, like for most other models, are usually estimated from available data or are based on a priori knowledge. This implies that parameters are subject to uncertainty and the chosen model is only one possible realization. If the optimal control policy is sensitive to small changes in the parameters or the level of uncertainty is high, then the policy computed for one MDP might show a bad behavior in other realizations of uncertainty.

In this paper we consider the analysis of MDPs under parameter uncertainty. Uncertainty is described in form of finitely many scenarios and the final goal is to find a policy that maximizes the weighted sum of rewards when applied to different scenarios. The paper considers discounted infinite and finite horizon problems.

Related Work: There is an enormous amount of papers on uncertainty in MDPs such that we can only mention a few important references. Older papers are [14,15,21], as more recent references we recommend [9,12,22]. Most of the papers consider robust optimization under parameter uncertainty which means that

© Springer Nature Switzerland AG 2020
H. Hermanns (Ed.): MMB 2020, LNCS 12040, pp. 37–53, 2020.
https://doi.org/10.1007/978-3-030-43024-5_3

the policy is computed which behaves best under the worst possible realization of uncertainty. The resulting optimization problem is of the max − min-type and can be solved efficiently for specific classes of uncertainty where (s, a)-rectangularity holds [9].

There are two shortcomings of the mentioned approaches to handle uncertainty. First, the computation of robust policies often results in a very pessimistic policy which behaves clearly sub-optimal for most realizations of uncertainty [3]. Furthermore, the assumption of (s, a)-rectangularity and even its extension [7,11,22] are restrictive. In (s, a)-rectangularity it is assumed that parameter uncertainty occurs independently for all transition probabilities and rewards belonging to a state action pair (s, a). Usually, uncertainty occurs according to some parameters of the model, e.g., failure or arrival rates, and not independently for states and decisions as assumed for (s, a)-rectangularity. However, as shown for some cases in [22] the computation of other than robust solutions or the relaxation of rectangularity makes the resulting optimization problems NP-hard.

In this paper we consider scenario based uncertainty which means that some scenarios are defined to describe the realization of uncertainty. Scenario based uncertainty is for example used for specific classes of problems in [1,2]. The class of Concurrent MDPs (CMDPs), which we use here, has been defined in [5,16] and independently under the name *Multi-Model MDP* in [18,20]. In both papers policies are computed that maximize the weighted sum of rewards over several MDPs sharing the same policy. Stationary policies over an infinite horizon are considered in [5,16], whereas [18,20] optimizes Markovian policies over a finite horizon. Both optimization problems are NP-hard and for both cases approximation methods are developed.

Contribution of the Paper: This paper extends and combines the results from [5,16] and [18,20]. For infinite horizons and discounted rewards it has been shown in [5,16] that the optimal stationary policy can be randomized, whereas [18,20] proves that an optimal Markovian deterministic policy exists for the finite horizon case. Here we consider discounted infinite horizon and finite horizon problems. We extend the class of policies to finite Markovian policies and show that these policies are at least as good as the best stationary randomized policy. We present an exact algorithm based on mixed integer programming to compute optimal finite Markovian policies. Additionally, we present an efficient approximation algorithm which extends the approximation algorithm from [5,16] and [18,20] and show that this approximation algorithm computes efficiently optimal or nearly optimal policies.

Structure of the Paper: In the next section basic definitions and results are introduced. Afterwards, in Sect. 3, the main algorithms to compute optimal policies are introduced. In Sect. 4 a new class of policies is defined followed by the introduction of a new approximate policy iteration approach. Then some examples are analyzed and the paper is concluded.

2   Background

We first introduce the basic notation used in the paper and then define the class of concurrent MDPs and rephrase the basic results for the model.

2.1   Notation

Vectors and matrices are denoted by capital and small boldface letters. Apart from $\mathbb{R}$ for the set of real numbers, sets are denoted by calligraphic letters. For some set $\mathcal{K}$, $\mathcal{K}^{n \times m}$ is the set of matrices with n rows and m columns with elements from $\mathcal{K}$. $\boldsymbol{P}(i\bullet)$ denotes row i of matrix $\boldsymbol{P}$ and $\boldsymbol{P}(\bullet i)$ column i. $\mathbb{1}$ is a column vector of 1 and $\boldsymbol{0}$ is a column vector or matrix with all elements equal to 0. $\boldsymbol{e}_i$ is the ith basic row vector.

2.2   Concurrent MDPs

We consider Markov Decision Processes over finite state and action spaces which are defined in the usual way [13], the only exception is the initial distribution which is assumed to be part of the definition.

Definition 1. *A Markov Decision Process (MDP) is a 4 tuple* $MDP = \left(\mathcal{S}, \boldsymbol{\alpha}, (\boldsymbol{P}^a)_{a \in \mathcal{A}}, (\boldsymbol{r}^a)_{a \in \mathcal{A}}\right)$ *where* $\mathcal{S} = \{1, \ldots, N\}$ *is the (finite) set of states,* $\mathcal{A} = \{1, \ldots, M\}$ *is the (finite) set of actions,* $\boldsymbol{\alpha} \in \mathbb{R}_{\geq 0}^{1 \times N}$ *with* $\boldsymbol{\alpha}\mathbb{1} = 1$ *is the initial distribution,* $\boldsymbol{P}^a \in \mathbb{R}_{\geq 0}^{N \times N}$ *is the stochastic transition matrix under action* a *and* $\boldsymbol{r}^a \in \mathbb{R}_{\geq 0}^{N \times 1}$ *is the decision dependent reward vector.*

An MDP is driven by some policy $\boldsymbol{\Pi}$. Different classes of polices exist (for a classification see [13, Sect. 2.1]). In stationary policies, the decision depends only on the current state, $\boldsymbol{\pi}(i, a)$ is the probability of choosing action a in state i. If $\boldsymbol{\pi}(i, a) = 1$ for some $a \in \mathcal{A}$, the policy is denoted as deterministic, otherwise it is a randomized policy. We analyze MDPs over several periods starting at $t = 1$ and ending in the finite horizon case at $t = T$, for infinite horizons t is unbounded. A policy is Markovian if the decisions depend on the state and the time step, i.e. $\boldsymbol{\pi}_t(i, a)$ is the probability to choose a in state i at period t. Again we can distinguish between Markov deterministic and Markov randomized policies. The most general class of policies are history dependent where the decision may depend on the whole history, i.e. the states and decisions on the way from the initial state to the current state. The set of all policies is denoted by $\mathcal{P}$. If necessary we restrict the set of policies by adding a postfix. Thus, $\mathcal{P}^S$ is the set of stationary policies, $\mathcal{P}^M$ the set of Markovian polices and $\mathcal{P}^{XD}$, $\mathcal{P}^{XR}$ where $X \in \{S, M\}$ are the sets of stationary/Markovian deterministic and randomized policies, respectively. For policies from $\mathcal{P}^S$ we have $\boldsymbol{\Pi} = (\boldsymbol{\pi}, \boldsymbol{\pi}, \ldots)$ such that the policy is completely characterized by $\boldsymbol{\pi}$, instead for policies from $\mathcal{P}^M$ we have the representation $(\boldsymbol{\pi}_1, \boldsymbol{\pi}_2, \ldots)$. In the sequel we denote by $\boldsymbol{\pi}$ and $\boldsymbol{\pi}_t$ a vector with elements $\boldsymbol{\pi}(i, a)$ or $\boldsymbol{\pi}_t(i, a)$ describing the probability of choosing action a in state i (at time t). The term *policy vector* is used for $\boldsymbol{\pi}$ or $\boldsymbol{\pi}_t$. A policy $\boldsymbol{\Pi}$ is built from T policy vectors, where $T = \infty$ for infinite horizons. For deterministic policies $\boldsymbol{\pi}(i, \bullet)$ describes a Dirac distribution and for a stationary policy all policy vectors $\boldsymbol{\pi}_t$ are identical. We use the term *deterministic policy vector* for vectors describing a Dirac distribution and *randomized policy vector* for general vectors defining a distribution over the set of actions.

For some policy vector $\boldsymbol{\pi}_t$ $(t = 1, 2, \ldots)$ the MDP defines a Markov reward process (MRP) with transition matrix $\boldsymbol{P}^{\boldsymbol{\pi}_t}$. If $\boldsymbol{\Pi} \in \mathcal{P}^S$, then the resulting MRP is homogeneous, otherwise it is inhomogeneous. In this paper we analyze the discounted reward that is defined for a policy $\boldsymbol{\Pi} = (\boldsymbol{\pi}_1, \boldsymbol{\pi}_2, \ldots, \boldsymbol{\pi}_T)$ as

$$\boldsymbol{g}^{\boldsymbol{\Pi}} = \sum_{t=1}^{T} \left(\prod_{s=1}^{t-1} \gamma \boldsymbol{P}^{\boldsymbol{\pi}_s} \right) \boldsymbol{r}^{\boldsymbol{\pi}_t} \text{ and } \boldsymbol{G}^{\boldsymbol{\Pi}} = \boldsymbol{\alpha} \boldsymbol{g}^{\boldsymbol{\Pi}} \tag{1}$$

with $\gamma \in (0, 1)$. For infinite horizons $T = \infty$. $\boldsymbol{G}^{\boldsymbol{\Pi}}$ is the reward of policy $\boldsymbol{\Pi}$. Then the following optimization problem is solved.

$$\boldsymbol{g}^* = \max_{\boldsymbol{\Pi} \in \mathcal{P}} \left(\boldsymbol{g}^{\boldsymbol{\Pi}} \right) \text{ and } \boldsymbol{\Pi}^* = \arg\max_{\boldsymbol{\Pi} \in \mathcal{P}} \left(\boldsymbol{g}^{\boldsymbol{\Pi}} \right) \tag{2}$$

The maximum is taken for each element of the vector. It is well known [13] that for the finite horizon case an optimal policy from $\mathcal{P}^{MD}$ exists and for the infinite horizon case an optimal policy from $\mathcal{P}^{SD}$ exists. In both cases the policy is optimal for each element in vector $\boldsymbol{g}$.

In an MDP it is assumed that all parameters are completely known which is often not the case in practice. Concurrent MDPs are one possibility to express this uncertainty.

Definition 2. *A Concurrent MDP (CMDP) consists of a finite set of MDPs* $\mathcal{M} = \left\{ \left(\mathcal{S}, \boldsymbol{\alpha}, \left(\boldsymbol{P}_k^a \right)_{a \in \mathcal{A}}, \left(r_k^a \right)_{a \in \mathcal{A}} \right)_{k=1,\ldots,K} \right\}$ *with a common state space, a common action space and a common initial distribution.*

CMDPs have been defined in [5, 16] and independently under the name multi-model MDPs in [18, 20]. The assumption is that a policy has to be selected before the exact model is known, and afterwards the selected policy is applied to one of the MDPs. This can be interpreted as scenario based uncertainty [1, 12].

Different optimization problems for concurrent MDPs can be defined. Here we consider the optimization of the weighted sum of rewards. Let $\boldsymbol{w} \in \mathbb{R}_{\geq 0}^{1 \times K}$ with $\boldsymbol{w}\boldsymbol{1} = 1$ be a weight vector. For some policy $\boldsymbol{\Pi}$ the weighted sum of rewards is defined as

$$\boldsymbol{g}^{\boldsymbol{\Pi}} = \sum_{k=1}^{K} \boldsymbol{w}(k) \left(\sum_{t=1}^{T} \left(\prod_{s=1}^{t-1} \gamma \boldsymbol{P}_k^{\boldsymbol{\pi}_s} \right) \boldsymbol{r}_k^{\boldsymbol{\pi}_t} \right) \text{ and } \boldsymbol{G}^{\boldsymbol{\Pi}} = \boldsymbol{\alpha} \boldsymbol{g}^{\boldsymbol{\Pi}}. \tag{3}$$

Again the problem can be defined for finite or infinite horizons. The optimization problem is then given by

$$G^* = \max_{\Pi \in \mathcal{P}} \left(G^{\Pi} \right) \text{ and } \Pi^* = \arg \max_{\Pi \in \mathcal{P}} \left(G^{\Pi} \right). \tag{4}$$

Observe that scalar G^{Π} rather than vector $\boldsymbol{g}^{\Pi}$ is optimized because a common policy maximizing all vector elements usually does not exist whereas an optimal policy for the scalar is available.

For later use we define the neighborhood of some policy Π as

$$\mathcal{N}(\Pi) = \left\{ \Pi' | \exists i \in \mathcal{S}, \exists a, b \in \mathcal{A} : \pi(j, c) = \pi'(j, c) \text{ if } i \neq j \text{ or } c \in \mathcal{S} \setminus \{a, b\} \right\}. \tag{5}$$

Thus, $\Pi' \in \mathcal{N}(\Pi)$ differs from Π in at most one decision. Policy Π is globally optimal if $G^{\Pi} \geq \max_{\Pi' \in \mathcal{P}} G^{\Pi'}$, it is locally optimal if $G^{\Pi} \geq \max_{\Pi' \in \mathcal{N}(\Pi)} G^{\Pi'}$. The definitions can be restricted to subclasses of policies, e.g. $\mathcal{P}^S$ or $\mathcal{P}^M$.

2.3 Some Results for Concurrent MDPs

We now briefly summarize the result from [5, 20]. The first theorem shows the complexity of the resulting optimization problems.

Theorem 1. *The solution of* (4) *is NP-hard.*

Proof. For finite horizons the proof can be found in [20, Prop. 6] and for infinite horizons in [5, Theo. 1].

Theorem 2. *For the finite horizon problem* (4) *an optimal Markovian deterministic policy exists and for the infinite horizon problem* (4) *the optimal stationary policy can be randomized.*

Proof. The proofs can be found in [20, Prop. 5] and [5].

A finite horizon problem can be transformed into an infinite horizon problem on an MDP with $TN + 1$ states and the following vectors and matrices

$$\breve{\alpha} = \begin{pmatrix} \alpha \\ 0 \\ \vdots \\ 0 \\ 0 \end{pmatrix}^T , \breve{P}_k^a = \begin{pmatrix} 0 & P_k^a & & \\ & \ddots & \ddots & \\ & & 0 & P_k^a \mathbb{1} \\ & & & 1 \end{pmatrix} , \breve{r}_k = \begin{pmatrix} r_k^a \\ \vdots \\ r_k^a \\ 0 \end{pmatrix} \tag{6}$$

It is also possible to add final cost as done in [20]. This representation is not necessarily intended to be used in algorithms, it helps to avoid the separate handling of the finite and infinite case.

2.4   An Example

As an example we consider a simple admission problem. The system is a single server system with capacity B. Tasks in the system have an exponentially distributed service time with rate μ and are served according to *processor sharing*. C classes of customers arrive to the system according to a Poisson process with rate λ^c for class c. Upon arrival a job can be admitted to the system or can be rejected. The reward of admitting a job of class c to the system with b jobs present equals $r^c(b) = (b_c + 1) \cdot \lambda^c / ((b+1) \cdot \sum_{c=1}^{C} \lambda^c)$, where b_c is the number of class c jobs in the system.

For fixed arrival rates the system defines a continuous time MDP with $\sum_{b=0}^{B} \binom{b+C-1}{n}$ states and 2^C actions. Using the uniformization, the continuous time MDP is transformed into an MPD in discrete time [17]. If the arrival rates are not known, they have to be estimated which usually means that confidence intervals rather than exact values are available. Assume that $\lambda^c \in [\lambda^{c-}, \lambda^{c+}]$. If the distribution of λ^c in $[\lambda^{c-}, \lambda^{c+}]$ is known (e.g. corresponds to a truncated normal or a uniform distribution), samples $\lambda^{c,i}$ ($i = 1, \ldots, k$) can be drawn and a CMDP with k MPDs, one for each sample, can be generated. Then an optimal policy can be computed for the CMDP which considers the distributional information that is available about uncertain parameters.

3   Computation of Optimal Policies

In this section we present three different types of algorithms to compute or approximate optimal policies for CMDPs. The algorithms correspond to the standard approaches used for optimization in MDPs, namely linear programming, value and policy iteration. However, in contrast to the much simpler computation of optimal policies in MDPs, now integer linear programs have to be solved, also policy iteration becomes more complex and computes only locally optimal solutions. Value iteration is not guaranteed to converge to a stationary policy and computes also at most only locally optimal solutions.

The basic solution algorithms have been proposed in [5,20], we present here several extensions in a unified framework and extend the classes of policies that are computed. First we consider stationary polices in this section. Observe that Markovian policies for finite horizons can be computed as stationary policies after the transformation (6). For stationary policies $\Pi = \{\pi, \ldots\}$, the policy is described by a single policy vector. In the infinite horizon case π is a vector of length N, in the finite horizon case, a vector length TN which consists of T subvectors π_t each of length N.

3.1   Integer Linear Programming

With integer linear programming only deterministic policies can be determined. We can set up the following ILP.

$$
\max \sum_{k=1}^{K} w(k)\alpha g_k
$$

s.t.$\forall k \in \{1, \ldots, K\}, \forall i \in \mathcal{S}, \forall a \in \mathcal{A}, \pi(i,a) \in \{0,1\}$:   (7)

$$
g_k(i) \le r_k^a(i) + \gamma \sum_{j \in \mathcal{S}} P^a(i,j)g_k(j) + (1 - \pi(i,a))M_k, \quad \sum_{a \in \mathcal{A}} \pi(i,a) = 1
$$

where M_k is an upper bound for $g_k(i)$, e.g., $M_k = \max_{i \in \mathcal{S}} \max_{a \in \mathcal{A}} r_k^a(i)/(1-\gamma)$. The proof of the validity of the MILP is a simple extension of [20, Prop. 7] and [5, Sect. 4.1]. Although much progress has been made in solving large ILPs [10] and ILP solvers provide estimates on the deviation from the optimal solution, the size of exactly solvable models is limited because the number of variables grows rapidly with N, M, K and T. By fixing decisions in some states i, the size of the ILP is reduced but the resulting solution is no longer globally optimal. Nevertheless, the computation of partial policies using ILPs is the basic step of branch and bound algorithms.

The solution of the ILP is an optimal policy in the finite horizon case and it is the best stationary deterministic policy for the infinite horizon case. As shown in [5] better stationary randomized policies may exist and as we will show below better deterministic policies which are not stationary may also exist for infinite horizons. This implies that in the finite horizon case, optimal policies can be computed for small problems and short horizons using ILP solvers, whereas no exact algorithm is available to compute an optimal policy in the uncountable set of randomized stationary or Markovian policies for infinite horizon problems.

3.2   Policy Iteration

Policy iteration improves a policy until no more improvements are possible. Improvements are local by computing for policy π a policy $\pi' \in \mathcal{N}(\pi)$ with a larger value of the objective function. In a convex problem this strategy results in the computation of the globally optimal solution. Since the overall problem for CMDPs is non-convex, the approach is not guaranteed to find a globally optimal solution in CMDPs. However, results from [5] indicate that often the global optimum is computed or the solution is very near to the global optimum which means that the reward of the policy computed with policy iteration is a good approximation for the optimal reward. Policy iteration has been proposed in [5] for infinite horizons and rewards that do not depend on the policy. It becomes with the following formulation also usable for problems with a finite horizon. Furthermore, we extend the algorithm here to problems where rewards may depend on the chosen action a. In [5] this case is handled by state space expansion which is not necessary in the improved approach.

First define the following matrices

$$
C_k^\pi = (I - \gamma P_k^\pi) \text{ and } \overline{C}_k^\pi = (C_k^\pi)^{-1}.
$$ (8)

The inverse matrix exists and is non-negative because C_k^{π} is an M-matrix for $0 \leq \gamma < 1$ [5] or if $\gamma = 1$ and the matrices have a structure as in (6). Then

$$G^{\pi} = \sum_{k=1}^{K} \boldsymbol{w}(k) \boldsymbol{\alpha} \overline{\boldsymbol{C}}_k^{\pi} \boldsymbol{r}_k^{\pi} = \sum_{k=1}^{K} \boldsymbol{w}(k) \boldsymbol{\alpha} \boldsymbol{g}_k^{\pi}. \tag{9}$$

A policy from $\boldsymbol{\pi}' \in \mathcal{N}(\boldsymbol{\pi})$ can be defined by selecting $i \in \mathcal{S}$, $a, b \in \mathcal{A}$ and $\lambda \in [0, \boldsymbol{\pi}(i, a)]$ such that

$$\boldsymbol{\pi}'(i, a) = \boldsymbol{\pi}(i, a) - \lambda, \boldsymbol{\pi}'(i, b) = \boldsymbol{\pi}(i, b) + \lambda, \boldsymbol{\pi}'(j, c) = \boldsymbol{\pi}(j, c) \text{ for } j \neq i \text{ or } c \notin \{a, b\}. \tag{10}$$

For $i \in \mathcal{S}$, $a, b \in \mathcal{A}$ define

$$
\begin{aligned}
\boldsymbol{u}_{k,i}^{a,b} &= \gamma \left(\boldsymbol{P}_k^a(i\bullet) - \boldsymbol{P}_k^b(i\bullet) \right), & \boldsymbol{v}_k &= \boldsymbol{\alpha} \overline{\boldsymbol{C}}_k^{\pi}(\bullet i) \boldsymbol{u}_{k,i}^{a,b} \overline{\boldsymbol{C}}_k^{\pi} \\
\zeta_k &= \boldsymbol{v}_k \boldsymbol{r}_k^{\pi} & \eta_k &= \boldsymbol{u}_{k,i}^{a,b} \overline{\boldsymbol{C}}_k^{\pi}(\bullet i) \\
\phi_k &= \boldsymbol{v}_k(i) \left(\boldsymbol{r}_k^b(i) - \boldsymbol{r}_k^a(i) \right) & \chi_k &= \left(\boldsymbol{\alpha} \overline{\boldsymbol{C}}_k^{\pi} \right)(i) \left(\boldsymbol{r}_k^b(i) - \boldsymbol{r}_k^a(i) \right)
\end{aligned} \tag{11}
$$

$$\Delta^{\pi}(i, a, b) = \max_{\lambda \in [0, \pi(i,a)]} \left(\lambda \sum_{k=1}^{K} \boldsymbol{w}(k) \left(\frac{\lambda \phi_k + \zeta_k}{1 - \lambda \eta_k} + \chi_k \right) \right).$$

This representation follows because the modification of some policy vector $\boldsymbol{\pi}$ to a policy vector $\boldsymbol{\pi}' \in \mathcal{N}(\boldsymbol{\pi})$ results in a rank-1 update of matrix $\boldsymbol{P}_k^{\pi}$ which results in the above modifications of the inverse matrix [8]. For rewards that do not depend on the action, ϕ_k and χ_k are 0. The computation or better approximation of the maximum is relatively cheap because the function to optimize has a single parameter λ. Let $\lambda^{\pi}(i, a, b)$ be the arg max of the equation. If $\Delta^{\pi}(i, a, b) > 0$, then the policy $\boldsymbol{\pi}'$ resulting from $\boldsymbol{\pi}$ by changing $\boldsymbol{\pi}'(i, a) = \boldsymbol{\pi}(i, a) - \lambda^{\pi}(i, a, b)$, $\boldsymbol{\pi}'(i, b) = \boldsymbol{\pi}(i, b) + \lambda^{\pi}(i, a, b)$ and leaving the remaining probabilities unchanged results in $G^{\pi'} = G^{\pi} + \Delta^{\pi}(i, a, b)$.

A policy iteration algorithm now checks for all pairs (i, a) with $\boldsymbol{\pi}(i, a) > 0$ whether $b \in \mathcal{A}$ exist such that $\Delta^{\pi}(i, a, b) > 0$ holds. If a triple (i, a, b) has been found, the new policy vector $\boldsymbol{\pi}'$ is used as starting point. If no triple can be found, the policy is locally optimal. As shown in [5] the neighborhood covers in this case all policies that result from $\boldsymbol{\pi}$ by a rank one update of matrix $\boldsymbol{C}_k^{\pi}$.

If only deterministic policies should be computed, then only $\lambda = \boldsymbol{\pi}(i, a) = 1$ is checked in (11). When applied to larger problems the approach is much more efficient than an ILP solver.

3.3   Value Iteration

The following value iteration algorithm is proposed in [18, 20] (denoted as WSU) to compute deterministic Markovian policies for finite horizons.

For finite horizon problems with horizon T the algorithm is stopped after T steps. In this case the algorithm computes an approximation of the optimal policy. For the infinite horizon case, $T = \infty$ and the algorithm has to be stopped according to some stopping criterion. For MDPs it is known [13] that the iteration

---

```
1: t = 0 ;
2: h_k^t = 0 ; /* for k = 1, ..., K */
3: for t = 0 to T do
4:     for i ∈ S do
5:         a_i = arg max_{a∈A} (∑_{k=1}^{K} w(k) (r_k^a(i) + γP_k^a(i•)h_k^t)) ;
6:         π_t(i, a_i) = 1 ;  π_t(i, b) = 0 ; /* for b ≠ a_i */
7:     for k = 1, ..., K do
8:         h_k^{t+1} = r_k + γP_k^{π^t} h_k^t ;
```

Algorithm 1: Improved version of the value iteration approach from [20]

is going to converge to an optimal stationary policy and the iteration can be stopped for $\|h_k^t - h_k^{t-1}\| < \epsilon$. For CMDPs convergence cannot be guaranteed. The problem is that no relation between the vectors h_k^t and h_k^{t-1} can be established. Thus, the iteration does not necessarily define a contraction mapping and may diverge. Even if it converges it is not guaranteed that the resulting policy is optimal.

4 Finite Expansion of Policies

As shown in the previous section, optimal stationary policies for CMDPs need not be deterministic. In this section we extend the approach by defining limited classes of Markovian policies. Then algorithms for policy evaluation are presented. Afterwards policy improvement and the computation or approximation of optimal policies is shown.

4.1 Expansion of CMDPs

A Markovian policy in general consists of an infinite sequence π_t of decision vectors. This is impractical for using and computing a general Markovian policy for large T or infinite horizons.

Definition 3. *For some MDP with state space $\mathcal{S}$, the class of finite randomized Markovian policies $\mathcal{P}^{fMR}$ is defined as the set of all policies $\Pi = \{(\pi_1, \pi_2, \ldots, \pi_T, \pi_T, \ldots)\}$ where π_t is a randomized policy vector over $\mathcal{S}$. Similarly the class of finite deterministic Markovian policies $\mathcal{P}^{fMD}$ can be defined by using deterministic policy vectors π_t.*

In a policy from $\mathcal{P}^{fMR}$ or $\mathcal{P}^{fMD}$, the decision rules potentially change in the first T steps and remain constant afterwards. T denotes the *length* of a policy. We denote by $\mathcal{P}_T^{fMD}$ and $\mathcal{P}_T^{fMR}$ the sets of finite Markovian deterministic and randomized policies of length T. A policy Π is denoted as ϵ-optimal if $|G^* - G^\Pi| < \epsilon$.

Theorem 3. *For any CMDP and any $\epsilon > 0$ a policy from $\mathcal{P}^{fMD}$ exists that is ϵ-optimal.*

Proof. According to Theorem 2 an optimal policy $\pi_1, \ldots, \pi_T$ exists for the finite horizon problem with horizon T. The additional value that is added after step T is bounded by $\gamma^{T+1} \max_{a \in \mathcal{A}} \max_{i \in \mathcal{S}} \left(\sum_{k=1}^{K} w(k) r_k^a(i) \right) / (1 - \gamma)$. Thus, by choosing

$$T > \frac{\epsilon(1 - \gamma)}{- \log(\gamma) \max_{a \in \mathcal{A}} \max_{i \in \mathcal{S}} \left(\sum_{k=1}^{K} w(k) r_k^a(i) \right)} - 1$$

we obtain a finite policy.

4.2   Matrix Structures

Finite policies for infinite horizons can be described by a new (C)MDP which is denoted as *state space expansion*. We begin with some CMDP

$$\mathcal{M} = \left\{ \left(\mathcal{S}, \alpha, (P_k^a)_{a \in \mathcal{A}}, (r_k^a)_{a \in \mathcal{A}} \right)_{k=1,\ldots,K} \right\}.$$

The corresponding CMDP for policies from $\mathcal{P}_T^{fMX}$ is

$$\widetilde{\mathcal{M}}_T = \left\{ \left(\tilde{\mathcal{S}}, \tilde{\alpha}, \left(\tilde{P}_k^a \right)_{a \in \mathcal{A}}, (\tilde{r}_k^a)_{a \in \mathcal{A}} \right)_{k=1,\ldots,K} \right\}$$

where $\tilde{\mathcal{S}} = \{1, \ldots, T\} \times \mathcal{S}$ and

$$\tilde{\alpha} = (\alpha, 0, \ldots, 0), \quad \tilde{P}_k^a = \begin{pmatrix} 0 & P_k^a & 0 & \cdots & 0 \\ \vdots & \ddots & \ddots & \ddots & \vdots \\ \vdots & \ddots & \ddots & P_k^a & 0 \\ \vdots & \ddots & \ddots & 0 & P_k^a \\ 0 & \cdots & \cdots & 0 & P_k^a \end{pmatrix}, \quad \tilde{r}_k^a = \begin{pmatrix} r_k^a \\ \vdots \\ \vdots \\ \vdots \\ r_k^a \end{pmatrix}.$$

In principle we can apply the algorithms presented in Sect. 3 to compute optimal policies for these CMDPs as already described for the finite horizon case using (6). The problem is that the state space grows with T. This has the consequence that MILP solvers are only usable for small state spaces and small T. The policy iteration approach is usable for significantly larger models but also reaches its limits because large inverse matrices have to be built. Only value iteration can be applied but usually results in sub-optimal policies. However, the CMDP $\widetilde{\mathcal{M}}_T$ contains a lot of structure which can be exploited for the computation of optimal or at least good policies.

4.3   Policy Evaluation

The computation of G^Π for CMDPs over an infinite horizon is given by (8) and (9). By using $\tilde{P}_k^a$ rather than P_k^a policies from $\mathcal{P}_T^{fMX}$ can be evaluated. For a more efficient computation, the matrix structures have to be exploited. For some $\boldsymbol{\Pi} \in \mathcal{P}_T^{fMX}$ we obtain

$$
G^{\boldsymbol{\Pi}} = \sum_{k=1}^{K} \boldsymbol{w}(k)\boldsymbol{\alpha} \left(\sum_{t=1}^{T-1} \left(\prod_{s=1}^{t-1} \gamma \boldsymbol{P}_k^{\boldsymbol{\pi}_s} \right) \boldsymbol{r}_k^{\boldsymbol{\pi}_t} + \left(\prod_{t=1}^{T-1} \gamma \boldsymbol{P}_k^{\boldsymbol{\pi}_t} \right) \left(\boldsymbol{I} - \gamma \boldsymbol{P}_k^{\boldsymbol{\pi}_T} \right)^{-1} \boldsymbol{r}_k^{\boldsymbol{\pi}_T} \right).
$$

$$(12)$$

The equation can be proved by showing that the first row of the inverse matrix $(\boldsymbol{I} - \gamma \tilde{\boldsymbol{P}}_k^{\boldsymbol{\Pi}})^{-1}$ is given by

$$
\left(\boldsymbol{I}, \gamma \boldsymbol{P}_k^{\boldsymbol{\pi}_1}, \ldots, \prod_{t=1}^{T-1} \gamma \boldsymbol{P}_k^{\boldsymbol{\pi}_t}, \left(\prod_{t=1}^{T-1} \gamma \boldsymbol{P}_k^{\boldsymbol{\pi}_t} \right) \left(\boldsymbol{I} - \gamma \boldsymbol{P}_k^{\boldsymbol{\pi}_T} \right)^{-1} \right).
$$

4.4 Policy Iteration for Policies from $\mathcal{P}^{fMX}$

As already mentioned optimal policies from $\mathcal{P}^{fMX}$ can be computed with the MILP solver (Sect. 3.1) or can be approximated with policy iteration (Sect. 3.2) or value iteration (Sect. 3.3). For policy iteration and in particular for the *exact* MILP solver the size solvable CMDPs is limited by the dimension of the inverse matrix and the number of variables and constraints in the MILP, respectively. The proposed value iteration approach is of limited use for infinite horizons because it often does not converge. There is only one recent paper [19] that defines a branch and bound approach for the optimization of CMDPs on finite horizon. Here we extend the proposed policy iteration by exploiting the specific structure of policies from $\mathcal{P}^{fMX}$.

To compute a policy $\boldsymbol{\Pi} \in \mathcal{P}^{fMX}$ first $\boldsymbol{\pi}_T$ is computed using the MILP solver (7) or the policy iteration (11) applied to the CMDP $\mathcal{M}$. Policy iteration is often preferable because it is more efficient, allows one to compute policies from $\mathcal{P}^{SR}$, and often yields a policy that is as good or better than the policy from $\mathcal{P}^{SD}$ computed by the MILP solver (see [5] for examples). In the following, we show a way to improve the computed policy $\boldsymbol{\pi}_T$ with a policy from $\mathcal{P}^{fMX}$.

To improve $\boldsymbol{\pi}_T$ we follow the idea of policy iteration based on the representation of $G^{\boldsymbol{\Pi}}$ given in (12). States are denoted by tuples (t, i) where $t \in \{1, \ldots, T\}$ and $i \in \mathcal{S}$. Define for $\boldsymbol{\Pi} \in \mathcal{P}^{fMX}$ the following vectors.

$$
\begin{aligned}
\boldsymbol{f}_{k,T} &= \left(\boldsymbol{I} - \gamma \boldsymbol{P}_k^{\boldsymbol{\pi}_T} \right)^{-1} \boldsymbol{r}_k^{\boldsymbol{\pi}_T}, & \boldsymbol{f}_{k,t} &= \gamma \boldsymbol{P}_k^{\boldsymbol{\pi}_t} \boldsymbol{f}_{k,t+1} \text{ for } 1 \le t < T \\
\boldsymbol{z}_{k,\ell,\ell} &= \boldsymbol{r}_k^{\boldsymbol{\pi}_\ell} \text{ for } 1 \le l \le T, & \boldsymbol{z}_{k,t,\ell} &= \gamma \boldsymbol{P}_k^{\boldsymbol{\pi}_\ell} \boldsymbol{z}_{k,t+1.\ell} \text{ for } 1 \le t < \ell \\
\boldsymbol{\beta}_{k,1} &= \boldsymbol{w}(k)\boldsymbol{\alpha}_k, & \boldsymbol{\beta}_{k,t} &= \boldsymbol{\beta}_{k,t-1} \gamma \boldsymbol{P}_k^{\boldsymbol{\pi}_{t-1}} \text{ for } 1 < t \le T
\end{aligned}
$$

Similar to (11) we compute $\lambda^{\boldsymbol{\pi}_t}$ and $\Delta^{\boldsymbol{\Pi}}((t,i),a,b)$ such that the $G^{\boldsymbol{\Pi}'} = G^{\boldsymbol{\Pi}} + \Delta^{\boldsymbol{\Pi}}((t,i),a,b)$ is the reward of policy $\boldsymbol{\Pi}'$ which results from $\boldsymbol{\Pi}$ by $\pi'_t(i,a) = \pi_t(i,a) - \lambda^{\boldsymbol{\pi}_t}$, $\pi'_t(i,b) = \pi'_t(i,b) + \lambda^{\boldsymbol{\pi}_t}$ and leaving the remaining values unchanged.

For states (T, i) the computation of λ^{π_t} and $\Delta^{\Pi}((T, i), a, b)$ corresponds to (11) where α is substituted by $\beta_{k,T}$ for the computation of v_k and χ_k. This results in the same optimization problem as above. For $1 \leq t < T$ it is

$$
\begin{aligned}
&\Delta^{\Pi}((t, i), a, b) \\
&= \max_{\lambda \in [0, \pi_t(i,a)]} -\lambda \sum_{k=1}^{K} \beta_{k,t}(i) \left(\sum_{\ell=t+1}^{T-1} u_{k,i}^{a,b} z_{k,t+1,\ell} + u_{k,i}^{a,b} f_{k,t+1} + r_k^a(i) - r_k^b(i) \right)
\end{aligned}
\tag{13}
$$

Observe that the function is linear in λ and the maximum can always be found in one of the two endpoints, 0 or $\pi_t(i, a)$, i.e. decisions in the first $T - 1$ steps are deterministic in an optimal policy.

As in the policy iteration approach presented above state action pairs $((t, i), a, b)$ with $\pi_t(i, a) > 0$ are checked for a possible improvement of the resulting reward until a local maximum is reached. Algorithm 2 formalizes this approach.

1: $\Pi \leftarrow (\pi_1, \ldots, \pi_T) = (\pi_T, \ldots, \pi_T)$ ▷ Initialize finite expansion policy
2: **repeat**
3:     done $\leftarrow$ true
4:     **for** $t \in \{1, \ldots, T - 1\}$ **do**
5:         **for** $i \in \{1, \ldots, N\}$ **do**
6:             **for** $a \in \{a \in \mathcal{A} \mid \pi_t(i, a) > 0\}$ **do**
7:                 $b \leftarrow \arg\max_b \Delta((t, i), a, b)$
8:                 **if** $\Delta((t, i), a, b) > 0$ **then**
9:                     $\pi_t(i, b) = \pi_t(i, b) + \pi_t(i, a); \pi_t(i, a) = 0$;
10:                    done = false
11: **until** done

Algorithm 2: Policy improvement algorithm for finite expansion policies

---

The algorithm can also be used for finite horizons. In this case the inverse matrix for the computation of π_T is not needed, i.e., vectors $f_{k,T} = r_k^{\pi_T}$ in (13). The resulting algorithm is an improvement of the basic value iteration approach proposed in [20]. Furthermore, it is possible to show that the algorithm computes finite expansion policies which are at least as good as policy π_T and often improve this policy.

Theorem 4. *Let π_T be any stationary policy vector and $\Pi_1 = (\pi_T, \ldots)$. Let $\Pi_2, \ldots, \Pi_T$ be the policies constructed in lines 4–10. Then it is $G^{\Pi_i} \leq G^{\Pi_{i+1}}$.*

Proof. The statement follows from the fact that $\Delta^{\Pi}(\cdot)$ depicts the difference in the resulting value. Thus, as only the improving changes with $\Delta^{\Pi}(\cdot) > 0$ are chosen, the constructed sequence of policies yields a non-decreasing sequence of values $G^{\Pi_1}, \ldots, G^{\Pi_T}$.

It is interesting to note that even if π_T is a randomized policy vector which is better than any stationary deterministic policy, the policy vectors $\pi_1, \ldots, \pi_{T-1}$

are deterministic. This implies that the best policy from $\mathcal{P}^{MD}$ is at least as good as the best stationary randomized policy.

5   Examples

We present two sets of examples. First, we consider random models to evaluate the effort and solution quality of the different algorithms. Afterwards the model proposed in Sect. 2.4 is analyzed in different configurations. All experiments are performed on a PC with Intel Xeon $E5 - 2690$ processor and 32 GByte of main memory running Debian Linux, *Matlab R 2017* and *CPLEX 12.6.2*.

5.1   Random MDPs

We first consider results for randomly generated CMDPs. Since the integer programs to compute exact solutions become very large, they usually cannot be solved until the optimality gap is closed (i.e., the exact solution is computed for sure). We stop the ILP-solver CPLEX after 1000 s of CPU time, which does not include the setup time for the ILP. Therefore the overall time of the exact solution becomes much longer than 1000 s for larger problems. In these cases, the ILP solver does, of course, not necessarily find the optimal solution. For the following experiments we generate for each instance 10 different random CMDPs which are analyzed. Then we show the mean CPU time required by the solver and the 95% confidence interval. Furthermore, we compute the mean reward reached by the computed policies and the 95% confidence interval. Rewards are normalized by the largest reward computed for an example.

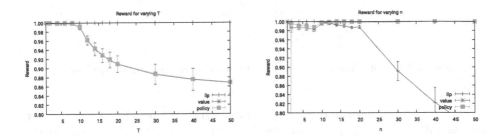

Fig. 1. Reward for random MDPs on finite horizons.

We first consider the finite horizon case with $\gamma = 1$. Results for two cases are shown in Fig. 1. In all experiments $M = K = 5$, in the first series of experiments $N = 5$ and T is varied from 1 through 50. Results are shown on the left side of Fig. 1. In the second series $T = 10$ and $N = 1, \ldots, 40$. Each configuration is solved by value iteration, policy iteration and the ILP solver. The CPU times required for the solutions are shown in Fig. 2.

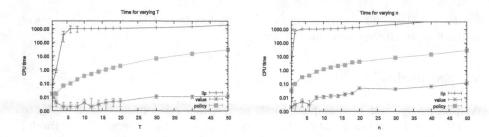

Fig. 2. Solution time for random MDPs on finite horizons.

It can be noticed that value and policy iteration are extremely fast requiring solution times of a few seconds or less, whereas the ILP solver reaches quickly the time limit. In particular for large values, the setup time for the ILP solver is significant such that the overall time is more than an hour. For a growing time horizon T, the local optimizers are not able to compute a policy which is as good as the policy resulting from the ILP solver. The situation is different for fixed T and growing N. In this case, the policy resulting from the ILP solver is worse than the results from value or policy iteration. In both cases, policy iteration results in slightly better policies than value iteration.

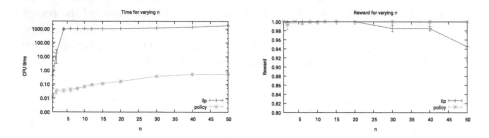

Fig. 3. Solution time and reward for random MDPs on infinite horizons.

For the infinite horizon case we compute Markovian policies of length 5 for models with $M = K = 5$ and varying N. Results and CPU time requirements are shown in Fig. 3. In this case only policy iteration and the ILP solver are applicable. It can be seen that both methods compute policies of a similar quality for smaller values of N. For larger N policy iteration finds better policies than the ILP solver within the time limit. In all cases policy iteration requires only at most a second whereas the ILP solver reaches quickly the time limit of 1000 s solution time which means up to an hour of solution time including setup times.

It should be mentioned that in all cases MDPs where K or M is increased and the other parameters remain fixed show a similar behavior than MDPs with for increasing N.

5.2 Admission Control Problem

As a second example we consider the example introduced in Sect. 2.4. We assume that $C = 3$ and $B = 8$ resulting in an MDP with 165 states and 8 actions. The service rate equals $\mu = 1$ and arrival rates are $\lambda^c \in [0,1]$ ($c \in \{1,2,3\}$). We analyze the MDP for an infinite horizon with discount factor $\gamma = 0.999$. Furthermore we assume that the initial distribution is uniform.

A simple approach is to set $\lambda^c = 0.5$, the mean value in the interval, and compute the optimal policy for this situation. Alternatively, one can sample K different realization of λ^c and build a CMDP with weights $K^{-1}\mathbb{1}$. For this CMDP the policy that maximizes the weighted sum of rewards over the sampled MDPs according to the initial distribution can be computed. Due to the size of the state space an exact ILP solution can only be used for very small sample sizes in the range of 2 or 3. Therefore we apply the local optimization method presented in this paper to compute the optimal policy.

Table 1. Computation time (in sec.) and reward for different policies applied to the admission example with uncertain arrival rates.

K	Normal		Uniform	
	Time	Reward	Time	Reward
1	2.489	206.97 ± 2.34	2.489	218.61 ± 2.20
3	17.63	204.65 ± 2.36	22.92	219.99 ± 2.98
5	40.40	206.93 ± 2.59	59.73	220.00 ± 1.89
10	98.20	208.76 ± 2.65	112.0	225.29 ± 2.55
20	186.6	208.04 ± 0.79	292.5	224.85 ± 2.78
30	276.2	209.14 ± 1.89	450.8	224.31 ± 1.30
50	585.1	210.08 ± 1.54	720.7	225.61 ± 2.89

For the following experiments we first compute an optimal policy for a CMDP resulting from sampling K different realizations of the arrival rates. Then the resulting policy is applied to 1000 MDPs resulting from sampling arrival rates according to the same distribution that has been used for the generation of the policy. This experiment is repeated 10 times for each sample size. From these experiments the mean reward and the 95% confidence interval are computed. As example distributions we use a truncated normal and a uniform distribution. Table 1 contains the results and the times to compute the optimal policy. It can be seen that with an increasing sample size, policies become better. The difference is moderate for the example and is larger for a uniform, than for a truncated normal distribution with more probability mass around the mean. It seems that 10 samples already improve the policy compared to the policy computed with respect to the expected parameter values, at least for the uniform distribution. For the normal distribution a larger sample size further increases the reward of the resulting policy. The price for enlarging the sample size is an additional effort to compute the policy by the local optimization method. However, since the local optimization algorithm can be easily parallelized, which we did not do yet, CMDPs with a few hundred states and sample sizes of about 100 can be handled with the approach.

6   Conclusion

This work extends the approaches of [5,16] and [19,20] for concurrent (or multi-model) Markov decision processes in several directions. First, the approach in [5,16] is generalized for action-dependent rewards. Second, the finite-horizon problem considered in [19,20] is taken in order to compute Markovian finite-memory policies for the discounted reward problem. The finite expansion approach is proven to provide locally optimal policies and seems also practically superior to the value iteration approach from [20], with the finite expansion providing better policies with an acceptable sacrifice in complexity.

For future work, the sampling approach, which is presented here for the second example model, should be further developed because it allows one to analyze systems with realistic parameter uncertainties covering several states of the stochastic process. The approach can be extended to other performance measure like the optimization of the reward for one scenario by guaranteeing lower bounds for other scenarios as done in a slightly different setting in [6]. *matlab* functions for the different functions described in this paper can be downloaded from [4].

References

1. Bertsimas, D., Mišić, V.V.: Robust product line design. Oper. Res. **65**(1), 19–37 (2017)
2. Bertsimas, D., Silberholz, J., Trikalinos, T.: Optimal healthcare decision making under multiple mathematical models: application in prostate cancer screening. Health Care Manag. Sci. **21**(1), 105–118 (2016)
3. Bertsimas, D., Sim, M.: The price of robustness. Oper. Res. **52**(1), 35–53 (2004)
4. Buchholz, P.: Markov decision processes with uncertain parameters. http://ls4-www.cs.tu-dortmund.de/download/buchholz/CMDP/CMDP_Description
5. Buchholz, P., Scheftelowitsch, D.: Computation of weighted sums of rewards for concurrent MDPs. Math. Methods Oper. Res. **89**(1), 1–42 (2019)
6. Buchholz, P., Scheftelowitsch, D.: Light robustness in the optimization of Markov decision processes with uncertain parameters. Comput. Oper. Res. **108**, 69–81 (2019)
7. Goyal, V., Grand-Clement, J.: Robust Markov decision process: Beyond rectangularity. CoRR, abs/1811.00215 (2019)
8. Hager, W.W.: Updating the inverse of a matrix. SIAM Rev. **31**(2), 221–239 (1989)
9. Iyengar, G.N.: Robust dynamic programming. Math. Oper. Res. **30**(2), 257–280 (2005)

10. Jünger, M., et al. (eds.): 50 Years of Integer Programming 1958–2008 - From the Early Years to the State-of-the-Art. Springer, Heidelberg (2010). https://doi.org/10.1007/978-3-540-68279-0
11. Mannor, S., Mebel, O., Xu, H.: Robust MDPs with k-rectangular uncertainty. Math. Oper. Res. **41**(4), 1484–1509 (2016)
12. Nilim, A., Ghaoui, L.E.: Robust control of Markov decision processes with uncertain transition matrices. Oper. Res. **53**(5), 780–798 (2005)
13. Puterman, M.L.: Markov Decision Processes. Wiley, New York (2005)
14. Rockafellar, R.T., Wets, R.J.: Scenarios and policy aggregation in optimization under uncertainty. Math. Oper. Res. **16**(1), 119–147 (1991)
15. Satia, J.K., Lave, R.E.: Markovian decision processes with uncertain transition probabilities. Oper. Res. **21**(3), 728–740 (1973)
16. Scheftelowitsch, D.: Markov decision processes with uncertain parameters. Ph.D. thesis, Technical University of Dortmund, Germany (2018)
17. Serfozo, R.F.: An equivalence between continuous and discrete time Markov decision processes. Oper. Res. **27**(3), 616–620 (1979)
18. Steimle, L.N.: Stochastic Dynamic Optimization Under Ambiguity. Ph.D. thesis, Industrial and Operations Engineering in the University of Michigan (2019)
19. Steimle, L.N., Ahluwalia, V., Kamdar, C., Denton, B.T.: Decomposition methods for multi-model Markov decision processes. Technical report, Optimization-online (2018)
20. Steimle, L.N., Kaufman, D.L., Denton, B.T.: Multi-model Markov decision processes. Technical report, Optimization-online (2018)
21. White, C.C., Eldeib, H.K.: Markov decision processes with imprecise transition probabilities. Oper. Res. **42**(4), 739–749 (1994)
22. Wiesemann, W., Kuhn, D., Rustem, B.: Robust Markov decision processes. Math. Oper. Res. **38**(1), 153–183 (2013)

A Stochastic Automata Network Description for Spatial DNA-Methylation Models

Alexander Lück[✉] and Verena Wolf

Department of Computer Science, Saarland University, Saarbrücken, Germany
alexander.lueck@uni-saarland.de

Abstract. DNA methylation is an important biological mechanism to regulate gene expression and control cell development. Mechanistic modeling has become a popular approach to enhance our understanding of the dynamics of methylation pattern formation in living cells. Recent findings suggest that the methylation state of a cytosine base can be influenced by its DNA neighborhood. Therefore, it is necessary to generalize existing mathematical models that consider only one cytosine and its partner on the opposite DNA-strand (CpG), in order to include such neighborhood dependencies. One approach is to describe the system as a stochastic automata network (SAN) with functional transitions. We show that single-CpG models can successfully be generalized to multiple CpGs using the SAN description and verify the results by comparing them to results from extensive Monte-Carlo simulations.

Keywords: DNA methylation · Stochastic automata networks · Spatial stochastic model

1 Introduction

The field of epigenetics investigates changes in gene function that are not related to the organism's genetic code but rely on epigenetic markers. DNA methylation is one of the main epigenetic markers regulating gene expression and controlling cell fate. The epigenetic code is passed along from one generation to the next but environmental factors such as diet, stress, and prenatal nutrition can modify such markers resulting, for instance, in the deactivation or activation of certain genes. In the case of DNA methylation, a marker is set by adding a methyl group to cytosine (C) bases on the DNA. The conversion of C to its methylated form (5-methylcytosine) is carried out by DNA methyltransferase (Dnmt) enzymes and the resulting methylation pattern determines the program and function of the corresponding cell.

Together with a subsequent guanine (G) and the corresponding GC-pair on the opposite strand, a cytosine base forms a so-called CpG, which may be methylated on none, one, or both DNA strands. Mechanistic models based on

© Springer Nature Switzerland AG 2020
H. Hermanns (Ed.): MMB 2020, LNCS 12040, pp. 54–64, 2020.
https://doi.org/10.1007/978-3-030-43024-5_4

Discrete-Time Markov Chains (DTMCs) have been developed to describe the temporal evolution of the methylation state of a CpG [1]. The goal of such models is to increase the understanding of methylation pattern formation. Due to the possible influence of the neighboring CpGs [14,17] generalizations of simple, single-CpG models have recently been developed, which take more than one CpG into account [3,18–20]. However, even for a small number of CpGs the size of the transition matrices grows rapidly and they are therefore hard to generate without suitable methods. One of these methods are the stochastic automata networks (SANs) [22,23], which have already been successfully applied in a variety a fields, like biology [9,24], geology [2] or performance evaluation of software development [7,11]. In this work we show how to successfully apply the SAN framework to Markov models for single CpGs in order to generalize them to multiple CpGs with the aid of suitable, neighbor state dependent rate functions.

This paper is organized is follows: In Sect. 2 we describe the model for a single CpG and show how to generalize it to several CpGs using the SAN framework. A comparison with Monte-Carlo simulations in order to verify the results of our generated matrices can be found in Sect. 3. In Sect. 4 we conclude our findings and give ideas for possible future work.

2   SANS

In order to describe the methylation dynamics of a CpG in terms of DTMCs, we consider CpGs on the double stranded DNA where each CpG contains two Cs (one on each strand), each of which can be either methylated or unmethylated. Therefore there are four possible states, i.e., both Cs unmethylated (state 1), only the C on the upper strand methylated (state 2), only the C on the lower strand methylated (state 3) and both Cs methylated (state 4). A sequence of CpGs, which can be described as a concatenation of states, is called a pattern. For a sequence of L CpGs there are 4^L possible patterns.

The processes that lead to state transitions are cell division, maintenance and *de novo* methylation. During cell division, one strand and its methylation state are kept as they are (parental strand), while the other strand is newly synthesized (daughter strand) with all Cs unmethylated. Maintenance methylation adds methylation to the C on the daughter strand if the corresponding C on the parental strand is already methylated in order to reestablish existing methylation patterns. In contrast to that, *de novo* methylation may occur on unmethylated Cs on both strands independent of the methylation state of the C on the opposite strand and is therefore responsible for creating new patterns. The transition probability matrices for these processes for a single CpG are listed in Table 1. In the left column the matrices concerning the upper strand are listed and in the right column the matrices for the lower strand.

It is biologically plausible to assume that cell division happens first, afterwards maintenance on the daughter strand and in the end *de novo* on both strands takes place. Note that the order of the two possible *de novo* events does not matter, i.e. $T_1 \cdot T_2 = T_2 \cdot T_1$. Since the strand that is kept after cell division is chosen randomly with equal probability, the total transition probability matrix P is given by

$$P = 0.5 \cdot (CD_1 \cdot M_1 + CD_2 \cdot M_2) \cdot T_1 \cdot T_2. \tag{1}$$

Table 1. Transition matrices for a single CpG. Note that the transition probabilities f may be functions of the reaction parameters, the CpG position and/or the states of the adjacent CpGs. The matrices in the left column represent the transitions on the upper and the matrices in the right column the transitions on the lower strand.

Cell Division

$$CD_1 = \begin{pmatrix} 1 & 0 & 0 & 0 \\ 1 & 0 & 0 & 0 \\ 0 & 0 & 1 & 0 \\ 0 & 0 & 1 & 0 \end{pmatrix} \qquad CD_2 = \begin{pmatrix} 1 & 0 & 0 & 0 \\ 0 & 1 & 0 & 0 \\ 1 & 0 & 0 & 0 \\ 0 & 1 & 0 & 0 \end{pmatrix}$$

Maintenance

$$M_1 = \begin{pmatrix} 1 & 0 & 0 & 0 \\ 0 & 1 & 0 & 0 \\ 0 & 0 & 1-f & f \\ 0 & 0 & 0 & 1 \end{pmatrix} \qquad M_2 = \begin{pmatrix} 1 & 0 & 0 & 0 \\ 0 & 1-f & 0 & f \\ 0 & 0 & 1 & 0 \\ 0 & 0 & 0 & 1 \end{pmatrix}$$

De Novo

$$T_1 = \begin{pmatrix} 1-f & f & 0 & 0 \\ 0 & 1 & 0 & 0 \\ 0 & 0 & 1-f & f \\ 0 & 0 & 0 & 1 \end{pmatrix} \qquad T_2 = \begin{pmatrix} 1-f & 0 & f & 0 \\ 0 & 1-f & 0 & f \\ 0 & 0 & 1 & 0 \\ 0 & 0 & 0 & 1 \end{pmatrix}$$

Given a sequence of L CpGs, each CpG can be described by the aforementioned DTMC, which gives us one automaton of the automata network. The structure of each automaton is independent of the automata describing neighboring CpGs, however, the transition probabilities may depend on their local states (functional transitions). A suitable method to combine these automata in order to capture the dynamics of whole sequences of CpGs is to consider them as an automata network. Within the SAN framework, the transition matrices of the individual automata are combined via the Kronecker product. Since in our case the transition matrix for one automaton is a product of the transition matrices for the different processes, we exploit some properties of the Kronecker product to generate the global transition matrix of the network. From

$$A \otimes (B \otimes C) = (A \otimes B) \otimes C \tag{2}$$
$$(AC) \otimes (BD) = (A \otimes B) \cdot (C \otimes D) \tag{3}$$

the following properties can be derived [8]

$$\left(\prod_{n=1}^{N} A_n\right) \otimes \left(\prod_{n=1}^{N} B_n\right) = \prod_{n=1}^{N} \left(A_n \otimes B_n\right), \tag{4}$$

$$\bigotimes_{m=1}^{M} \left(\prod_{n=1}^{N} A_n^{(m)}\right) = \prod_{n=1}^{N} \left(\bigotimes_{m=1}^{M} A_n^{(m)}\right). \tag{5}$$

Note that in Eqs. (3)–(5) the corresponding matrices have to be compatible under the standard matrix product.

As a consequence of Eq. (5) it is possible to obtain the total transition matrix P in two ways: First compute a transition matrix for a single CpG Eq. (1) and extend the result to several CpGs with the Kronecker product or calculate the transition matrices for the different processes for several CpGs first via the Kronecker product and combine them afterwards. Since the transition probabilities may depend on the neighbor states, i.e. the states of the adjacent automata, it is easier to choose the second possibility and construct the individual transition matrices for the different processes first. Another advantage is that the matrices for the different processes are sparse, while the total transition matrix is quite dense for a single CpG (see Table 1 and Fig. 1), such that we apply the Kronecker product to sparse matrices and multiply the (also sparse) results afterwards.

If we assume that all CpGs are methylated independent of their neighborhood, then no functional transitions are needed and the transition probabilities are constants. The construction of the global transition matrix is then straightforward by simply applying the Kronecker product. To model dependence, first observe that since only the transition probabilities, but not the transitions themselves, depend on the neighboring states, the structure of the global transition matrix is the same as in the independent case. By using functions instead of constant probabilities, we are able to capture the effect of the neighbors on the transition rates. Another advantage of the functions is that we can incorporate different model assumptions (like processivity) by using different functions without altering the structure of the transition matrices.

To shape the function $f := f(r, l, s_{l-1}, s_{l+1}) \in [0, 1]$ in the matrices in Table 1 to our needs, we use the following inputs:

- r is a vector with the reaction parameters,
- $l \in \{1, \ldots, L\}$ is the position of the CpG such that boundary ($l = 1, L$) and non-boundary ($l = 2, \ldots, L-1$) CpGs can be distinguished,
- s_{l-1} is the state of the left neighboring CpG and
- s_{l+1} is the state of the right neighboring CpG.

Depending on the methylation event (maintenance or *de novo*) different parameter vectors r can be chosen. Since in general all CpGs may undergo a reaction, the states of the neighboring CpGs that are used (before or after reaction) as an input for the function depend on the underlying assumptions. This will be demonstrated in the following.

We first note that the indices of the matrices in Table 1 correspond to the states before and after transition, i.e. the entry $a_{i,j}$ corresponds to the probability of going from state i to state j. Furthermore, there is a unique relation between the indices of the initial matrices and the indices of the result of their Kronecker product

$$a_{r,s} \cdot b_{v,w} = (A \otimes B)_{p(r-1)+v,q(s-1)+w}, \tag{6}$$

$$(A \otimes B)_{i,j} = a_{\lfloor (i-1)/p \rfloor +1, \lfloor (j-1)/q \rfloor +1} \cdot b_{i-\lfloor (i-1)/p \rfloor p, j-\lfloor (j-1)/q \rfloor q}, \tag{7}$$

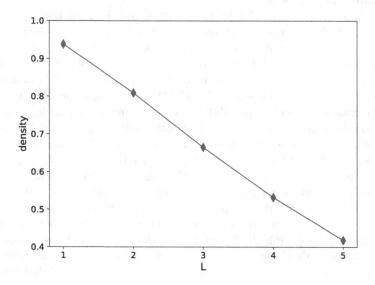

Fig. 1. Density of entries for the transition matrix P for different numbers of CpGs L.

where A is a $p \times q$ and B an arbitrary matrix. These formulas can easily be generalized such that for a Kronecker product of L matrices we know exactly the indices for each of the matrices and therefore the states before and after transition for each CpG. We then use this knowledge to choose the correct transition probability depending on our assumptions.

For the transition probabilities, we impose, depending on the neighbor states, the following forms [19]: For *de novo* methylation events (the state of the other strand does not matter) we have transition probabilities for non-boundary cases

$$\circ \circ \circ \to \circ \bullet \circ \qquad p_1 = 0.5 \cdot (\psi_L + \psi_R)\tau, \tag{8}$$

$$\bullet \circ \circ \to \bullet \bullet \circ \qquad p_2 = 0.5 \cdot (\psi_L + \psi_R)\tau + 0.5 \cdot (1 - \psi_L), \tag{9}$$

$$\circ \circ \bullet \to \circ \bullet \bullet \qquad p_3 = 0.5 \cdot (\psi_L + \psi_R)\tau + 0.5 \cdot (1 - \psi_R), \tag{10}$$

$$\bullet \circ \bullet \to \bullet \bullet \bullet \qquad p_4 = 1 - 0.5 \cdot (\psi_L + \psi_R)(1 - \tau), \tag{11}$$

where an empty circle represents an unmethylated and a filled circle a methylated C. The parameters ψ_L and ψ_R characterize the dependency on the neighbor state, where $\psi_i = 1$ means full independency and $\psi_i = 0$ full dependency.

The parameter τ corresponds to the *de novo* probability in the fully independent case.

For maintenance events, we replace the probability τ by μ and have the additional requirement that the C on the opposite strand must be methylated.

For boundary cases, i.e., the left- and rightmost CpG in a sequence of L CpGs, we have the probabilities

$$? \circ \circ \rightarrow ? \bullet \circ \qquad \tilde{p}_1 = (1 - \rho) \cdot p_1 + \rho \cdot p_2, \tag{12}$$

$$? \circ \bullet \rightarrow ? \bullet \bullet \qquad \tilde{p}_2 = (1 - \rho) \cdot p_3 + \rho \cdot p_4, \tag{13}$$

$$\circ \circ ? \rightarrow \circ \bullet ? \qquad \tilde{p}_3 = (1 - \rho) \cdot p_1 + \rho \cdot p_3, \tag{14}$$

$$\bullet \circ ? \rightarrow \bullet \bullet ? \qquad \tilde{p}_4 = (1 - \rho) \cdot p_2 + \rho \cdot p_4, \tag{15}$$

where we use the average methylation level ρ, since we do not have any information about the CpG on the left/right at the boundaries.

For a moderate number of CpGs (≈ 5) it is possible to explicitly construct the whole transition matrix with a simple algorithm. We first note that we have to apply the Kronecker product for the matrices in Table 1 L times with themselves for a sequence of L CpGs. We then apply the following scheme:

1. Identify the indices of the non-zero entries of the matrix.
2. Calculate the indices of the resulting matrix after applying the Kronecker product with Eq. (6) for the indices from step 1. Iteratively applying Eq. (6) L times leads to the final indices (u, v). For each (u, v) we get an ordered list ℓ containing the indices from the original matrices that lead to this index.
3. For each (u, v) calculate the matrix entry

$$m_{u,v} = \prod_{(i,j) \in \ell} a_{i,j}, \tag{16}$$

   where $a_{i,j}$ are the entries of the original matrix.
4. If $a_{i,j}$ contains the function f choose the neighbor states based on the assumption and the indices (states) from ℓ of the adjacent matrices.

Note that for real data we have to ensure that all CpGs of a given sequence originate from the same cell in order to properly investigate the neighborhood dependencies. Real data rarely covers states of more than a couple of successive CpGs from the same cell with sufficiently deep coverage. Therefore, the number of contiguous CpGs is usually very limited, such that the explicit construction of the transition matrix for short CpG sequences is feasible in most cases. For a possible larger number of CpGs from advanced measurement techniques we have to resort to more sophisticated methods to obtain the transition matrices or even avoid the generation completely and resort to matrix vector matrix products on the smaller component matrices [4–6, 10, 23].

Example: Processivity

The detailed mechanisms about the interaction of the Dnmts with the DNA remain elusive. The Dnmts may behave in a processive way, i.e., moving continuously on the DNA strand, or in a distributive manner without directed movement, where attachment and detachment occurs at arbitrary positions on the DNA strand. We therefore would like to test these different assumptions about the methylation mechanisms [13,15,19,21]. For the remainder of this paper, we assume *processivity from left to right*, which is a reasonable assumption for Dnmt1, due to its link to the replication machinery. The processivity from left to right implies, that a transition already happened at the left neighbor (position $l - 1$) but not yet at the right neighbor ($l + 1$). This means, given the list of indices $\ell = [\ldots, (i_{l-1}, j_{l-1}), (i_l, j_l), (i_{l+1}, j_{l+1}), \ldots]$ we choose j_{l-1} for the left neighbor state and i_{l+1} for the right neighbor state as an input for the function in step 4 of our algorithmic scheme. Consider for example the transition from a fully unmethylated sequence ($\circ\,\circ\,\circ$) to a fully methylated sequence ($\bullet\,\bullet\,\bullet$). In this case the correct order of (sub)transitions with their respective probabilities are:

$$\circ\,\circ\,\circ \;\xrightarrow{(12)}\; \bullet\,\circ\,\circ \;\xrightarrow{(9)}\; \bullet\,\bullet\,\circ \;\xrightarrow{(15)}\; \bullet\,\bullet\,\bullet$$

3 Results

In order to check the correctness of our dedicated implementation for generating matrices with the Kronecker product for L CpGs, we compare the resulting distributions with results from Monte-Carlo (MC) simulations. As initial distribution π_0 we use a discrete uniform distribution which assigns the same probability 4^{-L} to all possible methylation patterns. We then compute the transient distributions $\pi(t)$ after $t = 30$ cell division and subsequent methylation events via

$$\pi(t + 1) = \pi(t) \cdot P, \tag{17}$$

where P is the total transition matrix, where we assume processivity. Note that $t = 30$ cell divisions is well within the order of cell divisions for biological data [1], where the system still shows a transient behaviour. For a larger number of cell divisions the system may reach a stationary state. However, with the generated transition matrix a stationary analysis is also straightforward.

We perform the corresponding MC simulations of our model with $N = 10^6$ runs to get an independent estimation for the transient pattern probabilities. Note that for that many runs the results from MC simulations are already pretty stable, i.e., the confidence intervals for the estimated transient probabilities are small. In order to not overload the figures, we therefore do not show them here. The distributions for different parameter sets are shown in Fig. 2. Panels (a) and (b) show the fully dependent case, where the transition probabilities depend only on the neighbor states and not on the actual maintenance and *de novo* rates μ and τ. In Fig. 2(c) the transition probabilities are totally independent of the neighboring states and depend solely on μ and τ. This case is equivalent to the case where we replace the function f by the respective (constant) transition probabilities. Figure 2(d) shows a case with some dependency on both neighbor states, where the dependence to the left is slightly stronger. Choosing a wrong transition function in the matrix entries (compared to MC, where it is easier to ensure the correct choice) would affect the distribution in (a) and (b) the most, since there is a full dependency and hence the largest effect from the neighboring states. For the partial dependencies in (d) there should also be an effect if the choices were wrong. In the independent case (c) there can not be a wrong choice, since the transition function is a constant.

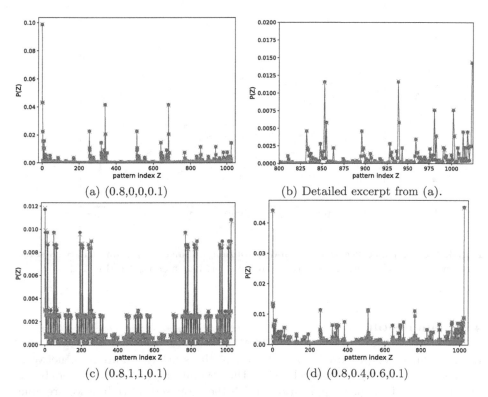

(a) (0.8,0,0,0.1)

(b) Detailed excerpt from (a).

(c) (0.8,1,1,0.1)

(d) (0.8,0.4,0.6,0.1)

Fig. 2. Comparison of distributions obtained from transition matrices generated from the SAN description (blue dots connected with solid lines) and from MC simulations (red crosses). The parameters for each subfigure are given in the form $(\mu, \psi_L, \psi_R, \tau)$. (Color figure online)

In all cases we observe an almost perfect agreement with only small deviations on some patterns on a very small scale. In order to exclude a flaw in the construction of the transition matrix we compute the Hellinger distance

$$H(P,Q) = \frac{1}{\sqrt{2}} \left(\sum_{i=1}^{k} (\sqrt{p_i} - \sqrt{q_i})^2 \right)^{\frac{1}{2}} \tag{18}$$

to compare the similarity of the distributions and to check if the deviations stem from the finite number of MC simulation runs. From Fig. 3 it is obvious that with an increasing number of runs the distributions become more and more similar such that we can indeed exclude a flaw in the matrix construction. The small deviations stem from the finite number of runs since for $N = 10^6$ there are still statistical inaccuracies and hence H is quite large (order of 10^{-2}).

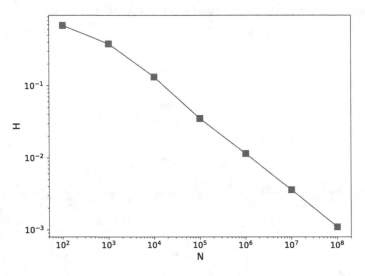

Fig. 3. Hellinger distance H between distribution obtained from numerical SAN solution and from MC simulations with N runs for the parameter set of Fig. 2(d).

4   Conclusion

In this paper, we propose an adaptation of the stochastic automata network framework to solve problems related to the generation of transition probability matrices for a biological application. With the proposed procedure we are able to describe the methylation dynamics of a sequence of several CpGs, given the matrices for a single CpG. The transition matrices form the basis for numerical solutions of mechanistic models, which allow to test assumptions about the functioning of methylation enzymes. The presented framework allows to consider longer CpG sequences and hence the proper investigation of larger genomic regions. The transition matrix for L CpGs can systematically be generated from the small single-CpG matrices and the generation is less prone to errors than an ad-hoc approach. It is also pretty easy to adapt the model to test different biological assumptions by using different functions in the transition matrices. In our example, we assumed processivity from left to right, but by changing the functions other assumptions like processivity from right to left (less biologically plausible) or even non-processive (e.g. distributive) behavior can be realized. It is also easily possible to introduce additional reaction parameters for each individual CpG within this framework to generalize the model. Using the same reaction parameters for all CpGs is a strong assumption, especially for the neighborhood dependencies, which should intuitively be different due to the (in general) different distances between CpGs or also due to different base sequences in the DNA.

Furthermore, it is also straightforward to apply the SAN approach to more complex methylation models in order to investigate possible neighborhood dependencies. This is especially useful when there are more than four states per CpG as with more states the transition matrix grows rapidly. Introducing additional hydroxylated Cs as in [12] the number of states per CpG grows from four to eight such that the transition matrix grows from $4^L \times 4^L$ to $8^L \times 8^L$ for L CpGs.

With even more possible modifications of C, such as the formylated form 5-formylcytosin, the number of possible states and hence the matrix size grows even more (16^L or $16^L \times 16^L$ respectively). In this case, the SAN description becomes even more useful as it would be very tedious to generate the transition matrix in other ways. It is also possible to apply the SAN approach to continuous time Markov chains or hybrid models as in [16]. Here, the discrete transition matrix was generated with a Kronecker product, while the continuous generator matrix can be generated with a Kronecker sum.

References

1. Arand, J., et al.: In vivo control of CpG and non-CpG DNA methylation by DNA methyltransferases. PLoS Genet. **8**(6), e1002750 (2012)
2. Assunçao, J., Espindola, L., Fernandes, P., Pivel, M., Sales, A.: A structured stochastic model for prediction of geological stratal stacking patterns. Electron. Notes Theor. Comput. Sci. **296**, 27–42 (2013)
3. Bonello, N., et al.: Bayesian inference supports a location and neighbour-dependent model of DNA methylation propagation at the MGMT gene promoter in lung tumours. J. Theor. Biol. **336**, 87–95 (2013)
4. Buchholz, P.: Equivalence relations for stochastic automata networks. In: Stewart, W.J. (ed.) Computations with Markov Chains, pp. 197–215. Springer, Boston (1995). https://doi.org/10.1007/978-1-4615-2241-6_13
5. Buchholz, P.: Hierarchical Markovian models: symmetries and reduction. Perform. Eval. **22**(1), 93–110 (1995)
6. Buchholz, P., Kemper, P.: Kronecker based matrix representations for large Markov models. In: Baier, C., Haverkort, B.R., Hermanns, H., Katoen, J.-P., Siegle, M. (eds.) Validation of Stochastic Systems. LNCS, vol. 2925, pp. 256–295. Springer, Heidelberg (2004). https://doi.org/10.1007/978-3-540-24611-4_8
7. Czekster, R.M., Fernandes, P., Lopes, L., Sales, A., Santos, A.R., Webber, T.: Stochastic performance analysis of global software development teams. ACM Trans. Softw. Eng. Methodol. **25**(3), 1–32 (2016)
8. Davio, M.: Kronecker products and shuffle algebra. IEEE Trans. Comput. **100**(2), 116–125 (1981)

9. DeRemigio, H., Kemper, P., LaMar, M.D., Smith, G.D.: Markov chain models of coupled intracellular calcium channels: Kronecker structured representations and benchmark stationary distribution calculations. In: Biocomputing 2008, pp. 354–365. World Scientific (2008)

10. Fernandes, P., Plateau, B., Stewart, W.J.: Efficient descriptor-vector multiplications in stochastic automata networks. J. ACM **45**(3), 381–414 (1998)

11. Fernandes, P., Sales, A., Santos, A.R., Webber, T.: Performance evaluation of software development teams: a practical case study. Electron. Notes Theor. Comput. Sci. **275**, 73–92 (2011)

12. Giehr, P., Kyriakopoulos, C., Ficz, G., Wolf, V., Walter, J.: The influence of hydroxylation on maintaining CpG methylation patterns: a hidden Markov model approach. PLoS Comput. Biol. **12**(5), e1004905 (2016)

13. Gowher, H., Jeltsch, A.: Molecular enzymology of the catalytic domains of the DNMT3A and DNMT3B DNA methyltransferases. J. Biol. Chem. **277**(23), 20409–20414 (2002)

14. Haerter, J.O., Lövkvist, C., Dodd, I.B., Sneppen, K.: Collaboration between CpG sites is needed for stable somatic inheritance of DNA methylation states. Nucleic Acids Res. **42**(4), 2235–2244 (2013)

15. Holz-Schietinger, C., Reich, N.O.: The inherent processivity of the human de novo methyltransferase 3A (DNMT3A) is enhanced by DNMT3L. J. Biol. Chem. **285**(38), 29091–29100 (2010)

16. Kyriakopoulos, C., Giehr, P., Lück, A., Walter, J., Wolf, V.: A Hybrid HMM Approach for the Dynamics of DNA Methylation. arXiv preprint arXiv:1901.06286 (2019)

17. Lövkvist, C., Dodd, I.B., Sneppen, K., Haerter, J.O.: DNA methylation in human epigenomes depends on local topology of CpG sites. Nucleic Acids Res. **44**(11), 5123–5132 (2016)

18. Lück, A., Giehr, P., Nordström, K., Walter, J., Wolf, V.: Hidden Markov modelling reveals neighborhood dependence of DNMT3A and 3B activity. IEEE/ACM Trans. Comput. Biol. Bioinform. **16**, 1598–1609 (2019)

19. Lück, A., Giehr, P., Walter, J., Wolf, V.: A stochastic model for the formation of spatial methylation patterns. In: Feret, J., Koeppl, H. (eds.) CMSB 2017. LNCS, vol. 10545, pp. 160–178. Springer, Cham (2017). https://doi.org/10.1007/978-3-319-67471-1_10

20. Meyer, K.N., Lacey, M.R.: Modeling methylation patterns with long read sequencing data. IEEE/ACM Trans. Comput. Biol. Bioinform. **15**(4), 1379–1389 (2017)

21. Norvil, A.B., Petell, C.J., Alabdi, L., Wu, L., Rossie, S., Gowher, H.: DNMT3B methylates DNA by a noncooperative mechanism, and its activity is unaffected by manipulations at the predicted dimer interface. Biochemistry **57**(29), 4312–4324 (2016)

22. Plateau, B., Atif, K.: Stochastic automata network of modeling parallel systems. IEEE Trans. Softw. Eng. **17**(10), 1093–1108 (1991)

23. Stewart, W.J., Atif, K., Plateau, B.: The numerical solution of stochastic automata networks. Eur. J. Oper. Res. **86**(3), 503–525 (1995)

24. Wolf, V.: Modelling of biochemical reactions by stochastic automata networks. Electron. Notes Theor. Comput. Sci. **171**(2), 197–208 (2007). Proceedings of the First Workshop on Membrane Computing and Biologically Inspired Process Calculi (MeCBIC 2006)

An ns-3 Model for Multipath Communication with Terrestrial and Satellite Links

Jörg Deutschmann$^{(\boxtimes)}$, Kai-Steffen Jens Hielscher, and Reinhard German

Department of Computer Science 7,
Computer Networks and Communication Systems,
University of Erlangen-Nürnberg,
Martensstraße 3, 91058 Erlangen, Germany
{joerg.deutschmann,kai-steffen.hielscher,reinhard.german}@fau.de

Abstract. Some terrestrial Internet access links provide only low data rates. Internet access via geostationary satellites on the other hand provides data rates of up to 50 Mbit/s, but suffers from high latencies. The combination of low data rate, low latency Internet access (e.g., DSL light) and high data rate, high latency Internet access (e.g., geostationary satellites) can utilize the advantages of both. We discuss multipath communication architectures and scheduling strategies for such heterogeneous link combinations. The solution described in this paper relies on Split TCP and Performance Enhancement Proxies. We implement and evaluate the solution with the network simulator ns-3. A well-established traffic model for loading websites is enhanced with different HTTP variants. The results show that the combination of heterogeneous link types can result in page load times close to as if there was a high data rate, low latency Internet access.

Keywords: Terrestrial and satellite networks · Multipath communication · Hybrid access · Network simulation

1   Introduction

Despite the ever-increasing demand for broadband Internet access, people in some areas still only have Internet access with data rates of a few Mbit/s [16]. Internet access via geostationary satellites provides data rates of up to 50 Mbit/s already today and more in the near future [10]. However, the large propagation delay leads to Round Trip Times (RTTs) of more than 600 ms, which can be problematic for some applications. Especially modern websites are very large regarding transferred data size (problematic for low data rate Internet access) and very interactive (problematic for high latency links). The approach in the *Transparent Multichannel IPv6* (TMC) project [12] is to combine low data rate, low latency Internet access (e.g., DSL light) with high data rate, high latency Internet access (e.g., geostationary satellites) as shown in Fig. 1. These very

© Springer Nature Switzerland AG 2020
H. Hermanns (Ed.): MMB 2020, LNCS 12040, pp. 65–81, 2020.
https://doi.org/10.1007/978-3-030-43024-5_5

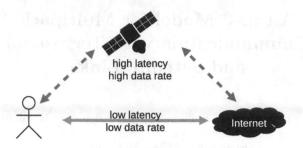

Fig. 1. TMC project concept

heterogeneous link characteristics are a challenge because data rates as well as delays differ by an order of magnitude. The TMC project accepts solutions that can be realized with IPv6 only, but for the moment, the solution described in this paper is compatible with IPv4 and IPv6.

This paper focuses on the modeling and evaluation of the TMC approach. Measurements of commercially available satellite Internet accesses were already presented in [11]. The main contributions of this paper are:

(1) A Split-TCP architecture for multipath communication with very heterogeneous links and a scheduling mechanism based on buffered data (backlog).
(2) A model of (1) and an enhanced HTTP traffic model, both implemented in the network simulator ns-3.
(3) Quality of Service evaluation given different HTTP variants and link configurations.

This paper is structured as follows: As part of the introduction, we introduce satellite Internet and Performance Enhancement Proxies (PEPs) as well as multipath communication concepts. In Sect. 2, related work with a focus on multipath communication and very heterogeneous links, especially terrestrial and satellite links, is reviewed. Based on this, we present the TMC solution in Sect. 3. The HTTP workload and TMC model is described in Sect. 4, the experiment setup in Sect. 5, and the evaluation in Sect. 6. Finally, Sect. 7 concludes this paper and gives directions for future work.

1.1 Satellite Internet and Performance Enhancement Proxies

TCP does not work very well over geostationary satellite links with RTTs larger than 600 ms [11]. To overcome TCP's performance degradations over high delay links, Performance Enhancement Proxies are deployed in every commercial satellite network [6]. PEPs use Split TCP as shown in Fig. 2. Clients and servers can use their default TCP stacks and parameters. On the satellite link, TCP with optimized parameters and congestion control (e.g., TCP Hybla [8]) or any other (maybe proprietary) protocol can be used. Virtual Private Networks and encrypted transport layer protocols (e.g., QUIC [20]) can not benefit from PEPs, which is also the reason why these protocols usually perform poorly when a satellite link is involved.

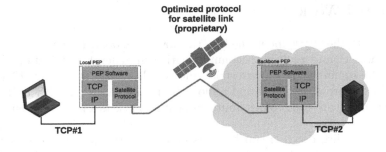

Fig. 2. Performance Enhancement Proxies (PEPs)

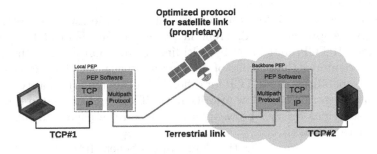

Fig. 3. PEPs with multiple (heterogeneous) links

1.2 Multipath Communication

There are approaches to multipath communication on different layers [22]. Besides reliability and mobility, bandwidth aggregation is often one of the main goals of multipath communication. However, with a combination of links as assumed in the TMC project, bandwidth aggregation seems to be less important. For example, the 1 Mbit/s of a DSL light access can be neglected compared to the 20 Mbit/s of a satellite Internet access.

Multipath TCP (MPTCP) [18], which is a transport layer approach, is in a very mature state. However, the more heterogeneous the paths are, the lower the overall performance is [17]. Originally designed for end hosts, MPTCP proxies have been designed to support hosts that are not MPTCP-enabled yet [25].

Multipath communication on the network layer is often referred to as *bonding*. It consists of a local and a backbone gateway connected via two or more paths (usually tunnels). At the ingress of the bond (local or remote side), received packets are encapsulated, labeled with a sequence number and scheduled among the links. To avoid reordering of packets caused by heterogeneous links, the egress of the bond buffers packets and delivers them in the order as they have been received. There are commercial solutions offering such bonding solutions (e.g., GRE Tunnel Bonding [21]). Bonding provides bandwidth aggregation and works for any transport layer protocol, but the overall latency of the bond is dominated by the link with the highest latency as soon as one packet is sent over the high latency link.

2   Related Work

In addition to the work mentioned in the introduction, which was related to satellite Internet and multipath communication in general, publications which consider the combination of terrestrial and satellite links are [3–5, 9, 13, 15, 19, 23]. In most approaches, local and remote/backbone gateways (either PEPs or MPTCP proxies) are used to distribute and gather packets among different paths (c.f. Fig. 3).

In [9] a satellite downstream boost is described. Whenever the throughput of a DSL link is not sufficient, flows are switched to the satellite link providing higher data rates. The paper uses a high-level simulation without specifying protocols or scheduling mechanisms.

Abdelsalam et al. [3–5] focus on bandwidth aggregation with terrestrial and satellite links. Approaches at different layers are discussed in [3, 4], including bonding and MPTCP, and in [4] a multi-link aggregation architecture is proposed which combines the benefits of different approaches. In [5] the bandwidth aggregation capabilities of MPTCP for different link combinations are evaluated. Bandwidth aggregation has a low priority in the TMC project, and in this paper we discuss strategies for web browsing and focus on the page load time (PLT) as performance metric.

In [23], the authors recognize that long objects benefit from the satellite link, whereas short objects benefit from the low latency link. MPTCP and a *path selection based on object length* (PSBOL) algorithm, which is based on inter-arrival times of packets, was used to combine satellite, LTE, and DSL links. The authors used artificial traffic patterns (short objects, long objects, and a mixture) for performance evaluation. In [15] a Quality of Experience (QoE) study was carried out based on [23]. Unfortunately, details regarding the link selection algorithm and information about the website structure (object sizes, HTTP variants) were not provided. [13] introduces a project which adds satellite links into the backhaul of 5G networks using the PSBOL algorithm. Different from [13, 15, 23], we suggest that it is much simpler to select the best link by looking at the outstanding amount of data among all flows (see Sect. 3 for details). We also provide a more detailed analysis and evaluation of web traffic.

In [19] the authors introduce *Accelerating Network Services by Adding a Short Path* (ASAP), a combination of low latency and satellite networks. The PLT is used as performance metric and like the TMC approach, the basic idea is to set up connections and send HTTP requests via the low latency terrestrial link and then switch to the satellite link. However, frequently switching among the links was not discussed. Regarding performance evaluation, real networks (i.e., 3G/4G cellular networks and a geostationary satellite network) were used without stating the link properties, but from the provided results a high data rate terrestrial link can be assumed. The authors have shown performance improvements in the PLT and handshake phase delay of four unspecified websites listed in the Alexa top U.S. sites.

3   The TMC Solution

The TMC solution consists of two rationales: First, use Split TCP to aggregate data received from a TCP sender. Second, use the aggregated data as link scheduling decision.

We initially considered a bonding architecture in combination with a specialized scheduler [12]. This would preserve the end-to-end principle and also work for any transport layer protocol. However, the flow control of end hosts usually handles sudden changes in the link characteristics not very well. With PEPs and Split TCP, which is deployed in satellite networks anyway, we gain more flexibility in the scheduling among very heterogeneous links. Thanks to Split TCP, as much transport layer payload from a sender as desired can be aggregated in the PEPs. Based on that aggregated data, a scheduling decision is made. This solution works purely on the transport layer (i.e., TCP) and does not need higher-layer protocol information (e.g., HTTP Content-Length). The resulting architecture is the one shown in Fig. 3.

One of the key elements of efficient multipath communication is scheduling among the paths. In our case, it is especially important because of the very heterogeneous links in terms of both delay and data rate. The very different link characteristics are illustrated in Fig. 4, which shows a transmission of a single

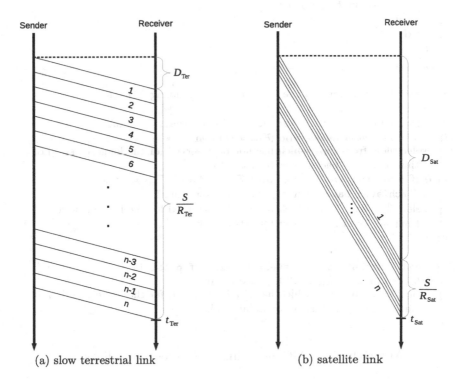

Fig. 4. Data transmission of n packets over (a) terrestrial link and (b) satellite link

Input: $\mathcal{F} = \{(flow_i, backlog_i);\ 1 \le i \le N\}$ // Set of all flows
Init: $\mathcal{F}_{\text{Ter}} \leftarrow \emptyset$ // Set of flows eligible for terrestrial link
    $\mathcal{F}_{\text{Sat}} \leftarrow \emptyset$ // Set of flows eligible for satellite link

// First part: Decide which flows are suitable for which link type

$totalBacklog = \sum_{i=1}^{N} backlog_i$
if $totalBacklog < S_{\text{Th,TerSat}}$ **then**
        // don't use sat link because total backlog is too small
        for $1 \le i \le N$ **do**
                if $backlog_i > 0$ **then**
                    | $\mathcal{F}_{\text{Ter}} = \mathcal{F}_{\text{Ter}} + flow_i$
                end
        end
else
        // consider sat link because total backlog is quite large
        for $1 \le i \le N$ **do**
                if $backlog_i > 0$ **and** $backlog_i < S_{\text{Th,SmallFlow}}$ **then**
                        // conn. setups and mice flows over the ter link
                    | $\mathcal{F}_{\text{Ter}} = \mathcal{F}_{\text{Ter}} + flow_i$
                else if $backlog_i > 0$ **then**
                        // suitable for satellite link
                    | $\mathcal{F}_{\text{Sat}} = \mathcal{F}_{\text{Sat}} + flow_i$
                end
        end
end

// Second part: Send packet(s) on corresponding link(s)

// always try to send a packet on the terrestrial link
if $terrestrial\ link\ available$ **and** $\mathcal{F}_{Ter} \ne \emptyset$ **then**
        select flow from $\mathcal{F}_{\text{Ter}}$ which has not been served for the longest period of
        time and send packet over terrestrial link
else if $terrestrial\ link\ available$ **and** $\mathcal{F}_{Ter} = \emptyset$ **and** $\mathcal{F}_{Sat} \ne \emptyset$ **then**
        // achieves bandwidth aggregation (optional)
        select flow from $\mathcal{F}_{\text{Sat}}$ which has not been served for the longest period of
        time and send packet over terrestrial link
end

// send a packet on the satellite link if possible
if $satellite\ link\ available$ **and** $\mathcal{F}_{Sat} \ne \emptyset$ **then**
        select flow from $\mathcal{F}_{\text{Sat}}$ which has not been served for the longest period of
        time and send packet over satellite link
end

Algorithm 1: TMC algorithm for heterogeneous links

object via a terrestrial and a satellite link, respectively. D_{Ter} and D_{Sat} is the one-way delay of the terrestrial and satellite link, respectively; R_{Ter} and R_{Sat} is the data rate of the terrestrial and satellite link, respectively; and S is the size of data which is sent. For now, it is assumed that protocol mechanisms (e.g., headers, acknowledgements, window sizes, etc.) are not relevant on the links interconnecting the PEPs. In case of multiple parallel flows, the outstanding data (backlog) of all flows has to be considered. It is then easy to calculate a threshold $S_{\text{Th,TerSat}}$ which describes over which link a transmission finishes first:

$$t_{\text{Ter}} = t_{\text{Sat}}$$

$$D_{\text{Ter}} + \frac{S}{R_{\text{Ter}}} = D_{\text{Sat}} + \frac{S}{R_{\text{Sat}}}$$

$$S = \frac{D_{\text{Sat}} - D_{\text{Ter}}}{R_{\text{Ter}}^{-1} - R_{\text{Sat}}^{-1}} =: S_{\text{Th,TerSat}} \tag{1}$$

Besides the threshold $S_{\text{Th,TerSat}}$, we introduce another threshold $S_{\text{Th,SmallFlow}}$ which is used to force connection setups and small flows, also known as mice, to the terrestrial link. The motivation for this is that connection setups should avoid high latency links and it can be assumed that mice flows are more time-sensitive than elephant flows [14]. Moreover, the terrestrial link may always be used to achieve bandwidth aggregation, whereas a falsely scheduled packet on the satellite link can delay the transmission of an object (c.f. bonding in Sect. 1.2). The final algorithm is shown in Algorithm 1, with N being the total number of flows handled by the PEPs. Practical realization and implementation aspects will be discussed in Sect. 4.2.

4   Modeling

Two key components are required for performance evaluation (Fig. 5). First, a traffic generation and workload model. It consists of one or more clients and one or more web servers. The traffic shall represent typical web browsing given different websites and HTTP variants. We emphasize that the workload model is the only component which includes randomness in our simulation. Second, a model of the TMC approach, i.e., both a local and backbone PEP connected

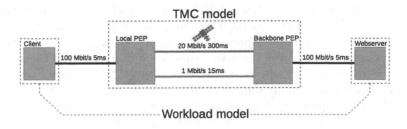

Fig. 5. Simulation model

Table 1. HTTP model parameters taken from [24]

Parameter	Mean	Median	Max	Standard deviation	Best fit
Main object size	31,561 Byte	19,471 Byte	8 MB	49,219 Byte	Weibull (28242.8, 0.814944)
Number of main objects	2.19	1	212	2.63	Lognormal $\mu = 0.473844$, $\sigma = 0.688471$
Inline object size	23,915 Byte	10,284 Byte	8 MB	128,079 Byte	Lognormal $\mu = 9.17979$, $\sigma = 1.24646$
Number of inline objects	31.93	22	1920	37.65	Exponential $\mu = 31.9291$

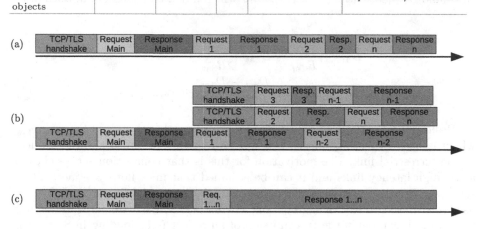

Fig. 6. Website loading strategies

via two or more heterogeneous links. The TMC model is completely determin-istic: For a specific input produced by the workload model, the same outcome is obtained. We use ns-3.29 to implement the models described in the following. The source code is available online.[1]

4.1   Traffic Generation and Workload Model

Internet browsing was identified to be an application which can highly benefit from the combination of satellite and terrestrial access networks. ns-3 provides a traffic generator for web browsing traffic [1], but the underlying 3GPP model from the year 2001 seems outdated. Instead, we use the HTTP model from [24], which was published in 2012. Although the complexity of websites has increased ever since, this seems to provide a good starting point. The authors distinguished between compressed and uncompressed objects, but as websites have become potentially larger in size over the past years, we only considered the uncom-pressed sizes. The parameters are reprinted in Table 1. Our concern regarding this workload model is the missing effect of parallel HTTP/1.1 connections and objects which are spread among different servers (both is mentioned but not modeled) as well as HTTP/2 with its multiplexing feature.

---

[1] https://github.com/cs7org/ns-3.29-tmc-mmb2020.

In order to consider different HTTP variants, we assume three strategies for loading websites. A connection setup is assumed to take two RTTs: One for the TCP handshake (40 byte in each direction) and another one for TLS (1000 byte in each direction). Afterwards, the main object is requested and received. Persistent HTTP connections are assumed with all strategies. Corresponding to Fig. 6, the HTTP strategies are:

(a) Sequential loading of all objects within one flow, which is a worst-case scenario.
(b) Parallel connections after receiving the base page. Opening multiple connections in order to request multiple objects in parallel is a common setting for web browsers. We allow eight parallel connections in total. The objects are requested round-robin style among the parallel connections.
(c) After receiving the base page, all embedded objects are requested as one large object. This mimicks a website where all content is served from a single HTTP/2 web server.

The size of an HTTP request is set to a constant value of 350 byte according to [1]. Domain Name System (DNS) queries/responses are neither considered in [24] nor [1], therefore we also do not model them. A more fine-tuned modeling of the connection setup and header sizes is subject to future work.

4.2   TMC Model

We have chosen a dumbbell topology as shown in Fig. 5. Client and server are connected via ns-3 point to point links (100 Mbit/s, 5 ms delay) to the local and backbone PEP, respectively. These links use ns-3's TCP/IP stack with default settings. Both PEPs are connected via two ns-3 point to point links: A terrestrial link (1 Mbit/s, 15 ms delay) and a satellite link (20 Mbit/s, 300 ms delay). The MTU size of a point to point links is set to the default value of 1500 bytes. There purposely is no randomness in the link characteristics, because we only want to compare different HTTP variants and different (ideal) link types interconnecting the PEPs. The effects of non-ideal link characteristics is subject to future work.

To the best of our knowledge, PEP implementations of satellite operators are not publicly available and there is no PEP implementation in ns-3. PEPsal [7], which is an open-source PEP implementation for Linux, uses TCP Hybla and large buffers for the satellite link. The basic operation of PEPsal is then to copy data from one socket to another as illustrated in Fig. 7(a). As shown in Fig. 7(b), the ns-3 TMC model has a slightly different design. The links interconnecting the PEPs do not use TCP/IP but directly access the ns-3 `NetDevice` structs. The reason for this is twofold: First, we assume that these two links are always connected and their characteristics are well-known, i.e., there is no need for TCP-like flow and congestion control. Second, we want to avoid buffers in the sending process: In our simulation model, every time a link becomes available, it is checked which packet should be sent to the other PEP according to Algorithm 1. If there are multiple outstanding packets from multiple flows, the

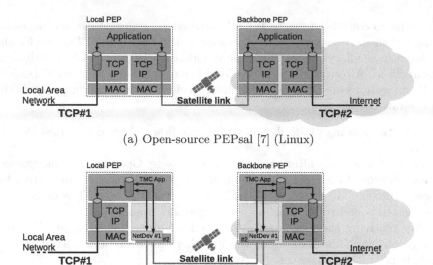

(a) Open-source PEPsal [7] (Linux)

(b) PEP with TMC (ns-3)

Fig. 7. Comparison of PEP implementations

flows are served in round-robin fashion. According to Eq. (1) from Sect. 3, the threshold for using the satellite link is set to $S_{\mathrm{Th,TerSat}} = 37.5$ kbyte. Based on the sizes for connection setups and HTTP requests, the threshold for forcing mice flows to the terrestrial link is $S_{\mathrm{Th,SmallFlow}} = 2$ kbyte. If the number of parallel connections p is very large it can happen that $p \cdot S_{\mathrm{Th,SmallFlow}} > S_{\mathrm{Th,TerSat}}$, which leads to suboptimal performance. This will not happen with the workload model from Sect. 4.1 because of a maximum number of $p = 8$ parallel connections, but must be considered in more complex setups. The terrestrial link is always used in order to achieve bandwidth aggregation, although the 1 Mbit/s of the terrestrial link does not add much to the 20 Mbit/s of the satellite link.

PEPs must provide a mapping between the flows of both sides and handle new and closed connections. In our ns-3 model, this is done by a simple protocol with the following header:

control (1 byte)	source IP	dest. IP	source port (2 byte)	dest. port (2 byte)	packet identifier (8 byte)	payload size (4 byte)

Source IP, destination IP, source port, and destination port (4-tuple, protocol is always TCP) uniquely identifies all flows handled by the PEPs. The source IP and destination IP field is either 4 byte for IPv4, or 16 byte for IPv6. New and closed TCP flows are signaled via control messages to the other side of the PEP, where connections are initiated and closed, respectively. The links between two PEPs are typically bottlenecks and therefore PEPs have to buffer packets received from end hosts. But also packets from one PEP to the other PEP can arrive out of order, because the terrestrial link has a lower delay than the satellite link. Similar to TCP's sequence number, the `packet identifier` is used for reordering packets before they are sent to an end host. With non-ideal links interconnecting the PEPs, a more sophisticated protocol between the interconnected PEPs would be required (e.g, handling packet loss), which is subject to future work.

5 Experiment Setup

We generate $5 \cdot 10^5$ websites (1000 websites multiplied by 500 independent replications) with the workload model described in Sect. 4.1. As recommended in the ns-3 manual [2], different run numbers are used to run independent replications. The websites are then loaded via different HTTP strategies (see also Sect. 4.1) and link configurations. The link configurations are:

- Bidirectional low data rate terrestrial link (1 Mbit/s, 15 ms delay). For this link, it has no significant performance impacts whether Split TCP is used or not.
- Bidirectional satellite link (20 Mbit/s, 300 ms delay). Split TCP is required to achieve good performance (Sect. 1.1).
- TMC combination of the terrestrial and the satellite link. PEPs and Split TCP is required by design.
- Bidirectional high data rate terrestrial link (20 Mbit/s, 15 ms delay). This serves as a benchmark for the TMC solution.

With 4 link configurations and 3 HTTP variants, a total of $3 \cdot 4 = 12$ experiments is run. The same workload is generated for each experiment.

6 Evaluation

For each experiment, the same set of websites is used. The generated objects match the statistics from Table 1. As shown in Fig. 8, almost 75% of the generated websites have a total size of less than 1 Mbyte.

Table 2 shows the total number of bytes sent from the backbone PEP to the local PEP, i.e., the traffic generated by the web server. The total number of bytes varies for different HTTP strategies: Parallel HTTP connections result in slightly more overhead compared to sequential HTTP. On the contrary, HTTP/2 has only one response header for all objects and therefore less overhead than the other two HTTP variants. From client to web server, only connection setups and HTTP requests were sent, and because of their small sizes they were always

Table 2. Data sent via TMC PEPs from web server to client

	Terrestrial	Satellite	Total Mbyte
Sequential HTTP	70%	30%	370,466
Parallel HTTP	36%	64%	373,772
HTTP/2	13%	87%	364,949

sent via the terrestrial link. In Sect. 3 we mentioned that the terrestrial link can always be utilized, which leads to bandwidth aggregation and is implemented in our TMC model. Without this feature, the terrestrial link would be used less often.

Figures 9, 10 and 11 show cumulative distribution functions (CDF) of the page load time. When the objects are loaded sequentially (Fig. 9), there is only a small performance gain of the TMC solution compared to a slow terrestrial Internet access. The reason for this is that most objects are rather small. Small objects are either not transmitted over the satellite link, which is confirmed by Table 2, or the scheduling over the satellite link does not lead to notable time savings. The gap towards a fast terrestrial access is rather large, more than 2 seconds for the median. The performance of the satellite link suffers a lot from the high delays. Luckily for satellite Internet users, plain sequential HTTP request(s)/response(s) are not the normal case for browsing websites given modern browsers and protocols.

The results for parallel HTTP connections are shown in Fig. 10. With up to 8 parallel HTTP connections, the performance of the TMC solution ranges between a fast terrestrial link and the other two link configurations. For large websites with a large PLT, the satellite link performs better than the low data rate terrestrial link and vice versa.

Lastly, we discuss the HTTP strategy where all embedded objects are requested at once, as it is done with HTTP/2. Fig. 11 shows that the satellite link performs better than the low data rate terrestrial link expect for very small websites with a low PLT. HTTP/2 is highly beneficial for loading websites when the Internet access is a satellite link because the price for the high latency has to be paid only once for all embedded objects. For medium-sized and large websites, the TMC solution is ahead of the satellite link by approximately $3 \cdot 600\,\mathrm{ms} = 1.8\,\mathrm{s}$ (two RTTs connection setup, one RTT for main object). For small websites, the TMC solution is better than a low data rate terrestrial link. From Table 2, one can also see that the satellite link is used to a great extent. All in all, the performance of the TMC solution is very close to a high data rate, low latency terrestrial link.

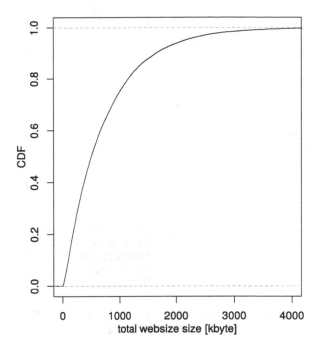

Fig. 8. Distribution of website sizes

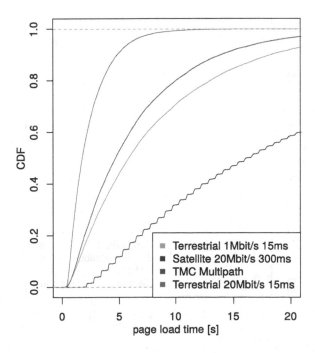

Fig. 9. Performance evaluation: Sequential HTTP request(s)/response(s)

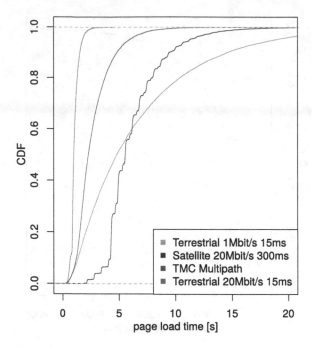

Fig. 10. Performance evaluation: Parallel HTTP request(s)/response(s)

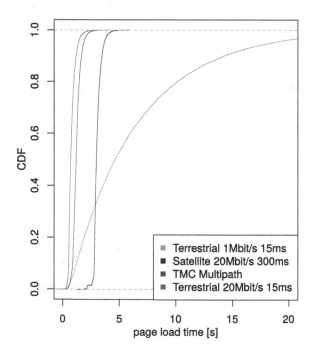

Fig. 11. Performance evaluation: Single request/response (HTTP/2)

7   Conclusion and Future Work

We have presented a multipath communication solution for very heterogeneous link types. The workload model from [24] generated mainly websites with a total size of less than 1 Mbyte. The TMC solution is always better than solely using a low data rate terrestrial link or a geostationary Internet access link, and the performance gain depends on the HTTP variant. According to the simulations, the TMC solution can provide significant lower page load times, especially for HTTP with parallel connections and HTTP/2.

The workload model should be updated in future work, as websites have become probably even larger and more complex over the past years. In this context, also the number of contacted servers, the amount of data required for connection setup, and the size of HTTP overhead for different HTTP variants should be modeled. Workload models other than web browsing are also worth being evaluated. The assumption of ideal links interconnecting the PEPs must be revisited, i.e., the impact of varying link characteristics must be evaluated. Finally, an implementation of the TMC solution in a real network stack is envisaged.

Acknowledgement. This work was funded by the German Ministry for Economic Affairs and Energy (BMWi) on the basis of a decision by the German Bundestag (FKZ 50YB1705).

Author contributions. All Internet links were last accessed on 2020-01-27.

References

1. NS-3 3GPP HTTP Applications. https://www.nsnam.org/docs/models/html/applications.html
2. NS-3.29 Manual: Random Variables. https://www.nsnam.org/docs/release/3.29/manual/html/random-variables.html
3. Abdelsalam, A., Luglio, M., Roseti, C., Zampognaro, F.: TCP connection management through combined use of terrestrial and satellite IP-Based links. In: 2017 40th International Conference on Telecommunications and Signal Processing (TSP), pp. 37–42, July 2017. https://doi.org/10.1109/TSP.2017.8075932
4. Abdelsalam, A., Luglio, M., Roseti, C., Zampognaro, F.: Analysis of bandwidth aggregation techniques for combined use of satellite and xDSL broadband links. Int. J. Satellite Commun. Netw. **37**(2), 76–90 (2018). https://doi.org/10.1002/sat.1242. https://onlinelibrary.wiley.com/doi/abs/10.1002/sat.1242
5. Abdelsalam, A., Luglio, M., Roseti, C., Zampognaro, F.: Linux MP-TCP performance evaluation in a combined terrestrial-satellite access. In: 2019 International Conference on Wireless Technologies, Embedded and Intelligent Systems (WITS), pp. 1–6, April 2019. https://doi.org/10.1109/WITS.2019.8723688
6. Border, J., Kojo, M., Griner, J., Montenegro, G., Shelby, Z.: Performance Enhancing Proxies Intended to Mitigate Link-Related Degradations. RFC 3135, June 2001
7. Caini, C., Firrincieli, R., Lacamera, D.: PEPsal: a performance enhancing proxy designed for TCP satellite connections. In: 2006 IEEE 63rd Vehicular Technology Conference, vol. 6, pp. 2607–2611, May 2006. https://doi.org/10.1109/VETECS.2006.1683339

8. Caini, C., Firrincieli, R.: TCP Hybla: a TCP enhancement for heterogeneous networks. Int. J. Satell. Commun. Netw. **22**(5), 547–566 (2004)
9. Cicconetti, C., et al.: Architecture and analysis of a satellite downstream boost for xDSL networks. In: 2014 7th Advanced Satellite Multimedia Systems Conference and the 13th Signal Processing for Space Communications Workshop (ASMS/SPSC), pp. 287–292, September 2014
10. De Gaudenzi, R., Angeletti, P., Petrolati, D., Re, E.: Future technologies for very high throughput satellite systems. Int. J. Satell. Commun. Netw. (2019). https://doi.org/10.1002/sat.1327. https://onlinelibrary.wiley.com/doi/abs/10.1002/sat.1327
11. Deutschmann, J., Hielscher, K., German, R.: Satellite internet performance measurements. In: 2019 International Conference on Networked Systems (NetSys), pp. 1–4, March 2019. https://doi.org/10.1109/NetSys.2019.8854494
12. Deutschmann, J., Hielscher, K., Keil, T., German, R.: Multipath communication over terrestrial and satellite links. In: 2018 IEEE International Symposium on Local and Metropolitan Area Networks (LANMAN), pp. 119–121, June 2018. https://doi.org/10.1109/LANMAN.2018.8475101
13. Diarra, M., Ottavj, L., Masson, T., Ismail, A.: 5G hybrid backhauling for better QoE. In: 25th Ka and Broadband Communications Conference (2019)
14. Divakaran, D.M., Altman, E., Vicat-Blanc Primet, P.: Size-based flow-scheduling using spike-detection. In: Al-Begain, K., Balsamo, S., Fiems, D., Marin, A. (eds.) ASMTA 2011. LNCS, vol. 6751, pp. 331–345. Springer, Heidelberg (2011). https://doi.org/10.1007/978-3-642-21713-5_24
15. Ekmekcioglu, E., et al.: Context-aware hybrid satellite-terrestrial broadband access. Int. J. Satell. Commun. Netw. **37**(6), 513–526 (2019). https://doi.org/10.1002/sat.1291. https://onlinelibrary.wiley.com/doi/abs/10.1002/sat.1291
16. Erhebung der atene KOM im Auftrag des Bundesministeriums für Verkehr und digitale Infrastruktur: Aktuelle Breitbandverfügbarkeit in Deutschland (Stand Ende 2018). https://www.bmvi.de/goto?id=451090
17. Ferlin, S., Dreibholz, T., Alay, O.: Multi-path transport over heterogeneous wireless networks: does it really pay off?, December 2014. https://doi.org/10.1109/GLOCOM.2014.7037567
18. Ford, A., Raiciu, C., Handley, M., Bonaventure, O.: TCP Extensions for Multipath Operation with Multiple Addresses. RFC 6824, January 2013
19. Hong, S.G., Su, C.: ASAP: fast, controllable, and deployable multiple networking system for satellite networks. In: 2015 IEEE Global Communications Conference (GLOBECOM). pp. 1–7, December 2015. https://doi.org/10.1109/GLOCOM.2015.7417041
20. Langley, A., et al.: The QUIC transport protocol: design and internet-scale deployment. In: SIGCOMM 2017, pp. 183–196 (2017)
21. Leymann, N., Heidemann, C., Zhang, M., Sarikaya, B., Cullen, M.: Huawei's GRE Tunnel Bonding Protocol. RFC 8157, May 2017
22. Li, M., et al.: Multipath transmission for the internet: a survey. IEEE Commun. Surv. Tutor. **18**(4), 2887–2925 (Fourthquarter 2016). https://doi.org/10.1109/COMST.2016.2586112
23. Ottavj, L., et al.: Intelligent gateways enabling broadband access via integrated terrestrial and satellite systems. In: Pillai, P., Hu, Y.F., Otung, I., Giambene, G. (eds.) WiSATS 2015. LNICST, vol. 154, pp. 92–102. Springer, Cham (2015). https://doi.org/10.1007/978-3-319-25479-1_7

24. Pries, R., Magyari, Z., Tran-Gia, P.: An HTTP web traffic model based on the top one million visited web pages. In: Proceedings of the 8th Euro-NF Conference on Next Generation Internet NGI 2012, pp. 133–139, June 2012. https://doi.org/10.1109/NGI.2012.6252145

25. Wei, X., Xiong, C., Lopez, E.: MPTCP proxy mechanisms. Internet-Draft draft-wei-mptcp-proxy-mechanism-02, IETF Secretariat, June 2015. http://www.ietf.org/internet-drafts/draft-wei-mptcp-proxy-mechanism-02.txt

Model-Based Performance Predictions for SDN-Based Networks: A Case Study

Stefan Herrnleben[1]([✉]), Piotr Rygielski[2], Johannes Grohmann[1],
Simon Eismann[1], Tobias Hoßfeld[1], and Samuel Kounev[1]

[1] University of Würzburg, Würzburg, Germany
{stefan.herrnleben,johannes.grohmann,
simon.eismann,tobias.hossfeld,samuel.kounev}@uni-wuerzburg.de
[2] D4L data4life gGmbH, Potsdam, Potsdam, Germany
piotr.rygielski@data4life.care

Abstract. Emerging paradigms for network virtualization like Software-Defined Networking (SDN) and Network Functions Virtualization (NFV) form new challenges for accurate performance modeling and analysis tools. Therefore, performance modeling and prediction approaches that support SDN or NFV technologies help system operators to analyze the performance of a data center and its corresponding network. The Descartes Network Infrastructures (DNI) offers a high-level descriptive language to model SDN-based networks, which can be transformed into various predictive modeling formalisms. However, these modeling concepts have not yet been evaluated in a realistic scenario.

In this paper, we present an extensive case study evaluating the DNI modeling capabilities, the transformations to predictive models, and the performance prediction using the OMNeT++ and SimQPN simulation frameworks. We present five realistic scenarios of a content distribution network (CDN), compare the performance predictions with real-world measurements, and discuss modeling gaps and calibration issues causing mispredictions in some scenarios.

Keywords: Network modeling · Performance prediction · Software-Defined Networking

1 Introduction

In recent years, data centers became increasingly dynamic due to the wide-spread adoption of virtualization technologies [10]. Virtual machines, data, and services can be offered on-demand and shared as well as migrated between different physical hosts to optimize resource utilization and hence costs while enforcing service-level agreements (SLAs). However, this forms new challenges for accurate and timely performance analyses of these virtualized units and the resulting data centers [3]. In addition to the virtualization of compute resources, the network infrastructures shift towards virtualization as well, with the emergence of

H. Hermanns (Ed.): MMB 2020, LNCS 12040, pp. 82–98, 2020.
https://doi.org/10.1007/978-3-030-43024-5_6

paradigms like Software-Defined Networking (SDN) and Network Functions Virtualization (NFV). Therefore, performance modeling and prediction approaches that support SDN or NFV technologies help system operators to analyze the performance of a data center and its corresponding network.

There exist multiple different modeling formalism to represent data center networks, like, domain-specific simulation models, stochastic Petri nets, queueing networks, and stochastic process algebras. However, modeling with a given formalism requires to understand the meta-model and the usual modeling steps of the respective approach. Thus, specific knowledge and experience with multiple modeling formalisms are required to benefit from the variety of their characteristics. Usually, such knowledge and experience is missing or limited to a single modeling formalism.

In [20], we introduce a modeling approach that models the network using DNI (Descartes Network Infrastructures), a high-level descriptive modeling language. A DNI model can be transformed to multiple predictive models, which enables the application of various modeling and analysis approaches without requiring in-depth expertise in the respective modeling formalisms. Furthermore, we extended the DNI to also capture SDN-based network solutions [22]. While the modeling concept of non-SDN networks was already evaluated in [21], the SDN models have not been evaluated yet.

In this paper, we present an extensive evaluation of the DNI, its proposed model-to-model transformations, and two simulation frameworks OMNeT++ [27] and SimQPN [16] in the context of a realistic case study. This case study models file download scenarios within a content distribution network (CDN). We compare their predictions with network measurements and use the results to identify modeling gaps and draw conclusions about directions for future work. We present five different scenarios, covering non-SDN-based networking, SDN-based networking using hardware tables, SDN-based networking using software tables, node virtualization, and routing via the SDN controller. By analyzing the above scenarios, we can compare the simulation techniques as well as the corresponding model-to-model transformations and therefore contribute to a better understanding of the respective techniques.

2   Performance Modeling and Prediction Methodology

In this section, we briefly introduce the main concepts of the *Descartes Network Infrastructure Modeling (DNI) language* and the corresponding performance prediction pipeline. The DNI meta-model is a descriptive model to describe a network infrastructure and covers the three main aspects of every data center network infrastructure: the topology, the configuration, and the traffic. The topology includes all nodes, links, and interfaces, which can either be physical or virtual. Nodes can be end nodes (e.g., virtual machine, server) or intermediate nodes (e.g., switch, router). SDN switches act as both intermediate and end nodes, as they are forwarding devices but also interact with the SDN controller. Figure 1 depicts an example of the infrastructure modeling. For every element in the

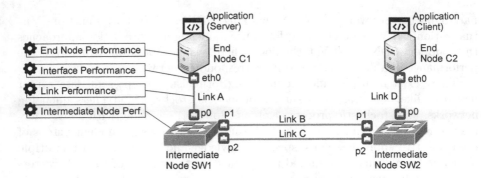

Fig. 1. Example DNI infrastructure model.

model, the performance-relevant parameters are described. The performance for each element has to be specified according to the vendor datasheet or by conducting tailored measurements. The DNI network modeling language considers different forwarding performance characteristics for SDN switches, depending on whether the packet is processed using hardware or software flow tables [23]. Sending the packet headers of unknown flows from an SDN switch to the SDN controller is also supported by DNI with a separate performance description. Traffic is modeled in DNI as flows that are linked to communicating applications, which are deployed on end nodes. Each flow has exactly one traffic source – the traffic generator – and multiple possible destinations. Flows can be composed into a workload model that defines the payload size as well as the temporal behavior by supporting sequences, loops, and branches. Lastly, the configuration of a network contains information about routes, protocols, and protocol stacks. The flexible modeling concept of DNI allows defining customized protocols and protocol stacks, including overheads by the data unit headers. The information of the configuration is used to calculate the paths in the topology graph and coarsely estimate the overheads introduced by the protocols. A route in DNI can either be described between a pair of nodes (source and destination) or flow-based, by defining a route for every flow individually. The flow-based routing representation enables the modeling of software-defined networks, which might use the OpenFlow protocol, for example.

The accuracy of the simulation – as well as the simulation time – is primarily dependent on the level of detail of the performance model. As highly detailed models require increased simulation time, they might not be applicable for large data center networks prediction; additionally, they require specifying many low-level parameters, which might be cumbersome for large networks. Therefore, DNI enables modeling in different levels of detail and therefore supports different use cases. Additionally, in order to predict the performance of a model, a transformation into a predictive model has to be performed, as shown in Fig. 2. The transformation from the descriptive model into a predictive model is performed by adapters, which can be supplemented by transformations into additional pre-

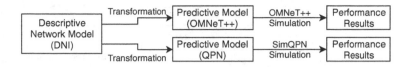

Fig. 2. Workflow from descriptive network model through transformation into a predictive model and simulation to performance results.

diction models. Currently, DNI supports transformations to Queueing Petri Nets (QPNs) [22] and to OMNeT++generic [20]. The generated models can be simulated using OMNeT++ [27] and SimQPN [16] (for QPN), respectively. This enables users to decide on the right simulation framework, depending on the specific requirements (in terms of, e.g., accuracy and simulation time) of the given use-case.

3   Case Study Design

In this section, we describe the base scenario of the case study presented in this work. The presented evaluation uses a file download scenario, where different file resources are requested by multiple clients over a specified network. As the file resources are redundantly located on the servers, client requests may be handled by one or more servers and thus provide the resources from an optimal network location. Typical examples for such distributed resource requests within a data center are cluster file systems or software-defined storage [5,7,28]. Content distribution networks (CDNs) [14,19] for files or streams are another example of such distributed file requests which are frequently used both inside and outside a data center. A client can request single or multiple resources, either as batch download or one by one, with a deterministic or exponentially distributed pause between each of the individual requests. The presented experiments are executed leveraging the L7sdntest software [24], which works similar to Uperf [25]. L7sdntest includes specialized SDN features, like support of the SNMP and OpenFlow protocols, the signaling between clients and servers to the SDN controller, and the management of SDN flow tables by the SDN controller. Additionally, the L7sdntest provides a central experiment controller to control complex experiments.

The structure of the used network is based on a representative data center layout and is visualized in Fig. 3. A redundant pair of distributions switches SW10 and SW00 represent the backbone of the network. The top-of-rack switches SW40, SW41, SW42, SW43, and SW35 are connected to each of these distribution switches. The nodes C10, C11, C12, C13, C17, C36, C37, C38, and C39 are connected to the top-of-rack switches and represent data center servers or clients. The role of the nodes can be freely configured, as L7sdntest software implements each client and server in a unified way so that each client has the functionality of a server and vice versa. The SDN controller, deployed on node C16, is directly connected to distribution switch SW00.

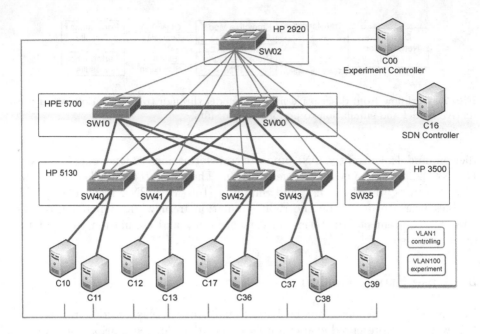

Fig. 3. Experimental testbed used for SDN experiments.

3.1   Hardware Testbed

For the hardware testbed, nine commodity servers (C10, C11, C12, C13, C17, C36, C37, C38, and C39) are used. Each server is equipped with a four-core CPU, 32 GB of memory, and a 1 Gbps Ethernet network interface. Eight of them are connected to HP 5130 top-of-rack switches SW40, SW41, SW42, and SW43, one of them to the SW35 HP 3500 switch, all with a bandwidth of 1 Gbps. The topology of the hardware testbed is shown in Fig. 3. The HP 5130 run the *Comware* switch operating system, the HP 3500 is controlled by the *ProVision* switch operating system. The top-of-rack switches are connected to the HP 5700 distribution switches SW10 and SW00 via 10 Gbps SFP+ DAC copper cables. The distribution switches are connected with each other using copper QSFP+ DAC with a maximum bandwidth of 40 Gbps. Depending on the required OpenFlow version, *Ryu* [26] was used for OpenFlow 1.0, and *HP SDN VAN Controller* [9] was used for OpenFlow 1.3. The SDN controller was deployed on the server C16. In order to isolate the experiment control traffic from the experiment traffic, two different VLANs and an additional switch SW02 are used. An experiment controller, deployed on server C00, manages the L7sdntest software, requests switch statistics via SNMP over the isolated control traffic network, and stores the results.

3.2 Modeling

Predict the performance of the network, requires building a corresponding DNI network model. As described in Sect. 2, all servers, switches, network interfaces, and links have to be mapped to their corresponding element in the model. While the servers C10, C11, C12, C13, C17, C36, C37, C38, and C39 act as end nodes that generate and consume traffic, the switches SW10, SW00, SW40, SW41, SW42, SW43, and SW35 are modeled as intermediate nodes which forward traffic. When the network operates in SDN mode, the switches also get the role of end nodes assigned as they communicate with the SDN controller via the Southbound API with a control channel protocol like, e.g., OpenFlow [12]. If virtual machines are used, they are modeled as nodes, each with an own performance description, and are assigned to a physical node. The SDN controller itself is modeled as an application on server C16. Network interfaces are also modeled as child entities of clients and servers. The connections between servers and switches are modeled as links with additional performance parameters. All end nodes get a performance description, specifying a software layer delay. The intermediate performance description for the switches defines the forwarding latency, switching capacity, and forwarding bandwidth. For SDN switches, the performance for processing the packets using hardware tables is specified together with the performance of using software tables. Switches of the same type each receive identical performance descriptions. For all network interfaces, the packet processing time and the interface throughput is defined within their performance description. Furthermore, for each link, a propagation delay as well as a maximal supported bandwidth is specified. The link from the server to the top of rack switches are configured by a maximal supported bandwidth of 1 Gbps and their uplink to the distribution switches with a maximal bandwidth of 10 Gbps. The link between the distribution switches SW10 and SW00 is specified using a maximal supported bandwidth of 40 Gbps in the network model. The SDN controller on server C16 is connected via a 1 Gbps link to the distribution switch SW00. In the protocol configuration, the L4 protocols TCP and UDP, with their underlying protocol stack, i.e., IP and MAC, each with their maximum data payload as well as the packet overhead, are modeled.

To transport the packages through the network, corresponding routes are configured. DNI supports two routing mechanisms: In the classical mode, routes are specified on each interface whereby at each interface, one route is marked as the default route. The classical routing mode is used for all non-SDN measurements. For the SDN scenarios, the second routing mechanism of DNI, the SDN flow rules, are used. An SDN flow rule refers to a node, a flow, as well as an SDN controller. A probability configuration attribute specifies whether the packet should be processed using hardware or using software tables. The last part of the model is the definition of the workload. Each request is mapped to a flow and the traffic sources and destinations are specified for all flows. Additionally, the size of the file to be transferred is specified for each flow.

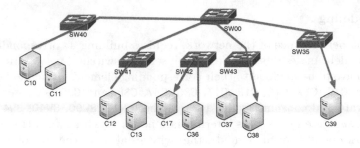

Fig. 4. Flows of server replies (denoted by arrows).

4   Case Study

In this section, we evaluate the prediction accuracy of predictive models obtained in the flexible performance prediction approach for SDN-based data center networks. The approach leverages DNI models instantiated from the DNI meta-model and obtains predictive models using model transformations. For each DNI model, we generate two predictive models using the *DNI-to-OMNeT++generic* and *DNI-to-QPN* model transformations. The generated models are solved with the respective OMNeT++generic and SimQPN solvers. Based on the base scenario introduced in Sect. 3, we analyze the following five scenarios:

Scenario #1 **Non-SDN Networking**
Scenario #2 **SDN Hardware Tables**
Scenario #3 **Node Virtualization**
Scenario #4 **Software Flow Tables**
Scenario #5 **SDN Controller**

Each scenario consists of at least 30 repetitions of the experiment scenario. A single repetition of an experiment scenario takes between 3 and 60 min, depending on the specific scenario. For the measured data, an average throughput is calculated for each second after removing the warm-up and cool-down periods. Finally, the average steady-state throughput, as well as confidence intervals and percentiles, are calculated. Additionally, all models used in this case study are available online[1].

4.1   Non-SDN Networking

In this scenario, three client applications are deployed on servers C39, C38, and C17. The clients request files from predefined servers: C10, C12, and C36. The clients request 100 times the same resource of size 20 MB, where each request is issued every 5 s. The breaks between requesting the resources are deterministic.

---

[1] https://gitlab2.informatik.uni-wuerzburg.de/descartes/dni-meta-model/tree/dev/examples/sdn-measurements.

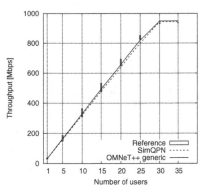
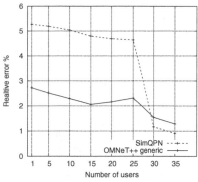

(a) Measured/predicted throughput.   (b) Relative prediction error.

Fig. 5. Network throughput of SW35 → C39 with non-SDN networking.

The communication pattern is presented in Fig. 4, where each gray arrow represents the reply of a server to the respective client. Each server reacts to the client requests immediately and starts transmission of the requested resource. The three pairs of servers communicate simultaneously and share the network infrastructure with each other. For each communicating pair, we measure the network capacity for 1, 5, 10, 15, 20, 25, 30, and 35 users. These measurements of reference throughput are obtained using SNMP-based monitoring procedures implemented in L7sdntest software.

Modeling. For this scenario, the DNI model described in Sect. 3.2 is used as a base. As this scenario investigates on a non-SDN network, we remove all model elements corresponding to SDN features, such as the SDN controller and the SDN applications on the switches. Additionally, the SDN flow rules are replaced by more coarse-grained interface-based route configurations.

Results. In this scenario, we compare the prediction accuracy of two predictive models: OMNeT++generic and QPN. Based on the obtained predictions, the network reaches its maximal capacity at the level of about 25–30 users. The Throughput does not increase beyond the maximum of 942 Mbps for 30 and 35 users. The measured and predicted throughput on a selected network interface (SW35 → C39) is presented in Fig. 5a, whereas the relative prediction error in Fig. 5b. The measurement results are stable and the size of confidence intervals does not exceed 60 Mbps. Both generated predictive models provided very good performance prediction accuracy. OMNeT++generic delivered predictions with lower error (at most 3%) than SimQPN (at most 5.2%). The maximal absolute prediction error was below 40 Mbps for SimQPN and 20 Mbps for OMNeT++generic. For the case of 1–25 users, both solvers underestimated the throughput, whereas, for a fully saturated network, the predictions were overestimating the measured capacity by up to 14 Mbps. Based on these measurements, we conclude that DNI correctly models the structure and performance properties of the traditional network.

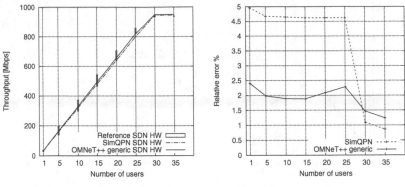

(a) Measured/predicted throughput.   (b) Relative prediction error.

Fig. 6. Network throughput of SW35 → C39 using SDN hardware tables.

4.2   SDN Hardware Tables

For this scenario, the switches from the previous experiment setup are reconfigured to work in SDN mode in order to evaluate the prediction accuracy for SDN-based networks. The SDN switching is based on flow rules that match the IP addresses of the traffic flows. This scenario assumes proactive flow insertion. Therefore, the flow rules are inserted by the SDN controller before the arrival of the traffic. In order to evaluate the performance predictions for hardware SDN modes, we assert that all flow rules are inserted into hardware flow tables of the respective switches and the table capacity is not exceeded.

Modeling. The DNI models adapted to SDN hardware mode by adding SDN flow rules and enable the processing of the rules in the hardware tables of the switches. Each SDN node in DNI gets assigned an additional SDN performance description. The official vendor data sheets do not include the performance of SDN, so we use the forwarding performance and other performance-relevant characteristics of the switches that have been published in [23].

Results. The measured and predicted throughputs on the network interface SW35 → C39 are presented in Fig. 6a. These results show that there is no significant difference in performance between the native and SDN hardware mode for the analyzed switches. The network gets saturated for 30 users and offers a maximum throughput of about 942 Mbps. The maximum relative deviation of offered throughput does not exceed 1%. However, the bounds of confidence intervals differ up to 7% for the measurement with five users. Therefore, the deviations likely stem from measurement errors. The predictions for SDN hardware mode provide almost identical capacity prediction. Both generated predictive models provide high accuracy with maximum prediction errors of 5% for SimQPN and 2.5% for OMNeT++generic. While the error for SimQPN is higher than for OMNeT++generic, we consider the prediction error as acceptable and therefore conclude that DNI provides the capability to model SDN hardware mode.

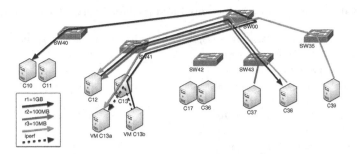

Fig. 7. Experimental testbed and file transfer flows with node virtualization.

4.3   Node Virtualization

SDN networks are often used in conjunction with virtualized compute resources, which results in different network routings. In this scenario, we introduce server virtualization on node C13 and modify the service deployment to obtain a new configuration of flows. Server C13 becomes a Xen [2] hypervisor that hosts two virtual machines C13a and C13b with four CPU cores and 8 GB memory each. The L7sdntest services are redeployed to leverage the high bandwidth of the 10 Gbps SFP+ links between the switch SW00 and switches SW4x. Additionally, we add multiple users that request the resources of diversified sizes: $r_1 = 1000$, $r_2 = 100$, and $r_3 = 10$ MB respectively (selected arbitrarily). We also configure a new flow of file resources that connects the virtual machines C13b and C13a to investigate the influence of the hypervisor on the network capacity. The full testbed configuration is presented in Fig. 7. We use the same measurements procedure as previously for all flows traversing a physical switch. Unfortunately, the SNMP implementation in the Xen hypervisor (node C13) cannot provide stable reports from virtual interface byte counters. Therefore, we measure flow C13b–C13a separately using Iperf [8] to estimate the maximal capacity of the VM-to-VM connection.

Modeling. The modeling of the server virtualization consists of defining the VMs, a virtual switch (a bridge running on the hypervisor), and virtual links connecting the VMs to the hypervisor bridge. The bandwidth of links and network interfaces is set to 1000 Gbps in both predictive models (as an approximation of infinity). The maximal bandwidth of the virtual hypervisor bridge was specified using forwarding delay. The value of forwarding delay was estimated using a controlled experiment and set to 1 µs for the Iperf workload. The experiment was executed under a repeatable constant level of computing load on the SDN controller.

Results. The measured and predicted throughputs are presented in Table 1. While both predictive models deliver predictions with low errors, the SimQPN solver performed better than OMNeT++generic and provided up to 2% more accurate predictions. The absolute prediction error of the high-bandwidth link

Table 1. Scenario #5: Measured and predicted network capacity.

Measured port	Reference *Mbps*		QPN *Mbps*	Relative error %	OMNeT *Mbps*		Relative error %
	lCI	uCI	avg		lCI	uCI	
Scenario #5A (no flow C13b → C13a)							
SW41 ● → SW00	1834	1888	1848	0.7	1879	1924	2.2
SW00 ● → SW41	171	196	192	4.9	163	232	7.9
SW41 ● → C12	152	174	176	7.8	154	208	11.0
SW41 ● → C13	18	22	16	19.6	14	19	17.4
SW00 ● → SW40	920	941	924	0.7	940	962	2.2
SW00 → ● SW43	917	944	924	0.7	938	961	2.1
SW43 ● → C38	917	942	924	0.6	945	954	2.2
Scenario #5B (flow C13b → C13a with *iperf*)							
C13b → ● C13	11052	11149	17040	54	16823	17987	57
C13 ● → C13a	11052	11149	10878	2.0	9999	10256	8.8

($SW41 \rightarrow SW00$) was low and did not exceed 40 Mbps on average. Anomalies can be observed for three of the monitored network interfaces. The flows sharing the path $SW00 \rightarrow SW41 \rightarrow C12$ and $C13$ consumed less network resources than predicted by the models. The total consumption of capacity on the link $SW00 \rightarrow SW41$ is expected in theory as maximally 192 Mbps. Despite the ideal prediction of SimQPN, the reference measurements provided larger confidence intervals and thus the average is reported below the expected 192 Mbps. OMNeT++generic, however, predicted a higher variation of the average consumed capacity and thus the prediction is provided with higher accuracy error. This phenomenon propagates further to the links $SW41 \rightarrow C12$ and $SW41 \rightarrow C13$, so higher prediction errors are observed. Note that the absolute prediction errors are low and do not exceed 25 Mbps and 5 Mbps for links $SW41 \rightarrow C12$ and $SW41 \rightarrow C13$, respectively. Despite the challenging calibration procedure, the performance predictions for the flow C13b → C13a that are measured using *iperf* return accurate results with 2% and 8.8% prediction error for SimQPN and OMNeT++generic respectively. The flow $C13b \rightarrow C13$, however, is affected by the TCP-UDP modeling gap, that is, the predictive models analyze the traffic in an UDP-fashion, whereas the reference communication runs over TCP and the throughput of the flow is limited by congestion control algorithms according to the bandwidth of a bottleneck resource.

4.4   Software Flow Tables

In this experiment, we reconfigure the SDN switches to forward the incoming traffic based on MAC addresses instead of IP addresses. This forces the $SW35$ switch to install the rules into the software flow table. The rest of the switches install the new rules in the hardware tables. Thus, for the switch $SW35$, we investigate the offered network capacity in the SDN software mode. The other switches contain only hardware flow tables, so their performance in SDN software mode cannot be analyzed.

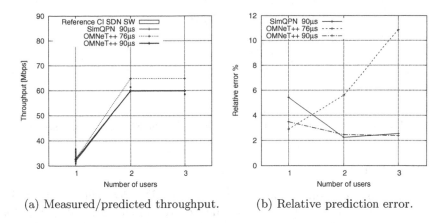

(a) Measured/predicted throughput.   (b) Relative prediction error.

Fig. 8. Network throughput of SW35 → C39 using SDN software tables.

Modeling. The software SDN forwarding mode is modeled in DNI by disabling the processing of the flow rules in the hardware table and thereby force usage of the software flow tables. The switching capacity for software switching is set to 10.000 packets per second in DNI. This represents the maximal switching capacity offered by the switch operating system. We experimentally estimated the forwarding in SDN software mode to 90 μs. Additionally, we also evaluate a forwarding delay of 76 μs (as estimated using the method presented in [22]).

Results. Setting the SDN forwarding mode to software switching causes a drastic drop in the offered throughput. The switch *SW*35 is able to deliver maximally 62 Mbps of throughput, which corresponds to 6.5% of the maximal throughput in the SDN hardware mode. There are two main factors that contribute to the observed performance drop. First, the switch operating system limits the maximum switching capacity to 10.000 packets per second. This limit is configurable and can be set to lower values, however for the maximum setting, the switch consumes already almost 90% of its CPU resources (as presented in [23]). Second, the software flow table is usually implemented using general-purpose SDRAM, so the lookup procedure consumes additional time to find a matching rule in the flow table. This incurs additional forwarding delay that needs to be estimated empirically. The measured and predicted throughputs are depicted in Fig. 8a, whereas the relative prediction errors in Fig. 8b. Both predictive models predict the drastic performance degradation and provide accurate estimates of the maximal network capacity. The OMNeT++generic simulation with forwarding delay 90 μs predicts the average throughput accurately with a prediction error below 4%. SimQPN performed similarly, however the prediction error reaches about 6% for a single user. The alternative method for calibrating the forwarding delay results in higher inaccuracies and the prediction error for OMNeT++ reaches 11%. This can still be considered an acceptable prediction accuracy under the assumption that the forwarding delay was calculated a priori using an analytical formula.

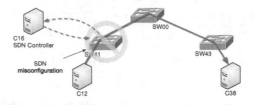

Fig. 9. Experimental testbed and network flows for the SDN controller scenario.

4.5 SDN Controller

In this scenario, we assume that an error in the SDN flow rule configuration causes all switches to misinterpret the rules located in the flow tables and forward all traffic via the SDN controller. This way, we indirectly examine the performance of the SDN controller in handling excessive *packet-in* traffic. The switches are configured to forward to the controller if no rule in the flow tables can be matched. Additionally, the SDN controller application returns the *flow-mod* messages that do not install any rules in the flow tables. Instead, the switch is instructed to forward each packet directly to the proper outgoing port. In this scenario, two servers are communicating via a network path containing three SDN switches, as shown in Fig. 9. Next, we enable SDN on switch $SW41$, whereas the other switches work in native mode. The *Ryu* SDN controller is connected directly to SW41 over a dedicated network link. Node C38 represents a single user requesting a 20 MB resource from C12 every five seconds. Unfortunately, L7sdntest could not establish a stable connection between the client and the server. Note that in each of 30 experiment repetitions, the software handles 100 consecutive file transfers and reports an experiment failure if any of the experiment repetition fails. Therefore, we use Iperf to emulate the user behavior for this scenario.

Modeling. In this scenario, we build the DNI model similarly as in the previously presented SDN scenario. The modeling consists of defining a flow between nodes C10 and C38 with respective SDN flow rules. But instead of processing flows in hardware or software tables within the data plane, the SDN devices are modeled to forward them to the controller by default. The modeling of an SDN controller faces similar challenges to the calibration of forwarding delay of the SDN switch working in SDN software mode. Therefore, we empirically estimate the per-packet processing delay by the SDN controller application to 8 ms.

Results. The reference measurements shown in Table 2 originate from three Iperf settings. First, we use the default Iperf command that measures the maximal capacity of the network connection. In this scenario, the average bandwidth of the path connecting node C10 and C38 is low and does not exceed 1.3 Mbps of stable traffic throughput. Both SimQPN and OMNeT++generic overestimate the throughput on link $C12 \rightarrow SW41$ due to the previously discussed differences between TCP and UDP. For the link $SW43 \rightarrow C38$, the high relative errors correspond to an acceptable absolute error of 0.15 Mbps and 1.18 Mbps respectively.

Table 2. Measured and predicted throughput in the SDN controller scenario.

Measured port	Reference *Mbps* avg	QPN *Mbps* avg	Relative error %	OMNeT *Mbps* lCI	uCI	Relative error %
Reference: default TCP *iperf*						
C12 → • SW41	1.24	32.00	2481	27.12	38.60	2550
SW43 • → C38	1.24	1.39	12	2.14	2.70	95
Reference: default UDP *"iperf-udp"*						
C12 → • SW41	1.03	32.00	3007	27.12	38.60	3090
SW43 • → C38	1.03	1.39	35	2.14	2.70	135
Reference: modified UDP *"iperf-udp-b 32000000"*						
C12 → • SW41	32.00	32.00	0	27.12	38.60	2.6
SW43 • → C38	2.19	1.39	57.5	2.14	2.70	10.5

Next, we switch the transport protocol to UDP and measure the available bandwidth. This however, does not allow Iperf to send more data than 1 Mbps unless the receiving side confirms successful receptions. The maximal non-interrupted transfer measured by Iperf limited the throughput to 1.03 Mbps. Iperf tries to transmit data with 2 Mbps but it returns to the throughput of 1 Mbps due to high packet losses [8]. The relative and absolute prediction errors are high and therefore opportunities for improvement in future work.

Finally, we force Iperf to send 32 Mbits of data without waiting for the confirmation of the receiving side. The switch SW41 forwards each packet to the SDN controller. After approximately 8 ms, the controller replies with a decision regarding the packet forwarding, which is not stored in the flow table. Therefore, each packet is delayed by at least 8 ms (plus additional network interface processing delays) and forwarded to the destination in C38. At the receiving end-point, Iperf reported maximal throughput of 2.19 Mbps with 130 ms jitter and packet loss rate of 92%. Iperf measures the performance at the receiver side until the sender side notifies it that the experiment ends. However, the notification is significantly delayed by the switch and the SDN controller, so it arrives at the receiver later. Due to this additional delay, an additional part of the datagrams queued at the SDN controller arrive at the receiver and are included in the statistics. As the behavior in this scenario is closely related to the modeled behavior, the utilized network capacity has been predicted exactly by SimQPN, whereas OMNeT++generic mispredicted it with 2.6% relative error (0.86 Mbps absolute error). While the relative prediction errors on link $SW43 \rightarrow C38$ were higher—57% for SimQPN and 10.5% for OMNeT++generic—the absolute errors of 0.8 Mbps and 0.23 Mbps can be considered acceptable.

5 Related Work

We group the related work into two clusters. First, we describe all related works modeling the performance of data center networks on an architecture level. Note that none of the approaches is able to capture SDN-based networks. Second, we list performance modeling approaches capable of modeling SDN-based networks. However, none of those include explicit architecture-level modeling like DNI does.

Architecture-Level Performance Modeling of Data Center Networks. Several approaches for modeling networks in data center networks have been proposed. In [29], the authors propose to extend the SDL and UML languages with performance annotations. In [6], the authors propose a modeling approach named Syntony. A similar approach is presented in [18]. Similar to [29], all approaches focus the modeling on the protocol-level. The authors of [13] present a stochastic model for the window dynamics in TCP and investigate the throughput performance of TCP-Tahoe. The I/O path model (IOPm) [17] was designed to model the architecture of parallel file systems. However, none of the above works are capable of modeling SDN networks.

Performance Modeling of SDN-Based Networks. The authors of [1] propose an analytical performance model based on network calculus. In contrast to our approach, the proposed model does not cover the computing infrastructure, the software architecture, and the hosted applications. The authors of [11] propose a performance model based on queueing theory to evaluate SDN-enabled switches. The evaluation focuses only on OpenFlow-enabled switches and controllers; the scope of the complete data center architecture is missing. Similarly, the authors of [4] focus only on a selected part of SDN-based networks, i.e., the data plane of a switch. The authors of [15] proposed an SDN extension to OMNeT++ simulation based on the INET library. Nevertheless, given the simulation at the protocol-level, their approach focuses on the specific network protocols supported by the INET library and misses the scope of the entire data center.

To the best of our knowledge, the only work considering modeling SDN-based networks at the architecture level is our prior work [22]. However, the prior work fails to exhaustively evaluate the performance of the modeling approach, which is what we are targeting in this work.

6   Conclusion

In this paper, we present an extensive case study evaluating performance predictions of SimQPN and OMNet++ on SDN-based networks. Both simulation models are created by model-to-model transformations based on the Descartes Network Infrastructure (DNI) model. We present five different scenarios, covering non-SDN-based networking, SDN-based networking using hardware tables, SDN-based networking using software tables, node virtualization, and routing via the SDN controller. Our results show that both simulation frameworks deliver comparable and sufficiently accurate predictions for most scenarios. However, we also identify some remaining challenges and open issues. For example, we notice the TCP-UDP-modeling gap. Here, if the predictive models simulate the traffic in an UDP-fashion, while TCP operated by the reference application limits the throughput of the flow using congestion control algorithms. Modeling of congestion control algorithms for network protocols in DNI would close this gap, which is planned as follow-up work. Additionally, the manual calibration of the forwarding delay parameter for SDN switches is cumbersome and error-prone. In the future, fully automated calibration approaches could be investigated.

Acknowledgements. This work was funded by the German Research Foundation (DFG) under grant No. (KO 3445/18-1).

References

1. Azodolmolky, S., Nejabati, R., Pazouki, M., Wieder, P., Yahyapour, R., Simeonidou, D.: An analytical model for software defined networking: a network calculus-based approach. In: IEEE Global Communications Conference (GLOBECOM), pp. 1397–1402, December 2013
2. Barham, P., et al.: Xen and the art of virtualization. SIGOPS Oper. Syst. Rev. **37**(5), 164–177 (2003)
3. Bezemer, C., et al.: How is performance addressed in DevOps? In: Proceedings of the 2019 ACM/SPEC International Conference on Performance Engineering, pp. 45–50 (2019). https://doi.org/10.1145/3297663.3309672
4. Bianco, A., Birke, R., Giraudo, L., Palacin, M.: OpenFlow switching: data plane performance. In: 2010 IEEE International Conference on Communications (ICC), pp. 1–5, May 2010
5. Clements, A.T., Ahmad, I., Vilayannur, M., Li, J., et al.: Decentralized deduplication in SAN cluster file systems. In: USENIX Annual Technical Conference, pp. 101–114 (2009)
6. Dietrich, I., Dressler, F., Schmitt, V., German, R.: SYNTONY: network protocol simulation based on standard-conform UML2 models. In: Proceedings of the ValueTools 2007, pp. 21:1–21:11 (2007)
7. Donvito, G., Marzulli, G., Diacono, D.: Testing of several distributed file-systems (HDFS, Ceph and GlusterFS) for supporting the HEP experiments analysis. In: Journal of Physics Conference Series, vol. 513, p. 042014. IOP Publishing (2014)
8. ESnet: NLANR/DAST: Iperf - the TCP/UDP bandwidth measurement tool. https://iperf.fr/. Accessed September 2016
9. HP: HP SDN controller architecture. Technical report, Hewlett-Packard Development Company, L.P., September 2013
10. Huber, N., von Quast, M., Hauck, M., Kounev, S.: Evaluating and modeling virtualization performance overhead for cloud environments. In: Proceedings of the 1st International Conference on Cloud Computing and Services Science, pp. 563–573 (2011)
11. Jarschel, M., Oechsner, S., Schlosser, D., Pries, R., Goll, S., Tran-Gia, P.: Modeling and performance evaluation of an OpenFlow architecture. In: 2011 23rd International Teletraffic Congress (ITC), pp. 1–7, September 2011
12. Jarschel, M., Zinner, T., Hoßfeld, T., Tran-Gia, P., Kellerer, W.: Interfaces, attributes, and use cases: a compass for SDN. IEEE Commun. Mag. **52**(6), 210–217 (2014)
13. Kaj, I., Olsén, J.: Throughput modeling and simulation for single connection TCP-Tahoe. In: de Souza, J.M., da Fonseca, N.L., de Souza e Silva, E.A. (eds.) Teletraffic Engineering in the Internet Era (2001). Teletraffic Sci. Eng. **4**, 705–718. Elsevier
14. Kangasharju, J., Roberts, J., Ross, K.W.: Object replication strategies in content distribution networks. Comput. Commun. **25**(4), 376–383 (2002)

15. Klein, D., Jarschel, M.: An OpenFlow extension for the OMNeT++ INET framework. In: Proceedings of the 6th International ICST Conference on Simulation Tools and Techniques, SimuTools 2013, pp. 322–329. ICST (Institute for Computer Sciences, Social-Informatics and Telecommunications Engineering), Brussels (2013). http://dl.acm.org/citation.cfm?id=2512734.2512780

16. Kounev, S., Buchmann, A.: SimQPN-a tool and methodology for analyzing queueing Petri net models by means of simulation. Perform. Eval. **63**(4–5), 364–394 (2006)

17. Kunkel, J., Ludwig, T.: IOPm - modeling the I/O path with a functional representation of parallel file system and hardware architecture. In: 2012 20th Euromicro International Conference on Parallel, Distributed and Network-Based Processing (PDP), pp. 554–561, February 2012

18. Mitschele-Thiel, A., Müller-Clostermann, B.: Performance engineering of SDL/MSC systems. Comput. Netw. **31**(17), 1801–1815 (1999)

19. Pallis, G., Stamos, K., Vakali, A., Katsaros, D., Sidiropoulos, A.: Replication based on objects load under a content distribution network. In: 22nd International Conference on Data Engineering Workshops (ICDEW 2006), p. 53. IEEE (2006)

20. Rygielski, P., Kounev, S., Tran-Gia, P.: Flexible performance prediction of data center networks using automatically generated simulation models. In: Proceedings of the Eighth International Conference on Simulation Tools and Techniques (SIMUTools 2015), pp. 119–128, August 2015. https://doi.org/10.4108/eai.24-8-2015.2260961

21. Rygielski, P., Kounev, S., Zschaler, S.: Model-based throughput prediction in data center networks. In: Proceedings of the 2nd IEEE International Workshop on Measurements and Networking (M&N 2013), pp. 167–172, October 2013

22. Rygielski, P., Seliuchenko, M., Kounev, S.: Modeling and prediction of software-defined networks performance using queueing petri nets. In: Proceedings of the Ninth International Conference on Simulation Tools and Techniques (SIMUTools 2016), pp. 66–75, August 2016. http://dl.acm.org/citation.cfm?id=3021426.3021437

23. Rygielski, P., Seliuchenko, M., Kounev, S., Klymash, M.: Performance analysis of SDN switches with hardware and software flow tables. In: VALUETOOLS (2016)

24. Stoll, J.: SDN-basierte Lastverteilung für Schicht-7 Anfragen (SDN Rechenzentrum Fallstudie). Bachelor thesis, University of Würzburg, Würzburg, Germany, March 2016

25. Performance Applications Engineering Group at Sun Microsystems: Uperf a network performance tool (2012). www.uperf.org. Accessed 28 Aug 2016

26. RYU Project Team: RYU SDN Framework - English Edition Release 1.0.osrg (2014). https://www.amazon.com/RYU-SDN-Framework-English-Edition-ebook/dp/B00IKME2FO, eBook

27. Varga, A.: OMNet++. In: Wehrle, K., Güneş, M., Gross, J. (eds.) Modeling and tools for network simulation, pp. 35–59. Springer, Heidelberg (2010). https://doi.org/10.1007/978-3-642-12331-3_3

28. Weil, S.A., Brandt, S.A., Miller, E.L., Long, D.D., Maltzahn, C.: Ceph: a scalable, high-performance distributed file system. In: Proceedings of the 7th Symposium on Operating Systems Design and Implementation, pp. 307–320. USENIX Association (2006)

29. de Wet, N., Kritzinger, P.: Using UML models for the performance analysis of network systems. Comput. Netw. **49**(5), 627–642 (2005)

Design of a Hybrid Genetic Algorithm for Time-Sensitive Networking

Anna Arestova$^{(\boxtimes)}$, Kai-Steffen Jens Hielscher, and Reinhard German

Department of Computer Science 7,
Computer Networks and Communication Systems,
University of Erlangen-Nürnberg,
Martensstraße 3, 91058 Erlangen, Germany
{anna.arestova,kai-steffen.hielscher,reinhard.german}@fau.de

Abstract. With Time-Sensitive Networking (TSN), the IEEE 802.1 Task Group is extending the Ethernet standard by time-sensitive capabilities to establish a common ground for real-time communication systems via Ethernet. The Time-Sensitive Networking Task Group introduces a time-triggered transmission approach in IEEE 802.1Qbv to enable a deterministic transmission of time-critical network traffic, which requires scheduling strategies. Genetic algorithms are qualified to solve these scheduling problems in Time-Sensitive Networks. The difficulty is to design the genetic algorithm to find an optimal or a near-optimal solution for different complex problems taking performance and quality of the schedule into account. The complexity of schedules for TSN depends on the decision space of a network designer comprising the possibility to combine a variable number of network participants, a variable number of TSN flows, as well as assuming fixed or flexible routes for the flows. In this paper, we discuss a design approach for a hybrid genetic algorithm including chromosome representation for the routing and scheduling problems in TSN, the choice of genetic operators, and a neighborhood search to find a near-optimal solution. Additionally, we introduce an approach to compress the resulting schedules. Our evaluations show that the proposed hybrid genetic algorithm is able to compete with the well-adapted NEH algorithm in terms of schedule quality, and it outperforms the NEH algorithm regarding the computing time.

1 Introduction

In application domains, such as industry, automotive, and railway, the number of intelligent devices and sensors is rising. To handle the huge amount of transmitted mixed-critical data between the devices, the requirements for deterministic network latency, jitter, and efficient bandwidth allocation in real-time communication systems have increased tremendously. The IEEE Time-Sensitive Networking (TSN) Task Group establishes a common ground for different real-time communication protocols based on Ethernet and for mixed-critical communication. It introduces new standards to satisfy the requirements of time-sensitive

© Springer Nature Switzerland AG 2020
H. Hermanns (Ed.): MMB 2020, LNCS 12040, pp. 99–117, 2020.
https://doi.org/10.1007/978-3-030-43024-5_7

traffic and to take best-effort traffic into account. To be able to give guaranteed latency bounds to communication flows with real-time requirements, the TSN working group introduced the substandard *802.1Qbv*, see Sect. 3.1, enabling a deterministic transmission of time-sensitive flows. As the standard does not provide scheduling strategies, it is left to the user to calculate a feasible global offline schedule for all involved periodic TSN flows. The calculation of the global schedule is an NP-complete problem [10] of finding the appropriate order of TSN flows in different topologies with diverse communication requirements. The complexity of the schedules increases with a rising number of communication devices, end-systems, and flows. Numerous works are dedicated to solving this problem, but most of them neglect the routing aspect for TSN flows.

In our paper, we solve the scheduling and routing problem for Time-Sensitive Networks applying the proposed hybrid genetic algorithm (HGA). Genetic Algorithms are randomized search techniques and are based on the idea of the evolution of nature. Starting from a population of several individuals, genetic algorithms create new offsprings by pairing or mutating existing individuals. Subsequently, genetic algorithms replace old individuals with their offsprings based on a fitness function. In our work, the coding of one individual represents the sequence of TSN flows in a schedule and their routes. Hybridization approaches for genetic algorithms, in turn, allow a more detailed exploration of existing solutions.

We take a closer look at the possibilities provided by genetic algorithms and propose which encoding and which genetic operators are suitable to solve the scheduling and routing problems in TSN. The objective of our algorithm is to optimize the computational performance of the HGA and the effective length of the schedule, the *makespan*. Additionally, we show how to compress a TSN schedule to provide a more efficient bandwidth allocation. To evaluate the performance and quality of the schedule, we compare our results to the proven, constructive algorithm *NEH* (Nawaz-Enscore-Ham), developed for solving the related Job Shop Scheduling problems.

2 Related Work

A comparable concept to scheduling flows in time-sensitive networks is the Job Shop Scheduling Problem (JSP). JSP describes the problem to schedule a set of jobs consisting of a sequence of operations on a set of machines with the goal to minimize the makespan. If the tasks can be executed on several machines, we talk about the Flexible Job Shop Scheduling Problem (FJSP). FJSP adds a routing aspect to the scheduling problem. Numerous works have addressed the JSP using genetic algorithms and turning (F)JSP into a permutation problem.

Chen et al. introduces the split representation of the chromosome for FJSP in [8] using one part of the chromosome for the assignment of tasks to machines and the second part defining the sequence of operations on each machine. The authors in [5, 13, 21, 25, 32] make use of a modified split representation of the chromosome. The chromosome consists of a string vector containing the assignment of tasks to machines and another string vector showing the order of the tasks. This chromosome design allows applying routing decision operators on the machine assignment vector independently of the task sequence vector. We transfer the latter representation to our TSN routing and scheduling problem by converting the machine to task assignment to a route assignment vector and the task order vector into a flow order vector.

The NEH algorithm proposed in [23] is a well-established population initialization heuristic in genetic algorithms. Reeves [29] uses the plain NEH heuristic and Ruiz et al. [30] apply a modified version in their genetic algorithms as part of the population initialization, which results in a more effective algorithm. In this paper, we apply a restricted NEH algorithm to support the initialization process. The restriction to NEH serves the purpose to save computation time.

Another hybridization method for genetic algorithms is the *Neighborhood Search* or *Local Search*. The authors in [18,22,28,30] add local search mechanisms to improve the solution space exploration of genetic algorithms for JSP. We integrate the neighborhood search by applying mutation operators to the best and worst solutions to provide a way to escape a local optimum.

Regarding the genetic operators, the authors in [6,27,33] give an overview of the applied genetic operators for permutation problems that comprises the subset of operators that is used in this paper.

For solving real-time scheduling problems in TSN, Craciunas et al. [9] introduce a scheduling approach considering scheduling constraints for deterministic Ethernet and IEEE 802.1Qbv [4] with fixed flow routes. They solve the problem with *Satisfiability Modulo Theories* (SMT) and *Optimisation Modulo Theories* (OMT). Dürr et al. map the TSN scheduling problem with predetermined TSN flow routes to the No-Wait Job Shop Scheduling Problem using a Tabu Search algorithm in [14]. Additionally, they provide a schedule compression approach to reduce the number of configurable *guard bands*. Our schedule compression approach is comparable to Dürr et al. The difference is that we apply the compression mechanisms during the calculation of the schedule, whereas Dürr et al. apply the approach after the schedule generation [14].

Regarding scheduling problems with flexible routing, the authors in [24] propose routing algorithms for IEEE 802.1Qbv networks using Integer Linear Programming (ILP). The ILP solver is known to be time-consuming but is able to deliver an optimal solution. The most related work is from Pahlevan et al. [26] showing how to solve the joint scheduling and routing problem in TSN using genetic algorithms and at the same time considering the distribution of real-time applications to end-systems. The described approach of M. Pahlevan et al. shows better schedule results compared to the list scheduler introduced in the same paper. The work of M. Pahlevan et al. do not elaborate on the configuration of genetic algorithms, choice of operators, and combinable approaches to improve the genetic algorithm itself. We intend to focus more on the design of the genetic algorithm to be able to explore the solution space of possible TSN schedules in a more efficient manner. We focus on solving scheduling and routing problems for TSN with a hybrid genetic algorithm optimizing the performance and quality of the schedule. Compared to other scheduling algorithms, a genetic algorithm can be configured to find a compromise between the quality of solution and the calculation time.

3   Time-Sensitive Networking

Time-Sensitive Networking offers deterministic services through IEEE 802 networks [2]. It extends the standard IEEE 802.1 by the aspects of:

- Synchronization of time (802.1AS, P802.1AS-REV)
- Reliability (802.1CB, 802.1Qci, etc.)
- Latency (802.1Qbv, 802.1Qav, 802.1Qcr, etc.)
- Resource Management (802.1Qcc, 802.1Qat, etc.)

In TSN, the source of data, the *talkers*, and the sink, the *listeners*, communicate via TSN flows. TSN flows can consist of several Ethernet frames and can be propagated over unicast to a dedicated listener or over multicast to a group of listeners. Our scheduling approach supports the generation of schedules for the time-triggered transmission introduced by the *Time-Aware Shaper* in 802.1Qbv.

3.1   Time-Aware Shaper

The IEEE 802.1Qbv standard [4] describes how time-triggered transmission of flows is realized in TSN. The Time-Aware Shaper (TAS) divides the time into several segments within a defined, repeatable cycle assigned to a transmission port of an end-system or switch device. Determined egress queues are allowed to

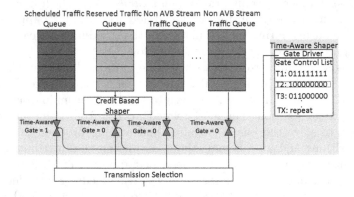

Fig. 1. Port egress queues with gating mechanism, see [4]

transmit packets within these time segments. To avoid an accidental interfering with packets from other queues, 802.1Qbv introduces the so-called *gates* associated each with one egress queue, see Fig. 1. The gates can have the states *open*

or "1" allowing packets from its queue to pass, and *closed* or "0" forbidding
the transmission of packets of the associated queue, see Fig. 1. The transmission selection does not consider packets from queues with closed gates. The
gate states at time *TX* are determined in a *gate control list*. In the literature,
typically one egress queue is dedicated to time-critical traffic [14] owning an
exclusive time window for transmission, see Fig. 2. Other queues can have their
own or shared transmission slots. The second important mechanism of 802.1Qbv
is the *guard band* that is available in each egress queue. Its function is to prevent traffic associated with one transmission slot from delaying traffic assigned
to the subsequent transmission window. The guard band suppresses the start of
transmission of packets for a defined time interval before the closing event of its
queue, see Fig. 2. Thus, the transmission of critical packets will not be delayed
by outstanding transfers.

To enable a global schedule, the involved devices require a common notion
of time. 802.1AS [3] and the project P802.1AS-Rev [1] provide mechanisms for
time synchronization for TSN.

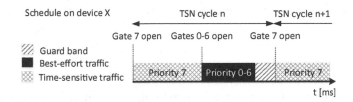

Fig. 2. Schedule with time slots for time-sensitive and best-effort traffic

3.2   Scheduling Constraints

The calculated schedule has to meet deterministic Ethernet and TSN constraints.
The overall goal is to calculate transmission offsets for TSN flows within their
transmission periods to guarantee a collision-free transmission of the flows. This
implies that whenever the transmission of a time-sensitive flow has started, it
should not experience additional delays except the simplified static network delay
comprising transmission delay $trans_{f_i,D_k}$ of flow f_i on device D_k[1], propagation
delay $prop_{D_k,D_l}$ on the transmission link between D_k and D_l, and processing
delay $proc_{D_k}$ on device D_k. We have designed our restrictions for store-and-
forward switching. Even though cut-through switching highly reduces end-to-
end latencies, it has not seen a wide support in TSN switches that are on the
market at the moment.

The restrictions are defined in more detail in [14] and are also comparable
to [9]. We combine the described restrictions from [14] and [9] and assume the
following ones:

---

[1] e_k for end-system and s_k for switch.

- The transmission of a flow f_i on a switch s_k cannot start until the transmission on switch s_{k-1}, the propagation of f_i towards switch s_k, and the processing on s_k have finished.
- Two conflicting TSN flows f_i and f_j that are transmitted over the same physical link must not overlap in time. The transmission of the second flow can not take place until the first flow has been completely put on the wire and after waiting for an interpacket gap interval. For hard determinism, we apply the flow isolation principle described in [9]. This even means that the second flow can not be enqueued in the egress queue before the first has left the queue. Thus, we assume no queuing delay.
- The end-to-end delay denoting the difference between the arrival time and the sending time of the flows [9] must be satisfied.
- Each flow f_i has a transmission period p_{f_i}. Thus, another constraint is that all packets must arrive at the destinations before the next transmission cycle. We simplify the scenario by assuming transmission periods that correspond to 2^x ms, $x \in \mathbb{Z}$, as opposed to [9].
- The flows are available for transmission at the beginning of their period.

We neglect the delays caused by time synchronization and deviation of different local clocks.

4   Genetic Algorithms

A Genetic algorithm (GA) is a randomized search technique simulating the biological evolution. The GA operates on a population consisting of individuals. Each individual has a fitness value that describes the quality of the individual. To create new individuals, the GA provides selection and variation operators consisting of crossover and mutation operators to pair and to evolve individuals of the population. To optimize the population, the parent individuals are replaced by their children based on a fitness evaluation and a replacing approach. The generational process is shown in Fig. 3. The GA stops if a condition is satisfied or after a certain number of generations. The individuals are represented by chromosomes in the biological context containing themselves genes. The genes are assigned values, so-called alleles, see Fig. 4. The following section describes a possible encoding scheme for TSN schedules.

4.1   Chromosome Encoding for TSN

We divide the encoding of a TSN schedule in a chromosome into two parts, the *Flow Permutation Vector* and the *Route Assignment Vector*. The Flow Permutation Vector tells which flow is allowed to be scheduled first in a global schedule. In Fig. 4, *Flow 2* is scheduled first, followed by *Flow 3*, and so on. Different permutations might lead to different schedules. We have chosen an integer encoding to identify the flows in the Flow Permutation Vector. Thus, the number 2 in a gene references *Flow 2*. If the flows are assigned fixed paths, the Route Assignment Vector is unnecessary. To give the possibility to select different routes for

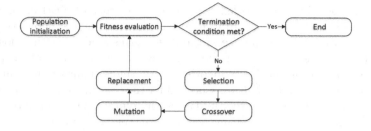

Fig. 3. Genetic algorithm, see [7]

the flows, we make use of an additional vector of the same length as the Flow Permutation Vector, the Route Assignment Vector. The Route Assignment Vector has a fixed assignment of a gene to a flow. The left gene of the routing vector in Fig. 4 describes that the currently selected path for Flow 1 is identified with number 1. Flow 1 has 3 alternative routes in our example. We assume in this example that each flow has one listener. In case of multicast flows, each gene of the Route Assignment Vector corresponds to an array of routes. Each element of the array represents the chosen path for one listener of the flow. The length of the array corresponds to the number of listeners. In our hybrid genetic algorithm, the fitness of a chromosome is described as makespan. The optimization goal is to minimize the makespan.

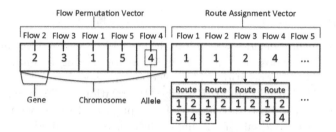

Fig. 4. Route assignment and flow permutation vector

4.2   Population Initialization

The initialization of the population has a big impact on the result of a GA. This step of the genetic algorithm creates the first generation of individuals that the crossover and mutation process is applied to. Heuristic approaches are often used to enrich the initial population with one or several good individuals. One of the most mentioned heuristics for population initialization is the constructive NEH algorithm introduced by Nawaz et al. in [23]. The NEH algorithm was developed for solving permutation flow shop scheduling problems (PFSP), a specific problem of JSP, with the aim to minimize the makespan. NEH has proven to be good in many works, see [29,30]. The steps of NEH are explained in Table 1. For our population initialization, we apply a restricted version of the NEH algorithm. The sequence of the flows corresponds to a chromosome in our algorithm. Instead of placing the next flow to be scheduled at all possible positions in *Step x* of the NEH algorithm, we define a maximum number of randomly chosen positions that are searched for the best makespan. The solution of the restricted NEH will be integrated as one individual in the initial population of our algorithm. The remaining individuals are created randomly.

Table 1. NEH algorithm

Step 1:	Generate a sequence of flows and sort the flows according to their earliest arrival time at the last node of their path. Assume that each flow has exclusive access to the network resources
Step 2:	Extract the two best flows and calculate the makespan with one flow starting first and then with the other. The schedule with the best makespan will be considered for further steps
Step x:	Take the next flow from the sorted sequence described in *Step 1* and calculate the resulting schedule placing the flow at all possible positions in the best schedule generated in *step x-1*. Do not swap the positions of already scheduled flows and continue with the best schedule. Repeat this step until all flows are scheduled

4.3 Selection

The selection method decides which individuals will be selected for mating. The primary goal is to choose the fitter individuals for mating to improve the population in the next generation. The selection method has a high impact on the so-called *selection pressure*. It describes the relationship between the probability of selecting the best individuals of a population to the average selection probability of all individuals [7]. A high selection pressure might lead to a fast convergence towards a local optimum, whereas a small selection pressure has a more global character, but might take more time to find an optimum. For our algorithm, we have chosen the *binary tournament selection*. In a binary tournament selection, two individuals are randomly selected in a tournament round, the number of tournament rounds is arbitrary. The better individual is selected with a fixed probability and the worse with the complimentary probability [16]. The advantage of this selection method is that a small number of competitors per tournament round leads to smaller selection pressure, and this approach is easy to implement in an efficient way [16].

4.4 Crossover Operators

A crossover operator combines the genes of two individuals by extracting information from both parents and recombining them into new offsprings. In our paper, we consider the following operators for the Flow Permutation Vector: The Partially-Mapped Crossover operator (PMX) [17], The Position-Based Crossover operator (PBX) [31], The Similar Block Order Crossover operator (SBOX) [30], The Order Crossover operator (OX) [11], and The Linear-Order Crossover (LOX) [15]. Moreover, we have developed an operator, the *RAO operator*, for the Route Assignment Vector. The OX, LOX, and RAO operator are further introduced in the following sections.

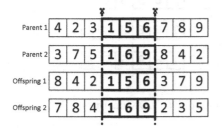

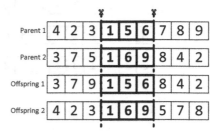

Fig. 5. OX operator example   **Fig. 6.** LOX operator example

OX and LOX Operator. The Order Crossover operator (OX) [11] and the Linear-Order Crossover (LOX) introduced in [15] define two cut points in both parents. The resulting offsprings keep the middle substring of one parent each. In our example, the Offspring 1 always inherits the slice between the two cutpoints from Parent 1, and Offspring 2 inherits from Parent 2. The remaining genes in the offsprings are filled with the missing values taken from the second parent. In OX, the missing values are taken from the second parent starting from the next position after the right cutpoint. Therefore, the left 3 genes in Offspring 1 are 842 in Fig. 5. In LOX, the filling starts from the left position to the right position of the second parent. In Fig. 6, the left 3 genes in Offspring 1 are 379, following the order from the left to the right in Parent 2.

RAO Operator. The *Routing Assignment Operator* (RAO) is an operator that we designed to determine the route of one flow in the Route Assignment Vector during runtime. We combine the route assignment process with the crossover process for the Flow Permutation Vector. Thus, according to Fig. 7, Offspring 1 inherits the routes 3, 1, and 2 (bold) of the inherited flows 1, 5, and 6 from Parent 1 in his Route Assignment Vector. The inherited flows have resulted from the crossover step of the Flow Permutation vector. The other, not inherited flows, are assigned the route with the least load one by one. The order of the route assignment is the same as the flow order in the Flow Permutation Vector of the offspring starting from the left to the right. Regarding Offspring 1, that means that after the inherited routes have been placed in the Route Assignment Vector of Offspring 1, the flow identified with number 3 is assigned the route 1 due to load balancing.[2] After, flow 7 is assigned the best possible route in terms of load balancing, and so on. The load of a route is determined as the sum of octets that is transmitted on the links of the route.

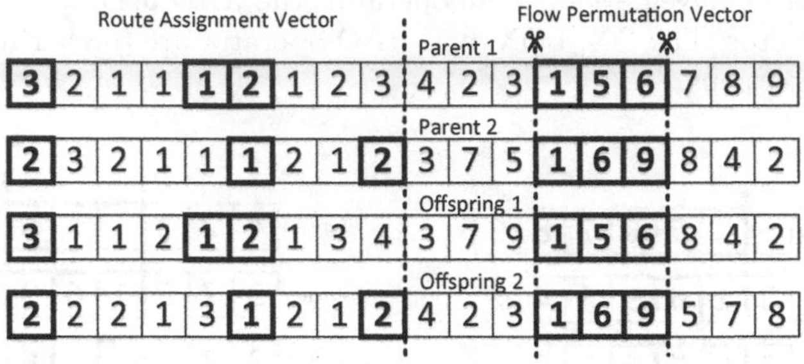

Route Assignment Vector | Flow Permutation Vector

Parent 1

| 3 | 2 | 1 | 1 | 1 | 2 | 1 | 2 | 3 | 4 | 2 | 3 | 1 | 5 | 6 | 7 | 8 | 9 |

Parent 2

| 2 | 3 | 2 | 1 | 1 | 1 | 2 | 1 | 2 | 3 | 7 | 5 | 1 | 6 | 9 | 8 | 4 | 2 |

Offspring 1

| 3 | 1 | 1 | 2 | 1 | 2 | 1 | 3 | 4 | 3 | 7 | 9 | 1 | 5 | 6 | 8 | 4 | 2 |

Offspring 2

| 2 | 2 | 2 | 1 | 3 | 1 | 2 | 1 | 2 | 4 | 2 | 3 | 1 | 6 | 9 | 5 | 7 | 8 |

Fig. 7. RAO operator in combination with LOX operator

4.5 Mutation

While crossover operators try to combine and preserve the genetic material of the population, mutation operators aim to evolve the individuals by introducing diversity from one generation to the next. The mutation process tries to avoid the convergence towards a local optimum. Mutation operators are applied with a rather small probability to the individuals [33]. For our algorithm, we decided to apply the *SWAP* mutation operator that randomly selects 2 positions within a chromosome and swaps the values at the positions and the *INVERSION* mutation operator that selects a substring within a chromosome and inverses the genes of the substring. While the SWAP mutation operator introduces a small change in a chromosome, the INVERSION operator is able to implicate a bigger change in the sequence of one chromosome. Both operators are used to manipulate the Flow Permutation Vector in our hybrid genetic algorithm.

4.6 Replacement Strategies

Replacement strategies describe how individuals of a population are selected for a new generation after new offsprings have been created. For our research, we are interested in replacement strategies introducing diversity to the population. In [12], the author describes a crowding approach to maintain the diversity of a population by replacing an individual out of a randomly chosen parent subpopulation that is most similar to the new offspring. We extend this approach by defining the rule that the offspring only replaces an individual if it provides a better fitness value. If it is not the case, we compare the fitness value of the offspring

---

[2] We assume that route 1 provides the least traffic load without giving a concrete example network.

to the worst makespan c_{worst} in the population and replace the individual with c_{worst} if the fitness value of the offspring is better. To determine the similarity, we measure the *hamming distance* [20] between the offspring and all individuals in the parent population. We call our approach the *modified crowding*.

4.7   GA Combined with Neighborhood Search

Neighborhood Search (NS) algorithms are widely applied to solve combinatorial optimization problems. In NS, starting from a solution x, the neighborhood solutions of x are explored. An adjacent solution x' can be reached directly from x by an operation called a move [28]. This move can also consist of applying a mutation operation to x [28]. For this purpose, we apply the SWAP mutation operator to 10% of the best solutions if the best solution of our HGA does not improve for n generations. Additionally, we use the INVERSION operator to explore the neighborhood of the worst 10% of individuals if the best fitness value does not improve for m generations. If the neighborhood contains a better solution, x will be replaced with x'.

5   Application of the Hybrid Genetic Algorithm in TSN

5.1   GA Settings

Our goal is to find the settings for a genetic algorithm to optimize the performance and the makespan for TSN schedules. To measure the optimization criteria, we compare the computation time of the fixed and flexible paths variant of our HGA to the computation time of NEH. The resulting makespan of our implementations is compared to the makespan of NEH. The GA is initialized

Table 2. GA settings

Population size	100
Generation number	Proportional to the number of flows
Crossover probability	0.9
Mutation probability	$\frac{1}{number\ of\ flows}$

with the values in Table 2. Before starting the genetic algorithm, we provide an initial solution by applying a restricted NEH algorithm, see Sect. 4.2. After that, the generational process starts, see Fig. 8. The fitness evaluation step of individuals is explained in Sect. 5.2. We apply the modified crowding approach described in Sect. 4.6 in order to introduce the diversity in the replacement process. If the best fitness value does not improve for a certain number of generations, we explore the neighborhood solutions of the best and worst individuals, see Sect. 4.7. The neighborhood search is implicitly applied to all selected best and worst individuals in comparison to the regular mutation process that takes place with a small probability. To determine the most suitable crossover operators, we execute the HGA alternating the crossover operators PMX, PBX, OX, LOX, and SBOX. We examine 10–100 flows in steps of 10 flows.

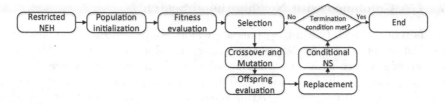

Fig. 8. Hybrid genetic algorithm

5.2   Schedule Calculation

The hybrid genetic algorithm delivers an ordered permutation of flows to the schedule calculation part during the fitness evaluation process. For the calculation, we introduce a global lower bound denoting the earliest possible transmission start times (*est*) and the global upper bound defining the latest transmission end times (*let*) of already scheduled or to be scheduled flows on all links, see Algorithm 1. The global bounds are realized using a vector notation. Each element of the vector corresponds to a transmission link and the value denotes the *est* or *let* on that link. We add the flows sequentially to the schedule and try to find the earliest transmission start times for each flow on its path links.[3] The global bounds change every time a new flow is scheduled. On the other hand, we apply steps to compress the schedule to avoid slacks. This might induce that the egress times of an already scheduled flow must be delayed. The goal is to create a schedule where the transmission start time of subsequent flows follow the transmission end times of the previous flows on intersecting network links as soon as possible [14]. This, in turn, implicates that several flows can be configured to use the same gate-open event for their transmission without introducing big slacks in the schedule [14], see Fig. 9a. Otherwise, subsequent time-triggered flows can be assigned different gate opening events on the same device. In this case, the slack between the transmissions should be big enough to fit at least one Ethernet packet in order to not waste bandwidth, see Fig. 9b. If the packet does not fit the slack, the transmission slot would be left unused.

Whenever we add a new flow f_{new} to the schedule in Algorithm 1, we check if the transmission times of f_{new} overlap with the previously added flows. First, we test if the global upper bound is smaller than the earliest transmission start times of f_{new} on all links of its route. If this occurs, we know that there is no

---

[3] The delay introduced between subsequent devices on a flow path is described as the static network delay from Sect. 3.2.

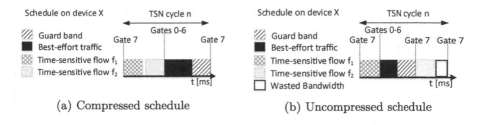

(a) Compressed schedule   (b) Uncompressed schedule

Fig. 9. Bandwidth allocation and gate event configuration

collision. Thus, we apply the compression step by raising the global bounds of all directly or indirectly affected links and all transmission times of the directly or indirectly affected scheduled flows by the difference *diffUpper*, compare [14]. The example in Fig. 10a and b shows that the *let* and *est* of transmission link tl_i increases after a new flow has been scheduled. The new flow can not be transmitted before $t = 6$, see Fig. 10a. Thus, the *est* of the link was raised to avoid small slacks between $t = 0$ and $t = 1$, and $t = 5$ and $t = 6$.

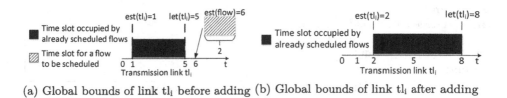

(a) Global bounds of link tl_i before adding   (b) Global bounds of link tl_i after adding
a new flow   a new flow

Fig. 10. Example showing the modification of the global bounds

Otherwise, we revise if f_{new} can finish its transmission before the global lower bound on its links. In this case, we delay f_{new} by *diffLower* in terms of schedule compression. If these cases do not apply, we know that a collision is inevitable. Thus, the transmission times of f_{new} have to be delayed by the absolute value of *diffUpper* in order to not collide with already scheduled flows. Finally, we have to merge the global upper and lower bound with the determined transmission times of f_{new} at the end of each step. A schedule is feasible if all contraints from Sect. 3.2 are fulfilled. Otherwise, a maximum high number is assigned to the makespan. For the sake of simplicity, the Algorithm 1 describes how to compute a schedule for TSN flows with the same flow period.

The presented HGA is able to compute the schedule for flows with periods that correspond to 2^x ms, $x \in \mathbb{Z}$, comparable to [19]. With this restriction, we have to check if all flows fit in the smallest available flow period. In this case, the procedure corresponds to Algorithm 1. If it is not the case, we have to consider our schedule in the next bigger period, in this case, 2 * (smallest available period). Thus, we have to build separate global upper and lower bounds for the first reduction of the bigger period containing all already scheduled flows that did not violate any restrictions and for the second reduction of the new

```
 1  take the first flow f₁;
 2  upperbound ← let(f₁);
 3  lowerbound ← est(f₁);
 4  while not all flows are scheduled do
 5      take the next flow fᵢ;
 6      diffUpper ← est(fᵢ) − upperbound;
 7      if diffUpper < 0 then
 8          diffLower ← lowerbound − let(fᵢ);
 9          if diffLower < 0 then
10              est(fᵢ) ← est(fᵢ) + (−diffUpper);
11              let(fᵢ) ← let(fᵢ) + (−diffUpper);
12          else
13              est(fᵢ) ← est(fᵢ) + diffLower;
14              let(fᵢ) ← let(fᵢ) + diffLower;
15          end
16      else
17          delay all transmission times of the affected previous flows by diffUpper;
18          lowerbound ← lowerbound + diffUpper;
19          upperbound ← upperbound + diffUpper;
20      end
21      merge(lowerbound, est(fᵢ));
22      merge(upperbound, let(fᵢ));
23      add fᵢ to schedule;
24  end
```

Algorithm 1: Calculation of the makespan

period containing flows that did not fit in the first reduction. The example in Fig. 11 shows that flow f_3 did not fit in the TSN cycle of 2 ms . Consequently, the global TSN cycle was expanded to 4 ms. To give another flow the chance to fit in the first reduction, we do not merge the global bounds of the reductions.

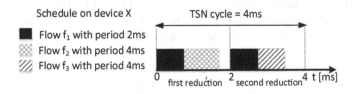

Fig. 11. Example of expanding the TSN cycle

6   Computational Results

We implemented our HGA on a Core i7-8550U CPU, 1.88 GHz processor and 24 GB RAM. The main emphasis was put on the evaluation of the performance and quality of the HGA using the ring and extended star network topology and a different number of flows. Additionally, we assume a fixed allocation of flows to devices. Our network consists of 10 switches and a maximum number of 5 end-systems per switch. Each TSN flow f_i contains one or two IEEE 802.1Q Ethernet frames and has a transmission period p_{f_i}, $p_{f_i} \in \{2 \text{ ms}, 4 \text{ ms}, 8 \text{ ms}\}$. We evaluated

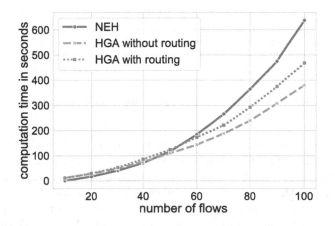

Fig. 12. Calculation time comparison

the execution time of all operators for the fixed and flexible routing variant. It turned out that the crossover operators show a similar time performance in each variant. The Fig. 12 sums up the performance of the operators used in the fixed and flexible routing implementation. Figure 12 points out that our algorithm shows a better time performance than NEH. The HGA without routing option provides the best results. We can state that the NEH algorithm rises exponentially with a bigger gradient than our HGA implementations. NEH performs a bit better for a small number of flows, but worse for a bigger number, because the number of flows has an exponential contribution to the execution time of NEH.

The computation time of our HGA for both variants depends on the number of generations when keeping the population size fixed. The number of generations rises with the number of flows, but does not have an exponential impact on the HGA. Additionally, it is easier to execute the HGA in a parallel manner, because the fitness value of a chromosome can be evaluated independently from other chromosomes for one generation. At the same time, our HGA implementations are able to compete with the NEH algorithm in terms of makespan quality, see Fig. 13a and b. We reference the quality measure to [26]:

$$quality_{makespan} = \frac{makespan_{NEH} - makespan_{HGA}}{makespan_{NEH}}$$

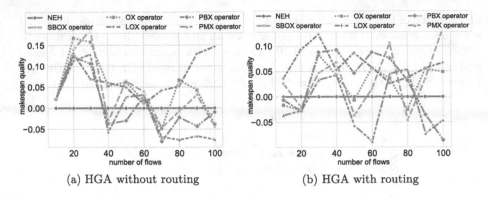

(a) HGA without routing   (b) HGA with routing

Fig. 13. Makespan quality of our HGA implementations

It is obvious in Fig. 13a and b that the makespan quality alternates for all crossover operators. The reason is that we still have a randomness factor using genetic operators. Additionally, the solution space grows faster than an exponential function with the increasing number of flows. A possible countermeasure is to raise the number of generations even more to explore a wider range of solutions. This, in turn, leads to higher computation time. Yet, our HGA is able to deliver comparable or even better results in terms of makespan quality using the settings in Table 2, especially when applying the LOX operator.

Regarding the different crossover operators, we can see that the LOX operator delivers the best makespan results on average, especially for a high number of flows, after running the evaluation for each number of flows about 30 times.

7   Conclusion

In our paper, we investigated the optimization possibilities given by genetic algorithms to solve scheduling and routing problems in TSN. We studied which encoding schemes are suitable for our problem, which operators are worth considering, and which hybrid approaches can be combined with genetic algorithms to find a near-optimal solution. Additionally, we introduced an approach to compress a schedule. The proposed HGA implementations were evaluated against the NEH algorithm that is a popular and efficient algorithm for permutation problems. We outperformed the NEH algorithm and showed that we can compete with NEH in terms of makespan quality. Additionally, we introduced a hybrid genetic algorithm to solve routing problems while keeping the network load balanced. We can state that the contribution of the hybridization approach and the schedule compression mechanism lead to a more efficient genetic algorithm. Furthermore, the compression approach has the effect of a better bandwidth utilization and thus, it is able to leave more bandwidth for non-critical network traffic. Our future work will focus more on the utilization of egress queue buffers of network devices and the integration of seamless redundancy into the schedule calculation process.

References

1. P802.1AS-Rev - Timing and Synchronization for Time-Sensitive Applications. https://1.ieee802.org/tsn/802-1as-rev/. Accessed 25 Oct 2019
2. Time-Sensitive Networking (TSN) Task Group. https://1.ieee802.org/tsn/. Accessed 25 Oct 2019
3. IEEE Standard for Local and metropolitan area networks- Timing and Synchronization for Time-Sensitive Applications in Bridged Local Area Networks. IEEE Std 802.1AS-2011 pp. 1–292, March 2011
4. IEEE Standard for Local and metropolitan area networks - Bridges and Bridged Networks - Amendment 25: Enhancements for Scheduled Traffic. IEEE Std 802.1Qbv-2015 (Amendment to IEEE Std 802.1Q-2014 as amended by IEEE Std 802.1Qca-2015, IEEE Std 802.1Qcd-2015, and IEEE Std 802.1Q-2014/Cor 1–2015) pp. 1–57, March 2016
5. Ak, B., Koc, E.: A guide for genetic algorithm based on parallel machine scheduling and flexible job-shop scheduling. Proc. - Soc. Behav. Sci. **62**, 817–823 (2012). http://www.sciencedirect.com/science/article/pii/S1877042812035793. World Conference on Business, Economics and Management (BEM-2012), May 4–6 2012, Antalya, Turkey
6. Anand, E., Panneerselvam, R.: A study of crossover operators for genetic algorithm and proposal of a new crossover operator to solve open shop scheduling problem. Am. J. Ind. Bus. Manage. **06**, 774–789 (2016)
7. Buttelmann, M., Lohmann, B.: Optimierung mit genetischen algorithmen und eine anwendung zur modellreduktion (optimization with genetic algorithms and an application for model reduction). At-automatisierungstechnik - AT-AUTOM **52**, 151–163 (2004)
8. Chen, H., Ihlow, J., Lehmann, C.: A genetic algorithm for flexible job-shop scheduling. In: Proceedings 1999 IEEE International Conference on Robotics and Automation (Cat. No.99CH36288C), vol. 2, pp. 1120–1125, May 1999
9. Craciunas, S.S., Oliver, R.S., Chmelík, M., Steiner, W.: Scheduling real-time communication in IEEE 802.1Qbv time sensitive networks. In: Proceedings of the 24th International Conference on Real-Time Networks and Systems, RTNS 2016, pp. 183–192. ACM, New York (2016)
10. Craciunas, S.S., Serna Oliver, R.: An overview of scheduling mechanisms for time-sensitive networks. In: Proceedings of the Real-time summer school L'École d'Été Temps Réel (ETR) (2017)
11. Davis, L.: Applying adaptive algorithms to epistatic domains. In: Proceedings of the 9th International Joint Conference on Artificial Intelligence, IJCAI 1985, vol. 1, pp. 162–164. Morgan Kaufmann Publishers Inc., San Francisco (1985). http://dl.acm.org/citation.cfm?id=1625135.1625164
12. De Jong, K.: An analysis of the behavior of a class of genetic adaptive systems (1975). https://books.google.de/books?id=4b9bNQcL6wMC
13. Demir, Y., İşleyen, S.K.: An effective genetic algorithm for flexible job-shop scheduling with overlapping in operations. Int. J. Prod. Res. **52**(13), 3905–3921 (2014). https://doi.org/10.1080/00207543.2014.889328
14. Dürr, F., Nayak, N.G.: No-wait packet scheduling for IEEE time-sensitive networks (TSN). In: Proceedings of the 24th International Conference on Real-Time Networks and Systems, RTNS 2016, pp. 203–212. ACM, New York (2016). https://doi.org/10.1145/2997465.2997494

15. Falkenauer, E., Bouffouix, S.: A genetic algorithm for job shop. In: Proceedings of the 1991 IEEE International Conference on Robotics and Automation, pp. 824–829 (1991)
16. Goldberg, D.E., Deb, K.: A comparative analysis of selection schemes used in genetic algorithms. In: Foundations of Genetic Algorithms, vol. 1, pp. 69–93. Elsevier (1991). http://www.sciencedirect.com/science/article/pii/B9780080506845500082
17. Goldberg, D.E., Lingle Jr., R.: Alleles, loci and the traveling salesman problem. In: Proceedings of the 1st International Conference on Genetic Algorithms, pp. 154–159. L. Erlbaum Associates Inc., Hillsdale (1985). http://dl.acm.org/citation.cfm?id=645511.657095
18. González Fernández, M.N., Vela, C., Arias, R.: A new hybrid genetic algorithm for the job shop scheduling problem with setup times, pp. 116–123, January 2008
19. Kopetz, H., Ademaj, A., Grillinger, P., Steinhammer, K.: The time-triggered ethernet (TTE) design. In: Eighth IEEE International Symposium on Object-Oriented Real-Time Distributed Computing (ISORC 2005), pp. 22–33, May 2005. https://doi.org/10.1109/ISORC.2005.56
20. Lozano, M., Herrera, F., Cano, J.R.: Replacement strategies to preserve useful diversity in steady-state genetic algorithms. Inform. Sci. **178**(23), 4421–4433 (2008). http://www.sciencedirect.com/science/article/pii/S0020025508002867. Including Special Section: Genetic and Evolutionary Computing
21. Moghadam, A.M., Wong, K.Y., Piroozfard, H.: An efficient genetic algorithm for flexible job-shop scheduling problem. In: 2014 IEEE International Conference on Industrial Engineering and Engineering Management, pp. 1409–1413 (2014)
22. Murata, T., Ishibuchi, H., Tanaka, H.: Genetic algorithms for flowshop scheduling problems. Comput. Ind. Eng. **30**(4), 1061–1071 (1996). http://www.sciencedirect.com/science/article/pii/0360835296000538
23. Nawaz, M., Enscore, E.E., Ham, I.: A heuristic algorithm for the m-machine, n-job flow-shop sequencing problem. Omega **11**(1), 91–95 (1983). EconPapers.repec.org/RePEc:eee:jomega:v:11:y:1983:i:1:p:91-95
24. Nayak, N., Dürr, F., Rothermel, K.: Routing algorithms for IEEE802.1Qbv networks. ACM SIGBED Rev. **15**, 13–18 (2017)
25. Nie, L., Gao, L., Li, P., Li, X.: A GEP-based reactive scheduling policies constructing approach for dynamic flexible job shop scheduling problem with job release dates. J. Intell. Manuf. **24**(4), 763–774 (2013). https://doi.org/10.1007/s10845-012-0626-9
26. Pahlevan, M., Obermaisser, R.: Genetic algorithm for scheduling time-triggered traffic in time-sensitive networks. In: 2018 IEEE 23rd International Conference on Emerging Technologies and Factory Automation (ETFA), vol. 1, pp. 337–344, September 2018
27. Potvin, J.Y.: Genetic algorithms for the traveling salesman problem. Ann. Oper. Res. **63**(3), 337–370 (1996). https://doi.org/10.1007/BF02125403
28. Reeves, C.R.: Genetic algorithms and neighbourhood search. In: Fogarty, T.C. (ed.) AISB EC 1994. LNCS, pp. 115–130. Springer, Heidelberg (1994). https://doi.org/10.1007/3-540-58483-8_10
29. Reeves, C.R.: A genetic algorithm for flowshop sequencing. Comput. Oper. Res. **22**(1), 5–13 (1995). http://www.sciencedirect.com/science/article/pii/030505489 3E0014K. Genetic Algorithms
30. Ruiz, R., Maroto, C., Alcaraz, J.: Two new robust genetic algorithms for the flowshop scheduling problem. Omega **34**, 461–476 (2006)
31. Syswerda, G.: Schedule optimization using genetic algorithms (1991)

32. Wang, X., Gao, L., Zhang, C., Shao, X.: A multi-objective genetic algorithm based on immune and entropy principle for flexible job-shop scheduling problem. Int. J. Adv. Manuf. Technol. **51**(5), 757–767 (2010). https://doi.org/10.1007/s00170-010-2642-2
33. Werner, F.: Genetic algorithms for shop scheduling problems: a survey. Preprint Ser. **11**, 1–66 (2011)

Performance Analysis for Loss Systems with Many Subscribers and Concurrent Services

Hans Daduna[1]([✉])[ID] and Ruslan Krenzler[2][ID]

[1] Department of Mathematics, Hamburg University,
Bundesstr. 55, 20146 Hamburg, Germany
`daduna@math.uni-hamburg.de`
[2] Institute for Information Systems, Leuphana University Lüneburg,
Universitätsallee 1, 21335 Lüneburg, Germany
`ruslan.krenzler@leuphana.de`

Abstract. We present models for performance analysis of IPTV services. The main topic is to model the interplay of the restricted number of channels, the larger number of available programs to be transmitted over the channels, and the concurrent access of many users to the same program, resp. channel (multicast services). In a simple Engset-like model we compute loss probabilities avoiding to count the number of concurrent users in the system. With a more detailed model where we explicitly count the number of concurrent users for the active channels we show how to compute revenue for the provider and loss probabilities as well. This model can be considered as a stratified system of different queueing systems. The main results are in both cases expressions for steady state distributions of simple structure, indicating separability.

Keywords: Loss probability · Concurrent services · Multichannel loss system · IPTV · Revenue · Separability · Insensitivity · Generalized Engset formula

1 Introduction

The following problem was communicated to us by Klaus Heidtmann from the Department of Informatics of Hamburg University.

An Internet Service Provider (ISP) offers television on demand over internet (IPTV) for S programs in parallel. Requested programs are transmitted over N parallel identical channels, where $N < S$. The services are provided as follows:

- If new demand of a user arrives for a program which is already attached to a channel (i.e., there is an ongoing transmission of that program for one

We thank Klaus Heidtmann for introducing us to this problem and pointing to us the relevance for research on IPTV. We thank four reviewers for their constructive comments which enhanced the paper.

H. Hermanns (Ed.): MMB 2020, LNCS 12040, pp. 118–135, 2020.
https://doi.org/10.1007/978-3-030-43024-5_8

or more other users), this user is immediately given access to the program (multicast transmission).

○ If new demand of a user for a program arrives which is not yet attached to a channel and if there is a free channel available, one channel is turned on and is busy with transmitting the required program and immediate access is given to the requesting user.

○ If new demand of a user for a program arrives which is not yet attached to a channel and if there is no free channel available, this demand is lost.

The main performance metric of interest is the overall loss probability of users' demand due to a request for a program which is not ongoing in a channel while all channels are busy (transmitting other programs) when the system is in its stationary state (blocking probability).

Related Problems and Literature. Loss systems are a classical topic in queueing theory and its applications, especially in telephony. For exponential loss systems $M/M/N/0$ (sometimes denoted as $M/M/N/N$) Erlang derived in 1917 the "loss formula" (now: Erlang's B-formula) [12, Sect. 3.7]: With arrival intensity λ and service intensity μ the stationary distribution for seeing N customers is

$$p(N) = \left(\frac{\lambda}{\mu}\right)^N \frac{1}{N!} \left\{ \sum_{\ell=0}^{N} \left(\frac{\lambda}{\mu}\right)^\ell \frac{1}{\ell!} \right\}^{-1}.$$

This is usually called the virtual loss probability (time-congestion) and this is (due to PASTA [23, Sect. 5.16]) for incoming requests the fraction of time all servers are busy and newly arriving customers are lost, for short the actual loss probability (customer-congestion) $P_L(N)$ satisfies $P_L(N) = p(N)$.

For several applications, e.g. in telephony, the assumption of a continuous arrival stream of demand has been considered inappropriate. Therefore the exponential Erlang model was modified for a finite number $S > N$ of customers calling for access to the $\circ/M/N/0$ server from time to time. The stationary distribution for seeing k customers is [12, p. 109]

$$\hat{p}(k) = \binom{S}{k} \left(\frac{\lambda}{\mu}\right)^k \left\{ \sum_{\ell=0}^{N} \binom{S}{\ell} \left(\frac{\lambda}{\mu}\right)^\ell \right\}^{-1}, \quad k = 0, 1, \ldots, N,$$

and therefore the virtual loss probability (time-congestion) is $\hat{p}(N)$. Engset computed the actual loss probability (customer-congestion) as the ratio between the rate of customers arriving when all channels are busy and the total rate of arrivals, which is different from $\hat{p}(N)$, see [26, Sect. 10].

There are many generalizations of these formulae available now because limited resources are typically restricting performance of systems and rejecting customers due to blocking of resources is a major point of customers' dissatisfaction.

Despite of the simplicity of the B-formula it turned out that for large numbers of servers combinatorial and numerical problems arise. This led to applying limit theorems, for a short review with more references see [22, Sect. 10.4.3, 10.4.4].

Closely related to loss service systems are finite buffer fluid systems, possibly with many sources (on-off processes), a typical demonstration of such asymptotic techniques and results is [10]. For the Engset loss formula and its generalizations the combinatorial and numerical problems are even harder [2].

Loss systems have been one of the sources of the so-called insensitivity theory for queueing systems and in reliability theory which roughly states (and proves) results like: The steady state probability for the number of busy channels in an $M/G/N/0$ system depends on the service time distribution only through the mean of the service time. The first general result in this direction was proved in [20], see also [9, Sect. 5.4]. This was generalized to more complex systems ("verallgemeinerte Bedienungsschemata") by König, Matthes, and Nawrotzki [14]. The systems investigated here will show such properties as well.

Although the problems of concurrent use combined with restricted availability of resources is a universal problem of Operations Research, the applications in IPTV have revived interest in such systems during the last decade considerably. The literature is overwhelming now, and we mention only a few. In [16] a short review of related early papers is given and a concise introduction into analytical modeling of unicast, broadcast, and multicast service schemes, see [1] for similar investigations. The investigation of multicast service there leads to investigation like ours. A more recent paper [17] generalizes [16] by including more technical details.

In this paper we do not consider the technical realization of the channels which in today's networks with e.g. mobile devices may be of complicated structure. If the channels are realized in mobile adhoc networks (MANETS) or are used for serving end users with IPTV services in VANETs (vehicular adhoc networks) availability is an important problem, for a short survey see the introduction in [24]. Availability problems, i.e. the number of accessible channels decreases from time to time due to breakdown of channels, will pose additional difficulties which are investigated e.g. in [24,25]. To include breakdown and repair into our models is part of our ongoing research. In this paper the channels are reliable: If a channel can transmit due to request of view times it will transmit.

Our Contributions. All classical loss models with discrete users where explicit (or limiting) performance metrics are available, partly described above, are considering the case: "One service channel for one user". The problem we are faced with is "one service channel for many users" (concurrent services), which makes the problem obviously much harder, see e.g. [16] for the case of exponential view times.

Nevertheless, even for non-exponential view times we are able to reduce our analysis of loss probabilities in the system with concurrent services to evaluation of a loss model of classical structure (generalized Engset model). This simple performance metric is of value because in case of our starting example, IPTV, the complementary metric, "availability", is a "highly important QoE measure for IPTV services" [24, p. 690].

Thereafter, in a second part we consider for more detailed analysis a new class of stratified models, discuss more complicated performance metrics in a general system and come up with some surprisingly simple formulas. We shall observe throughout insensitivity properties similar to those in "Verallgemeinerte Bedienungsschemata".

Structure of the Paper. We start in Sect. 2 with describing the general problem setting for the main body of the paper. In Sect. 3 we evaluate loss probabilities in a model where all users seeing the same program concurrently are lumped together as a super-user. This is possible because we identify the exact distribution for the time the super-user blocks the channel. In Sect. 4 we consider a model where all users viewing a program concurrently are traced individually. The stationary distribution as our main outcome shows that we have a stratified system of non-standard queueing systems. In Sect. 5 we consider a finite number of users in the system. We derive the stationary distribution under this restriction as well. In Sect. 6 we provide some short concluding remarks and point to unsolved problems which are situated in the neighbourhood of the present investigations.

Convention. cdf ≡ cumulative distribution function; empty products = 1.

2 Setting of the General Problem

We investigate our problem with a set $\mathcal{N}$ of identical resources (channels) and a class $\mathcal{S}$ of services for users (transmitting TV) and denote $S = |\mathcal{S}| > |\mathcal{N}| = N$. We identify users with their demanded service (program): If a user requests for program $c \in \mathcal{S}$, we say this user is of "class c". We assume first (Sects. 3 and 4) that there is no limit for the number of arriving users.

The assumptions for the system's behaviour with unbounded arrivals are

- users of class c arrive in a Poisson-$\lambda(c)$ stream, $0 < \lambda(c) < \infty$,
- the time a user of class c stays on with his selected program is generally distributed with cdf $H_c(t), t \geq 0$, which has mean $\mu(c)^{-1}$, $0 < \mu(c) < \infty$,
- all service times and all inter-arrival times are independent.

Because all channels have the same capacity we only need to maintain information about how many channels are busy, which programs are ongoing on busy channels, and

  o either how long the channel will be busy without interrupt (Sect. 3: loss probabilities),
  o or how many users are viewing the same program in parallel and their individual residual view times (Sect. 4: loss probabilities and revenue).

Remarks. The policy for dispatching channels to demand is myopic and greedy. No attempt is made to optimize the system's behaviour: Whenever a demand can be satisfied it will be satisfied. Clearly such a policy will not be cost optimal when costs are relevant for providing channels (of different capacity) and if users are willing to pay differently for different programs.

The arrival intensities $\lambda(c), c \in \mathcal{S}$, reflect an "important characteristic relevant for IPTV users" [24, p. 693]. Because the total arrival stream is Poisson with intensity $\lambda := \sum_{c \in \mathcal{S}} \lambda(c)$, and an arriving user selects program c with probability $p(c) := \lambda(c)/\lambda$, these probabilities $p(c)$ can be considered as "popularities" of the programs. Measurements have shown that the $p(c)$ often follow a Zipf distribution, see [24] and reference there.

Because all channels are identical we are allowed to set in force the

Assumption 1. *Channels are numbered* $\mathcal{N} := \{1, 2, \ldots, N\}$. *When* $n \leq N$ *different programs are ongoing they are associated to channels* $1, \ldots, n$.

When a user stops viewing and on departure leaves the channel, say number $m < n$, *behind empty, this idling channel is taken out of the count, i.e programs before on numbers* $m + 1, \ldots, n$ *are now located on positions* $m, \ldots, n - 1$.

When there are $n < N$ *programs busy and a new program is going to run, this program is formally inserted at random on one of the positions* $1, \ldots, n, n + 1$. *If this program is placed on position* $m \leq n$, *all programs associated to channels* $m, \ldots, n$ *are shifted one position up and counted now on* $m + 1, \ldots, n + 1$.

We emphasize that this regime of counting occupied channels is for book-keeping only, the physical realization might be quite different.

Performance Metrics. Beside of computing loss probabilities we are interested in the steady state mean number of lost demands per time unit. Existence of a stationary state is proved in Sect. 3, considering the rough model. A complementary performance metric of interest is the mean long-time revenue obtained from active users, resp. the stationary revenue, Sect. 4.

3 The Rough Model: Loss Probabilities

We describe the system's state in this part by sequences of lengths $n \leq N$

$$y = [c_1, t_1; \ldots; c_n, t_n], c_m \in \mathcal{S}, t_m > 0, m = 1, \ldots, n, c_m \neq c_{m'} \ \forall m \neq m', \quad (1)$$

where y at time t indicates that there are n busy channels with ongoing programs at time t, on position $\ell = 1, \ldots, n$ we see users of class c_ℓ. The respective number of users (≥ 1) are random and not specified, and the next time instant when no c_ℓ-users are present is $t + t_\ell$. If at time t there is no busy channel we will denote this by $y = [\emptyset]$. We denote the set of all such states by F.

A little reflection reveals that with these states a Markov process description of the system's evolution is possible **if we know the distribution of the time a channel will be continuously busy when it is started** for users of class $c, c \in \mathcal{S}$, and if we sample this duration when the channel starts transmitting (residual busy time). We denote this Markov process by $Y = (Y(t) : t \geq 0)$.

The proof of the next lemma is direct from the description of the multicast usage of channels by users of the same class.

Lemma 1. *The duration of time a channel will be continuously busy when it is started for users of class c is distributed as the busy period of an $M/G/\infty$ with Poisson-$\lambda(c)$ arrivals and generally distributed service times with cdf $H_c(\cdot)$. We denote the busy period cdf by $B_c(t), t \geq 0$, with mean $\beta(c)^{-1}$. It holds*

$$B_c(t) = 1 - \lambda(c)^{-1} \sum_{n=1}^{\infty} f_c^{n*}(t), \quad t \geq 0, \tag{2}$$

where f_c^{n*} denotes the n-fold convolution of the function f_c, which is given as

$$f_c(t) = \lambda(c)(1 - H_c(t)) \cdot \exp \left\{ -\lambda(c) \int_0^t (1 - H_c(x)) \, dx \right\}, \tag{3}$$

The mean value of the busy period is $E[B_c] = \beta(c)^{-1} = \dfrac{e^{\lambda(c)/\mu(c)} - 1}{\lambda(c)}$. $\tag{4}$

Proof. (2) is from [21, formula (3)], while (4) is from [8, formula (1.4)]. $\qquad\square$

Remark. Consider a time interval during which a channel is continuously busy for class-c users (without interrupt). We lump all these users into a single super-user having service time (view time) with cdf $B_c(\cdot)$ from Lemma 1. We equip this super-user with the same type c. We observe furthermore, that the influences of all arriving class-c users which occur during a class-c super-user's service are already encapsulated into its busy period distribution. Consequently, during service for a class-c super-user no new class-c super-users arrive (interrupted Poisson-$\lambda(c)$ stream).

Generalized Engset Model. Following the observation of the last remark we describe the system from the point of view of super-users as multi-type finite source model with blocking: We consider the system as an N-server queue which serves super-users where service requests of class-c super-users are generated by an external c-node (source) with exponentially-$\lambda(c)$ service times. If a class-c super-user is in service this source node is quiet, $c \in S$. On the other side, if a c-node generates a super-user's request and all N channels are busy this request is neglected and a new exponentially-$\lambda(c)$ inter-request time is started.

This system is an extension and generalization of the classical Engset model from telecommunication, [15, Sektion 7.5.3], [14, Sektion 1.9], [13, 26, Sekt. 10].

Proposition 1. *Consider a multiserver loss system $\circ/G/N/0$ with N service channels and (super-)users of different classes $c \in S$ requesting for service times with cdf $B_c(\cdot)$. This server is connected to a set of S single server exponential-$\lambda(c)$ source nodes (called c-nodes). For any $c \in S$, there is only one class-c (super-)user which cycles between the $\circ/G/N/0$ node and the c-node. Whenever the class-c (super-)user leaves its c-node and finds all channels of the $\circ/G/N/0$ node busy its stays-on at its c-node for another exponential-$\lambda(c)$ service time.*

With Assumption 1 for the service regime at the $\circ/G/N/0$ node this system can be described by a Markov process $Y = (Y(t) : t \geq 0)$ with state space F.

The asymptotic distribution of Y is independent of its initial distribution and is its stationary distribution as well. It is with normalization constant C (see Corollary 2) given by $\pi^Y[\emptyset] = C^{-1}$ for the empty system, and for $n = 1, \ldots, N$,

$$\pi^Y[(\{c_1\} \times [0, t_1]) \times \cdots \times (\{c_n\} \times [0, t_n])] = C^{-1} \frac{1}{n!} \prod_{\ell=1}^{n} \lambda(c_\ell) \int_0^{t_\ell} (1 - B_{c_\ell}(s)) ds. \quad (5)$$

Delete the residual times t_ℓ from Y to obtain the process $X = (X(t) : t \geq 0)$:

$$y = [c_1, t_1; \ldots; c_n, t_n] \rightarrow [c_1, \ldots; c_n] =: x$$

The stationary distribution of X is given by $\pi^X[\emptyset] = C^{-1}$, and for $n = 1, \ldots, N$

$$\pi^X[c_1, \ldots, c_n] = C^{-1} \frac{1}{n!} \prod_{\ell=1}^{n} \frac{\lambda(c_\ell)}{\beta(c_\ell)} \quad (6)$$

Proof. Due to Assumption 1 the server is symmetric in the sense of [11, Sect. 3.3]. Therefore (5) is (assuming the stationary distribution exists) a standard result for the generalized Engset scheme with (super-)users [14, 19, Sektion 1.9]. (6) follows from (5) for $t_\ell \rightarrow \infty, \ell = 1, \ldots, n$. The existence of the stationary distributions is direct from (6) and $N < \infty$. □

(6) shows that the unique stationary distribution of the marginal class process X depends on the mean values $\lambda(c_\ell)$ and $\beta(c_\ell)$ only. I.e., the stationary distribution of X is insensitive against variations of the shape of the B_{c_ℓ} as long as the means $\beta(c_\ell)^{-1}$ remain fixed. This proves the following corollary.

Corollary 1. *Consider the system from Proposition 1. Users of class $c \in S$ request for exponentially-$\beta(c)$ distributed service times, where $\beta(c_\ell)$ is given in (4). Then the class process X is a homogeneous Markov process with state space*

$$\widetilde{F} := \{[c_1; \ldots; c_n], c_m \in S, m = 1, \ldots, n, c_m \neq c_{m'} \forall m \neq m'\},$$

and unique stationary distribution given by $\pi^X[\emptyset] = C^{-1}$ and for $n = 1, \ldots, N$,

$$\pi^X[c_1, \ldots, c_n] = C^{-1} \frac{1}{n!} \prod_{\ell=1}^{n} \frac{\lambda(c_\ell)}{\beta(c_\ell)}.$$

Corollary 2. *Denote by $\mathcal{E}(S, N) := \{K \subseteq S : |K| \leq N\}$ the set of combinations of classes without repetition out of S of length N, the number of channels. The normalization constant for Y and X is for any selection of service time distributions with means $\beta(c)^{-1}, c \in S$,*

$$C =: C(S, N) := \sum_{K \in \mathcal{E}(S,N)} \prod_{c \in K} \frac{\lambda(c)}{\beta(c)}. \quad (7)$$

A further reduction of complexity is possible using state space $\mathcal{E}(S, N)$ for describing the loss system with exponential service time distributions.

Corollary 3. *Consider the system from Corollary 1 where users of class c request for exponentially-$\beta(c)$ distributed service times.*

The lumped class process $V := \kappa(X)$ obtained from X by applying the function $\kappa : \widetilde{F} \to \mathcal{E}(\mathcal{S}, N)$, $\kappa([c_1, \ldots, c_n]) := \{c_1, \ldots, c_n\}$, is a homogeneous Markov process with state space $\mathcal{E}(\mathcal{S}, N)$ and unique stationary distribution given by $\pi^V[\emptyset] = C^{-1}$ and with $\beta(c_\ell)$ as given in (4) for $n = 1, \ldots, N$

$$\pi^V\{c_1, \ldots, c_n\} = C^{-1} \prod_{\ell=1}^{n} \frac{\lambda(c_\ell)}{\beta(c_\ell)}. \tag{8}$$

Denote for $n = 0, 1, \ldots, N$ (for $n = 0$, recall that an empty product is 1)

$$c(\mathcal{S}, n) := \sum_{K \in \mathcal{E}(\mathcal{S},N), |K|=n} \prod_{c \in K} \frac{\lambda(c)}{\beta(c)},$$

then it holds $\qquad C(\mathcal{S}, N) := \sum_{n=0}^{N} c(\mathcal{S}, n) = C(\mathcal{S}, N-1) + c(\mathcal{S}, N).$

Corollary 4. *In the system with generally distributed view times the probability $p_b(\cdot)$ that all channels are busy (time-congestion) is*

$$p_b(\mathcal{S}, N) = \frac{c(\mathcal{S}, N)}{C(\mathcal{S}, N)} = \left(1 + \frac{C(\mathcal{S}, N-1)}{c(\mathcal{S}, N)}\right)^{-1}, \tag{9}$$

and the generalization of Erlang's B-formula, resp. the Engset formula, i.e. the stationary loss probability $p_L(\cdot)$ (program-congestion) is

$$p_L(\mathcal{S}, N) = C(\mathcal{S}, N)^{-1} \sum_{K \in \mathcal{E}(\mathcal{S},N), |K|=N} \left(\prod_{c \in K} \frac{\lambda(c)}{\beta(c)}\right) \left(\frac{\sum_{d \in \mathcal{S} \setminus K} \lambda(d)}{\sum_{d \in \mathcal{S}} \lambda(d)}\right). \tag{10}$$

Proof. We can not compute $p_L(\mathcal{S}, N)$ via Proposition 1 by the recipe to obtain the Engset loss formula. This would provide super-users' arrival distribution. Recall that the total arrival stream of users (programs) is Poisson-λ with $\lambda = \sum_{c \in \mathcal{S}} \lambda(c)$. These arrivals fulfill the PASTA property [23, Sect. 5.16], and the time stationary probabilities (5), resp. (8) provide information to finish the calculations. Denote by $\{A(t)\}$ the event that at time t an arrival occurs and by $\{A(t) = c\}$ the event that the arrival at t is of class $c \in \mathcal{S}$. Then

$$Pr\left(\{A(t) \text{ is lost}\}\right)$$

$$= Pr\left(\sum_{K \in \mathcal{E}(\mathcal{S},N), |K|=N} \sum_{d \in \mathcal{S} \setminus K} \{A(t) \text{ is lost}, V(t) = K, A(t) = d\}\right)$$

$$= Pr\left(\sum_{K \in \mathcal{E}(\mathcal{S},N), |K|=N} \sum_{d \in \mathcal{S} \setminus K} \{V(t) = K, A(t) = d\}\right)$$

which is (10) because the $\{A(t) = d\}$ are independent of $\{V(t) = K\}$.   □

Comment. The remarkable fact about the loss probability and the all-channels-busy probability of Corollary 4 is that it is a result for systems with many subscribers (with generally distributed view times!) and concurrent services. Nevertheless, numerically these probabilities can be obtained by computations in a simple exponential loss system with different classes. Astonishingly, the resulting "performance metrics" rely on mean values only.

Although (10) is simple, numerical issues arise with formulas of realistic sizes and are subject of intense investigations, see e.g. [2].

4   The Detailed Model: Revenue

In this section we consider all users individually and allow generally distributed view times. The system's states in this part are sequences of lengths $n \leq N$ where the elements of the sequences are subsequences $(c_m, t_{m1}, \ldots, t_{mk_m})$:

$$z = [c_1, t_{11}, \ldots, t_{1k_1}; \ldots; c_n, t_{n1}, \ldots, t_{nk_n}], \tag{11}$$
$$c_m \in \mathcal{S}, t_{mg} > 0, m = 1, \ldots, n, g = 1, \ldots, k_m, c_m \neq c_{m'} \forall m \neq m'.$$

Here z at time t indicates: n channels are busy with ongoing programs at t. At channel m we see k_m users of class c_m with residual view times $t_{m1}, \ldots, t_{mk_m}$.

If no channel is busy at time t, $z = [\emptyset]$, We denote by E the set of all such states.

Remark. For z in (11) the class sequence $[c_1; \ldots; c_n]$ are the states in $\widetilde{F}$ of the discrete state Markov models in Sect. 3. The supplementary variable vectors $[t_{11}, \ldots, t_{1k_1}], \ldots, [t_{n1}, \ldots, t_{nk_n}]$ in case of generally distributed view times can be considered as residual service time vectors of transient $M/G/\infty$ queues which live for just one busy period. More comments will be given later.

With these states a Markov process description of the system's evolution is possible which we denote by $Z = (Z(t) : t \geq 0)$. Z describes the evolution of a modified multiserver loss system $M/G/N/0$ with N service channels and with "supplemented queues" and users of different classes $c \in \mathcal{S}$. Users of class c arrive in a Poisson-$\lambda(c)$ stream and request for service times with cdf $H_c(t), t \geq 0$, with mean $\mu(c)^{-1} < \infty$. Arriving users of class c finding a channel busy with class c programs, i.e. observing a subsequence $[c, t_1, \ldots, t_k]$ with $k \geq 1$ in the arrival state of the system, join this channel concurrently to those already present there.

Arriving users of class c finding no channel busy with class c programs, and observe an idle channel enter an idle channel, i.e. add a pair $[c, t_1]$ to the arrival state of the system, where t_1 is sampled according to $H_c(\cdot)$.

Arriving users of class c finding no channel busy with class c programs, and observe all channels busy are lost.

Recording channels is organized according to Assumption 1. Moreover, for detailed book keeping we apply this counting regime (with insertion of new arrivals at random) to the supplementary sequences of residual view times as well.

Proposition 2. *Z has a unique stationary distribution π^Z. With normalization*

$$C = \sum_{K \in \mathcal{E}(\mathcal{S},N)} \prod_{c \in K} \left(e^{\lambda(c)/\mu(c)} - 1 \right) < \infty, \tag{12}$$

π^Z *is given by* $\pi^Z[\emptyset] = C^{-1}$ *and for* $z = [c_1, t_{11}, \ldots, t_{1k_1}; \ldots; c_n, t_{n1}, \ldots, t_{nk_n}]$

$$\pi^Z[\{c_1\} \times [0, t_{11}] \times \cdots \times [0, t_{1k_1}]; \ldots; \{c_n\} \times [0, t_{n1}] \times \cdots \times [0, t_{nk_n}]] \tag{13}$$

$$= C^{-1} \frac{1}{n!} \prod_{\ell=1}^n \frac{1}{k_\ell!} \prod_{g=1}^{k_\ell} \left(\lambda(c_\ell) \int_0^{t_{\ell g}} (1 - H_{c_\ell}(x)) \, dx \right), \quad n = 1, \ldots, N.$$

Before we prove Proposition 2 comments are necessary. The form of the stationary distribution is not intuitive although the components occur in stationary distributions of related models and so reflect structural connections.

The factor $1/n!, n \leq N$, clearly refers to the multiserver loss structure of the system of channels. The factors $\prod_{g=1}^{k_\ell} \left(\lambda(c_\ell) \int_0^{t_{\ell g}} (1 - H_{c_\ell}(x)) \, dx \right)$ are non-normalized stationary distributions of $M/G/\infty$ queues and seemingly (13) is therefore related to our approach in Sect. 3 where we argued that the time a channel is continuously busy is distributed according to a busy period distribution of an $M/G/\infty$ queue (=super-user's service times). Remarkable is that the channels do <u>not</u> behave like an $M/G/\infty$ because when a busy period of a channel expires the following idle periods have a complicated structure.

Summarizing, we have a stratified system where the basic stratum is a classical multiserver loss system where customers (not our users !) arrive and are served. These customers are infinite server queues for their own - which serve our users on the upper stratum. In case of exponential view times the problem simplifies.

Corollary 5. *Assume that in the setting of Proposition 2 class-c users have exponential-$\mu(c)$ view times. A description of the system's evolution by a Markov process X is possible without recording users' residual view times. States are $z = [\emptyset]$ and for $n = 1, \ldots, N : z = [c_1, k_1; \ldots; c_n, k_n]$ indicating that there are k_ℓ class-c_ℓ users, $\ell = 1, \ldots, n$. The unique stationary distribution is with normalization constant C from (12) given by $\pi^X[\emptyset] = C^{-1}$ and for $n = 1, \ldots, N$*

$$\pi^X[c_1, k_1; \ldots; c_n, k_n] = C^{-1} \frac{1}{n!} \prod_{\ell=1}^n \frac{1}{k_\ell!} \left(\frac{\lambda(c_\ell)}{\mu(c_\ell)} \right)^{k_\ell}. \tag{14}$$

If we do not respect the order of classes, we have unordered reduced states $z = \{(c_1, k_1), \ldots, (c_n, k_n)\}$ and the stationary distribution for the lumped states is

$$\pi^V\{(c_1, k_1), \ldots, (c_n, k_n)\} = C^{-1} \prod_{\ell=1}^n \frac{1}{k_\ell!} \left(\frac{\lambda(c_\ell)}{\mu(c_\ell)} \right)^{k_\ell}. \tag{15}$$

(15) is the result (30) in [16], where a different state space is used which can be transformed into the present lumped model.

Proof. For simplicity of the proof we assume that the view time distributions are finite mixtures of Erlang distributions, i.e.

$$H_c(t) = \sum_{h=1}^{K_c} r_c(h) \Gamma_{\eta(c),h}(t), \ t \geq 0, \tag{16}$$

where $r_c = (r_c(h) : h = 1, \ldots, K_c)$ is a probability mass function with $r_c(K_c) > 0$. $\Gamma_{\eta(c),h}(\cdot)$ is the Erlang (Gamma) distribution with h exponential-$\eta(c)$ phases.

The states of the process Z can then be converted to counting classes and number of residual phases, which a user of class c will stay-on viewing, each phase is exponential with mean $\eta(c)^{-1}$.

The meaning of state $z = [c_1, t_{11}, \ldots, t_{1k_1}; \ldots; c_n, t_{n1}, \ldots, t_{nk_n}]$, is now that n channels are busy with ongoing programs, at channel m we see k_m users of class c_m with residual numbers $t_{m1}, \ldots, t_{mk_m}$ of phases of $\exp(\eta(c_m))$ view times, $m = 1, \ldots, n$.

If no channel is busy, $z = [\emptyset]$. We denote the set of all such states by E.

The global balance equations of Z which determine the steady state distribution by flow-in = flow-out equations, are (with abbreviation $x(z) = x([c_1, t_{11}, .., t_{1k_1}; \ldots; c_n, t_{n1}, .., t_{nk_n}]) =: x[c_1, t_{11}, .., t_{1k1}; \ldots; c_n, t_{n1}, .., t_{nkn}]$ for the unknown solution vector)

- for $z = [\emptyset]$

$$x[\emptyset] \left(\sum_{c \in \mathcal{S}} \lambda(c) \right) = \sum_{c \in \mathcal{S}} x[c, 1] \eta(c), \tag{17}$$

- for $z = [c, t]$

$$x[c, t] \left(\lambda(c) + \sum_{d \in \mathcal{S} \setminus \{c\}} \lambda(d) + \eta(c) \right) \tag{18}$$

$$= x[\emptyset] \lambda(c) r_c(t) + 1_{(t < K_c)} x[c, t+1] \eta(c) + x[c, t, 1] \eta(c) + x[c, 1, t] \eta(c)$$

$$+ \sum_{d \in \mathcal{S} \setminus \{c\}} x[c, t; d, 1] \eta(d) + \sum_{d \in \mathcal{S} \setminus \{c\}} x[d, 1; c, t] \eta(d)$$

- and for $z = x[c_1, t_{11}, .., t_{1k1}; \ldots; c_n, t_{n1}, .., t_{nkn}]$ with $1 \leq n < N$

$$x[c_1, t_{11}, .., t_{1k1}; \ldots; c_n, t_{n1}, .., t_{nkn}] \left(\underbrace{\sum_{m=1}^{n} \lambda(c_m)}_{(A)} + \underbrace{\sum_{d \in \mathcal{S} \backslash \{c_1, \ldots, c_n\}} \lambda(d)}_{(B)} \right.$$

$$\left. + \underbrace{\sum_{m=1}^{n} 1_{(k_m > 1)} \eta(c_m) \cdot k_m}_{(C)} + \underbrace{\sum_{m=1}^{n} 1_{(k_m = 1)} \eta(c_m)}_{(D)} \right) \quad (19)$$

$$= \sum_{m=1}^{n} 1_{(k_m > 1)} \sum_{f=1}^{k_m} x[c_1, t_{11}, .., t_{1k1}; \ldots; c_m, t_{m1}, .., t_{mf-1}, t_{mf+1}, .. t_{mkm}; ..$$

$$.. ; c_n, t_{n1}, .., t_{nkn}] \lambda(c_m) \frac{1}{k_m} r_{c_m}(t_{mf}) \quad \text{(recall Assumption 1)} \quad (20)$$

$$+ \sum_{m=1}^{n} 1_{(k_m = 1)} x[c_1, t_{11}, .., t_{1k1}; \ldots; c_{m-1}, t_{m-1,1}, .., t_{m-1,km-1};$$

$$c_{m+1}, t_{m+1,1}, .., t_{m+1,km+1} \cdots ; c_n, t_{n1}, .., t_{nkn}] \lambda(c_m) \frac{1}{n} r_{c_m}(t_{m1}) \ (21)$$

$$+ \sum_{m=1}^{n} \sum_{f=1}^{k_m+1} x[c_1, t_{11}, .., t_{1k1}; \ldots; c_m, t_{m1}, .., t_{mf-1}, 1, t_{mf}, .. t_{mkm}; \ldots$$

$$\ldots ; c_n, t_{n1}, .., t_{nkn}] \eta(c_m) \quad (22)$$

$$+ \sum_{d \in \mathcal{S} \backslash \{c_1, \ldots, c_n\}} \sum_{m=1}^{n+1} x[c_1, t_{11}, .., t_{1k1}; \ldots; c_{m-1}, t_{m-1,1}, .., t_{m-1,km-1};$$

$$d, 1; c_m, t_{m,1}, .., t_{m,km-1}; \ldots; c_n, t_{n1}, .., t_{nkn}] \eta(d) \ (23)$$

$$+ \sum_{m=1}^{n} 1_{(k_m > 1)} \sum_{f=1}^{k_m} 1_{(t_{mf} < K_{c_m})} x[c_1, t_{11}, .., t_{1k1}; \ldots;$$

$$c_m, t_{m1}, .., t_{mf} + 1, t_{mf+1}, .. t_{mkm}; \ldots; c_n, t_{n1}, .., t_{nkn}] \eta(c_m) \quad (24)$$

$$+ \sum_{m=1}^{n} 1_{(k_m = 1)} \sum_{f=1}^{k_m} 1_{(t_{mf} < K_{c_m})} x[c_1, t_{11}, .., t_{1k1}; \ldots;$$

$$c_m, t_{m1}, .., t_{mf} + 1, t_{mf+1}, .. t_{mkm}; \ldots; c_n, t_{n1}, .., t_{nkn}] \eta(c_m) \quad (25)$$

- and for all channels busy with $z = x[c_1, t_{11}, .., t_{1k1}; \ldots; c_N, t_{N1}, .., t_{NkN}]$

$$
x[c_1, t_{11}, .., t_{1k1}; \ldots; c_N, t_{N1}, .., t_{NkN}] \left(\underbrace{\sum_{m=1}^{N} \lambda(c_m)}_{(A')} + \underbrace{\sum_{d \in \mathcal{S} \setminus \{c_1, \ldots, c_N\}} \lambda(d)}_{(B')} \right.
$$

$$
\left. + \underbrace{\sum_{m=1}^{N} 1_{(k_m > 1)} \eta(c_m) \cdot k_m}_{(C')} + \underbrace{\sum_{m=1}^{N} 1_{(k_m = 1)} \eta(c_m)}_{(D')} \right) \quad (26)
$$

$$
= \sum_{m=1}^{N} 1_{(k_m > 1)} \sum_{f=1}^{k_m} x[c_1, t_{11}, .., t_{1k1}; \ldots; c_m, t_{m1}, .., t_{mf-1}, t_{mf+1}, ..t_{mkm}; ..
$$

$$
\ldots; \quad c_n, t_{N1}, .., t_{NkN}] \lambda(c_m) \frac{1}{k_m} r_{c_m}(t_{mf})
$$

$$
+ \sum_{m=1}^{N} 1_{(k_m = 1)} x[c_1, t_{11}, .., t_{1k1}; \ldots; c_{m-1}, t_{m-1,1}, .., t_{m-1,km-1};
$$

$$
c_{m+1}, t_{m+1,1}, .., t_{m+1,km+1} \ldots; c_n, t_{N1}, .., t_{NkN}] \lambda(c_m) \frac{1}{N} r_{c_m}(t_{m1})
$$

$$
+ \sum_{m=1}^{N} \sum_{f=1}^{k_m+1} x[c_1, t_{11}, .., t_{1k1}; \ldots; c_m, t_{m1}, .., t_{mf-1}, 1, t_{mf}, ..t_{mkm}; \ldots
$$

$$
\ldots; c_N, t_{N1}, .., t_{NkN}] \eta(c_m) \eta(d)
$$

$$
+ \sum_{m=1}^{N} \sum_{f=1}^{k_m} 1_{(t_{mf} < K_{c_m})} x[c_1, t_{11}, .., t_{1k1}; \ldots; c_m, t_{m1}, .., t_{mf} + 1, t_{mf+1}, ..t_{mkm};
$$

$$
\ldots; c_N, t_{N1}, .., t_{NkN}] \eta(c_m).
$$

These global balance equations are solved by $x[\emptyset] = 1$ and for $n = 1, \ldots, N$ with $z = [c_1, t_{11}, .., t_{1k1}; \ldots; c_n, t_{n1}, .., t_{nkn}]$

$$
x[c_1, t_{11}, .., t_{1k1}; \ldots; c_n, t_{n1}, .., t_{nkn}] = \frac{1}{n!} \prod_{\ell=1}^{n} \frac{1}{k_\ell!} \prod_{g=1}^{k_\ell} \left(\frac{\lambda(c_\ell)}{\eta(c_\ell)} \sum_{h=t_{\ell g}}^{K_{c_\ell}} r_{c_\ell}(h) \right). \quad (27)
$$

The proof is now direct by inserting (27) into the global balance equations. For (17) and (18) correctness is immediate. We will check in detail equality for case $1 < n < N$. The demonstration is in parts tedious, but almost only simple algebra. For easier access we have grouped the lefthand side of the relevant equation accordingly. It holds

$$(22) = (A) \text{ and } (23) = (B) \text{ and } (20) + (24) = (C) \text{ and } (21) + (25) = (D).$$

Checking (26) is similar.

To obtain the non normalized solution in case of general cdf H_c in (13)

$$x[\{c_1\} \times [0, t_{11}] \times \cdots \times [0, t_{1k1}]; \ldots; \{c_n\} \times [0, t_{n1}] \times \cdots \times [0, t_{nkn}]] \quad (28)$$

$$= \frac{1}{n!} \prod_{\ell=1}^{n} \frac{1}{k_\ell!} \prod_{g=1}^{k_\ell} \left(\lambda(c_\ell) \int_0^{t_{\ell g}} (1 - H_{c\ell}(x)) \, dx \right),$$

we approximate the H_c by a sequence of finite mixtures of Erlang distributions in the sense of weak convergence. This is always possible, see [18, Sect. I.6]. That the solutions of the global balance equations converge follows by continuity of the transformations which transform the underlying stochastic data of the processes to the respective $x[\cdot]$-measures. This is proved in [3] for networks of queues in the sense of [11] and [4] and can be shown for our systems as well.

To check ergodicity we show that the solution $x[\cdot]$ is summable. The sum is the normalization constant. In a first step we integrate to obtain

$$x[\{c_1\} \times [0, \infty)^{k_1}; \ldots; \{c_n\} \times [0, \infty)^{k_n}] =: x[c_1, k_1 \ldots; c_n, k_n] \quad (29)$$

$$= \frac{1}{n!} \prod_{\ell=1}^{n} \frac{1}{k_\ell!} \prod_{g=1}^{k_\ell} \left(\lambda(c_\ell) \int_0^{\infty} (1 - H_{c\ell}(x)) \, dx \right) = \frac{1}{n!} \prod_{\ell=1}^{n} \frac{1}{k_\ell!} \left(\frac{\lambda(c_\ell)}{\mu(c_\ell)} \right)^{k_\ell}.$$

With $\mathcal{E}(\mathcal{S}, N)$, the set of all subsets of $\mathcal{S}$ with cardinality $\leq N$ we have

$$C =: C(\mathcal{S}, N) = 1 + \sum_{n=1}^{N} \frac{1}{n!} \sum_{[c_1,\ldots,c_n]} \sum_{k_1=1}^{\infty} \cdots \sum_{k_n=1}^{\infty} \prod_{\ell=1}^{n} \left(\frac{\lambda(c_\ell)}{\mu(c_\ell)} \right)^{k_\ell} \frac{1}{k_\ell!}$$

$$= 1 + \sum_{n=1}^{N} \frac{1}{n!} \sum_{[c_1,\ldots,c_n]} \prod_{\ell=1}^{n} \left(e^{\lambda(c_\ell)/\mu(c_\ell)} - 1 \right)$$

$$= \sum_{K \in \mathcal{E}(\mathcal{S}, N)} \prod_{c \in K} \left(e^{\lambda(c)/\mu(c)} - 1 \right) < \infty. \qquad \square$$

From (13) we can compute the probability of all channels busy and the loss probability similar to Corollary 4. At a first glance these expressions look different, but the reader should note that in (13) we have expected service times $\mu(c)^{-1}$ while in (6) of Proposition 1 we have expected service times $\beta(c)^{-1}$. This resolves the problem as discussed in the remark at the end of this section.

Comparing (14) for the system with exponential view times with (29) from the system with general view times shows that we have in the detailed model a strong insensitivity property, similar to that in the rough model from Sect. 3.

Recording classes and counting the number of users of the same class only leads to stationary probabilities which depend only on the means of the view time distributions: Varying shapes of the view time distributions do not change the stationary distribution of the reduced states as long as the means are invariant.

As an application of our explicit results on the number of users applying concurrently for IPTV service at the same channel we assume that the provider obtains as revenue from each active user of class c a payment $\theta(c)$ per time unit. We recur to the stationary distribution of the number of users of the respective classes, which was computed en passant in (29), and denote the total cost function by θ as well and obtain $\theta[\emptyset] = 0$ and

$$\theta[c_1, k_1; \ldots; c_n, k_n] = \sum_{\ell=1}^{n} \theta(c_\ell) \cdot k_\ell, \quad [c_1, k_1; \ldots; c_n, k_n] \in E.$$

The provider's total expected revenue in $[0, T]$ is $E\left[\int_0^T Z(t) \cdot \theta(Z(t)) \, dt\right]$, which is for large T by the mean ergodic theorem for Markov processes approximately $T \cdot \left[\sum_{z \in E} \pi(z) \cdot \theta(z)\right]$. We compute the expectation over the state space in the squared brackets of this expression of the mean costs per time unit.

$$\sum_{n=1}^{N} \sum_{[c_1, k_1; \ldots; c_n, k_n] \in E} \pi[c_1, k_1; \ldots; c_n, k_n] \cdot \theta[c_1, k_1; \ldots; c_n, k_n]$$

$$= C^{-1} \sum_{n=1}^{N} \sum_{[c_1, k_1; \ldots; c_n, k_n] \in E} \frac{1}{n!} \prod_{\ell=1}^{n} \left(\frac{\lambda(c_\ell)}{\mu(c_\ell)}\right)^{k_\ell} \cdot \frac{1}{k_\ell!} \cdot \left(\sum_{\ell=1}^{n} \theta(c_\ell) \cdot k_\ell\right)$$

$$= C^{-1} \sum_{n=1}^{N} \sum_{\{c_1 \ldots, c_n\}} \prod_{\ell=1}^{n} \left(e^{\lambda(c_\ell)/\mu(c_\ell)} - 1\right) \left(\sum_{g=1}^{n} \frac{\theta(c_g) \cdot \frac{\lambda(c_g)}{\mu(c_g)} e^{\lambda(c_g)/\mu(c_g)}}{e^{\lambda(c_g)/\mu(c_g)} - 1}\right)$$

In a similar way we can compute costs for the provider when a user is lost due to all channels busy and his selected program is not among the programs online.

Remark. Combining our two approaches from Propositions 1 and 2 to the same system we have an interesting conclusion. We consider the simplest system with one channel $N = 1$ and one customer class $\mathcal{S} = \{c\}$ and note that in Corollary 1 of Proposition 1 the state space is $\widetilde{F} = \{\emptyset, [c]\}$. Then the stationary probability for an empty system is

$$\pi[\emptyset] = (1 + \frac{\lambda(c)}{\beta(c)})^{-1}, \tag{30}$$

by standard insensitivity arguments and using the exponential system with mean $\beta(c)^{-1}$ of the relevant busy period distribution. The point is: We need not to know the value of $\beta(c)$, because (30) holds for any service time distribution in the Engset model and carries over to the exponential system by insensitivity. Considering now the detailed system from Proposition 2. Here we do not need to know the value of $\beta(c)$ to obtain the stationary probability for the system to be empty. This probability is by (13) and (12)

$$\pi[\emptyset] = \left(1 + \left(e^{\frac{\lambda(c)}{\mu(c)}} - 1\right)\right)^{-1}, \tag{31}$$

Equating (30) and (31) and solving for $\beta(c)^{-1}$ yields

$$\beta(c)^{-1} = (e^{\lambda(c)/\mu(c)} - 1)/\lambda(c),$$

which is the result (4) of Daley, who obtained it using renewal theory – derived here anew by queueing theoretical principles. Note, we do not use the explicit series expression (with an infinite number of convolutions) given in (2).

5 Finite Population: Limited Number of Subscribers

We consider now the situation where the provider admits only a bounded number $U > 1$ of users subscribing for the multi-channel IPTV system. For simplicity of presentation we consider only exponential-$\mu(c)$ view times. Obviously, this problem can not be dealt with in the rough model from Sect. 3 because there we neglected counting the number of users present and introduced the super-user. We therefore reenter the realm of Proposition 2.

Lemma 2. *The Markov process Z from Proposition 2 with exponential view times and states $[c_1, k_1; \ldots; c_n, k_n]$ is reversible with respect to the stationary distribution π obtained from (29) in case of exponential view times.*

Proof. Check that $\pi[c_1, k_1; \ldots; c_n, k_n] = \frac{1}{n!} \prod_{\ell=1}^{n} \frac{1}{k_\ell!} \left(\frac{\lambda(c_\ell)}{\mu(c_\ell)}\right)^{k_\ell}$ from (14) fulfills the local balance equations (see [11, Sect. 1.2]).   □

For a reversible Markov process Z with stationary distribution π on a discrete state space E it is possible to truncate E to a non empty subset $E_U \subset E$. For our purpose, E_U is the set of states with at most U users present.

Proposition 3. *Consider a multiserver loss system with N service channels and "supplemented queues" as described in Proposition 2. Define Markov process $Z_U = (Z_U(t) : t \geq 0)$ by truncation of the reversible Markov process Z on E to $E_U := \{[c_1, k_1; \ldots; c_n, k_n] \in E : \sum_{\ell=1}^{n} k_\ell \leq U\}$. Reduce Z to E_U as follows:*

Arriving users of class c seeing on their arrival $< U$ users in the system behave in the same way as in the unrestricted system.

Arriving users of class c seeing on their arrival U users in the system are not admitted to enter and lost.

Z_U is ergodic with stationary distribution which is with normalization constant C_U given by $\pi_U[\emptyset] = C_U^{-1}$ and for $n = 1, \ldots, N$ with $z = [c_1, k_1; \ldots; c_n, k_n] \in E_U$

$$\pi_U[c_1, k_1; \ldots; c_n, k_n] = C_U^{-1} \frac{1}{n!} \prod_{\ell=1}^{n} \left(\frac{\lambda(c_\ell)}{\mu(c_\ell)}\right)^{k_\ell} \cdot \frac{1}{k_\ell!}. \tag{32}$$

Proof. The proof elaborates on [11, Sect. 1.6]: If the truncated transition intensity matrix reduced to E_U is irreducible the unique stationary distribution of the truncated process Z_U is obtained as the reduction of π by conditioning on E_U, which includes renormalization. Irreducibility of Z_U is obvious.   □

6 Concluding Remarks

We have demonstrated with different level of detail an analysis of concurrent services (with non-exponential view times) at common channels with restricted access due to limited resources. We obtained in a first step results by transforming the model into a classical multi-class loss system with finite population.

In a second step we invented a new stratified non-exponential queueing model to prove and compute much more detailed performance metrics.

Review of related applications (not necessarily infotainment related) of concurrent use of common channels under capacity constraints showed that a challenging research project is to consider the situation where the channels can break down and are repaired after some time. E.g., this would be an abstract model for MANETs where due to moving devices the transmission over a (multi-hop) channel is not possible without interrupt. This is part of our ongoing research. Within these applications the restriction to finite population models seems to be not realistic. Our approach offers (as can seen from our results) a way to search for stationary behaviour, and, if results are available at all, the hope for smooth performance metric computations even in the more complicated situation. In [24] availability in infotainment applications is declared to be an important issue.

Non-availability of channels in the model brings the classical reader-writer problem into the realm of our model: Readers for a data base are the concurrent users while the writers, modeled as breakdown of a channel (which can occur only when the channel is idle) take the data base out of use for readers [7].

We have computed normalization constants explicitly during our investigations. Nevertheless, we point out that computing the stationary probabilities obtained in Propositions 1 and 2 will need additional effort for large numbers of channels and programs - as is known for closed networks of queues with finite but large number of customers and queues. But our formulas offer the possibility to derive numerical schemes similar to those which are well known for multi-class closed queueing networks, see e.g. [5] or [6].

References

1. Abdollahpouri, A., Wolfinger, B.E.: Measures to quantify the gain of multicast with application to IPTV transmissions via WiMax networks. Telecommun. Syst. **55**(2), 185–198 (2014)
2. Azimzadeh, P., Carpenter, T.: Fast Engset computation. Oper. Res. Lett. **44**(3), 313–318 (2016)
3. Barbour, A.D.: Networks of queues and the method of stages. Adv. Appl. Probab. **8**, 584–591 (1976)

4. Baskett, F., Chandy, M., Muntz, R., Palacios, F.G.: Open, closed and mixed networks of queues with different classes of customers. J. Assoc. Comput. Mach. **22**, 248–260 (1975)
5. Bruell, S.C., Balbo, G.: Computational Algorithms for Closed Queueing Networks. North-Holland, New York (1980)
6. Bolch, G., Greiner, S., de Meer, H., Trivedi, K.S.: Queueing Networks and Markov Chains, 2nd edn. Wiley, New York (2006)
7. Courtois, P.-J., Heymans, F., Parnas, D.: Concurrent control with "readers" and "writers". Commun. ACM **14**, 667–668 (1971)
8. Daley, D.J.: The busy period of the M/GI/∞ queue. Queueing Syst.: Theory Appl. **38**, 195–204 (2001)
9. Gnedenko, B.W., Kowalenko, I.N.: Einführung in die Bedienungstheorie. Akademie-Verlag GmbH, Berlin (1974)
10. Jelenković, P., Momčilović, P.: Asymptotic loss probabilities in a finite buffer fluid queue with heterogeneous heavy-tailed on-off processes. Ann. Appl. Probab. **13**, 576–603 (2003)
11. Kelly, F.P.: Reversibility and Stochastic Networks. Wiley, Chichester (1979)
12. Kleinrock, L.: Queueing Theory, vol. I. Wiley, New York (1975)
13. König, D.: Verallgemeinerungen der Engsetschen Formeln. Math. Nachr. **28**(3–4), 145–155 (1964)
14. König, D., Matthes, K., Nawrotzki, K.: Unempfindlichkeitseigenschaften von Bedienungsprozessen. In: Gnedenko, B.W., Kowalenko, I.N. (eds.) Einführung in die Bedienungstheorie, 2nd edn, pp. 358–450. Akademie Verlag, Berlin (1974)
15. König, D., Stoyan, D.: Methoden der Bedienungstheorie. Vieweg, Braunschweig (1976)
16. Li, M.: Analysis of blocking rate and bandwidth usage of mobile IPTV services in wireless cellular networks. Sci. World J. **2014**, 1–9 (2014). Article ID 215710
17. Li, M., Wu, Y.-H.: Performance analysis of adaptive multicast streaming services in wireless cellular networks. IEEE Trans. Mob. Comput. **18**(11), 2616–2630 (2019)
18. Schassberger, R.: Warteschlangen. Springer, Wien (1973)
19. Schassberger, R.: Insensitivity of steady-state distributions of generalized semi-Markov processes, part I. Ann. Prob. **5**, 87–99 (1977)
20. Sevastyanov, B.: An ergodic theorem for Markov processes and its application to telephone systems with refusal. Theory Probab. Appl. **2**, 104–112 (1957)
21. Stadje, W.: The busy period of the queueing system M/G/∞. J. Appl. Probab. **22**, 697–704 (1985)
22. Whitt, W.: Stochastic Process Limits. Springer, Berlin (2002). https://doi.org/10.1007/b97479
23. Wolff, R.W.: Stochastic Modeling and the Theory of Queues. Prentice-Hall International Editions, Englewood Cliffs (1989)
24. Wolfinger, B., Hübner, A., Momeni, S.: A validated analytical model for availability prediction of IPTV services in VANETs. Electronics **3**, 689–711 (2014)
25. Wolfinger, B., Baez, E.E., Wilzek, N.R.: A generalized approach to predict the availability of IPTV services in vehicular networks using an analytical model. In: Proceedings International Conference on Networks, ICN 2015, pp. 163–170. IARIA (2015). ISBN 978-1-61208-398-8
26. Zukerman, M.: Introduction to queueing theory and stochastic teletraffic Models. Lecture Notes. City University of Hong Kong, EE Department. arXiv:1307.2968v22 (2019)

On the Stochastic End-to-End Delay Analysis in Sink Trees Under Independent and Dependent Arrivals

Paul Nikolaus and Jens Schmitt[✉]

Distributed Computer Systems (DISCO) Lab, TU Kaiserslautern,
Kaiserslautern, Germany
{nikolaus,jschmitt}@cs.uni-kl.de

Abstract. Sink trees are a frequent topology in many networked systems; typical examples are multipoint-to-point label switched paths in Multiprotocol Label Switching networks or wireless sensor networks with sensor nodes reporting to a base station. In this paper, we compute end-to-end delay bounds using a stochastic network calculus approach for a flow traversing a sink tree.

For n servers with one flow of interest and n cross-flows, we derive solutions for a general class of arrivals with moment-generating function bounds. Comparing algorithms known from the literature, our results show that, e.g., pay multiplexing only once has to consider less stochastic dependencies in the analysis.

In numerical experiments, we observe that the reduced dependencies to consider, and therefore less applications of Hölder's inequality, lead to a significant improvement of delay bounds with fractional Brownian motion as a traffic model. Finally, we also consider a sink tree with dependent cross-flows and evaluate the impact on the delay bounds.

Keywords: Network calculus · Sink trees · Moment-generating functions · Hölder's inequality · Fractional Brownian motion

1 Introduction

1.1 Background

The stochastic network calculus (SNC) offers a versatile uniform framework to compute probabilistic performance bounds in networked systems. The most prominent goal is to control tail probabilities for the end-to-end (e2e) delay, i.e., probabilities for rare events shall be bounded, e.g., $P(\text{e2e delay} > 10 \text{ ms}) \leq 10^{-6}$. Many modern systems are eager after such performance guarantees, as exemplified in application visions like, e.g., Tactile Internet [17], Industrial IoT [8], or Internet at the speed-of-light [43].

Over almost three decades, the development of SNC has progressed with the pioneering work by [11,15,45], and important contributions in [9,13,18,23,28]

ⓒ Springer Nature Switzerland AG 2020
H. Hermanns (Ed.): MMB 2020, LNCS 12040, pp. 136–154, 2020.
https://doi.org/10.1007/978-3-030-43024-5_9

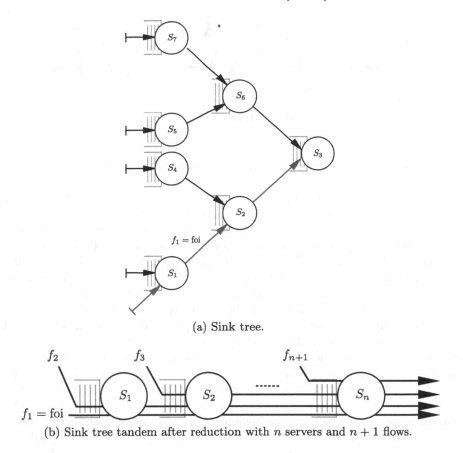

(a) Sink tree.

(b) Sink tree tandem after reduction with n servers and $n+1$ flows.

Fig. 1. Sink tree reduction.

to name a few, see also [14,19] for a guide and some perspectives. Two flavors of SNC have evolved: arrival and service processes characterized either by tail bounds [13,15,23] or by moment-generating function (MGF) bounds [12,18]. While tail bounds offer a wider modeling scope, they have been shown to result in more conservative bounds in scenarios where independence between stochastic processes can be assumed [37]. In this paper, we focus on the SNC with MGF bounds.

1.2 E2E Analysis in SNC – State of Affairs

When performing an SNC analysis given a network of servers with a set of flows routed over subsets of theses servers, the first step is to reduce the network to the tandem of servers which are traversed by a certain flow of interest (foi), see also Fig. 1. To that end, arrival bounds for each cross-flow with which the foi shares a subset of servers need to be computed at the point when it joins the foi. Conceptually, this simple, but important step just requires the computation

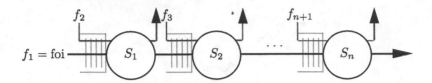

Fig. 2. Tandem in [18].

of output bounds for the cross-flows and has recently been improved by the use of Lyapunov's inequality in [34].

While, in this paper, we assume this reduction from network to tandem has already been performed, an important observation has to be made: Even under the assumption that all flows are independent when entering the network, some of them become dependent when traversing a shared server. These stochastic dependencies between cross-flows severely aggravate the e2e analysis for the foi. In the SNC based on MGF bounds, one can resort to use Hölder's Inequality to deal with dependent scenarios. However, the inequality is known to be very conservative and, if invoked too often in the e2e analysis, loosens the performance bounds considerably. This was shown in a simple tandem of servers traversed by many parallel flows in [32]. In that paper, it was demonstrated that two different ways of doing the e2e delay analysis, known from the deterministic network calculus (DNC) as separated flow analysis (SFA) and pay multiplexing only once (PMOO), result in very different bounds. In these simple tandems, PMOO completely avoids the usage of Hölder's inequality if all flows are originally independent whereas SFA requires the inequality's invocation at each server; consequently, PMOO clearly outperforms SFA in the quality of the bounds (and also in run times). This shows the importance of a careful e2e analysis and has been investigated extensively in DNC literature, see, e.g., [5,7,41]. Yet, to the best of our knowledge, it has not been investigated much in the literature on SNC with MGF bounds.

In existing work on the SNC based on MGF bounds [18], a tandem as in Fig. 2 was analyzed with all flows being independent and a nice linear scaling of the e2e delay bound was shown. Yet, such a tandem, if being the result of a network reduction, is likely to be crossed by dependent flows based on their previous entanglement. Apart from the work mentioned above [32], there is also some work to deal with stochastic dependencies in the analysis [6,16,33]. Overall, it must be concluded that the e2e analysis in SNC still faces many open problems.

1.3   Motivation and Contribution

In this paper, we take the next step in tackling the SNC e2e delay analysis by providing results for a particular topology: sink trees. Sink trees are interesting for a number of application scenarios:

- Classically, in Multiprotocol Label Switching (MPLS) networks there is the option to set up multipoint-to-point label-switched paths between several ingress edge routers and one egress edge router [39], thus creating a sink tree.
- Multi-hop wireless sensor networks with a central base station collecting data from sensor nodes induce a sink tree topology and have been investigated using network calculus methods previously, see, e.g., [25,40]. More generally, any data collection by a central point results in a sink tree and if time-critical decisions are made based on that data, performance guarantees are desirable, see, e.g., [47].
- Network-on-Chip architectures frequently employ tree topologies and have been analyzed using network calculus methods previously, see, e.g., [21,36].
- Switched Ethernets set up spanning trees to avoid cycles in frame forwarding, hence, again sink trees emerge as a natural choice to support resource allocation in such installations [22].
- Sink trees are also related to so-called fat trees in supercomputing [26]; in fact, fat trees have also been proposed in data center interconnects and have been subject to SNC-based analysis in [44,46], recently.

Hence, from an application perspective, it is clearly interesting to provide an e2e delay analysis for sink trees. While we constrain the topology for the SNC e2e analysis to sink trees, we want to remain as flexible as possible with respect to arrival and service models. In particular, we intentionally do not restrict to linear MGF bounds as provided by the so-called (σ, ρ)-bounds from [12], but derive the e2e delay bounds for general MGF bounds on arrivals and service. For instance, this includes a traffic model based on fractional Brownian motion (fBm). FBm has been shown to be useful for Internet traffic modeling [20,35], because it can capture the typical long-range dependence, which is why we also use it in our numerical experiments. On the other hand, it is a non-trivial traffic type for SNC to deal with and we do not provide stationary (time-independent) delay bounds (for Hurst parameter $H > 0.5$), but transient (time-dependent) delay bounds only. Having said that, it is interesting to note that some applications are actually more interested in transient bounds and corresponding developments have been reported in [2,4,10,29].

1.4   Outline

In Sect. 2, we provide the necessary SNC background and notations used throughout the paper. Section 3 presents the derivations for the e2e delay analysis of sink tree tandems under independent and dependent cross-flows using different algorithms (SFA and PMOO). In Sect. 4, numerical evaluations of different aspects are provided: influence of the time horizon on the transient delay bounds, effects of traffic parameters and sink tree depths, comparisons between different analysis algorithms and the independent and dependent scenarios. Section 5 concludes the paper.

2   SNC Background and Notation

We use the MGF-based SNC in order to bound the probability that the delay exceeds a given value $T \geq 0$. The MGF bound on a probability is established by applying Chernoff's bound [31]

$$P(X > a) \leq e^{-\theta a} \, \mathrm{E}\big[e^{\theta X}\big], \quad \theta > 0.$$

Definition 1 (Arrival Process). *We define an* arrival flow *by the stochastic process A with discrete time space $\mathbb{N}_0$ and continuous state space $\mathbb{R}_0^+$ as*

$$A(s,t) := \sum_{i=s+1}^{t} a_i, \tag{1}$$

with $a_i \geq 0$ as the traffic increment process in time slot i.

Network calculus provides an elegant system-theoretic analysis by employing min-plus algebra.

Definition 2 (Convolution and Deconvolution in Min-Plus Algebra [1]). *Let $x(s,t)$ and $y(s,t)$ be real-valued, bivariate functions. The* min-plus convolution *of x and y is defined as*

$$x \otimes y\,(s,t) := \inf_{s \leq u \leq t} \{x(s,u) + y(u,t)\}.$$

The min-plus deconvolution *of x and y is defined as*

$$x \oslash y\,(s,t) := \sup_{0 \leq u \leq s} \{x(u,t) - y(u,s)\}.$$

The characteristics of the service process are captured by the notion of a dynamic S-server.

Definition 3 (Dynamic S-Server [12]). *Assume a service element has an arrival flow A as its input and the respective output is denoted by D. Let $S(s,t)$, $0 \leq s \leq t$, be a stochastic process that is nonnegative and increasing in t. The service element is a* dynamic S-server *iff for all $t \geq 0$ it holds that*

$$D(0,t) \geq A \otimes S\,(0,t) = \inf_{0 \leq s \leq t} \{A(0,s) + S(s,t)\}.$$

Definition 4 (Work-Conserving Server [12,18]). *For any $t \geq 0$ let $\tau := \sup\{s \in [0,t] : D(0,s) = A(0,s)\}$ be the beginning of the last backlogged period before t. Assume again the service $S(s,t)$, $0 \leq s \leq t$, to be a stochastic process that is nonnegative and increasing in t with $S(\tau,\tau) = 0$. A server is said to be* work-conserving *if for any fixed sample path the server is not idle in $(\tau,t]$ and uses the entire available service, i.e., $D(0,t) = D(0,\tau) + S(\tau,t)$.*

The analysis is based on a per-flow perspective. That is, we consider a certain flow, the so-called *flow of interest* (foi). Throughout this paper, for the sake of simplicity, we assume the servers' scheduling to be arbitrary multiplexing [41].

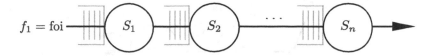

Fig. 3. Tandem of n servers.

Proposition 1 (Leftover Service under Arbitrary Multiplexing [18]).
Let flow f_2 be prioritiz ed over flow f_1 at a work-conserving dynamic S-server with service process S. Then, the corresponding arrival A_1 sees under arbitrary multiplexing the leftover service

$$S_{\text{l.o.}}(s,t) = [S(s,t) - A_2(s,t)]^+.$$

Definition 5 (Virtual Delay). *The virtual delay at time $t \geq 0$ is defined as*

$$d(t) := \inf\{\tau \geq 0 : A(0,t) \leq D(0,t+\tau)\}.$$

It can briefly be described as the time it takes for the cumulated departures to "catch up with" the cumulated arrivals.

Theorem 1 (Output and Delay Bound [12,18]). *Consider an arrival process $A(s,t)$ with dynamic S-server $S(s,t)$.*
The departure process D is upper bounded for any $0 \leq s \leq t$ according to

$$D(s,t) \leq A \oslash S(s,t). \tag{2}$$

The delay at $t \geq 0$ is upper bounded by

$$d(t) \leq \inf\{\tau \geq 0 : A \oslash S(t+\tau,t) \leq 0\}.$$

We focus on the stochastic analogue of Theorem 1 for moment-generating functions:

Theorem 2 (MGF Delay Bound [3,18]). *Let $\theta \geq 0$. For the assumptions as in Theorem 1, we obtain:*
The violation probability of a given stochastic delay bound $T \geq 0$ at time $t \geq 0$ is bounded by

$$P(d(t) > T) \leq E\left[e^{\theta(A \oslash S(t+T,t))}\right]. \tag{3}$$

In order to obtain the tightest possible result, the bound in Eq. (3) should be optimized in θ.

The next theorem shows how network calculus leverages min-plus algebra to derive end-to-end results.

Theorem 3 (End-to-End Service [18]). *Consider a flow f crossing a tandem of n work-conserving servers with service processes $S_i, i = 1, \ldots, n$ as in Fig. 3. Then, the overall service offered to f can be described by the end-to-end service*

$$S_{\text{e2e}}(s,t) = \bigotimes_{i=1}^{n} S_i(s,t) := S_1 \otimes S_2 \otimes \cdots \otimes S_n(s,t).$$

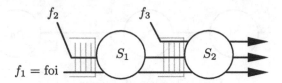

Fig. 4. Sink tree with 3 flows and 2 servers.

In the following definition, we introduce (σ, ρ)-constraints [12] as they are often used to compute time-independent, stationary bounds under stability.

Definition 6 $((\sigma, \rho)$-**Bound** [12]). *An arrival flow is $(\sigma_A(\theta), \rho_A(\theta))$-bounded for some $\theta > 0$, if for all $0 \leq s \leq t$*

$$\mathrm{E}\left[e^{\theta A(s,t)}\right] \leq e^{\theta \rho_A(\theta)(t-s) + \theta \sigma_A(\theta)}.$$

Theorem 4 (Generalized Hölder Inequality [30]). *Let $X_1, \ldots, X_n \geq 0$ be random variables such that $\mathrm{E}[X_i^{p_i}] < \infty$. Then we have*

$$\mathrm{E}\left[\prod_{i=1}^{n} X_i\right] \leq \prod_{i=1}^{n} \mathrm{E}[X_i^{p_i}]^{\frac{1}{p_i}}$$

with $\sum_{i=1}^{n} \frac{1}{p_i} = 1$ and $p_i > 1$.

3   Sink Tree End-to-End Delay Bound

In this section, we provide stochastic delay bounds for sink trees for the separated flow analysis (SFA) and pay multiplexing only once (PMOO) e2e analysis algorithms as known from DNC [42]. All topologies in this paper assume the servers to be work-conserving and independent of the arrivals. We start the analysis with independent cross-flows, but forego this assumption at the end of the section.

3.1   Two-Server Sink Tree

We start the sink-tree analysis with the two-server case (Fig. 4) as an illustrative example, since it already enables us to point at some key differences between SFA and PMOO. We extend the results to general sink trees in the following subsection.

Separated Flow Analysis (SFA). Here, we compute the leftover service at each server (assuming arbitrary multiplexing) until we convolve all service processes in a final step.

For the two-server sink tree in Fig. 4, SFA yields the end-to-end service

$$S_{e2e} = [S_1 - A_2]^+ \otimes [S_2 - (A_3 + (A_2 \oslash S_1))]^+.$$ (4)

Observe that the arrival process A_2 appears twice. For the analysis, this means that we need to invoke Hölder's inequality to upper bound the MGF of dependent processes. It follows for the delay bound, that

$$P(d(t) > T)$$

$$\overset{(3)}{\leq} E\left[e^{\theta(A_1 \oslash S_{e2e}(t+T,t))}\right]$$

$$\overset{(4)}{=} E\left[e^{\theta\left(A_1 \oslash [S_1 - A_2]^+ \otimes [S_2 - (A_3 + (A_2 \oslash S_1))]^+(t+T,t)\right)}\right]$$

$$\vdots$$

$$\leq \sum_{s_0=0}^{t} E\left[e^{\theta A_1(s_0,t)}\right]$$

$$\cdot \left(\sum_{s_1=s_0}^{t+T} E\left[e^{p_1\theta A_2(s_0,s_1)}\right]^{\frac{1}{p_1}} E\left[e^{e^{-p_1\theta S_1(s_0,s_1)}}\right]^{\frac{1}{p_1}} E\left[e^{p_2\theta A_3(s_1,t+T)}\right]^{\frac{1}{p_2}}\right.$$

$$\left.\cdot \left(\sum_{s_2=0}^{s_1} E\left[e^{p_2\theta A_2(s_2,t+T)}\right] E\left[e^{-p_2\theta S_1(s_2,s_1)}\right]\right)^{\frac{1}{p_2}} E\left[e^{-p_2\theta S_2(s_1,t+T)}\right]^{\frac{1}{p_2}}\right),$$

where $1/p_1 + 1/p_2 = 1$.

Pay Multiplexing Only Once (PMOO). In contrast to SFA, in PMOO, we first convolve and then subtract. However, we only obtain a rigorous bound if we convolve servers that share the same set of cross-flows. Therefore, one has to first subtract all flows that are not in this intersection of cross-flows. For sink trees, there is still a unique outcome when applying the PMOO algorithm, since there is no overlapping interference. The analysis can become much more complex when considering general topologies [42].

It is known in deterministic network calculus, that neither of the analyses is strictly better than the other [41], though for many topologies PMOO yields a better delay bound [42].

For the two-server sink tree, PMOO yields the end-to-end service

$$S_{e2e} = \left[\left([S_2 - A_3]^+ \otimes S_1\right) - A_2\right]^+.$$ (5)

In contrast to SFA, A_2 appears only once.

$P(d(t) > T)$

$\overset{(3)}{\leq} E\left[e^{\theta(A_1 \oslash S_{e2e}(t+T,t))}\right]$

$\overset{(5)}{=} E\left[e^{\theta\left(A_1 \oslash \left[(S_1 \otimes [S_2 - A_3]^+) - A_2\right]^+(t+T,t)\right)}\right]$

$\leq \sum_{s_0=0}^{t} E\left[e^{\theta A_1(s_0,t)}\right] E\left[e^{-\theta\left[(S_1 \otimes [S_2 - A_3]^+) - A_2\right]^+(s_0,t+T)}\right]$

$\leq \sum_{s_0=0}^{t} E\left[e^{\theta A_1(s_0,t)}\right] E\left[e^{\theta A_2(s_0,t+T)}\right] E\left[e^{-\theta\left((S_1 \otimes [S_2 - A_3]^+)\right)(s_0,t+T)}\right]$

$\leq \sum_{s_0=0}^{t} E\left[e^{\theta A_1(s_0,t)}\right] E\left[e^{\theta A_2(s_0,t+T)}\right] \left(\sum_{s_1=s_0}^{t+T} E\left[e^{-\theta S_1(s_1,t+T)}\right] \cdot E\left[e^{-\theta[S_2 - A_3]^+(s_0,s_1)}\right]\right)$

$\leq \sum_{s_0=0}^{t} E\left[e^{\theta A_1(s_0,t)}\right] E\left[e^{\theta A_2(s_0,t+T)}\right] \left(\sum_{s_1=s_0}^{t+T} E\left[e^{-\theta S_1(s_1,t+T)}\right] E\left[e^{\theta A_3(s_0,s_1)}\right]\right.$

$\left. \cdot E\left[e^{-\theta S_2(s_0,s_1)}\right]\right).$

Even though we consider only a two-server sink tree, we can already observe the key difference between SFA and PMOO, as only the SFA has to apply Hölder's inequality. We see in the following subsection, that this insight is even more evident in the general sink tree.

3.2   The General Case

In this subsection, we generalize the two-server sink tree to the sink tree with n servers, as in Fig. 1b. The proof follows lines similar to the one of Proposition 3 and is therefore omitted.

Proposition 2 (Delay Bound with SFA).   *With the SFA, the end-to-end service for $n + 1$ arrival flows and n servers in a sink tree is*

$$S_{e2e} = [S_1 - A_2]^+ \otimes [S_2 - (A_3 + (A_2 \oslash S_1))]^+$$

$$\cdots \otimes \left[S_n - \left(A_n + (A_{n-1} \oslash S_{n-1}) + \cdots + \left((A_1 \oslash S_1) \oslash [S_2 - A_2]^+\right) \oslash\right.\right.$$

$$\left.\left.\cdots \oslash [S_{n-1} - (A_2 + \cdots + A_{n-1})]^+\right)\right]^+.$$

$$(6)$$

This yields for the delay bound

$$\mathrm{P}(d(t) > T)$$

$$\overset{(6)}{\leq} \sum_{s_0=0}^{t} \mathrm{E}\left[e^{\theta A_1(s,t)}\right] \left(\sum_{s_1=s_0}^{t+T} \cdots \sum_{s_{n-1}=s_{n-2}}^{t+T} \mathrm{E}\left[e^{p_1\theta A_2(s_0,s_1)}\right]^{\frac{1}{p_1}} \mathrm{E}\left[e^{-p_1\theta S_1(s_0,s_1)}\right]^{\frac{1}{p_1}} \right.$$

$$\cdots \mathrm{E}\left[e^{p_n\theta\left(A_{n+1}+(A_n\oslash S_{n-1})+\cdots+(((A_2\oslash S_1)\oslash[S_2-A_3]^+)\oslash\cdots\oslash[S_{n-1}-(A_3+\cdots+A_n)]^+))(s_{n-1},t+T)\right]}\right]^{\frac{1}{p_n}}$$

$$\left. \cdot \mathrm{E}\left[e^{-p_n\theta S_n(s_{n-1},t+T)}\right]^{\frac{1}{p_n}} \right)$$

with $\sum_{i=1}^{n}\frac{1}{p_i} = 1$.

The PMOO, on the other hand, does not have to take into account the dependencies between cross-flows that share servers.

Proposition 3 (Delay Bound with PMOO). *With the PMOO, the end-to-end service for $n+1$ arrival flows and n servers in a sink tree is*

$$S_{e2e} = \left[\left(\left[\left([S_n - A_{n+1}]^+ \otimes S_{n-1} \right) - A_n \right]^+ \otimes \cdots \otimes S_1 \right) - A_2 \right]^+. \quad (7)$$

This yields for the delay bound

$$\mathrm{P}(d(t) > T)$$

$$\overset{(7)}{\leq} \sum_{s_0=0}^{t} \mathrm{E}\left[e^{\theta A_1(s_0,t)}\right] \mathrm{E}\left[e^{\theta A_2(s_0,t+T)}\right] \left(\sum_{s_1=s_0}^{t+T} \mathrm{E}\left[e^{-\theta S_1(s_1,t+T)}\right] \mathrm{E}\left[e^{\theta A_3(s_0,s_1)}\right] \right.$$

$$\cdot \left(\sum_{s_2=s_0}^{s_1} \mathrm{E}\left[e^{-\theta S_2(s_2,s_1)}\right] \mathrm{E}\left[e^{\theta A_4(s_0,s_2)}\right] \right) \cdots \left(\sum_{s_k=s_0}^{s_{k-1}} \mathrm{E}\left[e^{-\theta S_k(s_k,s_{k-1})}\right] \mathrm{E}\left[e^{\theta A_{k+2}(s_0,s_k)}\right] \right)$$

$$\cdots \left. \left(\sum_{s_{n-1}=s_0}^{s_{n-2}} \mathrm{E}\left[e^{-\theta S_{n-1}(s_{n-1},s_{n-2})}\right] \mathrm{E}\left[e^{\theta A_{n+1}(s_0,s_{n-1})}\right] \mathrm{E}\left[e^{-\theta S_n(s_0,s_{n-1})}\right] \right)\right)\right).$$

Proof. See Appendix A.1.

3.3   Delay Bounds with PMOO Under Dependent Cross-flows

So far, the analysis only considered originally independent arrival flows. Now, if we assume the cross-flow arrivals to be dependent, even with the PMOO, we have to apply Hölder's inequality. Such dependencies may be due to resource sharing between cross-flows before they hit the foi, or simply because the original data sources are already dependent, as, e.g., in an environmental sensor network where the range of sensor nodes is overlapping and, thus, an observed physical phenomenon is reported by several neighboring nodes at the same time.

Proposition 4 (Delay Bound with PMOO and Dependent Cross-flows). *If all n cross-flows are dependent, the PMOO yields*

$$P(d(t) > T)$$

$$\leq \sum_{s_0=0}^{t} \mathrm{E}\big[e^{\theta A_1(s,t)}\big] \left(\mathrm{E}\big[e^{p_1\theta A_2(s,t+T)}\big]\right)^{\frac{1}{p_1}}$$

$$\cdot \left(\sum_{s_1=s_0}^{t+T} \mathrm{E}\big[e^{-p_2\theta S_1(s_1,t+T)}\big] \left(\mathrm{E}\big[e^{p_2p_3\theta A_3(s_0,s_1)}\big]\right)^{\frac{1}{p_3}} \right.$$

$$\cdots \left(\sum_{s_{k-1}=s_0}^{s_{k-2}} \mathrm{E}\big[e^{-p_2p_4\cdots p_{2k-2}\theta S_{k-1}(s_{k-1},s_{k-2})}\big] \left(\mathrm{E}\big[e^{p_2p_4\cdots p_{2k-2}p_{2k-1}\theta A_{k+1}(s_0,s_{k-1})}\big]\right)^{\frac{1}{p_{2k-1}}} \right.$$

$$\cdots \left(\sum_{s_{n-2}=s_0}^{s_{n-3}} \mathrm{E}\big[e^{-p_2p_4\cdots p_{2n-4}\theta S_{n-2}(s_{n-2},s_{n-3})}\big] \right.$$

$$\cdot \left(\mathrm{E}\big[e^{p_2p_4\cdots p_{2n-4}p_{2n-3}\theta A_n(s_0,s_{n-1})}\big]\right)^{\frac{1}{p_{2n-3}}}$$

$$\left(\sum_{s_{n-1}=s_0}^{s_{n-2}} \mathrm{E}\big[e^{-p_2p_4\cdots p_{2n-2}\theta S_{n-1}(s_{n-1},s_{n-2})}\big] \mathrm{E}\big[e^{p_2p_4\cdots p_{2n-2}\theta A_{n+1}(s_0,s_{n-1})}\big] \right.$$

$$\left. \cdot \mathrm{E}\big[e^{-p_2p_4\cdots p_{2n-2}\theta S_n(s_0,s_{n-1})}\big] \right)^{\frac{1}{p_{2n-2}}} \cdots \right)^{\frac{1}{p_{2k-2}}} \right)^{\frac{1}{p_4}} \Bigg)^{\frac{1}{p_2}},$$

where $\frac{1}{p_1} + \frac{1}{p_2} = 1, \ldots, \frac{1}{p_{2n-1}} + \frac{1}{p_{2n-2}} = 1.$

4   Numerical Evaluation

In this section, we evaluate and compare the delay bounds in sink trees for different algorithms and parameters. At the beginning, all flows are assumed to be independent. At first, we investigate the impact of the transient time horizon t on the bound and how it relates to the assumed fractional Brownian motion traffic model. Then, we compare the SFA with the PMOO, before taking a look at the sensitivity of the model with respect to the fBm parameters. Furthermore, we consider the scaling behavior when increasing the tree depth. In the last experiment, we relax the independence assumption and consider the case of dependent cross-flows.

We assume the arrivals to be of the form (as in [27, 35, 38])

$$A(0,t) := \lambda t + \sigma Z(t), \tag{8}$$

where $Z(t)$ is a normalized fractional Brownian motion, λ is the mean arrival rate and $\sigma^2 > 0$ is the variance of $A(0,1)$. The fBm $Z(t)$ is governed by the Hurst parameter $H \in (0,1)$ that, in turn, is independent of the other parameters [35]. This arrival process, also called fBm traffic model [27], has been shown to have the following MGF [24] for $t \geq 0$:

$$\mathrm{E}\big[e^{\theta A(0,t)}\big] = e^{\lambda\theta t + \frac{\theta^2\sigma^2}{2}t^{2H}}. \tag{9}$$

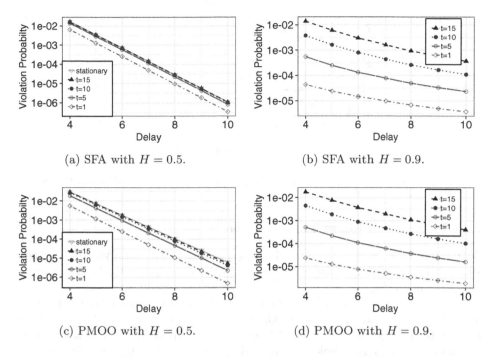

Fig. 5. Delay violation probability for two servers and different t.

For $H \in (0.5, 1)$, fBm exhibits a property called long-range dependence (LRD). If not mentioned otherwise, throughout the experiments, we choose $\lambda = 1, \sigma^2 = 1$, and $H = 0.7$.

Given the continuous nature of fBm, the arrivals in Eq. (8) are a continuous-time process

$$A(s, t) = \int_s^t a(x) \mathrm{d}x, \text{ where } 0 \le s \le t,$$

that has to be discretized in order to be applicable to our discrete-time arrival model (cf. Eq. (1)).

We proceed as in [13]. Let $\tau > 0$ be a discretization parameter and $t \ge 0$. Then, assuming a dynamic S-server, it can be shown for the delay bound that

$$P(d(t) > T) \le \sum_{j=0}^{\lfloor \frac{t}{\tau} \rfloor} \mathrm{E}\left[e^{\theta A(t-(j+1)\tau, t)}\right] \mathrm{E}\left[e^{-\theta S(t-j\tau, t+T)}\right].$$

The rest follows along similar lines as in the discrete-time case.

If not explicitly specified, by default, the cross-flows are assumed to be independent and t is equal to 20. The server rate (we assume homogeneous sink trees) is denoted by $c > 0$. Further, all results are obtained by numerically optimizing θ and the Hölder parameters p_i.

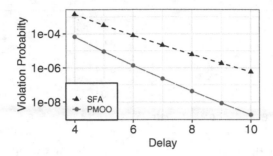

Fig. 6. Comparison between delay violation probabilities using SFA and PMOO.

4.1 Impact of a Finite Time Horizon

We compare the delay bounds for different time horizons t, applying the bounds for SFA (Proposition 2) and PMOO (Proposition 3), respectively. The results are depicted in Fig. 5.

We observe that the delay bounds do not change significantly for larger t when the Hurst parameter $H = 0.5$ (Fig. 5a and c). Since for this particular H, the fBm traffic model is (σ, ρ)-bounded (Definition 6), we can also derive stationary bounds that hold for all t. However, for $H = 0.9$ (Fig. 5b and d), when the fBm traffic model exhibits a long-range dependence, the delay bounds vary strongly for different t. This indicates that, if one is aiming at transient bounds, results obtained from a stationary analysis may be too conservative.

4.2 Comparison Between SFA and PMOO

For a sink tree with two servers, we compare the delay bounds using SFA and PMOO. To that end, we consider a three-server sink tree with server rate $c = 6.0$.

The results in Fig. 6 indicate a significant gap in the delay bounds. While the difference in the violation probability is about two orders of magnitude, in the delay space, the PMOO bound exhibits an improvement of roughly 30%. This is caused by the additional application of Hölder's inequality, that is only necessary in the SFA. Hence, in the following experiments, we only use PMOO.

4.3 Parameter Sensitivity of Fractional Brownian Motion

In this subsection, we investigate the impact of the fBm traffic model parameters on the delay bounds. Therefore, for a three-server sink tree, we fixed the server rates to $c = 9.0$ and varied the parameters separately by 0.2. The results are shown in Fig. 7.

We see that, while all parameters clearly influence the outcome, the parameter sensitivity significantly differs. As expected, it is evident that, at the same load, the Hurst parameter H can be decisive whether the system suffers from long queues ($H = 0.9$), or hardly sees any queueing effects ($H = 0.5$) (Fig. 7c).

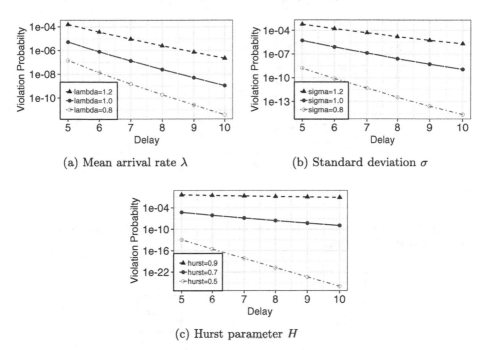

Fig. 7. Parameter sensitivity of fractional Brownian motion on the delay bounds.

4.4   Scaling Effects of PMOO

In this experiment, we focus on how the delay violation probability scales with the number of servers for a delay of $T = 4$. Further, we keep the utilization at the last server (since it is the server with the heaviest load in a homogeneous sink tree, $\frac{(n+1)\lambda}{c}$) constant, i.e. we scale its capacity with the number of flows.

The results in Fig. 8 show that the delay bounds improve with the number of servers. This improvement is due to statistical multiplexing effects as the number of flows grows.

4.5   Comparison Between Independent and Dependent Cross-flows

So far, all experiments considered the cross-flows to be independent. In this last experiment, we now omit the independence assumption, i.e., we apply Hölder's inequality to the MGF of the cross-flows. The delay bounds for a sink tree of three servers with server rate $c = 9.0$ are depicted in Fig. 9.

As expected, the impact of dependence (and therefore Hölder's inequality) is strong. The delay violation probability is about 9 orders of magnitude higher compared to the independent case. This indicates the importance of treating and, if possible, avoiding the invocation of Hölder's inequality.

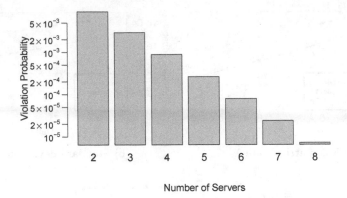

Fig. 8. Delay violation probability of the sink tree for different lengths and constant utilization at the last server.

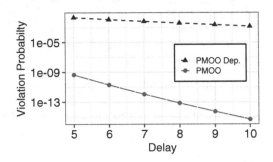

Fig. 9. Comparison between delay violation probabilities for independent and dependent cross-flows using PMOO.

5   Conclusion

In this paper, we have derived end-to-end delay bounds for a flow traversing a sink tree using a stochastic network calculus approach. It has been shown that pay multiplexing only once has to consider less stochastic dependencies, and therefore applies less Hölder inequalities in the analysis. Further, our numerical experiments with a fractional Brownian motion traffic model indicate that each application of Hölder's inequality significantly worsens the delay bound.

Overall, the e2e analysis still imposes many open problems in the stochastic network calculus. The most striking one is clearly how to take stochastic dependence into account. One possible approach could be to leverage negative dependence as in [33].

A   Appendix

A.1   Proof of Proposition 3

Proof. We prove the theorem via induction. The base case $n = 2$ is already treated in Subsect. 3.1.

Assume now that the induction hypothesis (IH) is true for some $n \in \mathbb{N}$. We denote the end-to-end service of tandems of length n by S_{e2e}^n. Observe that extending the sink tree basically means that we prolong all flows and add one flow that only traverses the last hop. Therefore, we apply the induction hypothesis on the last server n servers $S_2, \ldots, S_{n+1}$ and receive S_{e2e}^n. Afterwards, we basically apply the base case, as the network is reduced to the network consisting of S_1 and S_{e2e}^n. This gives

$$S_{e2e}^{n+1} = [(S_{e2e}^n \otimes S_1) - A_2]^+$$

$$\stackrel{(IH)}{=} \left[\left(\left[\left(\left[\left([S_{n+1} - A_{n+2}]^+ \otimes S_n \right) - A_{n+1} \right]^+ \otimes \cdots \otimes S_2 \right) - A_3 \right]^+ \otimes S_1 \right) - A_2 \right]^+.$$

For the delay bound, it follows that

$$P(d(t) > T)$$

$$\stackrel{(3)}{\leq} E\left[e^{\theta(A_1 \oslash S_{e2e}(t+T,t))} \right]$$

$$\leq \sum_{s_0=0}^{t} E\left[e^{\theta A_1(s_0,t)} \right]$$

$$\cdot E\left[e^{-\theta \left[\left(\left[\left(\left[(S_{n+1}-A_{n+2}]^+ \otimes S_n \right) - A_{n+1} \right]^+ \otimes \cdots \otimes S_2 \right) - A_3 \right]^+ \otimes S_1 \right) - A_2 \right]^+ (s_0,t+T)} \right]$$

$$\stackrel{(IH)}{\leq} \sum_{s_0=0}^{t} E\left[e^{\theta A_1(s_0,t)} \right] E\left[e^{\theta A_2(s_0,t+T)} \right] \left(\sum_{s_1=s_0}^{t+T} E\left[e^{-\theta S_1(s_1,t+T)} \right] E\left[e^{\theta A_3(s_0,s_1)} \right] \right.$$

$$\cdot \left(\sum_{s_2=s_0}^{s_1} E\left[e^{-\theta S_2(s_2,s_1)} \right] E\left[e^{\theta A_4(s_0,s_2)} \right] \cdots \left(\sum_{s_{n-1}=s_0}^{s_{n-2}} E\left[e^{-\theta S_{n-1}(s_{n-1},s_{n-2})} \right] \right.\right.$$

$$E\left[e^{\theta A_{n+1}(s_0,s_{n-1})} \right] \cdot E\left[e^{-\theta \left([S_{n+1}-A_{n+2}]^+ \otimes S_n \right)(s_0,s_{n-1})} \right] \bigg) \Bigg) \Bigg)$$

$$\leq \sum_{s_0=0}^{t} E\left[e^{\theta A_1(s_0,t)} \right] E\left[e^{\theta A_2(s_0,t+T)} \right] \left(\sum_{s_1=s_0}^{t+T} E\left[e^{-\theta S_1(s_1,t+T)} \right] E\left[e^{\theta A_3(s_0,s_1)} \right] \right.$$

$$\cdot \left(\sum_{s_2=s_0}^{s_1} E\left[e^{-\theta S_2(s_2,s_1)} \right] E\left[e^{\theta A_4(s_0,s_2)} \right] \cdots \left(\sum_{s_{n-1}=s_0}^{s_{n-2}} E\left[e^{-\theta S_{n-1}(s_{n-1},s_{n-2})} \right] \right.\right.$$

$$E\left[e^{\theta A_{n+1}(s_0,s_{n-1})} \right] \cdot \left(\sum_{s_n=s_0}^{s_{n-1}} E\left[e^{-\theta S_n(s_n,s_{n-1})} \right] E\left[e^{\theta A_{n+2}(s_0,s_n)} \right] E\left[e^{-\theta S_{n+1}(s_0,s_n)} \right] \right) \bigg) \Bigg) \Bigg).$$

This finishes the proof.

References

1. Baccelli, F., Cohen, G., Olsder, G.J., Quadrat, J.P.: Synchronization and Linearity: An Algebra for Discrete Event Systems. Wiley, Hoboken (1992)
2. Beck, M.: Towards the analysis of transient phases with stochastic network calculus. In: IEEE 17th International Network Strategy and Planning Symposium (Networks 2016) (2016)
3. Beck, M.A.: Advances in theory and applicability of stochastic network calculus. Ph.D. thesis, TU Kaiserslautern (2016)
4. Becker, N., Fidler, M.: A non-stationary service curve model for performance analysis of transient phases. In: 2015 27th International Teletraffic Congress, pp. 116–124. IEEE (2015)
5. Bondorf, S., Nikolaus, P., Schmitt, J.B.: Quality and cost of deterministic network calculus - design and evaluation of an accurate and fast analysis. Proc. ACM Meas. Anal. Comput. Syst. (POMACS) 1(1), 34 (2017)
6. Bouillard, A., Comte, C., de Panafieu, É., Mathieu, F.: Of kernels and queues: when network calculus meets analytic combinatorics. In: 2018 30th International Teletraffic Congress (ITC 30), vol. 2, pp. 49–54. IEEE (2018)
7. Bouillard, A., Thierry, É.: Tight performance bounds in the worst-case analysis of feed-forward networks. Discrete Event Dyn. Syst. 26(3), 383–411 (2016)
8. Boyes, H., Hallaq, B., Cunningham, J., Watson, T.: The industrial internet of things (IIOT): an analysis framework. Comput. Ind. 101, 1–12 (2018)
9. Burchard, A., Liebeherr, J., Ciucu, F.: On superlinear scaling of network delays. IEEE/ACM Trans. Netw. 19(4), 1043–1056 (2010)
10. Champati, J.P., Al-Zubaidy, H., Gross, J.: Transient delay bounds for multi-hop wireless networks. CoRR (2018)
11. Chang, C.S.: Stability, queue length, and delay of deterministic and stochastic queueing networks. IEEE Trans. Autom. Control 39(5), 913–931 (1994)
12. Chang, C.S.: Performance Guarantees in Communication Networks. Springer, London (2000). https://doi.org/10.1007/978-1-4471-0459-9
13. Ciucu, F., Burchard, A., Liebeherr, J.: Scaling properties of statistical end-to-end bounds in the network calculus. IEEE Trans. Inf. Theory 52(6), 2300–2312 (2006)
14. Ciucu, F., Schmitt, J.: Perspectives on network calculus - no free lunch, but still good value. In: Proceedings of the ACM Conference on Applications, Technologies, Architectures, and Protocols for Computer Communications (SIGCOMM 2012), New York, NY, USA, pp. 311–322 (2012)
15. Cruz, R.L.: Quality of service management in integrated services networks. In: Proceedings of the Semi-Annual Research Review, CWC, UCSD (1996)
16. Dong, F., Wu, K., Srinivasan, V.: Copula analysis for statistical network calculus. In: Proceedings of the IEEE INFOCOM 2015, pp. 1535–1543 (2015)
17. Fettweis, G.P.: The tactile internet: applications and challenges. IEEE Veh. Technol. Mag. 9(1), 64–70 (2014)
18. Fidler, M.: An end-to-end probabilistic network calculus with moment generating functions. In: Proceedings of the IEEE IWQoS 2006, pp. 261–270 (2006)
19. Fidler, M., Rizk, A.: A guide to the stochastic network calculus. IEEE Commun. Surv. Tutor. 17(1), 92–105 (2015)
20. Fonseca, N.L., Mayor, G.S., Neto, C.A.: On the equivalent bandwidth of self-similar sources. ACM Trans. Model. Comput. Simul. (TOMACS) 10(2), 104–124 (2000)
21. Jafari, F., Lu, Z., Jantsch, A., Yaghmaee, M.H.: Buffer optimization in network-on-chip through flow regulation. IEEE Trans. Comput. Aided Des. Integr. Circuits Syst. 29(12), 1973–1986 (2010)

22. Jasperneite, J., Neumann, P., Theis, M., Watson, K.: Deterministic real-time communication with switched ethernet. In: 4th IEEE International Workshop on Factory Communication Systems, pp. 11–18. IEEE (2002)
23. Jiang, Y., Liu, Y.: Stochastic Network Calculus, vol. 1. Springer, London (2008). https://doi.org/10.1007/978-1-84800-127-5
24. Kelly, F.P.: Notes on effective bandwidths. In: Kelly, F.P., Zachary, S., Ziedins, I. (eds.) Stochastic Networks: Theory and Applications. Royal Statistical Society Lecture Notes Series, vol. 4, pp. 141–168. Oxford University Press, Oxford (1996)
25. Koubaa, A., Alves, M., Tovar, E.: Modeling and worst-case dimensioning of cluster-tree wireless sensor networks. In: 2006 27th IEEE International Real-Time Systems Symposium (RTSS 2006), pp. 412–421. IEEE (2006)
26. Leiserson, C.E.: Fat-trees: universal networks for hardware-efficient supercomputing. IEEE Trans. Comput. **100**(10), 892–901 (1985)
27. Li, C., Burchard, A., Liebeherr, J.: A network calculus with effective bandwidth. IEEE/ACM Trans. Netw. **15**(6), 1442–1453 (2007)
28. Liebeherr, J., Burchard, A., Ciucu, F.: Delay bounds in communication networks with heavy-tailed and self-similar traffic. IEEE Trans. Inf. Theory **58**(2), 1010–1024 (2012)
29. Mellia, M., Stoica, I., Zhang, H.: Tcp model for short lived flows. IEEE Commun. Lett. **6**(2), 85–87 (2002)
30. Mitrinovic, D.S., Vasic, P.M.: Analytic Inequalities, vol. 1. Springer, Heidelberg (1970)
31. Nelson, R.: Probability, Stochastic Processes, and Queueing Theory: The Mathematics of Computer Performance Modeling. Springer, New York (1995). https://doi.org/10.1007/978-1-4757-2426-4
32. Nikolaus, P., Schmitt, J.: On per-flow delay bounds in tandem queues under (in)dependent arrivals. In: Proceedings of 16th IFIP Networking 2017 Conference (NETWORKING 2017). IEEE (2017)
33. Nikolaus, P., Schmitt, J., Ciucu, F.: Dealing with dependence in stochastic network calculus - using independence as a bound. Technical report, 394/19, TU Kaiserslautern, Department of Computer Science (2019). https://disco.cs.uni-kl.de/discofiles/publicationsfiles/NSC19-1_TR.pdf
34. Nikolaus, P., Schmitt, J., Schütze, M.: h-Mitigators: improving your stochastic network calculus output bounds. Comput. Commun. **144**, 188–197 (2019)
35. Norros, I.: On the use of fractional Brownian motion in the theory of connectionless networks. IEEE J. Sel. Areas Commun. **13**(6), 953–962 (1995)
36. Qian, Z., Bogdan, P., Tsui, C.Y., Marculescu, R.: Performance evaluation of NoC-based multicore systems: From traffic analysis to noc latency modeling. ACM Trans. Des. Autom. Electron. Syst. (TODAES) **21**(3), 52 (2016)
37. Rizk, A., Fidler, M.: Leveraging statistical multiplexing gains in single-and multi-hop networks. In: Proceedings of the IEEE Nineteenth IEEE International Workshop on Quality of Service (IWQoS 2011), pp. 1–9 (2011)
38. Rizk, A., Fidler, M.: Non-asymptotic end-to-end performance bounds for networks with long range dependent fbm cross traffic. Comput. Netw. **56**(1), 127–141 (2012)
39. Rosen, E., Viswanathan, A., Callon, R.: Multiprotocol label switching architecture. RFC 3031, RFC Editor (2001)
40. Schmitt, J., Bondorf, S., Poe, W.Y.: The sensor network calculus as key to the design of wireless sensor networks with predictable performance. J. Sensor Actuator Netw. **6**(3), 21 (2017)

41. Schmitt, J., Zdarsky, F.A., Fidler, M.: Delay bounds under arbitrary multiplexing: When network calculus leaves you in the lurch ... In: Proceedings of the IEEE International Conference on Computer Communications (INFOCOM 2008), Phoenix, AZ, USA, pp. 1669–1677 (2008)
42. Schmitt, J., Zdarsky, F.A., Martinovic, I.: Improving performance bounds in feed-forward networks by paying multiplexing only once. In: Proceedings of the GI/ITG Conference on Measurement, Modeling, and Evaluation of Computer and Communication Systems (MMB 2008), pp. 1–15 (2008)
43. Singla, A., Chandrasekaran, B., Godfrey, P.B., Maggs, B.: The internet at the speed of light. In: Proceedings of the ACM Workshop on Hot Topics in Networks 2014, pp. 1–7. HotNets-XIII (2014)
44. Wang, H., Shen, H., Wieder, P., Yahyapour, R.: A data center interconnects calculus. In: 2018 IEEE/ACM 26th International Symposium on Quality of Service (IWQoS), pp. 1–10. IEEE (2018)
45. Yaron, O., Sidi, M.: Performance and stability of communication networks via robust exponential bounds. IEEE/ACM Trans. Netw. **1**(3), 372–385 (1993)
46. Zhu, T., Berger, D.S., Harchol-Balter, M.: SNC-meister: admitting more tenants with tail latency SLOs. In: Proceedings of the ACM Symposium on Cloud Computing (SoCC 2016), pp. 374–387 (2016)
47. Zografos, K.G., Androutsopoulos, K.N., Vasilakis, G.M.: A real-time decision support system for roadway network incident response logistics. Transp. Res. Part C: Emerg. Technol. **10**(1), 1–18 (2002)

Graph-Based Mobility Models: Asymptotic and Stationary Node Distribution

Hans Daduna[✉][iD]

Department of Mathematics, Hamburg University,
Bundesstr. 55, 20146 Hamburg, Germany
daduna@math.uni-hamburg.de

Abstract. Under standard assumptions on the stochastic behaviour of mobile nodes in a graph-based mobility model we derive the stationary distribution for the network. This distribution describes as well the asymptotic behaviour of the system. We consider closed (fixed number of moving nodes) as well as open (nodes arrive and depart from the graph-structured area) systems. The stationary state shows that these graph-based models for mobile nodes are separable, i. e. the stationary distribution is for the open system the product of independent coordinate processes and for the closed system holds conditional independence.

Keywords: Mobility models · MANET · Stationary state · Separability

1 Introduction

In wireless mobile adhoc networks (MANETs) it is important to understand the interaction of the moving units in space and time. Bai and Helmy [5, p. 1–2] state in their "Survey of mobility models": "To thoroughly and systematically study a new Mobile Adhoc Network protocol, it is important to simulate this protocol ... and evaluate its protocol performance. Protocol simulation has several key parameters, including mobility model...", and: "...to model and analyze the mobility models in MANET, we are interested in the movement of individual nodes on the microscopic-level, including node location and velocity relative to other nodes."

From the relevant literature it is visible that the same principles and guide lines apply to performance evaluation of opportunistic networks, and especially in this connection for human mobility, see the introductory Sections 1 and 2 of [21].

I am greatful to Ralf Lehnert (TU Dresden) and Andreas Timm-Giel (TU Hamburg-Harburg) for helpful discussions on mobility models for delay-tolerant networks. – I thank four reviewers for their constructive comments which enhanced the paper.

© Springer Nature Switzerland AG 2020
H. Hermanns (Ed.): MMB 2020, LNCS 12040, pp. 155–172, 2020.
https://doi.org/10.1007/978-3-030-43024-5_10

We focus on "Pathway Mobility Models" with random influences, especially their long-time behaviour and stationary state. We do not consider classical "random waypoint models" (RWPs) as described in [5, Section 2] which in many situations seem to be unrealistic, see [24] where the authors proposed a graph-based mobility model under stochastic influences.

Graph-based mobility models where mobile nodes are considered as random walkers with geographic constraints are now a popular scheme for helping to understand performance behaviour of communication networks which are based on transmission of mobile senders and receivers. Literature on graph-based mobility models is now overwhelming, for an overview see the books [5,18,19].

Mobility models are used as input for simulation tools of irregular communication infrastructures where nodes are moving according to rules which are determined by a mobility module. In [22] mobility modules are structured by defining sub-modules: Spatial model, user trip model, and movement dynamics model, see Sect. 3 for more details. Due to complexity of the geographically distributed communication system it is hard to determine the long-time behaviour even of mobility modules. That control of the asymptotic behaviour of mobility modules is an important issue can be seen from the RWP, which delivered unexpected spatial node distributions in the long run [6].

For graph-based mobility models analytical results for their long time behaviour seem to be not at hand. The aim of the present paper is to remedy this situation: We take the standard description of mobility models for simulation modules and translate the description into a construction of a Markov process in continuous time. The main result is to determine analytically the exact stationary and asymptotic behaviour. This allows to sample for graph-based mobility models an initial state which reflects already its asymptotic behaviour and which is stationary for simulation of e.g. MANETs' behaviour in the same way as it is argued in [6,16] for the RWP. Consequently, when starting a simulation with the stationary mobile node distribution over the mobility graph the usual deletion of an initial transient (instationary) period is not necessary. That neglecting the transient initial period can have severe consequences is discussed in [17,27].

Usually the number of mobile nodes in the observation area is fixed (closed system), we consider also open systems where nodes enter and leave the area from/to the exterior. Our theorems cover both cases, and reveal that these distributions are surprisingly simple: The distributions are separable which makes computations for performance evaluation simple. Separability means: For open systems the multidimensional distribution has independent coordinates, while for the closed system conditional independence holds. Separability is well known in network theory for open Jackson and closed Gordon-Newell networks [4,10].

Related literature is numerous. Papers driving our investigation are referenced in Sect. 2. We mention here additionally [15] where stability and simulation of a class of RWP-related models are investigated. A Jackson-network-inspired model for mobile networks is used in [23] to find stability conditions.

Structure of the Paper: In Sect. 2 we describe graph-based models. In Sect. 2.1 we define the underlying graph, in Sect. 3 we consider the standard graph-based model with fixed number of mobile nodes and compute the stationary node distribution. Additionally we discuss in Sect. 3.2 the inverse problem to our main theorem. In Sect. 4 we allow mobile nodes to enter the graph from the exterior and to depart from it and compute the stationary node distribution. In Sect. 5 we comment on extensions.

2 Pathway Mobility Models

Following the graph-based mobility model of Tian, Hähner, Becker, Stepanov, and Rothermel in [24], Bai and Helmy [5, Section 5.1] describe a "Pathway Mobility Model" as special case of mobility models with geographic constraints by restricting the nodes' movement "to the pathways in the map". The structure of feasible movements is described by an underlying random graph. Vertices of the graph usually represent buildings or street intersections of a city and the edges represent streets and freeways between these buildings, resp. intersections. Initially the nodes are distributed randomly over the vertices of the graph. (For discussion of problems with to initialize a simulation of mobility models with a uniform distribution (=total random) of the mobile entities, see [21, Section 3]).

Then iterate for all nodes:

- A mobile node at vertex i stays there for a random time,
- chooses randomly vertex j to be visited next (typically: uniformly distributed on the set of all vertices),
- travels with constant speed $v_{(i,j)}$ on a shortest path $i \longrightarrow j$,
- speed $v_{(i,j)}$ is typically uniformly distributed in a set (v_{min}, v_{max}) of preferred velocities,
- arriving at j the mobile node waits for a (random) pause time,
- then the node selects randomly its next destination vertex k, and so on, ...

We will elaborate on this scenario. Before, we sketch examples which at first glance are not in the realm of systems defined by pathways. But the graphs constructed can be considered as functions of geographic scenarios.

Example 1. [26] Given an area which is cell-partitioned into disjoint (non-overlapping) cells (subareas) collected in the set $\{1, \ldots, J\}$. "Delay/fault-tolerant mobile sensors" initially are distributed randomly over the cells, and each sensor is associated to a home cell. The probability $r(k; i, j)$ that a sensor with home cell k, staying in cell i moves to cell j is inverse-proportional to the distance between cells k and j, $r(k; i, j) \simeq d(k, j)^{-1}$, for some distance $d(\cdot, \cdot)$. In [25] this model of a cell-partitioned area is used to analyze movements in the ZebraNet.

Example 2. An "obstacle mobility model" with geographic constraints is described in [5, Section 5.2]. The obstacles are buildings in an area and the pathways are found by constructing the Voronoi diagram with edges between the vertices defined by the buildings. The mobile nodes are only allowed to move between the buildings on the Voronoi pathways: Whenever a node leaves a vertex after staying a random time there it selects its next building randomly and moves towards this vertex on a shortest path over the edges.

Summarizing the scenarios, we have in any case a finite set of vertices connected by a structured set of edges. While in [24] and in Example 2 buildings and street intersections can naturally be considered as vertices (points), in the Example 1 we generate vertices by contracting the cell to a point, which is in line with the analytical investigation in [26].

The number of nodes may be fixed or varying, possibly without bound. The first case describes an invariant node population in the area, while in the second case nodes may enter the vertices and edges of the area from the outside and eventually leave the area after a finite sojourn time.

2.1   The Graph for Graph-Based Mobility Models

Following [24, Section 2] our fundamental structure is a mobility graph, i.e. a directed labeled graph $G = (V, E, L)$ with vertex set $V \neq \emptyset$, $E \subseteq V^2$ the set of edges between nearest neighbours of the graph, and with non negative labels (weights) $L = \{w(e) \geq 0 : e \in E\}$ for the edges. We identify edges with the pairs of nodes they connect: $e = (i, j) \in V^2$ denotes the directed edge (path) from vertex i to vertex j, and the weight $w(e) = w(i, j) \geq 0$ indicates the (not necessarily Euclidean) distance between i and j. By definition, edges in E connect nearest neighbours, and $(i, j) \neq (j, i)$ for $i, j \in V, i \neq j$, and, moreover, in general $w(i, j) \neq w(j, i)$. We define formally $w(i, i) := 0$.

We assume throughout that G is strongly connected, i.e. for any pair $i, j \in V$ there exists a directed path from i to j, but G is in general not complete.

The graph G characterizes the fundamental geographic structure of the region where the nodes are traveling. G is the "spatial sub-model" of a mobility model in the classification of [22].

We are interested in describing the joint behaviour of the nodes within the region of interest and assume throughout that nodes which move from vertex i to a distant vertex j will do this on a shortest path from i to j, which is determined by the sum of the weights in L on the path of G.

For simplicity of notation we extend the notion of weights $w(i, j) \in L$ from nearest neighbours to any two nodes $i, j \in V$. Then we fix $w(i, j)$ as the length of a shortest path from i to j, i.e. the sum of the weights on the (shortest) path.

We assume that in our models the shortest path is always uniquely determined. (If this is not the case, i.e. there are several shortest path between, say, node i and node j, a specific one can be fixed for traveling from i to j, or a random decision of where to travel can be made after leaving i.)

Conventions. cdf $\equiv$ cumulative distribution function; $V_-^2 := V^2 \setminus \{(i, i) : i \in V\}$.

3   Fixed Population: Closed Graph-Based Mobility Model

Almost all mobility scenarios feature a fixed population of moving nodes (users, entities) which cycle forever in the area of interest. Consequently, we have a fixed set of moving nodes $\overline{M} = \{1, 2, \ldots, M\}$ which cycle on the mobility graph G

according to the following rules (for easier reading we shall use $m, m', n, n', \cdots \in \overline{M}$ as names or types of the respective moving nodes):

If node $m \in \overline{M}$ enters vertex $i \in V$ it stays there for a random pause time, distributed according to the cdf $F(m, i)$ on $[0, \infty)$ with finite mean $\mu(m, i)^{-1}$. If this pause time expires m selects its new destination, say j, which is not necessarily a nearest neighbour, with probability $r_m(i, j)$. This selection is, given i, independent of the history of the system. $r_m = (r_m(i, j) : i, j \in V)$ is a stochastic matrix. We allow immediate feedback, $r_m(i, i) > 0$, and note that feedback of a node means that an additional pause time is set. For asymptotic and steady state analysis we can and will assume that all r_m are irreducible on a possibly m-dependent subset of V. We allow for $m, m' \in \overline{M}, m \neq m'$, that $r_m = r_{m'}$ holds.

Having fixed destination node $j \neq i$, the node m selects its velocity $v \in \mathcal{V}(m, (i, j))$, with probability $s_m((i, j), v))$ to travel the shortest path of length $w(i, j)$ from i to j. Here $\mathcal{V}(m, (i, j))$ is a countable set of preferred velocities to travel from i to j for m, and it holds $\sum_{v \in \mathcal{V}(m, (i, j))} s_m((i, j), v) = 1$.

When node m arrives at j it enters immediately that vertex and selects a random pause time distributed according cdf $F(m, j)$. If this pause time expires m selects its new destination, say k, with probability $r_m(j, k)$, and so on.

All nodes in $\overline{M}$ travel independently of one another, and we assume that all pause times and all travel times are independent (random) variables.

3.1 State Space for the Markov Model: Closed Area

We consider the mobile nodes from $\overline{M}$ as random walkers on $V \cup V_-^2$, which on their itineraries are equipped with tags. The tags carry supplementary information describing the status of a mobile nodes, e.g. its actual location. Tags change over time and space according to random rules which generate the graph based mobility behaviour. We use the following tags of node $m \in \overline{M}$:

(T1) $i \in V$ indicates that m resides at vertex $i \in V$ for a random pause time,
(T2) $((i, j), v) \in V_-^2 \times \mathcal{V}(m, (i, j))$ indicates that m is traveling on the shortest path from i to j with speed v.

Observing the sequence of tags associated to m over time will indicate its rough localization sequence and time development. It is possible that m visits only a strict subset of nodes in V and travels only a strict subset of V_-^2. We denote the set of realizible tags for m by

$$K_m \subseteq V \cup \bigcup_{(i,j) \in V_-^2} \{(i, j)\} \times \mathcal{V}(m, (i, j)).$$

The development of m's tags over time describes routing decisions and decisions for admissible speeds. This "user trip model" (sub-module [22]) is determined by stochastic routing matrices P_m on K_m for $m \in \overline{M}$ as follows.

$$P_m(i; i) = r_m(i, i), \quad i \in V, \tag{1}$$
$$P_m(i; (i, j), v) = r_m(i, j) \cdot s_m((i, j), v), \quad i \neq j \in V, \quad v \in \mathcal{V}(m, (i, j))$$
$$P_m((i, j), v; j) = 1. \quad i \neq j \in V, \quad v \in \mathcal{V}(m, (i, j))$$

Because r_m is irreducible on an m-dependent subset of V, P_m is irreducible on K_m.

The "movement dynamics model" (sub-module, [22]) reflects position changes of nodes: Dwell times of customer m equipped with tag i at node $i \in V$ are sampled according to cdf $F(m, i)$, whereas dwell times of m equipped with tag $((i, j), v)$ i.e. traveling from i to j with velocity v is deterministic $w(i, j)/v$.

"Static nodes" stay-on on a fixed position [6], in our model: If node $m_s \in \overline{M}$ is static on vertex $i \in V$ then $P_{m_s}(i; i) = r_{m_s}(i, i) = 1$, which implies $K_{m_s} = \{i\}$.

From the independence assumptions for pause times and setting in force the usual conditional independence assumptions for the (Markovian) tag changes we obtain a Markovian description of the time evolution of the system as follows. The global states of the Markovian graph-based mobility process are compounded of local states which refer to the individual vertices, resp. shortest paths. We refer henceforth to vertices, resp. shortest paths shortly as locations. For unified notation we use $\kappa \in V \cup V_-^2$ for locations, i.e., κ stands either for $\kappa = i \in V$ or for $\kappa = (i, j) \in V_-^2$. We proceed with notational conventions:

1. For each location $\kappa \in V \cup V_-^2$ with $n(\kappa)$ mobile nodes present we generate a sequence of positions $1, 2, \ldots, n(\kappa)$ where the nodes reside;
2. for location $\kappa = i \in V$ on each position we record the "type" (number in $\overline{M}$) of the node there;
3. for location $\kappa = (i, j) \in V_-^2$ on each position we record the "type" (number in $\overline{M}$) of the nodes there and their selected speeds;
4. in any case, for each mobile node we record as a supplementary variable the residual pause time, resp. residual travel time it still has to obtain.

We next construct local state spaces E_κ for the locations $\kappa \in V \cup V_-^2$. For location $\kappa = i \in V$ with $n(i) > 0$ mobile nodes present a typical local state is

$$z_i = [t_{i1}, \zeta_{i1}; \ldots; t_{in(i)}, \zeta_{in(i)}] \in E_i, \tag{2}$$

where $t_{i1} \in \overline{M}$ is the type of the mobile node on position 1, and this node will continue its ongoing pause for ζ_{i1} time units, $\ldots$, and $t_{in(i)} \in \overline{M}$ is the type of the node on the last occupied position $n(i)$, and this node will continue its ongoing pause for $\zeta_{in(i)}$ time units.

For location $\kappa = (i, j) \in V_-^2$ with $n(i, j) > 0$ mobile nodes present, a typical local state is

$$z_{(i,j)} = [t_{(i,j)1}, v_{(i,j)1}, \zeta_{(i,j)1}; \ldots; t_{(i,j)n(i,j)}, v_{(i,j)n(i,j)}, \zeta_{(i,j)n(i,j)}] \in E_{(i,j)}, \tag{3}$$

where $t_{(i,j)1} \in \overline{M}$ is the type of the mobile node on position 1, who travels with the selected velocity $v_{(i,j)1}$, and this node still has to travel $\zeta_{(i,j)1}$ time units, $\ldots$, and $t_{(i,j)n(i,j)} \in \overline{M}$ is the type of the mobile node on the last occupied position

$n(i, j)$, who travels with the selected velocity $v_{(i,j)n(i,j)}$, and this node still has to travel for $\zeta_{(i,j)n(i,j)}$ time units.

If a location is empty we denote this as $e_i \in E_i$, respectively $e_{(i,j)} \in E_{(i,j)}$.

Global states of the network are compounded of local states, and the global state space E of the network contains all feasible states of the form

$$z = [z_\kappa : \kappa \in V \cup V_-^2] \in E \subseteq \prod_{\kappa \in V \cup V_-^2} E_\kappa \qquad (4)$$

We introduce furthermore reduced local state spaces E_κ^{red} for $\kappa \in V \cup V_-^2$ which encompass the marginal state description of states in E_κ without the residual time variables, i.e. for $i \in V$ with $n(i) > 0$:
$z_i = [t_{i1}, \zeta_{i1}; \ldots; t_{in(i)}, \zeta_{in(i)}] \in E_i$, is reduced to $x_i = [t_{i1}, \ldots, t_{in(i)}] \in E_i^{red}$, and
for $(i, j) \in V_-^2$ with $n(i, j) > 0$:
$z_{(i,j)} = [t_{(i,j)1}, v_{(i,j)1}, \zeta_{(i,j)1}; \ldots; t_{(i,j)n(i,j)}, v_{(i,j)n(i,j)}, \zeta_{(i,j)n(i,j)}] \in E_{(i,j)}$, is reduced to $x_{(i,j)} = [t_{(i,j)1}, v_{(i,j)1}; \ldots; t_{(i,j)n(i,j)}, v_{(i,j)n(i,j)}] \in E_{(i,j)}^{red}$.

The global reduced state space contains all compounded feasible reduced states

$$x = [x_\kappa : \kappa \in V \cup V_-^2] \in E^{red} \subseteq \prod_{\kappa \in V \cup V_-^2} E_\kappa^{red}. \qquad (5)$$

Clearly, not all elements from $\prod_{\kappa \in V \cup V_-^2} E_\kappa$ are feasible for E: any mobile node can and must occur in a global state exactly once, and mobile node m can only occur at those locations which it can enter by following the r_m-regime.

Remark. Local reduced states encompass implicitly the complete tags of all the nodes present. E.g. for $i \in V$ the full state $z_i = [t_{i1}, \zeta_{i1}; \ldots; t_{in(i)}, \zeta_{in(i)}]$ carries the same information as $z_i = [t_{i1}, \mathbf{i}, \zeta_{i1}; \ldots; t_{in(i)}, \mathbf{i}, \zeta_{in(i)}]$.

3.2 Stationary Behaviour of Closed Graph-Based Mobility Models

For definiteness of the model's dynamics, scheduling of nodes inside the locations is determined according to the "shift-protocol" [10, p. 58, 59] which means:

SP1. If at location $\kappa \in V \cup V_-^2$ there are $n(\kappa)$ nodes present a newly arriving node is placed on position $\ell \in \{1, 2, \ldots, n(\kappa) + 1\}$ with probability $(n(\kappa) + 1)^{-1}$, and nodes, previously staying on positions $h \in \{\ell, \ldots, n(\kappa)\}$ are shifted one position up to places $h + 1 \in \{\ell + 1, \ldots, n(\kappa) + 1\}$.

SP2. If at location $\kappa \in V \cup V_-^2$ there are $n(\kappa)$ nodes present and the node on position $\ell \in \{1, 2, \ldots, n(\kappa)\}$ departs from the location, nodes previously on positions $h \in \{\ell + 1, \ldots, n(\kappa)\}$ are shifted one position down to places $h - 1 \in \{\ell, \ldots, n(\kappa) - 1\}$.

We emphasize that fixing dynamics inside locations via shift protocol is for book-keeping only. The physical realization of placements of mobile nodes on the streets and inside the vertices may be quite different. The main performance indices will not depend on the sequencing of the nodes on e.g. a lane. It is even possible to construct a model without any sequencing, e.g. using set-valued lane or vertex populations.

With these states and regulations a Markov process description of the graph based mobility network's evolution is possible. For compact description of the equilibrium behaviour of the network we define local measures $\widetilde{\xi}_\kappa$ the structure of which depend on the internal structure of the nodes $\kappa \in V \cup V_{-}^2$.

The final result (9) shows that the stationary distribution is the product of the $\widetilde{\xi}_\kappa$ conditioned on the number of mobile nodes. Such structure of a distribution is usually referred to as "separable system structure".

Theorem 1. *For the closed graph-based mobility network model let*

$$Z = (Z(t) = (Z_\kappa(t) : \kappa \in V \cup V_{-}^2) : t \geq 0)$$

denote the supplemented joint location process of the network. The local supplemented "node-tag-(residual pause/travel time) process" $Z_\kappa = (Z_\kappa(t) : t \geq 0)$ lives on a subset of E_κ, the specific form of which depends on whether node κ is a vertex $i \in V$, experiencing nodes' pauses, or a pair $(i,j) \in V_{-}^2$, indicating a traveling node on a shortest path from i to j. Z is irreducible on E.

For all mobile nodes $m = 1, \ldots, M$ we define traffic equations and their stochastic solutions $\alpha_m = (\alpha_m(t) : t \in K_m)$ by

$$\alpha_m = \alpha_m \hat{P}_m, \quad m = 1, \ldots, M. \tag{6}$$

If location $\kappa = i$ is in V the local measure $\widetilde{\xi}_i$ on E_i at i is $\widetilde{\xi}_i(e_i) = 1$, and for generic local state $z_i = [t_{i1}, \zeta_{i1}; \ldots; t_{in(i)}, \zeta_{in(i)}] \in E_i$,

$$\widetilde{\xi}_i[t_{i1}, \zeta_{i1}; ..; t_{in(i)}, \zeta_{in(i)}] = \prod_{\ell=1}^{n(i)} \frac{\alpha_{t_{i\ell}}(i)}{\mu(t_{i\ell}, i) \cdot \ell} \left\{ \mu(t_{i\ell}, i) \int_0^{\zeta_{i\ell}} (1 - F(t_{i\ell}, i)(y)) dy \right\} \tag{7}$$

is the measure for the event that at position 1 of location i resides mobile node with type $t_{i1} \in \overline{M}$, and this node will continue its ongoing pause for at most ζ_{i1} time units, $\ldots$, and that on the last occupied position $n(i)$ of location i, the type of the node is $t_{in(i)} \in \overline{M}$, and this node will continue its ongoing pause for at most $\zeta_{in(i)}$ time units.

If location (i,j) is in V_{-}^2 the local measure $\widetilde{\xi}_{(i,j)}$ on $E_{(i,j)}$ at (i,j) is $\widetilde{\xi}_{(i,j)}(e_{(i,j)}) = 1$, and for generic local state $z_{(i,j)} = [t_{(i,j)1}, v_{(i,j)1}, \zeta_{(i,j)1}; \ldots; t_{(i,j)n(i,j)}, v_{(i,j)n(i,j)}, \zeta_{(i,j)n(i,j)}] \in E_{(i,j)}$,

$$\widetilde{\xi}_{(i,j)}[t_{(i,j)1}, v_{(i,j)1}, \zeta_{(i,j)1}; \ldots; t_{(i,j)n((i,j))}, v_{(i,j)n((i,j))}, \zeta_{(i,j)n(i,j)}] \tag{8}$$

$$= \prod_{\ell=1}^{n(i,j)} \frac{\alpha_{t_{(i,j)\ell}}((i,j), v_{(i,j)\ell}) \cdot w(i,j)}{v_{(i,j)\ell} \cdot \ell} \left\{ (v_{(i,j)\ell}/w(i,j)) \cdot \left(\zeta_{t_{(i,j)\ell}} \wedge \frac{w(i,j)}{v_{(i,j)\ell}} \right) \right\}$$

is the measure of the event that on position 1 resides a mobile node with type $t_{(i,j)1} \in \overline{M}$, who travels with the selected velocity $v_{(i,j)1}$, and this node still has

to travel at most $\zeta_{(i,j)1}$ time units, ..., and on the last occupied position $n(i,j)$
resides a mobile node of type $t_{(i,j)n(i,j)} \in \overline{M}$ who travels with the selected velocity
$v_{(i,j)n(i,j)}$, and this node still has to travel for at most $\zeta_{(i,j)n(i,j)}$ time units.
Z is ergodic and the unique limiting and stationary distribution ξ of Z is with
normalization constant C

$$\xi[z_\kappa : \kappa \in V \cup V_-^2] = \prod_{\kappa \in V \cup V_-^2} \widetilde{\xi}_\kappa(z_\kappa) \cdot C^{-1}, \quad z = [z_\kappa : \kappa \in V \cup V_-^2] \in E. \quad (9)$$

Proof. The proof is direct and tedious. In a first step consider the case when
the pause time distributions and the travel time distribution are of phase-type
with a finite number of phases, i.e. finite mixtures of Erlangian distributions, see
[20, Section I.6]. Then the state space of Z is countable and ergodicity follows
directly by summation and bounding the sum from above. Write down the global
balance equations for Z, plug in (9) with (7) and (8) and check equality. In the
second step approximate pause time distributions and travel time distributions
by finite mixtures of Erlangian distributions. These are dense with respect to
convergence in distribution in the set of all distributions on $[0, \infty)$. Convergence
of processes follows along the lines of the proof in [1].   □

Notation. Expressions (7) and (8) should be read carefully. We explain for
$\kappa = i \in V$: The local state $z_i = [t_{i1}, \zeta_{i1}; \ldots; t_{in(i)}, \zeta_{in(i)}] \in E_i$, is an element of
$(\overline{M} \times [0, \infty))^{n(i)}$ while the local measure $\xi_i[t_{i1}, \zeta_{i1}; \ldots; t_{in(i)}, \zeta_{in(i)}]$ determines
the local measure of the event $(\{t_{i1}\} \times [0, \zeta_{i1}]) \times \cdots \times (\{t_{in(i)}\} \times [0, \zeta_{in(i)}])$.
  We shall maintain the abbreviated expressions like (7) instead.

Remark. The closed graph-based mobility networks resemble systems from
stochastic network theory, especially the celebrated BCMP networks [4] and
Kelly networks [9]. In fact, with considerable effort it is possible to transform the
structure of graph-based mobility systems into the notational range of [4] or [9].
The feature not covered by these sources is usage of general pause times, respectively deterministic travel times. While in the original BCMP's, resp. Kelly's
work different phase type distributions are used for supplementary time variables, our extension follows Barbour [1]. Due to the increased notational complexity we preferred the direct approach to present our results here.
  For applications, considering residual pause times is natural, while for the
traveling sensor nodes it might be more natural to record the residual distance
still to travel (or already traveled) by the node instead of residual travel times.
We have this information encoded in the combination of residual time to travel
and the selected speed as part of the nodes' tag, so it can be extracted easily.
E.g., if a node's residual travel time on the path (i,j) from vertex i to vertex
j is at most $\zeta_{(i,j)\ell}$ and this node has decided to travel this path with velocity
$v_{(i,j)\ell}$ its (residual) distance to destination vertex j is at most $\zeta_{(i,j)\ell} \cdot v_{(i,j)\ell}$.
  The redundant expressions in (7) and (8) clarify with taking $\zeta_{(i,j),\ell} \to \infty$ and
$\zeta_{i\ell} \to \infty$ the rough local measures for the types under stationary distribution
because the expressions in the waved backets are in the limit $= 1$. This yields
the next result.

Corollary 1. *For the closed graph-based mobility network model let* $X = (X(t) = (X_\kappa(t) : \kappa \in V \cup V_-^2) : t \geq 0)$ *denote the joint reduced location process of the network. The local "node-tag-process"* $X_\kappa = (X_\kappa(t) : t \geq 0)$ *lives on a subset of* E_κ^{red}, *the specific form of which depends on whether node* κ *is a vertex* $i \in V$ *or a pair* $(i,j) \in V_-^2$.

If location $\kappa = i \in V$ *the local reduced measure* $\widetilde{\xi}_i^{red}$ *on* E_i^{red} *at* i *is* $\widetilde{\xi}_i^{red}(e_i) = 1$, *and for reduced local state* $[t_{i1}, \dots, t_{in(i)}] \in E_i^{red}$,

$$\widetilde{\xi}_i^{red}[t_{i1}, \dots, t_{in(i)}] = \lim_{\zeta_{i1} \to \infty} \cdots \lim_{\zeta_{in(i)} \to \infty} \xi_i[t_{i1}, \zeta_{i1}; \dots; t_{in(i)}, \zeta_{in(i)}] = \prod_{\ell=1}^{n(i)} \frac{\alpha_{t_{i\ell}}(i)}{\mu(t_{i\ell}, i) \cdot \ell}$$

If location (i,j) *is in* V_-^2 *the local measure* $\widetilde{\xi}_{(i,j)}^{red}$ *on* $E_{(i,j)}^{red}$ *at* (i,j) *is* $\widetilde{\xi}_{(i,j)}^{red}(e_{(i,j)}) = 1$, *and for reduced local state* $[t_{(i,j)1}, v_{(i,j)1}; \dots; t_{(i,j)n(i,j)}, v_{(i,j)n(i,j)}] \in E_{(i,j)}^{red}$,

$$\widetilde{\xi}_{(i,j)}^{red}[t_{(i,j)1}, v_{(i,j)1}; \dots; t_{(i,j)n((i,j))}, v_{(i,j)n((i,j))}]$$
$$= \lim_{\zeta_{(i,j)1} \to \infty} \cdots \lim_{\zeta_{(i,j)n(i)} \to \infty}$$
$$\widetilde{\xi}_{(i,j)}[t_{(i,j)1}, v_{(i,j)1}, \zeta_{(i,j)1}; \dots; t_{(i,j)n((i,j))}, v_{(i,j)n((i,j))}, \zeta_{(i,j)n(i,j)}]$$
$$= \prod_{\ell=1}^{n(i,j)} \frac{\alpha_{t_{(i,j)\ell}}((i,j), v_{(i,j)\ell}) \cdot w(i,j)}{v_{(i,j)\ell} \cdot \ell}.$$

X *has unique limiting and stationary distribution* ξ^{red}

$$\xi^{red}[x_\kappa : \kappa \in V \cup V_-^2] = \prod_{\kappa \in V \cup V_-^2} \widetilde{\xi}_\kappa^{red}(x_\kappa) \cdot (C^{red})^{-1}, \quad x = [x_\kappa : \kappa \in V \cup V_-^2] \in E^{red},$$

with normalization constant $C = C^{red}$ *which is that of* Z.

Corollary 2. *The structure of the local measures* (7) *and* (8) *shows with Corollary 1 that the normalization constant* C^{red} *of the stationary distribution of* X *is amenable to generalized convolution algorithms similar to standard algorithms for computing normalization constants in multi-class closed queueing networks, see [2,3]. This solves the computational problem for* C *in Theorem 1 as well.*

Nevertheless, a detailed analysis of the complexity of an adapted algorithm is still needed - but beyond the scope of this paper.

The form of the local measure in (7) shows in conjunction with Corollary 1 that the stationary distribution of the type-tag processes (derived from ξ of Z by considering the reduced measures of X) is insensitive against variations of the pause time distributions as long as the means are fixed. E.g., the stationary probability to find at location $i \in V$ a sequence of types $[t_{i1}, \dots; t_{in(i)}]$ is with normalization constant C_i^{-1}

$$\xi_i^{red}[t_{i1}, \dots; t_{in(i)}] = C_i^{-1} \prod_{\ell=1}^{n(i)} \frac{\alpha_{t_{i\ell}}(i)}{\mu(t_{i\ell}, i) \cdot \ell}.$$

An Inverse Problem for Theorem 1. Kraaier and Killat tackled in a sequence of papers the inverse problem of Theorem 1: They start from a predetermined "stationary distribution of mobile users in wireless networks" on a street pattern which usually is obtained by statistical measurements. The street map network consists of bidirectional streets with intersections. The "inverse problem" of Theorem 1 is to find "turning probabilities" (routing probabilities - our r_m) for the mobile users at intersections and pause time probabilities such that under some additional simplifying assumptions a simulation model fed with these turning and pause probabilities will reproduce the predetermined stationary user distribution, see for more details and further references [11–13].

The initial information obtained from the measurements are stationary user flows $\phi_{(.)}$ (throughputs) on the lanes, the lengths $\ell_{(.)}$ of the streets and the mean street specific user velocities $v_{(.)}$. This allows to compute the stationary mean total number of users on the streets (sum over both directions) ($\pi_s : s \in S$) ($S =$ set of streets).

The obtained routing probabilities $p_{(ij)}$ are used as input for the simulation of the stationary user distribution in a "Random Direction City Model". The additional assumptions put on the models are similar to ours, e.g.

- users are independent of each other,
- speed is street specific with mean $\nu_{(.)}$ and uniformly distributed on 20% interval around mean,
- turning of users is only possible on intersections and at an intersection of i and j users from lane i turn to j with probability $p_{(ij)}$ - given i the decision is independent of the history of the system,
- users pause at intersections for intersection specific random times.

Noticing that in steady state $\sum_{s \in S} \pi_s = constant(=: M)$, we conclude that we have obtained a closed graph-based mobility model with M nodes as described in this section. Theorem 1 states that the information put into the simulation model will result in a stationary distribution of product form given here.

The point is: Starting from the data on mean values obtained from measurement of flows and putting the additional assumptions of [13] into the model, Theorem 1 provides the total stationary distribution without any simulation. This opens the path to obtain analytically e.g. comparison results for correlations over time under perturbation of the data, see e.g. [8].

Remark. In [13] the pause time at an intersection may depend on the lane on which the node arrived at the intersection. This feature can be incorporated into our model by extending the tag sets of the mobile nodes. The street specific speed which is uniformly distributed on 20% interval around mean $\nu_{(.)}$ can be approximated by uniform distribution on discrete subsets of $[0.9 \cdot \nu_{(.)}, 1.1 \cdot \nu_{(.)}]$.

4   Varying Population: Open Graph-Based Mobility Model

Recently, Kriege [14] emphasized that in many applications the number of moving nodes in the area is varying in time. He investigated "open" mobility models where mobile nodes can leave the observation area and newly arriving nodes may enter this area, travel for some time inside the area, and eventually depart from it. Kriege's approach is oriented towards simulation: He generated departure and arrival modules which can be combined with any existing mobility simulation program. A simple open graph-based mobility model was investigated in [7]. Following the ideas in [7,14] we incorporate varying numbers of mobile nodes into the setting of Sect. 3.

We consider the geographical structure from Sect. 2.1, described by graph $G = (V, E, L)$. Mobile nodes arrive from the exterior at vertices of G in independent Poisson streams and are characterized by types from $\overline{M} = \{1, 2, \ldots, M\}$. The type of a node is invariant during that nodes' sojourn in the system.

Nodes of type $m \in \overline{M}$ arrive at node $a(m) \in V$ with rate $\lambda_m > 0$ and are routed during their sojourn in the area according to a strictly substochastic matrix $r_m = (r_m(i,j) : i, j \in V)$ similar to movements as described in Sect. 3. We define the departure probabilities for type-m nodes by

$$r_m(i, 0) := 1 - \sum_{j \in V} r_m(i, j), \quad i \in V,$$

and set formally $r_m(0, a(m)) = 1$. We assume that the so defined stochastic matrix $r_m = (r_m(i,j) : i, j \in V \cup \{0\})$ is irreducible on a possibly m-dependent subset (which includes 0) of $V \cup \{0\}$. This guarantees that the mobile nodes will leave the area after a sojourn time which has finite expectation. Inside the graph-structured area, nodes behave in the same way as in the closed graph-based mobility setting on page 4.

4.1   State Space for the Markov Model: Open Area

Assuming that mobile nodes travel independently of another and that all pause times and travel times are independent (random) variables we construct a Markov process to describe the evolution over time of the moving nodes.

The difference to the closed system is that we may observe many mobile nodes of the same types (all out of $\overline{M}$) as random walkers on $V \cup V_-^2$ at the same time. On the other side, it is possible that for some finite time no node of type $m \in \overline{M}$ is present in the graph-based area.

Mobile nodes on their paths are equipped with the same tags as in Sect. 3.1. We denote the admissible tag set for mobile nodes of type $m \in \overline{M}$ by

$$K_m \subseteq V \cup \bigcup_{(i,j) \in V_-^2} \{(i,j)\} \times \mathcal{V}(m, (i,j)),$$

where the tags are the same as in T1, T2 on page 5. The development of tags of a type-m node is determined by a stochastic routing matrix P_m on K_m

$$P_m(i; i) = r_m(i, i), \quad i \in V, \tag{10}$$
$$P_m(i; (i,j), v) = r_m(i,j) \cdot s_m((i,j), v), \quad i \neq j \in V, \ v \in \mathcal{V}(m, (i,j))$$
$$P_m((i,j), v; j) = 1. \quad i \neq j \in V, \ v \in \mathcal{V}(m, (i,j))$$
$$P_m(i, 0) = r_m(i, 0) \quad i \in V.$$

P_m is irreducible on K_m. For all types $m = 1, \ldots, M$ we define traffic equations and their solutions $\alpha_m = (\alpha_m(t) : t \in K_m)$

$$\alpha_m(t) = \lambda_m \cdot 1_{(t=a(m))} + \sum_{t' \in K_m} \alpha_m(t')P_m(t', t), \quad m = 1, \ldots, M. \tag{11}$$

Dwell times of an m-type node equipped with tag i at node $i \in V$ have cdf $F(m, i)$, whereas dwell times of an m-type node equipped with tag $((i, j), v)$, i.e. traveling from i to j with velocity v, are deterministic $w(i, j)/v$. We use the conventions on page 6 with Properties 1–4 here as well.

The global states of the resulting Markov process are compounded of local states. For to prove the next theorem below we exploit a product structure of the global and the local state spaces. These are as follows.

For $\kappa = i \in V$ with $n(i) > 0$ mobile nodes a typical local state is

$$z_i = [t_{i1}, \zeta_{i1}; \ldots; t_{in(i)}, \zeta_{in(i)}] \in E_i, \tag{12}$$

with the same interpretation as (2). If location i is empty we denote this as $e_i \in E_i$. The realizable types at i are

$$T_i := \{m \in \overline{M} : \alpha_m(i) > 0\},$$

and we have with support $[0, S(m, i)]$ of $F(m, i)$

$$E_i = \{e_i\} \cup \bigcup_{n=0}^{\infty} \{[t_{i1}, \zeta_{i1}; \ldots; t_{in(i)}, \zeta_{in(i)}] : t_{i\ell} \in T_i, \zeta_{i\ell} \in [0, S(t_{i\ell}, i)], \ell = 1, \ldots, n\}.$$

We further define the type space for vertex i

$$E_i^{red} = \{e_i\} \cup \bigcup_{n=0}^{\infty} T_i^n.$$

For $\kappa = (i, j) \in V_-^2$ with $n(i, j) > 0$ mobile nodes a typical local state is

$$z_{(i,j)} = [t_{(i,j)1}, v_{(i,j)1}, \zeta_{(i,j)1}; \ldots; t_{(i,j)n(i,j)}, v_{(i,j)n(i,j)}, \zeta_{(i,j)n(i,j)}] \in E_{(i,j)}, \tag{13}$$

with the same interpretation as (3). If location (i, j) is empty we denote this as $e_{(i,j)} \in E_{(i,j)}$. The realizable types-speed pairs at (i, j) are

$$T_{(i,j)} := \{(m, v) : m \in \overline{M}, v \in \mathcal{V}(m, (i, j)) : \alpha_m(m, (i, j),) > 0\},$$

and we have

$$E_{(i,j)} = \{e_{(i,j)}\} \cup \bigcup_{n=0}^{\infty} \{[t_{(i,j)1}, v_{(i,j)1}, \zeta_{(i,j)1}; \ldots; t_{(i,j)n}, v_{(i,j)n}, \zeta_{(i,j)n}] :$$
$$(t_{(i,j)\ell}, v_{(i,j)\ell}) \in T_{(i,j)}, \zeta_{(i,j),\ell} \in [0, w(i, j)/v_{(i,j)\ell}], \ell = 1, \ldots, n\}.$$

We further define the type space for lane (i, j)

$$E_{(i,j)}^{red} = \{e_{(i,j)}\} \cup \bigcup_{n=0}^{\infty} T_{(i,j)}^n.$$

The global state space E of the network contains all states of the form

$$z = [z_\kappa : \kappa \in V \cup V_-^2] \in \prod_{\kappa \in V \cup V_-^2} E_\kappa =: E. \tag{14}$$

4.2   Stationary Behaviour of Open Graph-Based Mobility Models

Recall that scheduling nodes inside the locations is according to "shift-protocol" as described in SP1, SP2 on page 7. We define local measures $\widetilde{\xi}_\kappa, \kappa \in V \cup V_-^2$, and paste these together to obtain the global stationary distribution. The (non normalized) local measures look like local measures in the closed graph-based model, but are different because identical types may occur in the same state.

Theorem 2. *For the open graph-based mobility model denote by*

$$Z = (Z(t) = (Z_\kappa(t) : \kappa \in V \cup V_-^2) : t \geq 0)$$

the supplemented joint location process of the network, and the local "type-tag-(residual pause/travel time) processes" by $Z_\kappa = (Z_\kappa(t) : t \geq 0)$ on E_κ, similar as in Theorem 1. Z is irreducible on E.
   For $\kappa = i \in V$, the local measure $\widetilde{\xi}_i$ on E_i at i is $\widetilde{\xi}_i(e_i) = 1$, and for local state $z_i = [t_{i1}, \zeta_{i1}; \ldots ; t_{in(i)}, \zeta_{in(i)}] \in E_i$,

$$\widetilde{\xi}_i[t_{i1}, \zeta_{i1}; \ldots ; t_{in(i)}, \zeta_{in(i)}] = \prod_{\ell=1}^{n(i)} \frac{\alpha_{t_{i\ell}}(i)}{\mu(t_{i\ell}, i) \cdot \ell} \left(\mu(t_{i\ell}, i) \int_0^{\zeta_{i\ell}} (1 - F(t_{i\ell}, i)(y)) dy \right)$$

has word-by-word the same interpretation as (7).
   For $(i, j) \in V_-^2$ the local measure $\widetilde{\xi}_{(i,j)}$ on $E_{(i,j)}$ at (i, j) is $\widetilde{\xi}_{(i,j)}(e_{(i,j)}) = 1$, and for local state $z_{(i,j)} = [t_{(i,j)1}, v_{(i,j)1}, \zeta_{(i,j)1}; \ldots ; t_{(i,j)n(i,j)}, v_{(i,j)n(i,j)}, \zeta_{(i,j)n(i,j)}] \in E_{(i,j)}$,

$$\widetilde{\xi}_{(i,j)}[t_{(i,j)1}, v_{(i,j)1}, \zeta_{(i,j)1}; \ldots ; t_{(i,j)n((i,j))}, v_{(i,j)n((i,j))}, \zeta_{(i,j)n(i,j)}]$$
$$= \prod_{\ell=1}^{n(i,j)} \frac{\alpha_{t_{(i,j)\ell}}((i,j), v_{(i,j)\ell}) \cdot w(i,j)}{v_{(i,j)\ell} \cdot \ell} \left(v_{(i,j)\ell}/w(i,j) \cdot (\zeta_{t_{(i,j)\ell}} \wedge \frac{w(i,j)}{v_{(i,j)\ell}}) \right).$$

has word-by-word the same interpretation as (8).
Z is ergodic with limiting and stationary distribution ξ for $[z_\kappa : \kappa \in V \cup V_-^2] \in E$

$$\xi[z_\kappa : \kappa \in V \cup V_-^2] = \left(\prod_{\kappa \in V \cup V_-^2} \widetilde{\xi}_\kappa(z_\kappa) \right) \cdot C^{-1} = \prod_{\kappa \in V \cup V_-^2} \left(\widetilde{\xi}_\kappa(z_\kappa) \cdot C_\kappa^{-1} \right), \tag{15}$$

where the local normalization constants are for $\kappa \in V \cup V_-^2$

$$C_i = \exp\left(\sum_{t\in\overline{M}} \frac{\alpha_t(i)}{\mu(t,i)}\right) < \infty, \quad \kappa = i \in V, \tag{16}$$

and for $\quad \kappa = (i,j) \in V_-^2:$

$$C_{(i,j)} = \exp\left(\sum_{(t,v)\in\bigcup_{m\in\overline{M}^n}(\{m\}\times V(m,(i,j)))} \frac{\alpha_t((i,j),v)\cdot w(i,j)}{v}\right) < \infty. \tag{17}$$

Note that (16) and (17) are finite without additional assumptions. This is a result of the locations' structure which resemble infinite server queues $\circ/G/\infty$. Before proving the theorem we provide a corollary about reduced measures.

Corollary 3. *For the open graph-based mobility network model denote by $X = (X(t) = (X_\kappa(t) : \kappa \in V \cup V_-^2) : t \geq 0)$ the joint reduced location process of the network, and by $X_\kappa = (X_\kappa(t) : t \geq 0)$ the local "type-tag-processes" on E_κ^{red}. For $\kappa = i \in V$ the local reduced measure $\widetilde{\xi}_i^{red}$ on E_i^{red} at i is $\widetilde{\xi}_i^{red}(e_i) = 1$, and for reduced local state $x_i = [t_{i1}, \ldots, t_{in(i)}] \in E_i^{red}$,*

$$\widetilde{\xi}_i^{red}[t_{i1}, \ldots, t_{in(i)}]$$

$$= \lim_{\zeta_{i1}\to\infty\ldots\zeta_{in(i)}\to\infty} \widetilde{\xi}_i[t_{i1}, \zeta_{i1}; \ldots; t_{in(i)}, \zeta_{in(i)}] = \prod_{\ell=1}^{n(i)} \frac{\alpha_{t_{i\ell}}(i)}{\mu(t_{i\ell}, i)\cdot\ell}$$

For location $(i,j) \in V_-^2$ the local measure on $E_{(i,j)}^{red}$ is $\widetilde{\xi}_{(i,j)}^{red}(e_{(i,j)}) = 1$, and for reduced local state $x_{(i,j)} = [t_{(i,j)1}, v_{(i,j)1}; \ldots; t_{(i,j)n(i,j)}, v_{(i,j)n(i,j)}] \in E_{(i,j)}^{red}$,

$$\widetilde{\xi}_{(i,j)}^{red}[t_{(i,j)1}, v_{(i,j)1}; \ldots; t_{(i,j)n((i,j))}, v_{(i,j)n((i,j))}]$$

$$= \lim_{\zeta_{(i,j)1},\to\infty} \cdots \lim_{\zeta_{(i,j)n(t)}\to\infty}$$

$$\widetilde{\xi}_{(i,j)}[t_{(i,j)1}, v_{(i,j)1}, \zeta_{(i,j)1}; \ldots; t_{(i,j)n((i,j))}, v_{(i,j)n((i,j))}, \zeta_{(i,j)n(i,j)}]$$

$$= \prod_{\ell=1}^{n(i,j)} \frac{\alpha_{t_{(i,j)\ell}}((i,j), v_{(i,j)\ell})\cdot w(i,j)}{v_{(i,j)\ell}\cdot\ell}.$$

X has unique limiting and stationary distribution

$$\xi^{red}[x_\kappa : \kappa \in V \cup V_-^2] = \prod_{\kappa\in V\cup V_-^2} \widetilde{\xi}_\kappa^{red}(x_\kappa)\cdot(C^{red})^{-1}, \quad [x_\kappa : \kappa \in V \cup V_-^2] \in E^{red},$$

where $C^{red} = C$ is the normalization constant which is that of Z, and it holds moreover for $\kappa \in V \cup V_-^2: C_\kappa = C_\kappa^{red}$.

The distribution of X is invariant under varying shapes of the pause time distributions as long as the mean pause times do not change.

Proof. The proof of Theorem 2 is similar to the proof of Theorem 1 with respect to proving that (15) solves the balance equations. The problem is to prove ergodicity which turns to proving summability of the $\prod_{\kappa \in V \cup V_-^2} \tilde{\xi}_\kappa(z_\kappa)$. By Corollary 3 we can reduce this to summing the reduced non-normalized measures

$$\tilde{\xi}^{red}[x_\kappa : \kappa \in V \cup V_-^2] := \prod_{\kappa \in V \cup V_-^2} \tilde{\xi}_\kappa^{red}(x_\kappa), \quad x = [x_\kappa : \kappa \in V \cup V_-^2] \in E^{red},$$

with $\tilde{\xi}_\kappa^{red}(x_\kappa)$ from Corollary 3. Due to the product structure of E^{red} and $\tilde{\xi}^{red}$

$$\sum_{[x_\kappa : \kappa \in V \cup V_-^2] \in E^{red}} \tilde{\xi}^{red}[x_\kappa : \kappa \in V \cup V_-^2]$$

$$= \sum_{[x_\kappa : \kappa \in V \cup V_-^2] \in \prod_{\kappa \in V \cup V_-^2} E_\kappa^{red}} \prod_{\kappa \in V \cup V_-^2} \xi_\kappa^{red}(x_\kappa) = \prod_{\kappa \in V \cup V_-^2} \left[\sum_{x_\kappa \in E_\kappa^{red}} \xi_\kappa^{red}(x_\kappa) \right].$$

Summing up the squared brackets yields (16) and (17). □

5   Concluding Remarks

In [6] an expression for the stationary distribution of mobile nodes in an RWP model is given. The authors emphasize that in MANET simulations sampling the initial configuration according this distribution "puts the system immediately into its 'steady state', thus avoiding the number of movement periods needed to make the system converge to this state." [6, p. 264]. Clearly, this holds for our theorems which, moreover, offer hints to sampling the initial node distribution:

In open systems we sample for any location the nodes and their properties in isolation due to the independence structure of the stationary distribution (15).

For the closed system sampling suffers from computation of the normalization constant, but there are established schemes to simulate such distribution with conditionally independent coordinates.

On the other side it would be of value to develop adapted schemes for computing normalization constants in Theorem 1 exploiting the model-specific properties of the closed graph-based mobility models. This will need a detailed analysis and was out of the scope of the present paper.

In a similar way as for closed and open graph-based mobility schemes it is possible to construct models where some nodes stay forever on the graph and others arrive from the exterior, travel for some finite time and eventually depart from the graph-based network. The stationary mobile node distribution will be a composition of the distributions obtained in Theorems 1 and 2.

Another extension which is direct but will need some technical effort: Nodes may interact by generating traffic jams which reduce their pace. Separability will be maintained formally.

Although our results on the stationary distributions are explicit it seems to be challenging to use these formulas for computing analytically performance metrics for MANETs (availability of communication routes) or for opportunistic networks (inter-contact times, contact durations) [21].

References

1. Barbour, A.D.: Networks of queues and the method of stages. Adv. Appl. Probab. **8**, 584–591 (1976)
2. Bolch, G., Greiner, S., de Meer, H., Trivedi, K.S.: Queueing Networks and Markov Chains, 2nd edn. Wiley, New York (2006)
3. Bruell, S.C., Balbo, G.: Computational Algorithms for Closed Queueing Networks. North-Holland, New York (1980)
4. Baskett, F., Chandy, M., Muntz, R., Palacios, F.G.: Open, closed and mixed networks of queues with different classes of customers. J. Assoc. Comput. Mach. **22**, 248–260 (1975)
5. Bai, F., Helmy, A.: A survey of mobility models in wireless adhoc networks. In: Wireless Ad-Hoc Networks, chap. 1, pp. 1–30. Kluwer Academic Publisher, Dordrecht (2006)
6. Bettstetter, C., Resta, G., Santi, P.: The node distribution of the random waypoint mobility model for wireless ad hoc networks. IEEE Trans. Mob. Comput. **2**(3), 257–269 (2003)
7. Daduna, H.: Moving queue on a network. In: Remke, A., Haverkort, B.R. (eds.) MMB&DFT 2016. LNCS, vol. 9629, pp. 40–54. Springer, Cham (2016). https://doi.org/10.1007/978-3-319-31559-1_5
8. Daduna, H., Szekli, R.: Impact of routeing on correlation strength in stationary queueing networks processes. J. Appl. Probab. **45**, 846–878 (2008)
9. Kelly, F.: Networks of queues. Adv. Appl. Probab. **8**, 416–432 (1976)
10. Kelly, F.P.: Reversibility and Stochastic Networks. Wiley, Chichester/New York/Brisbane/Toronto (1979)
11. Kraaier, J., Killat, U.: Calculating mobility parameters for a predefined stationary user distribution. In: Proceedings of 2004 12th IEEE International Conference on Networks (ICON 2004) (IEEE Cat. No.04EX955), vol. 1, pp. 41–45, November 2004
12. Kraaier, J., Killat, U.: The random waypoint city model : User distribution in a street-based mobility model for wireless network simulations. In: Proceedings of the 3rd ACM International Workshop on Wireless Mobile Applications and Services on WLAN Hotspots, WMASH 2005, p. 100–103. ACM, New York (2005)
13. Kraaier, J., Killat, U.: Controlling the stationary distribution of mobile users in wireless network simulations. In: 2007 IEEE 66th Vehicular Technology Conference, pp. 804–808 (2007)
14. Kriege, J.: Combining mobility models with arrival processes. In: Remke, A., Haverkort, B.R. (eds.) MMB&DFT 2016. LNCS, vol. 9629, pp. 107–121. Springer, Cham (2016). https://doi.org/10.1007/978-3-319-31559-1_10
15. Le Boudec, J., Vojnovic, M.: Perfect simulation and stationarity of a class of mobility models. In: Proceedings IEEE 24th Annual Joint Conference of the IEEE Computer and Communications Societies, vol. 4, pp. 2743–2754, March 2005
16. Navidi, W., Camp, T.: Stationary distribution for the random waypoint mobility model. IEEE Trans. Mob. Comput. **3**(1), 99–108 (2004)
17. Navidi, W., Camp, T., Bauer, N.: Improving accuracy of random waypoint simulations through steady-state initialization. Technical report, Colorado School of Mines, Golden, CO, June 2006

18. Nikoletseas, S., Rolim, J.D.P.: Theoretical Aspects of Distributed Computing in Sensor Networks. Monographs in Theoretical Computer Science. An EATCS Series. Springer, Heidelberg (2011). https://doi.org/10.1007/978-3-642-14849-1
19. Roy, R.R.: Handbook of Mobile Ad Hoc Networks for Mobility Models. Springer, Heidelberg (2011). https://doi.org/10.1007/978-1-4419-6050-4
20. Schassberger, R.: Warteschlangen. Springer, Wien (1973)
21. Schwamborn, M., Aschenbruck, N.: On modeling and impact of geographic restrictions for human mobility in opportunistic networks. Perform. Eval. **130**, 17–31 (2019)
22. Stepanov, I., Marron, P.J., Rothermel, K.: Mobility modeling of outdoor scenarios for manets. In: Proceedings of the 38th Annual Symposium on Simulation, ANSS 2005, pp. 312–322. IEEE Computer Society, Washington (2005)
23. Simatos, F., Tibi, D.: Study of a stochastic model for mobile networks. SIGMETRICS Perform. Eval. Rev. **36**(2), 122–124 (2008)
24. Tian, J., Hähner, J., Becker, C., Stepanov, I., Rothermel, K.: Graph-based mobility model for mobile ad hoc network simulation. In: Proceedings of the 35th Annual Simulation Symposium, SS 2002, pp. 337–344. IEEE Computer Society, Washington (2002)
25. Wang, Y., Dang, H., Wu, H.H.: A survey on analytic studies of delay-tolerant mobile sensor networks. Wirel. Commun. Mob. Comput. **7**(10), 1197–1208 (2007)
26. Wu, H., Wang, Y., Dang, H., Lin, F.: Analytic, simulation, and empirical evaluation of delay/fault-tolerant mobile sensor networks. IEEE Trans. Wirel. Commun. **6**(9), 3287–3296 (2007)
27. Yoon, J., Liu, M., Noble, B.: A general framework to construct stationary mobility models for the simulation of mobile networks. IEEE Trans. Mob. Comput. **5**(7), 1–12 (2006)

Parallelization of EM-Algorithms for Markovian Arrival Processes

Andreas Blume$^{(\boxtimes)}$, Peter Buchholz$^{(\boxtimes)}$, and Jan Kriege

Informatik IV, Technical University of Dortmund, 44221 Dortmund, Germany
{andreas.blume,peter.buchholz,jan.kriege}@cs.tu-dortmund.de

Abstract. Markovian Arrival Processes (MAPs) are widely used stochastic models to describe correlated events. For the parameter fitting of MAPs according to measured data, the expectation-maximization (EM) algorithm is commonly seen as the best approach. Unfortunately, EM algorithms require a huge computational effort if the number of data points is large or the MAP has a larger dimension. The classical EM algorithm runs sequentially through the data which is necessary to consider dependencies between data points.

In this paper we present a parallel variant of the EM algorithm for MAPs with a general structure. The parallel version of the algorithm is developed for multicore systems with shared memory. It is shown that the parallel algorithm yields a significant speedup compared to its sequential counterpart.

Keywords: Markovian Arrival Process · EM algorithm · Parallel algorithms · Traffic modeling

1 Introduction

Markovian Arrival Processes (MAPs) [20,21] are an often used stochastic model to describe correlated events in various application areas like traffic modeling in computer networks or failure modeling in dependable systems. MAPs have a simple structure, can be easily analyzed and can be used as arrival or service processes of queues which may be analyzed with efficient matrix analytical techniques. Additionally, MAPs can be used in discrete event simulation models to generate correlated event streams.

For the practical use of MAPs, the parameters of the model have to be chosen in such a way that the behavior of some real event stream is adequately described. This is usually done by fitting or estimating the parameters with respect to some measured trace. This can be either done by choosing parameters such that some derived quantities like moments and joint moments are met or approximated by the MAP, or it can be done by maximizing the likelihood of generating the measured event sequence by the MAP. Both approaches require the solution of non-linear optimization problems. However, the fitting of derived quantities, in particular lower order moments or joint moments [9,12,15], is much more

© Springer Nature Switzerland AG 2020
H. Hermanns (Ed.): MMB 2020, LNCS 12040, pp. 173–189, 2020.
https://doi.org/10.1007/978-3-030-43024-5_11

efficient than the maximization of the likelihood which is usually done with EM-algorithms [3,7,8,16]. Unfortunately, algorithms maximizing the likelihood usually yield much better results [17].

Consequently, there is a need to improve the efficiency of EM-algorithms for MAP fitting. For the parameter fitting of phase type distributions, which have similar characteristics than MAPs, but do not model correlations, efficient versions of the EM algorithm are available [23,26]. These algorithms are based on restricted structures of phase type distributions that are general and flexible enough to model real traces. Additionally, the algorithms are easy to parallelize because correlation between events in the trace is neglected and data can be handled in arbitrary order and can be first aggregated without reducing the fitting quality [18,24] as long as the elements in the trace do not spread too much.

The idea of using restricted structures to improve parameter fitting has also been applied to MAPs. In this case the so called Erlang distributed continuous-time Markov chain (CHMM) and its extended version has been proposed [14,22]. Due to the specific structure of CHMMs, the EM-algorithm can be parallelized and realized on GPUs [6]. Different variants·of the algorithm are proposed in [6] and show a remarkable speed-up on GPUs.

In this paper we also consider the parallelization of the EM-algorithm for MAPs. Based on the serial algorithm proposed in [8] different parallel variants are developed. In contrast, to [6] we do not restrict the class of MAPs and we allow arbitrary structures. The current implementation of the parallel EM algorithm runs on multi-core processors and is implemented using OpenMP. Therefore, we cannot expect to reach speed ups as in [6]. Nevertheless, the results show that there is some potential for parallelization.

The paper is structured as follows. In the next section the basic definitions are given and the notation is fixed. In Sect. 3 the EM-algorithm that we use in the parallel variant is introduced. Afterwards we develop in Sect. 4 different parallel versions of the algorithm. Then experiments with the parallel and sequential variant of the algorithm are presented. The paper is concluded with a short summary and directions for future research.

2 Background

In this section we define MAPs together with the basic notation. Afterwards the analysis of MAPs is briefly introduced. Further details can be found in the literature [10].

2.1 Basic Definitions and Notation

Vectors and matrices are denoted by bold face small and capital letters. I is the identity matrix, $\mathbb{1}$ is a column vector of 1s, all other vectors are row vectors. $\mathbf{0}$ is a matrix or vector containing only 0 elements. $\boldsymbol{a}^T$ describes the transposed of vector $\boldsymbol{a}$. $\mathbb{R}^{N \times N}$ is the set of $N \times N$ matrices. A generator is a matrix $\boldsymbol{Q} \in \mathbb{R}^{N \times N}$

with row sum zero (i.e., $\boldsymbol{Q}\mathbb{1} = \boldsymbol{0}$) and $\boldsymbol{Q}(i,j) \geq 0$ for $i \neq j$. $\boldsymbol{Q}$ is a sub-generator if $\boldsymbol{Q}\mathbb{1} \leq \boldsymbol{0}$ and some $i \in \{1, \ldots, N\}$ exists such that $\boldsymbol{Q}(i\bullet)\mathbb{1} < 0$ where $\boldsymbol{Q}(i\bullet)$ denotes row i of $\boldsymbol{Q}$. $\boldsymbol{Q}$ is irreducible if between every pair of states i, j a path $i = i_0, i_1, \ldots, i_k = j$ exists such that $\boldsymbol{Q}(i_{h-1}, i_h) > 0$ for $h = 1, \ldots, k$.

Different ways to characterize a MAP exist. The probably most intuitive is the definition as an irreducible CTMC with marked transition. Let $\boldsymbol{Q}$ be an irreducible generator matrix of a CTMC with n states and let $\boldsymbol{Q} = \boldsymbol{D}_0 + \boldsymbol{D}_1$ where $\boldsymbol{D}_0$ is a sub-generator and $\boldsymbol{D}_1$ is non-negative. Then $\phi\boldsymbol{Q} = \boldsymbol{0}$, $\phi\mathbb{1} = 1$ is the unique stationary vector of the CTMC. $\boldsymbol{D}_0$ is non-singular and $-\boldsymbol{D}_0^{-1}$ is non-negative. $(\boldsymbol{D}_0, \boldsymbol{D}_1)$ describes a Markovian Arrival Process (MAP). The behavior of the process is as follows: If a transition from $\boldsymbol{D}_0$ occurs, it is internal and not visible, whereas transitions from $\boldsymbol{D}_1$ trigger an event which can be an arrival, end of a service, failure etc.

MAPs are very general and allow one to approximate a wide class of stochastic processes and describe many workloads in a realistic way [10,11,21]. An additional advantage is that they can be used in models that are analyzed numerically, by matrix-analytical techniques, as well as in simulation models [10].

2.2 Analysis of MAPs

A MAP describes a stochastic process that generates events. Inter-event times (i.e., the times between two events) t_i have a phase type distribution. Let $\boldsymbol{P} = -\boldsymbol{D}_0^{-1}\boldsymbol{D}_1$ be the transition matrix of the embedded DTMC describing the behavior of the MAP at event times. Let $\boldsymbol{\pi} = \phi\boldsymbol{D}_1/(\phi\boldsymbol{D}_1\mathbb{1})$, then $\boldsymbol{\pi} = \boldsymbol{\pi}\boldsymbol{P}$ and $\boldsymbol{\pi}$ describes the stationary probability distribution over the states of the MAP immediately after an event. The inter-event time is phase type distributed with phase type distribution $(\boldsymbol{\pi}, \boldsymbol{D}_0)$ and the moments and probability density function are given by

$$E[T^i] = \boldsymbol{\pi}\left(-\boldsymbol{D}_0\right)^{-i} \text{ and } f(t) = \boldsymbol{\pi}e^{t\boldsymbol{D}_0}\boldsymbol{d}_1 \text{ with } \boldsymbol{d}_1 = \boldsymbol{D}_1\mathbb{1}. \tag{1}$$

Sequences of inter-event times generated by MAPs are usually not independent. Let $X_1, \ldots, X_k$ be a sequence of k consecutive inter-event times and X an arbitrary inter-event time. Then the joint density, joint moments and coefficient of autocorrelation of lag-k are given by

$$f(t_1, t_2, \ldots, t_k) = \boldsymbol{\pi}e^{t_1\boldsymbol{D}_0}\boldsymbol{D}_1 e^{t_2\boldsymbol{D}_0}\boldsymbol{D}_1 \ldots e^{t_k\boldsymbol{D}_0}\boldsymbol{D}_1\mathbb{1} \text{ for } t_1, \ldots, t_k \geq 0,$$

$$E[X_1^{i_1}, X_2^{i_2}, \ldots, X_k^{i_k}] = i_1!i_2! \ldots i_k!\boldsymbol{\pi}(-\boldsymbol{D}_0)^{-i_1}\boldsymbol{P}(-\boldsymbol{D}_0)^{-i_2} \ldots \boldsymbol{P}(-\boldsymbol{D}_0)^{-i_k}\mathbb{1}, \tag{2}$$

$$\rho_k = \frac{E[X_1, X_{1+k}] - (E[X])^2}{E[X^2] - (E[X])^2} = \frac{\boldsymbol{\pi}(-\boldsymbol{D}_0)^{-1}\boldsymbol{P}^k(-\boldsymbol{D}_0)^{-1}\mathbb{1} - \left(\boldsymbol{\pi}(-\boldsymbol{D}_0)^{-1}\mathbb{1}\right)^2}{2\boldsymbol{\pi}(-\boldsymbol{D}_0)^{-2}\mathbb{1} - \left(\boldsymbol{\pi}(-\boldsymbol{D}_0)^{-1}\mathbb{1}\right)^2}.$$

Thus, all quantities related to MAPs can be easily analyzed using standard numerical methods.

3   EM-Algorithms for MAPs

To apply MAPs in stochastic models, their parameters have to be selected such that an event stream generated by the MAP is similar to some measured event stream. We consider here approaches that maximize the likelihood of generating the observed event stream from the MAP. This usually is the approach that gives the best results [17]. In this section we first introduce the basic problem setting, present afterwards the basic EM-algorithm and consider finally implementation issues.

3.1   Likelihood Optimization

Let $\mathcal{T} = \{t_1, \ldots, t_M\}$ be a sequence of M inter-event times which is denoted as a trace. Let $(\boldsymbol{D}_0, \boldsymbol{D}_1)$ be some MAP. The likelihood of the MAP according to trace $\mathcal{T}$ is based on the joint density in (2) and is defined as

$$\mathcal{L}((\boldsymbol{D}_0, \boldsymbol{D}_1)|\mathcal{T}) = \boldsymbol{\pi} \left(\prod_{i=1}^{M} \left(e^{t_i \boldsymbol{D}_0} \boldsymbol{D}_1 \right) \right) \mathbb{1}. \tag{3}$$

The best MAP that maximizes $\mathcal{L}((\boldsymbol{D}_0, \boldsymbol{D}_1)|\mathcal{T})$ results from the optimization problem

$$(\boldsymbol{D}_0, \boldsymbol{D}_1)^* = \arg \max_{(\boldsymbol{D}_0, \boldsymbol{D}_1)} \left(\boldsymbol{\pi} \left(\prod_{i=1}^{M} e^{t_i \boldsymbol{D}_0} \boldsymbol{D}_1 \right) \mathbb{1} \right) \tag{4}$$

with the additional constraints that $\boldsymbol{D}_0$ is a sub-generator, $\boldsymbol{D}_1 \geq 0$ and $\boldsymbol{D}_0 + \boldsymbol{D}_1$ is an irreducible generator matrix.

3.2   An EM Algorithm

Computation of the optimal MAP according to (4) requires the solution of a non-linear optimization problem which cannot be solved for global optimality. Instead the EM-algorithm is applied as a local optimization algorithm with a guaranteed but often slow convergence to a local optimum [27]. Different EM-algorithms have been proposed for MAPs [7,8,10,16]. We use here the basic approach from [10] and define

- B_i is the number of times the process starts in state i,
- Z_i is the total time spent in state i,
- N_{ij} equals the number of jumps from state i to state j without generating an event $(i \neq j)$, and
- M_{ij} is the total observed number of jumps from state i to j when generating an event.

In terms of these quantities the likelihood function can be expressed as

$$\mathcal{L}((\boldsymbol{D}_0, \boldsymbol{D}_1)|\mathcal{T}) =$$
$$\prod_{i=1}^{N} (\boldsymbol{\pi}(i))^{B_i} \prod_{i=1}^{N} e^{Z_i \boldsymbol{D}_0(i,i)} \prod_{i=1}^{N} \prod_{j=1, j \neq i}^{N} \boldsymbol{D}_0(i,j)^{N_{ij}} \prod_{i=1}^{N} \prod_{j=1, j \neq i}^{N} \boldsymbol{D}_1(i,j)^{M_{ij}} \mathbb{1}. \tag{5}$$

The forward and backward vectors and the flow matrix of each event $k = 1, \ldots, M$ are then given by

$$\boldsymbol{ff}_{(D_0,D_1)}^{(k)} = \begin{cases} \boldsymbol{\pi} & \text{if } k = 1 \\ \boldsymbol{ff}_{(D_0,D_1)}^{(k-1)} e^{t_{k-1}D_0} \boldsymbol{D}_1 & \text{if } 1 < k \leq M \end{cases}$$

$$\boldsymbol{bb}_{(D_0,D_1)}^{(k)} = \begin{cases} \boldsymbol{d}_1 & \text{if } k = M \\ \boldsymbol{D}_1 e^{t_{k+1}D_0} \boldsymbol{bb}_{(D_0,D_1)}^{(k+1)} & \text{if } 1 \leq k < M \end{cases} \tag{6}$$

$$\boldsymbol{f}_{(D_0,D_1),t}^{(k)} = \boldsymbol{ff}_{(D_0,D_1)}^{(k)} e^{tD_0}, \ \boldsymbol{b}_{(D_0,D_1),t}^{(k)} = e^{tD_0} \boldsymbol{bb}_{(D_0,D_1)}^{(k)}, \text{ and}$$

$$\boldsymbol{F}_{(D_0,D_1),t}^{(k)} = \int_0^t \left(\boldsymbol{f}_{(D_0,D_1),t-u}^{(k)} \right)^T \left(\boldsymbol{b}_{(D_0,D_1),u}^{(k)} \right)^T du.$$

From the forward vectors, backward vectors and the flow matrix the expectations of the characteristic quantities defined above can be computed for the MAP (D_0, D_1).

$$E_{(D_0,D_1),\mathcal{T}}[Z_i] = \sum_{k=1}^{M} \frac{F_{(D_0,D_1),t_k}^{(k)}(i,i)}{\pi b_{(D_0,D_1),t_1}^{(1)}},$$

$$E_{(D_0,D_1),\mathcal{T}}[N_{ij}] = \sum_{k=1}^{M} \frac{D_1(i,j)F_{(D_0,D_1),t_k}^{(k)}(i,j)}{\pi b_{(D_0,D_1),t_1}^{(1)}}, \tag{7}$$

$$E_{(D_0,D_1),\mathcal{T}}[M_{ij}] = \sum_{k=1}^{M-1} \frac{f_{(D_0,D_1),t_k}^{(k)}(i)D_1(i,j)b_{(D_0,D_1),t_{k+1}}^{(k+1)}}{\pi b_{(D_0,D_1),t_1}^{(1)}} + \frac{f_{(D_0,D_1),t_M}^{(M)}(i)D_1(i,j) \mathbb{1}}{\pi b_{(D_0,D_1),t_1}^{(1)}}.$$

The computed values are the expected values that result from the MAP (D_0, D_1) applied to trace $\mathcal{T}$. This step is denoted as the expectation or E-step of the algorithm. In the maximization or M-step values are improved such that the likelihood value of the MAP is increased.

$$\hat{D}_0(i,j) = \frac{E_{(D_0,D_1),\mathcal{T}}[N_{ij}]}{E_{(D_0,D_1),\mathcal{T}}[Z_i]} \text{ for } i \neq j,$$

$$\hat{D}_1(i,j) = \frac{E_{(D_0,D_1),\mathcal{T}}[M_{ij}]}{E_{(D_0,D_1),\mathcal{T}}[Z_i]}, \tag{8}$$

$$\hat{D}_0(i,i) = -\left(\sum_{j=1,i\neq j}^{n} \hat{D}_0(i,j) + \sum_{j=1}^{n} \hat{D}_1(i,j) \right).$$

The local convergence of the EM algorithm assures that $\mathcal{L}((\hat{D}_0, \hat{D}_1)|\mathcal{T}) \geq \mathcal{L}((D_0, D_1)|\mathcal{T})$ [27]. After the M-step $D_0 = \hat{D}_0$, $D_1 = \hat{D}_1$ and the next E-step is performed. (7) and (8) are iterated until the norm difference between new and old matrix fall below some threshold. This generates a sequence of MAPs with an increasing likelihood value.

3.3 Implementation Issues

Although the basic steps of the EM-algorithm for MAPs are simple, their concrete implementation has to be done carefully. There are several numerical issues which are briefly considered in this section and the effort for the expectation step is high, in particular the computation of the flow matrix is cumbersome. This aspect is considered in the following section when we describe a parallel implementation.

For the evaluation of the matrix exponentials usually uniformization is applied. First define the following vectors for $k = 1, \ldots, M$

$$
\boldsymbol{v}^{(l)}[k] = \begin{cases} \boldsymbol{ff}^{(k)}_{(D_0, D_1)} & \text{if } l = 0 \\ \boldsymbol{v}^{(l-1)}[k] \boldsymbol{P}_0 & \text{if } l > 0 \end{cases}, \quad
\boldsymbol{w}^{(l)}[k] = \begin{cases} \boldsymbol{bb}^{(k)}_{(D_0, D_1)} & \text{if } l = 0 \\ \boldsymbol{P}_0 \boldsymbol{w}^{(l-1)}[k] & \text{if } l > 0 \end{cases} \tag{9}
$$

where $\boldsymbol{P}_0 = \boldsymbol{D}_0/\alpha + \boldsymbol{I}$ and $\alpha \geq \max |\boldsymbol{D}_0(i,i)|$. From these vectors, the required forward and backward vectors can be computed.

$$
\begin{aligned}
\boldsymbol{ff}^{(k)}_{(D_0, D_1)} &= \left(\sum_{l=0}^{\infty} \beta(\alpha t_{k-1}, l) \boldsymbol{v}^{(l)}[k-1] \right) \boldsymbol{D}_1, \\
\boldsymbol{f}^{(k)}_{(D_0, D_1), t} &= \sum_{l=0}^{\infty} \beta(\alpha t, l) \boldsymbol{v}^{(l)}[k], \\
\boldsymbol{bb}^{(k)}_{(D_0, D_1)} &= \boldsymbol{D}_1 \left(\sum_{l=0}^{\infty} \beta(\alpha t_{k+1}, l) \boldsymbol{w}^{(l)}[k+1] \right), \\
\boldsymbol{b}^{(k)}_{(D_0, D_1), t} &= \sum_{l=0}^{\infty} \beta(\alpha t, l) \boldsymbol{w}^{(l)}[k],
\end{aligned} \tag{10}
$$

where $\beta(\alpha t, l) = e^{-\alpha t}(\alpha t)^l / l!$ is the probability that a Poisson process with rate α generates l events in the interval $(0, t]$. Poisson probabilities can be computed in an efficient and numerically stable way [13]. Furthermore, it is possible to truncate the above infinite sums according to a predefined error bound [25]. The flow matrix can be computed similarly

$$
\boldsymbol{F}^{(k)}_{(D_0, D_1), t} = \frac{1}{\alpha} \sum_{l=0}^{\infty} \beta(\alpha t, l+1) \sum_{h=0}^{l} \left(\boldsymbol{v}^{(h)}[k] \right)^T \left(\boldsymbol{w}^{(l-h)}[k] \right)^T. \tag{11}
$$

With this representation the flow matrix has to be computed consecutively for the elements in $\mathcal{T}$. However, the flow matrix is only needed to determine $E[N_{ij}]$ the expected number of jumps from i to j without an event and $E[Z_i]$ the expected sojourn time in i. The expected values can as well be computed from the phase type distribution $(\boldsymbol{\pi}, \boldsymbol{D}_0)$ which results from MAP $(\boldsymbol{D}_0, \boldsymbol{D}_1)$ with $\boldsymbol{\pi} = \boldsymbol{\pi}(-\boldsymbol{D}_0)^{-1} \boldsymbol{D}_1$. Then the computation of the flow matrix becomes

$$
\boldsymbol{F}^{(k)}_{(\pi, D_0), t} = \frac{1}{\alpha} \sum_{l=0}^{\infty} \beta(\alpha t, l+1) \sum_{h=0}^{l} \left(\boldsymbol{x}^{(h)} \right)^T \left(\boldsymbol{y}^{(l-h)} \right)^T, \text{ where}
$$
$$
\boldsymbol{x}^{(l)} = \begin{cases} \boldsymbol{\pi} & \text{if } l = 0 \\ \boldsymbol{x}^{(l-1)} \boldsymbol{P}_0 & \text{if } l > 0 \end{cases}, \quad
\boldsymbol{y}^{(l)} = \begin{cases} \boldsymbol{d}_1 & \text{if } l = 0 \\ \boldsymbol{P}_0 \boldsymbol{y}^{(l-1)} & \text{if } l > 0. \end{cases} \tag{12}
$$

This flow matrix can then be used in (7) to compute $E[N_{ij}]$ and $E[Z_i]$. The advantage of (12) compared to (11) is that the flow matrices can be computed in arbitrary order, the consecutive vectors $\boldsymbol{ff}^{(k)}_{(D_0, D_1)}$, $\boldsymbol{bb}^{(k)}_{(D_0, D_1)}$ are no longer required and if $t_k = t_l$ the resulting matrix is identical and need not be recomputed which does not hold for (11).

It might seem to be surprising that flow matrices for a MAP can be computed without considering the dependence between consecutive arrivals. The reason is that these dependencies result from matrix D_1 which does not depend on the flow matrix. Thus, (11) and (12) will not necessarily result in identical matrices but results are very similar and it cannot be said that one approach is better than the other. Some examples in combination with trace aggregation can be found in [18].

Uniformization is a numerically stable algorithm such that in a single step stable results are computed. Nevertheless, for longer and realistic traces, likelihood values tend to become very large or very small and numerical under- or overflows occur. Thus, values have to be scaled during computations which means that after each step (i.e., computation for an element in the trace), the size of the maximum element in the vectors and matrices has to be determined. If this value becomes too large or too small, all values need to be multiplied by a scaling factor (see the description in [6] for further details about scaling).

4   Parallel EM-Algorithm

We now consider a parallel implementation of the EM algorithm introduced in the previous section. Results are based on [5]. We first describe the parallel computation of the flow vectors, then we consider the computation of the flow matrix and finally the complete algorithm. The current implementation of the approach is realized for multicore processors with shared memory which implies a moderate level of parallelism. A future realization on GPUs probably allows a much higher level of parallelism.

In the following we assume that we have T threads and each thread handles between $\lfloor M/T \rfloor$ and $\lceil M/T \rceil$ consecutive elements from the trace. For simplicity we assume that $L = M/T$ is an integer such that each thread handles L elements from $\mathcal{T}$.

4.1   Computation of Forward and Backward Vectors

The forward and backward vectors $\boldsymbol{ff}^{(k)}_{(D_0,D_1)}$ and $\boldsymbol{bb}^{(k)}_{(D_0,D_1)}$ are defined in (6) and are usually computed with uniformization as shown in (10). Now define the following matrices

$$\boldsymbol{F}[t] = e^{tD_0}\boldsymbol{D}_1 = \left(\sum_{l=0}^{\infty} \beta(\alpha t, l)\boldsymbol{P}_0^l\right)\boldsymbol{D}_1 \quad \text{and}$$
$$\boldsymbol{B}[t] = \boldsymbol{D}_1 e^{tD_0} = \boldsymbol{D}_1\left(\sum_{l=0}^{\infty} \beta(\alpha t, l)\boldsymbol{P}_0^l\right). \tag{13}$$

From these matrices we can define

$$\boldsymbol{F}[u, v] = \prod_{z=u}^{v} \boldsymbol{F}[z] \text{ and } \boldsymbol{B}[u, v] = \prod_{z=u}^{v} \boldsymbol{B}[z] \tag{14}$$

with the common assumption $\boldsymbol{F}[u, v] = \boldsymbol{B}[u, v] = \boldsymbol{I}$ for $v < u$. Then we have

$$\boldsymbol{ff}^{(k)}_{(D_0,D_1)} = \boldsymbol{\pi}\boldsymbol{F}[1, k-1] \text{ and } \boldsymbol{bb}^{(k)}_{(D_0,D_1)} = \boldsymbol{B}[k+1, M]\boldsymbol{d}_1. \tag{15}$$

In our setting thread $h \in \{1, \ldots, T\}$ is responsible for the computations related to the matrices

$$\boldsymbol{U}[h] = \boldsymbol{F}[(h-1) \cdot L + 1, h \cdot L] \text{ and } \boldsymbol{V}[h] = \boldsymbol{B}[(h-1) \cdot L + 1, h \cdot L]. \quad (16)$$

For thread h the local initial backward and forward vectors are given by

$$\boldsymbol{\pi}^{(h)} = \begin{cases} \boldsymbol{\pi} & \text{if } h = 1 \\ \boldsymbol{\pi}^{(h-1)} \boldsymbol{U}[h-1] & \text{otherwise} \end{cases} \text{ and } \boldsymbol{d}_1^{(h)} = \begin{cases} \boldsymbol{d}_1 & \text{if } h = T \\ \boldsymbol{V}[h+1] \boldsymbol{d}_1^{(h+1)} & \text{otherwise.} \end{cases} \quad (17)$$

If the matrices $\boldsymbol{U}[h]$ and $\boldsymbol{V}[h]$ are all available, the parallel computation of the vectors corresponds to a parallel prefix computation [19] which can be easily realized on shared memory systems. Knowing $\boldsymbol{\pi}^{(h)}$ and $\boldsymbol{d}_1^{(h)}$ thread h can compute backward and forward vectors with the indices $k = (h-1)L + 1, \ldots, hL$ using

$$\boldsymbol{ff}_{(D_0,D_1)}^{(k)} = \boldsymbol{\pi}^{(h-1)} \boldsymbol{F}[(h-1)L + 1, k] \text{ and } \boldsymbol{bb}_{(D_0,D_1)}^{(k)} = \boldsymbol{B}[k, hL] \boldsymbol{d}_1^{(h)}. \quad (18)$$

Vectors $\boldsymbol{f}_{(D_0,D_1),t}^{(k)}$ and $\boldsymbol{b}_{(D_0,D_1),t}^{(k)}$ can then be computed from $\boldsymbol{ff}_{(D_0,D_1)}^{(k)}$ and $\boldsymbol{bb}_{(D_0,D_1)}^{(k)}$ using (10).

1: compute $\boldsymbol{U}[h]$ and $\boldsymbol{V}[h]$ from (16);
2: compute $\boldsymbol{\pi}^{(h)}$ and $\boldsymbol{d}_1^{(h)}$ using a parallel prefix algorithm;
3: compute $\boldsymbol{bb}_{(D_0,D_1),t_l}^{(l)}$ and $\boldsymbol{b}_{(D_0,D_1),t_l}^{(l)}$ for $l = hL, \ldots, (h-1)L + 1$ starting from $\boldsymbol{d}_1^{(h)}$;
4: synchronize all threads;
5: compute $\boldsymbol{ff}_{(D_0,D_1),t_l}^{(l)}, \boldsymbol{f}_{(D_0,D_1),t_l}^{(l)}$ and $m_{ij}^l = \boldsymbol{f}_{(D_0,D_1),t_l}^{(l)} \boldsymbol{D}_1(i,j) \boldsymbol{b}_{(D_0,D_1),t_{l+1}}^{(l+1)}$ for $l = (h-1)L + 1, \ldots, hL$ starting from $\boldsymbol{\pi}^{(h)}$;
6: compute $\boldsymbol{M}^{(h)}(i,j) = \sum_{l=(h-1)L+1}^{hL} m_{ij}^l$ $(i,j = 1, \ldots, N)$ and accumulate $\boldsymbol{M} = \sum_{h=1}^{T} \boldsymbol{M}^{(h)} / (\boldsymbol{\pi} \boldsymbol{b}_{(D_0,D_1),t_1}^{(1)})$ in thread 1;

Algorithm 1: Computation of the forward and backward vectors for thread h

---

Each thread h $(\in \{1, \ldots, T\})$ runs the program shown in Algorithm 1. The threads run in parallel and synchronize implicitly after step 2 by performing the parallel prefix operation and explicitly in step 4. After step 6, matrix $\boldsymbol{M}$ contains $E_{(D_0,D_1),T}[M_{ij}] = \boldsymbol{M}(i,j)$.

Observe that vectors $\boldsymbol{b}_{(D_0,D_1),t_l}^{(l)}$ are computed in step 3 and are used in the steps 5 and 6 such that these vectors have to be stored whereas vectors $\boldsymbol{f}_{(D_0,D_1),t_l}^{(l)}$ are only needed to compute m_{ij}^l and $\boldsymbol{f}_{(D_0,D_1),t_l}^{(l+1)}$, afterwards they may be deleted. Vectors $\boldsymbol{bb}_{(D_0,D_1),t_l}^{(l)}$ and $\boldsymbol{ff}_{(D_0,D_1),t_l}^{(l)}$ are stored for the computation of the flow matrices, if the standard approach for computing flow matrices is applied (see next paragraph).

Matrices $\boldsymbol{F}[l]$ and $\boldsymbol{B}[l]$ are used for the computation of the matrices $\boldsymbol{U}[h]$ and $\boldsymbol{V}[h]$ in step 1 of the algorithm and for the computation of the vectors $\boldsymbol{b}_{(\boldsymbol{D}_0,\boldsymbol{D}_1),t_l}^{(l)}$ and $\boldsymbol{f}_{(\boldsymbol{D}_0,\boldsymbol{D}_1),t_l}^{(l)}$ in the steps 3 and 5. The matrices can be either stored requiring additional memory or recomputed requiring additional time. We consider the following three variants of the parallel algorithm:

PAREM-MAP: matrices $\boldsymbol{F}[l]$ and $\boldsymbol{B}[l]$ are recomputed. Thus, only the memory consumption of $\boldsymbol{b}_{(\boldsymbol{D}_0,\boldsymbol{D}_1),t_l}^{(l)}$, $\boldsymbol{bb}_{(\boldsymbol{D}_0,\boldsymbol{D}_1),t_l}^{(l)}$, $\boldsymbol{ff}_{(\boldsymbol{D}_0,\boldsymbol{D}_1),t_l}^{(l)}$ and $\boldsymbol{F}_{(\boldsymbol{D}_0,\boldsymbol{D}_1),t_l}^{(l)}$ depend on M and N whereas the memory consumption of the other vectors (e.g. $\boldsymbol{\pi}^{(h)}$ and $\boldsymbol{d}_1^{(h)}$) and matrices (e.g. $\boldsymbol{U}[h]$ and $\boldsymbol{V}[h]$) depend on T and N.

PAREM-MAP_D: matrix exponentials $e^{t_l \boldsymbol{D}_0}$ are stored and can be used to compute $\boldsymbol{F}[l]$ and $\boldsymbol{B}[l]$ using matrix multiplication (additional memory requirements of $M \cdot N^2$ double values over all threads).

PAREM-MAP_D2: matrices $\boldsymbol{F}[l]$ and $\boldsymbol{B}[l]$ are stored (additional memory requirements of $2M \cdot N^2$ double values over all threads).

4.2   Computation of the Flow Matrices

If flow matrices are computed with (9) and (11), then vectors $\boldsymbol{ff}_{(\boldsymbol{D}_0,\boldsymbol{D}_1)}^{(k)}$ and $\boldsymbol{bb}_{(\boldsymbol{D}_0,\boldsymbol{D}_1)}^{(k)}$ are available from the previous computation of the forward and backwards vectors. Vectors $\boldsymbol{v}^{(l)}[k]$ and $\boldsymbol{w}^{(l)}[k]$ are usually recomputed although they have already been computed for the vectors $\boldsymbol{ff}_{(\boldsymbol{D}_0,\boldsymbol{D}_1)}^{(k)}$ and $\boldsymbol{bb}_{(\boldsymbol{D}_0,\boldsymbol{D}_1)}^{(k)}$ because the complete storage of these vectors exhausts available memory capacity for longer traces. This, of course, also holds for the sequential implementation of the algorithm.

1: compute $\boldsymbol{F}_{(\boldsymbol{D}_0,\boldsymbol{D}_1),t_l}^{(l)}$ and let $n_{ij}^l = \boldsymbol{F}_{(\boldsymbol{D}_0,\boldsymbol{D}_1),t_l}^{(l)}(i,j)$ for $i,j = 1,\ldots,N$;
2: compute $\boldsymbol{N}^{(h)}(i,j) = \sum_{l=(h-1)L+1}^{hL} n_{ij}^l$ $(i,j = 1,\ldots,N)$ and accumulate $\boldsymbol{N} = \sum_{h=1}^{T} \boldsymbol{N}^{(h)}/(\boldsymbol{\pi}\boldsymbol{b}_{(\boldsymbol{D}_0,\boldsymbol{D}_1),t_1}^{(1)})$ in thread 1;

Algorithm 2: Computation of the flow matrices for thread h

Algorithm 2 shows the algorithm that is performed on any thread to obtain flow matrices and the expected values resulting from the flow matrices. Flow matrices can be computed in any order for the threads, no matter whether (11) or (12) is used for their computation. However, if (11) is used, $2MN$ double values are required to store the vectors $\boldsymbol{ff}_{(\boldsymbol{D}_0,\boldsymbol{D}_1)}^{(k)}$ and $\boldsymbol{bb}_{(\boldsymbol{D}_0,\boldsymbol{D}_1)}^{(k)}$. This is not necessary if (12) is used. The algorithm computes a matrix $\boldsymbol{N}$ that contains in position $\boldsymbol{N}(i,j)$ the expectation $E_{(\boldsymbol{D}_0,\boldsymbol{D}_1),T}[N_{ij}]$ if $i \neq j$. For $i = j$ we have $E_{(\boldsymbol{D}_0,\boldsymbol{D}_1),T}[Z_i] = \boldsymbol{N}(i,i)$.

4.3   The Complete Algorithm

1: initialize $(D_0^{(0)}, D_1^{(0)})$ randomly and set $r = 0$;
2: **repeat**
3:     **parallel for** $h = 1 \rightarrow T$ **do**
4:         perform Algorithm 1 for h ;
5:     **end parallel for**
6:     **parallel for** $h = 1 \rightarrow T$ **do**
7:         perform Algorithm 2 for h ;
8:     **end parallel for**
9:     compute sequentially new matrices $D_0^{(r+1)}, D_1^{(r+1)}$ using (8) and set $r := r+1$;
10: **until** $\|D_0^{(r)} - D_0^{(r-1)}\| + \|D_1^{(r)} - D_1^{(r-1)}\| \leq \epsilon$
11: **return** $(D_0^{(r)}, D_1^{(r)})$;

Algorithm 3: Parallel EM Algorithm for MAPs using T threads.

Algorithm 3 is the overall parallel algorithm. It is, of course, also possible to compute the new matrices $D_0^{(r+1)}$, $D_1^{(r+1)}$ in parallel but the size of the MAPs is usually too small to obtain any gain from a parallel computation.

5   Examples

The following experiments have been performed on workstations with Intel Xeon Platinum 8160 CPUs with 24 physical cores (48 logical) running at 2.10 GHz and 512 GB RAM. Programs are written in C++ using OpenMP and are compiled with the GCC version 6.3.0.

As examples we use two old but often used benchmark traces from the internet traffic archive [1]. The trace BC-pAug89 with $1,000,000$ entries and the trace LBL-TCP3 with around $1,800,000$ entries.

5.1   Results for the Trace BC-pAug89

MAP of Order 4. We start with the trace BC-pAug89 and fit the parameters of a MAP of order 4. The sequential EM-algorithm from the tool ProFiDo [4], which is the basic implementation from where the parallel algorithm has been derived, requires 11,230 s and 264 MB of memory. The resulting MAP has a log-likelihood value of $-818,063$ which is achieved after 239 iterations.

Results for the different variants of the parallel EM algorithm are shown in Table 1. All parallel variants require 239 iterations to compute a MAP with the same likelihood as the sequential algorithm. This shows that the parallel implementation of the algorithm works correctly. The results of the runtime of the parallel algorithms show a significant speedup. Thus, using 48 rather than 2 threads in algorithm PAREM-MAP reduces the runtime from 27,722 to 1,621 s

Table 1. Time in seconds and memory requirements in MB for the different variants of the parallel EM algorithm applied to the trace BC-pAug89 to fit the parameters of a MAP of dimension 4. Sequential algorithm: 11,230 s and 264 MB of memory.

Threads	PAREM-MAP		PAREM-MAP_D		PAREM-MAP_D2	
	Time	Memory	Time	Memory	Time	Memory
2	27,722	212	22,973	344	22,839	608
4	14,336	212	11,818	344	11,755	608
8	7,539	212	6,253	344	6,424	608
16	3,854	213	3,202	345	3,169	609
24	2,667	213	2,197	345	2,174	609
32	2,130	213	1,759	345	1,726	609
48	1,621	214	1,339	346	1,331	610

which corresponds to a speedup of 17.1 using 24 times as many threads. Results for the other parallel variants are similar. However, this is obviously not the right benchmark because we have to compare the results with the sequential implementation of the algorithm. Since the EM algorithm contains some sequential parts, we cannot expect to obtain such high speedups. To beat the runtime of the sequential algorithm 8 threads are required. With 48 threads we obtain a speedup of 6.92 with PAREM-MAP and of 8.39 with PAREM-MAP_D compared to the sequential algorithm. The use of PAREM-MAP_D2 is not really recommended because it is not faster than PAREM-MAP_D but requires more memory. The basic parallel variant requires slightly less memory than the sequential implementation. The reason seems to be that some vectors can be released by the threads earlier, than in the sequential implementation.

MAP of Order 8. In a second series of experiments a MAP of order 8 is fitted to the trace. For this MAP the sequential algorithm took too long. Thus, only the parallel variants are applied. Results are shown in Table 2. All parallel algorithms require 480 iterations to compute a MAP that reaches a log-likelihood of $-768,958$ which is an increase compared to the MAP with 4 states. The speedups going from 16 to 48 threads equal 2.42, 2.65 and 2.43 for the algorithm PAREM-MAP, PAREM-MAP_D and PAREM-MAP_D2, respectively. Again it can be seen that the parallel algorithm scales sufficiently well.

Table 2. Time in seconds and memory requirements in MB for the different variants of the parallel EM algorithm applied to the trace BC-pAug89 to fit the parameters of a MAP of dimension 8.

Threads	PAREM-MAP		PAREM-MAP_D		PAREM-MAP_D2	
	Time	Memory	Time	Memory	Time	Memory
16	41,981	664	39,851	1,180	35,931	2,212
48	17,292	670	14,993	1,186	14,768	2,218

5.2   Results for the Trace LBL-TCP3

Now we consider the trace LBL-TCP3 and fit again the parameters of a MAP of order 4. The sequential algorithm requires 320 iterations in 34,961 s and 473 MB memory. The resulting MAP has a log-likelihood of $-1.62243e + 6$.

Table 3. Time in seconds and memory requirements in MB for the different variants of the parallel EM algorithm applied to the trace LBL-TCP3 to fit the parameters of a MAP of dimension 4. Sequential algorithm: 34,961 s and 473 MB memory.

Threads	PAREM-MAP		PAREM-MAP_D		PAREM-MAP_D2	
	Time	Memory	Time	Memory	Time	Memory
2	91,847	380	77,613	616	80,203	1,088
4	46,976	380	39,659	616	39,945	1,088
8	24,705	380	20,908	616	20,702	1,089
16	12,662	380	10,680	616	11,561	1,089
24	8,650	380	7,253	617	7,285	1,089
32	6,915	380	5,848	617	5,820	1,089
48	5,280	381	4,469	617	4,450	1,090

Results for the trace LBL-TCP3 confirm the previous results. The parallel algorithm also requires 320 iterations to obtain the same likelihood as the sequential algorithm. Results are summarized in Table 3. Again the parallel algorithm requires 8 threads to beat the sequential algorithm. However, with 48 threads we obtain a speedup between 6.62 and 7.85 over the sequential algorithm which is acceptable. The parallel algorithms scale well because we obtain a speedup of about 17.5 when going from 2 to 48 threads. We also observe that PAREM-MAP requires less memory than the sequential algorithm.

5.3   Comparison with the Parallel EM Algorithm from [6]

We finally present a comparison with the parallel EM algorithm from [6]. A C++ implementation of the algorithm using CUDA for parallelization on the GPU is available in github [2]. We run the algorithm on a computing node with Intel Xeon E5-2640 v4 CPU and two NVIDIA Tesla K40m GPUs with 2880 cores and 12 GB RAM. We configured the system to use all cores for the algorithm.

It is, of course, problematic to compare two different algorithms on completely different hardware using different model structures. However, a comparison will give a first hint of the advantages of using GPUs and it will show some differences of the MAP structures.

The first aspect which came up was the different data format. Our algorithm uses double precision to store vectors and matrices, whereas the implementation of [2] uses only single precision. This is, of course, a tribute to the use of GPUs.

The number of FLOPs in single precision is three times the number of FLOPs in double precision and memory consumption might become a problem too. This had a concrete effect on our example because we were not able to compute MAPs from the complete traces, the likelihood values became 0 in between. Thus, we decided to compare the algorithms on the first 10,000 elements of each trace which implies that the GPU memory is sufficient for the data structures and we can expect very fast computations whereas a longer trace requires time consuming on- and off-loading of data.

Table 4. Log-likelihood values achieved by the different methods for the two traces.

Method/Structure	BC-pAug89	LBL-TCP-3
PAREM-MAP	−6605.22	−10470.80
3-1	−7475.09	−11169.00
2-2	−7223.30	−11358.77
2-1-1	−6497.92	−10563.29
1-1-1-1	−7011.23	−10469.73

In [6] different variants of the parallel algorithm are introduced. In all variants the basic hyper-Erlang structure of matrix D_0 has to be predefined. However, usually it is not known which structure results in the best fitting and the algorithms test all or a subset of the possible structures. For a MAP of order 4 only four different possibilities exist (the structures 3-1, 2-2, 2-1-1 and 1-1-1-1) to distribute the states among the phases. Table 4 includes the log-likelihood values that are achieved for the different configurations and the first 10,000 entries of the traces. It can be seen that the values of the best MAP of type CHMM, achieved with 2-1-1 (BC-pAug89) and 1-1-1-1 (LBL-TCP-3), has a slightly better likelihood than the general MAP from our approach. Thus, we do not profit from the more general structure, at least not for this data.

The Tables 5, 6 and 7 contain the results for the trace BC-pAug89. The algorithm from [6] is analyzed in the available five different parallel version (P-1, P-2, P-2-D, P-3, P-3-D) on the above introduced GPU and it is run sequentially on the CPU. For comparison the overall time has to be taken because all variants have to be checked to obtain the best likelihood. It can be seen that the sequential variant of the algorithm from [6] is much faster than our parallel algorithm running on 16 threads. Even if the times are not directly comparable because the hardware differs and single instead of double precision is used, the specific structure of CHMMs allows a more efficient realization at least as long the number of variants of the hyper-Erlang structure is not too large. For $N = 8$ the number of variants grows to 20 which may reduce the difference between both algorithms. Another aspect is that the computation of the flow matrix in our algorithm can be made more efficient as already outlined above. The parallel variants of the algorithm from [6] are all extremely fast since they exploit the

Table 5. Time (in seconds) and memory requirements (in MB) for the different versions of PAREM-MAP applied to the first 10,000 elements of the trace BC-pAug89.

Threads	PAREM-MAP		PAREM-MAP_D		PAREM-MAP_D2	
	Time	Memory	Time	Memory	Time	Memory
16	55.21	2.446	44.90	3.763	44.25	6.399
48	33.29	3.034	23.50	4.348	24.55	6.975

Table 6. Runtimes (in seconds) for different versions of the algorithm from [6] applied to the first 10,000 elements of the trace BC-pAug89.

Structure	Sequential	P-1	P-2	P-2-D	P-3	P-3-D
3-1	0.830	0.310	0.230	0.220	0.160	0.150
2-2	0.110	0.040	0.030	0.040	0.030	0.020
2-1-1	0.340	0.300	0.140	0.140	0.070	0.070
1-1-1-1	3.700	0.010	0.000	0.010	0.000	0.010
Overall	4.980	0.660	0.400	0.410	0.260	0.250

Table 7. Memory requirements (in MB) for different versions of the algorithm from [6] applied to the first 10,000 elements of the trace BC-pAug89.

Structure	Sequential	P-1	P-2	P-2-D	P-3	P-3-D
3-1	0.343	0.782	0.553	0.630	0.668	0.744
2-2	0.343	0.782	0.553	0.630	0.668	0.744
2-1-1	0.458	2.519	1.145	1.260	0.992	1.107
1-1-1-1	0.572	6.736	2.157	2.309	1.393	1.546

large level of parallelism available on the GPU. This shows that if it is possible to implement the algorithm in a numerical stable way on a GPU than this implementation cannot be beaten, at least as long as sufficient memory is available on the GPU. Memorywise is the algorithm PAREM-MAP competitive to the algorithm from [6], in particular if one takes into account that double instead of single precision is used.

The Tables 8 and 9 include the results for the second trace, LBL-TCP3. The results confirm the results from trace BC-pAug89.

Table 8. Time (in seconds) and memory requirements (in MB) for the different versions of PAREM-MAP applied to the first 10,000 elements of the trace LBL-TCP3.

Threads	PAREM-MAP		PAREM-MAP_D		PAREM-MAP_D2	
	Time	Memory	Time	Memory	Time	Memory
16	121.36	2.471	102.71	3.789	102.08	6.425
48	58.77	3.106	44.16	4.420	44.48	7.047

Table 9. Runtimes (in seconds) for different versions of the algorithm from [6] applied to the first 10,000 elements of the trace LBL-TCP3.

Structure	Sequential	P-1	P-2	P-2-D	P-3	P-3-D
3-1	0.130	0.030	0.020	0.030	0.020	0.020
2-2	0.130	0.050	0.040	0.030	0.030	0.030
2-1-1	0.370	0.270	0.130	0.130	0.070	0.060
1-1-1-1	2.060	0.030	0.010	0.010	0.000	0.000
Overall	2.690	0.380	0.200	0.200	0.120	0.110

6   Conclusion

In this paper we present a parallel implementation of the EM algorithm for MAPs of a general structure for multicore systems with shared memory which are the common architecture nowadays. Examples show that the algorithm scales sufficiently well such that a large number of cores can be utilized. The results also indicate that the implementation is numerically stable.

However, the presented examples that use realistic network traces with a large number of elements also show that MAP fitting is cumbersome and requires a huge effort in time and memory. In contrast to EM algorithms for phase type distributions which are available in very efficient variants, the parameter fitting for MAPs is much more challenging because the sequence of arrivals defines the correlation and needs to be considered in detail. This introduces an inherently sequential part in any fitting algorithm. In so far the results presented in the paper are satisfactory. However, they are definitely not enough to apply the method in practice to large traces.

To reduce the speed and also the memory requirements of the algorithm several possibilities exist. A first and quite natural step would be to go from a multicore processor to a GPU, as done in [6]. All computations are fairly regular such that we can expect a significant speedup using the much higher computing power of a GPU. However, in this case numerical stability and the limited memory of GPUs could become a problem. We plan to extend the implementation in this direction to test whether this is a useful extension.

There are other possibilities to improve the algorithm. A first step is to compute the flow matrix from the embedded phase type distribution which reduces memory requirements and possibly also the runtime slightly. Another possibility is to use trace aggregation that allows one to drastically reduce the number of time consuming computations of matrix exponentials. This has shown to be a good way to speed up computations without reducing the likelihood value of the resulting MAP [18]. Trace aggregation can also be used in the parallel implementation which will be done in future research.

References

1. The internet traffic archive. http://ita.ee.lbl.gov/
2. The parmap software. https://github.com/minbraz/parmap/
3. Asmussen, S., Nerman, O., Olsson, M.: Fitting phase-type distributions via the EM-algorithm. Scand. J. Stat. **23**(4), 419–441 (1996)
4. Bause, F., Buchholz, P., Kriege, J.: ProFiDo - the processes fitting toolkit Dortmund. In: QEST 2010, Seventh International Conference on the Quantitative Evaluation of Systems, Williamsburg, Virginia, USA, 15–18 September 2010, pp. 87–96. IEEE Computer Society (2010)
5. Blume, A.: Parallelisierung von Methoden zur Parameteranpassung von MAPs. Master's thesis, Fakultät für Informatik, TU Dortmund (2019)
6. Brazenas, M., Horvath, G., Telek, M.: Parallel algorithms for fitting Markov arrival processes. Perform. Eval. **123–124**, 50–67 (2018)
7. Breuer, L.: An EM algorithm for batch Markovian arrival processes and its comparison to a simpler estimation procedure. Ann. OR **112**(1–4), 123–138 (2002)
8. Buchholz, P.: An EM-algorithm for MAP fitting from real traffic data. In: Kemper, P., Sanders, W.H. (eds.) TOOLS 2003. LNCS, vol. 2794, pp. 218–236. Springer, Heidelberg (2003). https://doi.org/10.1007/978-3-540-45232-4_14
9. Buchholz, P., Kemper, P., Kriege, J.: Multi-class Markovian arrival processes and their parameter fitting. Perform. Eval. **67**(11), 1092–1106 (2010)
10. Buchholz, P., Kriege, J., Felko, I.: Input Modeling with Phase-Type Distributions and Markov Models - Theory and Applications. Springer, New York (2014)
11. Casale, G.: Building accurate workload models using Markovian arrival processes. In: Merchant, A., Keeton, K., Rubenstein, D. (eds.) Proceedings of the 2011 ACM SIGMETRICS International Conference on Measurement and Modeling of Computer Systems SIGMETRICS 2011, San Jose, CA, USA, 07–11 June 2011 (Co-located with FCRC 2011), pp. 357–358. ACM (2011)
12. Casale, G., Zhang, E.Z., Smirni, E.: KPC-toolbox: simple yet effective trace fitting using Markovian arrival processes. In: QEST, pp. 83–92 (2008)
13. Fox, B.L., Glynn, P.W.: Computing poisson probabilities. Commun. ACM **31**(4), 440–445 (1988)
14. Horváth, G., Okamura, H.: A fast EM algorithm for fitting marked markovian arrival processes with a new special structure. In: Balsamo, M.S., Knottenbelt, W.J., Marin, A. (eds.) EPEW 2013. LNCS, vol. 8168, pp. 119–133. Springer, Heidelberg (2013). https://doi.org/10.1007/978-3-642-40725-3_10
15. Horváth, G., Telek, M., Buchholz, P.: A MAP fitting approach with independent approximation of the inter-arrival time distribution and the lag-correlation. In: QEST, pp. 124–133. IEEE CS Press (2005)
16. Klemm, A., Lindemann, C., Lohmann, M.: Modeling IP traffic using the batch Markovian arrival process. Perform. Eval. **54**(2), 149–173 (2003)
17. Kriege, J., Buchholz, P.: An empirical comparison of MAP fitting algorithms. In: Müller-Clostermann, B., Echtle, K., Rathgeb, E.P. (eds.) MMB&DFT 2010. LNCS, vol. 5987, pp. 259–273. Springer, Heidelberg (2010). https://doi.org/10.1007/978-3-642-12104-3_20
18. Kriege, J., Buchholz, P.: PH and MAP fitting with aggregated traffic traces. In: Fischbach, K., Krieger, U.R. (eds.) MMB&DFT 2014. LNCS, vol. 8376, pp. 1–15. Springer, Cham (2014). https://doi.org/10.1007/978-3-319-05359-2_1
19. Ladner, R.E., Fischer, M.J.: Parallel prefix computation. J. ACM **27**(4), 831–838 (1980)

20. Lucantoni, D.M., Meier-Hellstern, K.S., Neuts, M.F.: A single-server queue with server vacations and a class of non-renewal arrival processes. Adv. Appl. Probab. **22**(3), 676–705 (1990)
21. Neuts, M.F.: A versatile Markovian point process. J. Appl. Probab. **16**, 764–779 (1979)
22. Okamura, H., Dohi, T.: Faster maximum likelihood estimation algorithms for Markovian arrival processes. In: 2009 Sixth International Conference on the Quantitative Evaluation of Systems, pp. 73–82, September 2009
23. Okamura, H., Dohi, T., Trivedi, K.S.: A refined EM algorithm for PH distributions. Perform. Eval. **68**(10), 938–954 (2011)
24. Panchenko, A., Thümmler, A.: Efficient phase-type fitting with aggregated traffic traces. Perform. Eval. **64**(7–8), 629–645 (2007)
25. Stewart, W.J.: Introduction to the Numerical Solution of Markov Chains. Princeton University Press, Princeton (1994)
26. Thümmler, A., Buchholz, P., Telek, M.: A novel approach for phase-type fitting with the EM algorithm. IEEE Trans. Dep. Sec. Comput. **3**(3), 245–258 (2006)
27. Wu, C., Yang, C., Zhao, H., Zhu, J.: On the convergence of the EM algorithm: a data-adaptive analysis (2016)

It Sometimes Works: A Lifting Algorithm for Repair of Stochastic Process Algebra Models

Amin Soltanieh and Markus Siegle[✉]

Universität der Bundeswehr München, 85577 Neubiberg, Germany
{amin.soltanieh,markus.siegle}@unibw.de

Abstract. The paper presents an algorithm for lifting rate modification information from a flat Markovian model to its high-level modular description, specified with the help of a Stochastic Process Algebra (SPA). During the lifting, a specific set of transition rates in the model components is changed, and – if necessary – also the interaction between the components will be modified, in order to realise context-dependent rate modifications. It is shown that the proposed algorithm cannot always find a suitable lifting, but if such a lifting exists, the algorithm is guaranteed to find one. Furthermore, the paper shows that for a certain class of SPA product form models, the lifting algorithm will always find a solution.

Keywords: Markov chains · Stochastic Process Algebra · Probabilistic model checking · Compositional model repair · Product form

1 Introduction

For the specification of performance and dependability models, Stochastic Process Algebra (SPA) such as PEPA [1], EMPA [2] or CASPA [3], are often used, since they allow users to specify complex models in a modular and hierarchical way. Probabilistic model checking, implemented in tools such as PRISM [4] and STORM [5], is a powerful technique to reason about the properties of a system which is modelled, for example, with the help of an SPA. Although those specifications are compositional, model checking usually takes place at the level of the flat state space, i.e. at the level of a monolithic Continuous-Time Markov Chain (CTMC), labelled with atomic state properties. (In this paper, we focus on fully probabilistic systems, as opposed to, say, Markov Decision Processes.)

In case a model does not satisfy a given requirement, the user may want to modify it, such that the modified model will indeed satisfy the requirement. This process is referred to as model repair. While different strategies exist for carrying out model repair (see e.g. [6–8]), we focus on model repair by rate modification. This means that during model repair, the structure of the model is preserved, only some of the transition rates of the Markov chain are modified in such a

© Springer Nature Switzerland AG 2020
H. Hermanns (Ed.): MMB 2020, LNCS 12040, pp. 190–207, 2020.
https://doi.org/10.1007/978-3-030-43024-5_12

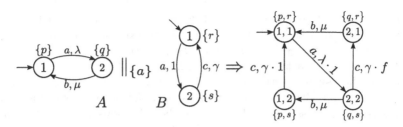

Fig. 1. Processes A and B and the resultant flat model

way that the probabilities of the satisfying paths will be affected in a positive way. Earlier work on model repair by rate modification has been published in [9] for time-unbounded CSL [10] and asCSL [11] requirements, and in [12] for CSL Until requirements with upper or lower time bound. Those works addressed the problem of model repair at the level of a flat state-labelled Markov chain.

In this paper, we do not deal with the question of how to modify the transition rates of a Markovian model in order to satisfy a given requirement. We rather assume that the rate modification factors for the low-level flat Markov chain are already given. The question we address is the following: How, and under which conditions, is it possible to lift the information about rate modification from the level of the flat transition system to the level of the modular model specification? This is an important issue, since users do not want to work at the level of the flat Markov chain, they do not even want to see that low-level model. Users rather want to work with their high-level model specification, i.e. they wish to know how to change their model specification, in order to get a particular requirement satisfied. We now illustrate this problem by a motivating example.

In Fig. 1, inspired by [13], two processes A and B which are synchronised over action a, and also the resultant flat model are drawn. Each transition is specified by a tuple of the form (a, λ), where a is the action name and λ is the transition rate, and each state is labelled by atomic propositions (for the moment, the atomic propositions can be ignored). Now assume that – for the purpose of model repair – the rate of only one of the two c-transitions in the combined transition system should be multiplied by the factor f (as highlighted in Fig. 1), while the transition rate of the other c-transition should remain unchanged (thus the factor 1 in the figure). But both of these transitions stem from the same c-transition in component B. Therefore, a local repair, changing only the rate of the c-transition in component B, is not possible, since this would affect both c-transitions in the flat model. Whether or not to apply factor f depends on the context: On the c-transition originating in state $(2, 2)$ the factor should be applied, but in the one originating in $(1, 2)$ it should not.

This example shows that model repair at the level of the flat transition system, in general, cannot be lifted in a straight-forward way to the high-level model. Having realised this fact, the questions to be answered by this paper are: Is there a technique to make such a lifting possible? Is it always possible to find a suitable lifting? How does the algorithm work that decides whether lifting is possible, and how does such an algorithm construct a valid lifting?

This paper develops an algorithm that lifts rate modification information from the level of the flat Markov chain to the level of the compositional model specification. It is assumed that the model is specified with the help of a Markovian SPA, where, in particular, processes interact via action synchronisation. It turns out that such a lifting is not always possible, but our algorithm will detect this and stop with a suitable error message. Then, of course, the question arises whether it is possible to characterise the situations where the algorithm will be successful by suitable conditions. While we are not able to give necessary and sufficient conditions that cover all possible cases, Sect. 4 of the paper shows that for the class of SPA product-form models regarded in [14], the algorithm is always guaranteed to find a lifting.

This paper is structured as follows: Sect. 2 provides some background information on Stochastic Process Algebra and on model repair by rate modification. Section 3, the main section of the paper, contains the description of the new lifting algorithm. It starts by taking up the example from the introduction, before the actual algorithm is presented and discussed. Section 3 also contains a worked example where all the different cases occuring during the course of the algorithm are illustrated. In Sect. 4, we focus on a class of product form models, previously regarded in [14], for which, under some mild conditions, the lifting algorithm is always guaranteed to find a solution. Finally, Sect. 5 concludes the paper with a summary and a view into future extensions.

2   Modelling Framework and State of the Art

2.1   Stochastic Process Algebra (SPA)

We assume that the model to be analysed is specified with the help of a stochastic process algebra (SPA) such as PEPA [1], EMPA [2] or CASPA [3], where each transition is labelled by an action and a rate, the latter specifying an exponentially distributed delay. Complex models are constructed by parallel composition of components, which interact via action synchronisation. This yields an overall model with a modular or even hierarchical structure. The states of the overall model are tuples (i.e. vectors) of states of the constituent processes, and the semantic model is a Markovian (multi-)transition system [1].

For action synchronisation in SPA, different semantics have been discussed and compared in the past, concerning the rate of the synchronised transition (also called combined transition) as a function of the rates of the partner processes [15]. In this paper, we assume that the rate of a combined transition is calculated as the product of the rates of the transitions to be synchronised. Rate multiplication can be used, for instance, in such a way that during action synchronisation, one partner determines the basic rate and the other partner(s) are either passive (rate 1) or may contribute a factor (accelerating/decelerating) to the resulting rate. Technically, this is realised by rate factor multiplication. However, it is important to point out that the algorithm presented in Sect. 3 will also work for different synchronisation semantics, for instance if the combined rate is determined as the minimum of the two partner rates, or by consideration of the apparent rate of a given action type within the partner processes as in [1].

We do not go into the details of the syntax or semantics of stochastic process algebra. We only give the formal semantics (SOS rules) for parallel composition, since this is needed to understand the algorithm in Sect. 3:

$$\frac{P\xrightarrow{a,\lambda}P',Q\xrightarrow{a,\mu}Q'}{P\|_{\Sigma_s}Q\xrightarrow{a,op(\lambda,\mu)}P'\|_{\Sigma_s}Q'}\quad(a\in\Sigma_s)$$

$$\frac{P\xrightarrow{a,\lambda}P'}{P\|_{\Sigma_s}Q\xrightarrow{a,\lambda}P'\|_{\Sigma_s}Q}\quad(a\notin\Sigma_s)\qquad\frac{Q\xrightarrow{a,\mu}Q'}{P\|_{\Sigma_s}Q\xrightarrow{a,\mu}P\|_{\Sigma_s}Q'}\quad(a\notin\Sigma_s)$$

In these rules, P and Q are processes, $\|$ is the parallel composition operator, $\Sigma_s\subseteq Act$ is the set of synchronising actions, $a\in Act$ is an action, and λ,μ are transition rates. The first rule realises the actual synchronisation via action a, where the resulting rate is obtained by combining the two partner rates by the binary operator op (which, as already said, we simply replace by multiplication). The other two (fully symmetrical) rules represent a move of one partner process while the other one remains stable.

2.2 Model Repair by Rate Modification

The concept of model repair by rate modification has been developed in earlier works. In [9], the authors studied the model checking of action- and state-labelled CTMCs against requirements specified by the temporal logics CSL [10] and asCSL [11] (as CSL is an extension of CSL which allows one to describe complex path requirements, specified by regular expressions over action labels and state formulas). In particular, the paper [9] focused on time-unbounded CSL Until formulas and time-unbounded asCSL path requirements, to be checked on flat CTMC models. The central idea of the approach is as follows: If a given CSL requirement is violated, some specific transition rates in the model are changed deliberately, in order to affect the satisfaction probabilities in a positive way. For a violated CSL requirement, the model repair strategy of [9] consists of determining a particular subset of the CTMC's transitions whose rates should be reduced by a common factor. For violated asCSL requirements, the idea in [9] is similar, but the model repair algorithm is more complicated since it involves a product construction with a non-deterministic automaton representing the asCSL path formula.

In [12] similar approaches were developed, but for state-labelled CTMCs to be checked against CSL Until requirements with upper time bound. Again, the model repair strategy consists of determining rate reduction factors by which the transition rates between certain classes of states should be reduced. The theoretical background of perturbing the transition rates of a CTMC by a common factor, with applications to model repair, has been studied in [16].

While some previous work on model repair only considered rate reduction, in this work we allow rate modifications in both directions, i.e. the rate of a specific transition can be either reduced or increased. However, we do not allow reducing a rate to zero (thereby effectively deleting a transition in the CTMC), which guarantees that the graph of the CTMC is not changed by the repair.

Importantly, as already mentioned in the introduction, this paper does not concern itself with the question which rates of a given model should be modified, in order to satisfy the requirement at hand. It is assumed that the rate modification factors have already been determined by a model repair algorithm such as the ones mentioned above. But all mentioned previous work considered the problem of model repair at the level of a monolithic, flat model, which means that the rate modification factors are only known at the level of the flat model. However, when models are constructed from a modular or compositional model specification such as SPA, model repair should take place at the level of the high-level model, not at the level of the flat state space. This is the focus of the present paper: Answering the question if and how model repair information (in the form of transition rate modifications) can be lifted from the flat low-level model to the high-level model specification.

3   A Lifting Algorithm for Modular Model Repair

3.1   Motivating Examples

We return to the example from Sect. 1 and show how it can be fixed. In Fig. 1, we saw that local repair of just one component (component B) is not possible, since only one of the two c-transitions in the flat model should be changed. This means that there exists a context-dependency for the repair factor. We can implement this context-dependency by adding action c to the synchronisation set and inserting c-self-loops at the states of component A, as shown in Fig. 2. The such repaired components are now denoted A' and B'. The rates of those self-loops correspond to the desired modification factors. We can describe this approach mathematically by the following system of equations:

$$x_{11} \cdot y_{21} = \gamma \cdot 1$$
$$x_{22} \cdot y_{21} = \gamma \cdot f$$

where the x_{ii} are the rates of the self-loops in component A', and y_{21} is the rate of the c-transition in component B'. One solution to this system is $x_{11} = 1$, $x_{22} = f$ and $y_{21} = \gamma$, as depicted in Fig. 2.

These modifications obviously solve the model repair lifting problem for the example of Fig. 1. Unfortunately, such a solution is not always possible, as an extension of the same example shows (see Fig. 3). In this extended example, component A remains unchanged, but component B has been extended by a third state, as shown in Fig. 3. Now suppose that the two transitions $(2,2) \xrightarrow{c,\gamma} (2,1)$ and $(1,2) \xrightarrow{c,\gamma} (1,3)$ should both be multiplied each by factor f. Both of these transitions stem from component B, but again one can easily argue that a local repair, changing only component B, is not possible. Trying to solve the context-dependency by a similar approach as before will not work either for this example. The reason is that the context (the state of component A) is contradictory in the following sense: When component A is in state 1, only the

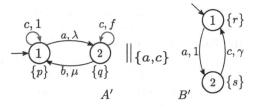

Fig. 2. Processes A' and B' with added self-loops and modified synchronising set

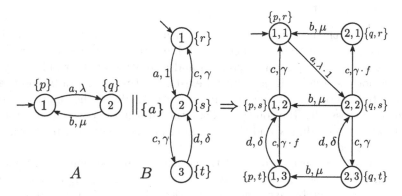

Fig. 3. Extended example

B-transition $2 \xrightarrow{c} 3$ should be modified, but not the B-transition $2 \xrightarrow{c} 1$, but when component A is in state 2, it is exactly the other way around! This cannot be controlled by c-self-loops on the states of component A. One can easily show this contradiction mathematically by the following system of nonlinear equations

$$x_{11} \cdot y_{21} = \gamma \cdot 1$$
$$x_{11} \cdot y_{23} = \gamma \cdot f$$
$$x_{22} \cdot y_{21} = \gamma \cdot f$$
$$x_{22} \cdot y_{23} = \gamma \cdot 1$$

where, as before, x_{ii} are the rates of the c-self-loops that would be added to states of component A, and y_{21} and y_{23} are the rates of the c-transitions in component B. For $f \neq 1$, this system of equations does not possess a solution.

3.2 Idea of the Algorithm

We present an algorithm which, for given rate multiplication factors, decides whether or not a lifting to the compositional model, by applying certain measures, is possible. If it is possible, the algorithm proposes a modification to the compositional high-level model, i.e. how exactly it should be changed. We now explain the general idea of the algorithm.

As its input, the algorithm takes a flat transition system whose states are n-tuples, each element characterising the current state of one of the n constituent processes. In order to keep the description simple, we assume for now that $n = 2$, but the algorithm can be extended to the case $n > 2$ in a rather straight-forward way. In addition to the flat transition system, the information about the rate modification factors is also given, i.e. it is known which transition rate of the flat model should be multiplied by which factor. The algorithm looks at the transitions whose rates are to be modified in a one by one fashion. A distinction is made, depending on whether the currently processed transition is a synchronising transition where several components are involved, or a local transition of only one single component.

Case (1): In case the currently processed transition is a synchronising transition, all transitions with the same action label are processed at once. For each of them, a nonlinear equation is created and a solution of the resulting system of equations is sought. If no solution exists, a lifting of the rate modification factors to the constituent components is not possible, so the algorithm terminates unsuccessfully. If a solution exists, the rates in the constituent processes are modified accordingly and the algorithm proceeds with the next transition to be modified.

Case (2): If the currently processed transition is a non-synchronising one, the algorithm first tries to fix its rate locally (i.e. by modifying only one of the components), thereby avoiding the creation of a (possibly large) system of equations. Such a local solution, however, is only possible if all modification factors of "parallel" transitions are identical, where "parallel" means that one component makes a specific move while the other component remains in any arbitrary fixed state. If a local solution is not possible, the modification factor of a non-synchronising transition depends on the context, i.e. the state of the other component. In this case, all transitions with the same action label are treated at once. The idea now is to change the transition from a non-synchronising transition to a synchronising one, thereby making it possible to control the modification factor depending on the context. For this reason, self-loops in the other component are added. In this case, a system of equations is created and solved. Again, it is possible that no solution exists, in which case a lifting is not possible.

3.3   Lifting Algorithm

In order to keep the notation simple, we present the algorithm, assuming that the states of the flat transition system are 2-tuples. If the states are n-tuples, the algorithm can be adapted canonically.

We first introduce the notation used in the algorithm: Let M_1 and M_2 be two Markovian transition systems and $\Sigma_s \subseteq Act$ a set of (synchronising) actions. The flat transition system of $M_1||_{\Sigma_s} M_2$ is given by the set of tuples

$$T \subseteq (S_1 \times S_2) \times Act \times \mathbb{R}^{>0} \times (S_1 \times S_2)$$

where the first two elements denote the source state tuple, the last two elements denote the target state tuple, and the two elements in the middle denote the action label and the rate. Let S denote the reachable subset of $S_1 \times S_2$. Consider a subset of transitions $T_{mod} \subseteq T$. The rate of each transition $t_i \in T_{mod}$ is to be modified by an individual multiplicative factor $factor(t_i) \in \mathbb{R}^{>0} \setminus \{1\}$. For convenience, for transitions which are not to be modified, i.e. transitions $t_i \in T \setminus T_{mod}$, we define the modification factor as $factor(t_i) = 1$. For a combined transition $t = ((s, u) \xrightarrow{c, \gamma} (s', u')) \in T$, we use the following notation:

$$source(t) := (s, u), \ source_1(t) := s, \ source_2(t) := u$$

$$target(t) := (s', u'), \ target_1(t) := s', \ target_2(t) := u'$$

$$action(t) = c, \ rate(t) = \gamma$$

If for a transition $t \in T_{mod}$ we write $t = ((s, u) \xrightarrow{c, \gamma \cdot f} (s', u'))$ then we mean that $rate(t) = \gamma$ and $factor(t) = f \neq 1$ (although strictly speaking the modification factor is not stored as part of T_{mod}). If we write the same for a transition $t \in T \setminus T_{mod}$, then $factor(t) = f = 1$.

Given the desired rate modification factors for the flat composed model, the following algorithm computes the modified rates for M_1 and M_2, if a solution exists. Apart from changing rates in M_1 and M_2, the algorithm may also insert some self-loops and add actions to the synchronisation set Σ_s, in order to control the context in which a previously non-synchronising action takes place, which means controlling its rate in a context-dependent way. In other words, the algorithm lifts a given model repair strategy from the flat model to the compositional model, if such a lifting is possible at all. If successful, the algorithm returns the modified processes M_1' and M_2', as well as the potentially augmented synchronisation set Σ_s'. We now present the algorithm in pseudocode, where the explanation of all essential steps is given by the comments.

1: **Algorithm** RepairLifting $(M_1, M_2, \Sigma_s, T, T_{mod}, factor)$
2: // T is the flat Markovian transition system of $M_1 \|_{\Sigma_s} M_2$.
3: // The algorithm lifts the repair information given in the form of
4: // rate modification factors $factor(t)$ for transitions $t \in T_{mod} \subseteq T$
5: // to the high-level components M_1 and M_2, if possible.
6: // The repaired system is returned as M_1', M_2' and Σ_s'.
7: $M_1' := M_1, \ M_2' := M_2, \ \Sigma_s' := \Sigma_s$ // initialisation
8: **while** $T_{mod} \neq \emptyset$ **do**

9:     choose $\hat{t} := ((\hat{s}, \hat{u}) \xrightarrow{c, \hat{\gamma} \cdot \hat{f}} (\hat{s}', \hat{u}'))$ from T_{mod}
10:    // $\hat{t}$ is the transition processed during one iteration of the while-loop
11:
12:    // Case (1):
13:    **if** $action(\hat{t}) =: c \in \Sigma_s$ **then**
14:        // a synchronising transition needs to be modified
15:        $T_c := \{t \in T \mid action(t) = c\}$ // all c-transitions considered at once
16:        $T_{mod} := T_{mod} \setminus T_c$ // remove considered transitions from T_{mod}

```
17:        for each t := ((s, u) --c,γ·f--> (s', u')) ∈ T_c do
18:            create an equation x_{ss'} · y_{uu'} = γ · f = rate(t) · factor(t)
19:            // or more general: create an equation op(x_{ss'}, y_{uu'}) = γ · f
20:            // where op is the operator determining the resulting rate (see Sec. 2.1)
21:        end for
22:        solve the system of nonlinear equations, i.e. find all x_{ss'} and y_{uu'}
23:        if no solution exists then
24:            return "impossible"
25:        else
26:            for each t := ((s, u) --c,γ·f--> (s', u')) ∈ T_c do
27:                in M'_1 set s --c,x_{ss'}--> s'
28:                in M'_2 set u --c,y_{uu'}--> u'
29:            end for
30:        end if
31:
32:    // Case (2):
33:    else if action(t̂) =: c ∉ Σ_s ∧ ŝ ≠ ŝ' then
34:        // a non-synchronising M_1-transition needs to be modified,
35:        // the algorithm first tries to do this locally in M_1
36:        // by considering all "parallel" transitions at once
37:        T_{c,ŝ,ŝ'} := {t ∈ T | action(t) = c ∧ source_1(t) = ŝ ∧ target_1(t) = ŝ'}
38:        if ∃f_{com} ∈ ℝ : ∀t ∈ T_{c,ŝ,ŝ'} : factor(t) = f_{com} then
39:            // there exists a common factor f_{com} for all transitions in T_{c,ŝ,ŝ'}
40:            in M'_1 set ŝ --c,γ_1·f_{com}--> ŝ' (where γ_1 is the current rate in M'_1)
41:            T_{mod} := T_{mod} \ T_{c,ŝ,ŝ'}
42:            for each t ∈ T_{c,ŝ,ŝ'} do
43:                factor(t) := 1
44:                // the modification factor of the fixed transitions is changed to 1,
45:                // which is important in case they are considered again
46:                // when dealing with another c-transition from T_{mod} later
47:            end for
48:        else
49:            // if the local fix in M_1 was not possible,
50:            // since non-synchronising action c can also occur in M_2,
51:            // the algorithm now tries to modify all c-transitions at once
52:            // by making c into a synchronising action.
53:            // but this only makes sense if there is no reachable combined state
54:            // from which c-transitions in both M_1 and M_2 are possible
55:            // (because if such a state existed, making c into a synchronising
56:            // action would generate spurious (i.e. wrong) transitions)
57:            if ∃(s, u) ∈ S : ∃t_1, t_2 ∈ T : (t_1 = ((s, u) --c,γ_1--> (s', u)) ∧ t_2 =
                ((s, u) --c,γ_2--> (s, u'))) then
58:                return "impossible"
59:            end if
```

```
60:        T_c := {t ∈ T | action(t) = c}
61:        T_mod := T_mod \ T_c
62:        for each t := ((s, u) --c,γ·f--> (s', u)) ∈ T_c do
63:            // an M_1-move
64:            create an equation x_ss' · y_uu = γ · f = rate(t) · factor(t)
65:        end for
66:        for each t := ((s, u) --c,γ·f--> (s, u')) ∈ T_c do
67:            // an M_2-move
68:            create an equation x_ss · y_uu' = γ · f = rate(t) · factor(t)
69:        end for
70:        solve the system of nonlinear equations, i.e. find all x_ss, x_ss', y_uu, y_uu'
71:        if no solution exists then
72:            return "impossible"
73:        else
74:            for each t := ((s, u) --c,γ·f--> (s', u)) ∈ T_c do
75:                in M'_1 set s --c,x_ss'--> s'
76:                in M'_2 add self-loop u --c,y_uu--> u
77:            end for
78:            for each t := ((s, u) --c,γ·f--> (s, u')) ∈ T_c do
79:                in M'_2 set u --c,y_uu'--> u'
80:                in M'_1 add self-loop s --c,x_ss--> s
81:            end for
82:            Σ'_s := Σ'_s ∪ {c} // add action c to the synchronisation set
83:        end if
84:    end if
85:
86:    // Case (2), symmetrical case:
87:    else if action(t̂) =: c ∉ Σ_s ∧ û ≠ û' then
88:        // an M_2-transition needs to be modified
89:        // this case is fully symmetrical to the previous case,
90:        // the code is analogous to lines 32-84
91:        ...
92:    end if
93: end while
94: return M'_1, M'_2, Σ'_s
```

3.4 Remarks on the Algorithm

We now comment on the way the algorithm works and give some insight into how it can be made to work efficiently:

– The flat transition system T is not modified by the algorithm. That means for $t \in T$: $rate(t)$ stays unmodified during the course of the algorithm. The algorithm assigns new rates (which are the solutions of the systems of equations) to some transitions of M'_1 and/or M'_2 and possibly adds actions to the set of synchronising actions $Σ'_s$.

– The algorithm cannot always find a solution, in which case it returns "impossible" (lines 24, 58 and 72). However, the algorithm can always decide whether or not a solution exists, and if it exists the algorithm will find it.
– It is possible that the same transition rate in M_i' changes twice in the course of the algorithm. This will occur if a non-synchronising transition is first changed locally and needs to be considered again later, when another transition with the same action label cannot be changed locally. This is the reason, why resetting the modification factor of already fixed transitions in line 42 is necessary.
– The algorithm is not a truly compositional algorithm, but only a lifting algorithm, which has the disadvantage that the low-level model needs to be constructed. Thus, practical use of the algorithm is limited in case state space explosion occurs.
– Various optimisations of the algorithm are possible. E.g. there are conditions which can be checked in order to decide a priori whether the system of equations in lines 21 or 69 possesses a solution. In some cases, it is also possible to split a large system of equations into several smaller systems, thus reducing the effort to solve the equations. Elaborating on the details of such optimisations would be beyond the scope of the present paper.
– It is natural to ask for necessary/sufficient conditions under which the algorithm will find a solution. These could be conditions concerning the composition structure and other characteristics of the overall model, but also conditions on the requirement whose violation during model checking caused the need for the model to be repaired (e.g., if the requirement only refers to state properties of only a single model component). Ideally, one should be able to check those conditions at the specification level. The goal is to identify special classes of models which can be repaired at the specification level without having to analyse the low-level model. One such candidate is the class of product form models discussed in Sect. 4.

3.5   Illustration of the Algorithm

In the following example we try to cover all possible cases which might occur during the course of the algorithm. Figure 4 shows two processes M_1 and M_2, synchronised over actions a and b, and also the resultant flat model. Assume that all rates are equal to 1, and so also the rates in the flat model are all 1.

Model Repair of Synchronising Transitions
Let us assume that we need to modify the rates of a-transitions where a is a synchronising action. According to the algorithm (Case (1)), we create an equation for each of the a-transitions.

In this example there are six a-transitions in the flat model. Table 1 shows those transitions and the system of nonlinear equations created according to lines 17–21 of the algorithm. The rate modification factors are $f_1, \ldots, f_6$, and Fig. 5 shows M_1' and M_2' with only a-transitions where $x_{ss'}$ and $y_{uu'}$ are the modified rates.

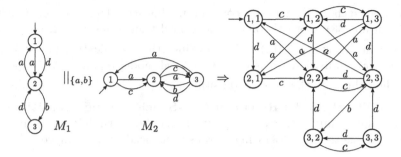

Fig. 4. Processes M_1 and M_2 and the resultant flat model

Table 1. a-transitions and the system of nonlinear equations.

$(1,1) \xrightarrow{a,1 \cdot f_1} (2,2) \Longrightarrow x_{12} \cdot y_{12} = f_1$

$(1,2) \xrightarrow{a,1 \cdot f_2} (2,3) \Longrightarrow x_{12} \cdot y_{23} = f_2$

$(1,3) \xrightarrow{a,1 \cdot f_3} (2,1) \Longrightarrow x_{12} \cdot y_{31} = f_3$

$(2,1) \xrightarrow{a,1 \cdot f_4} (1,2) \Longrightarrow x_{21} \cdot y_{12} = f_4$

$(2,2) \xrightarrow{a,1 \cdot f_5} (1,3) \Longrightarrow x_{21} \cdot y_{23} = f_5$

$(2,3) \xrightarrow{a,1 \cdot f_6} (1,1) \Longrightarrow x_{21} \cdot y_{31} = f_6$

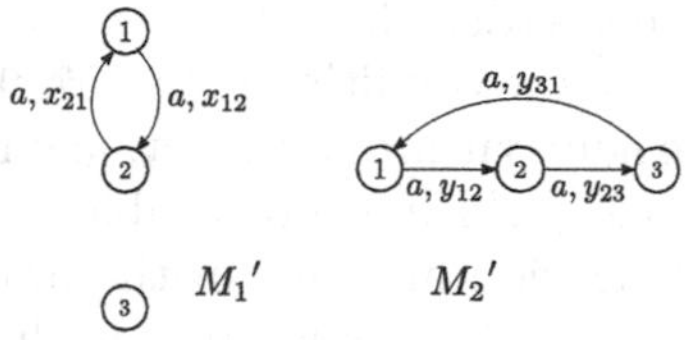

Fig. 5. Processes M_1' and M_2' with only a-transitions shown in Case (1).

The necessary condition for the system of equations in Table 1 to have a solution is $\frac{f_1}{f_4} = \frac{f_2}{f_5} = \frac{f_3}{f_6}$ (*). If this condition holds, one of the unknowns can be chosen freely, e.g. $x_{21} := 1$, and then the other unknowns are determined:

$$x_{12} = f_1/f_4$$
$$y_{12} = f_4/x_{21} = f_4$$
$$y_{23} = f_5/x_{21} = f_5$$
$$y_{31} = f_6/x_{21} = f_6$$

So, if the modification factors are such that condition (*) is satisfied, there exists a solution and lifting is possible.

Local Repair of Non-synchronising Transitions

Let us assume that we need to modify two of the d-transitions with common modification factor f:

$$(3,2) \xrightarrow{d,1 \cdot f} (2,2) \qquad (3,3) \xrightarrow{d,1 \cdot f} (2,3)$$

Following the algorithm, at first one of those d-transitions is picked from T_{mod}. Since action d is non-synchronising, the possibility of local model repair in one of the components should be tested. For that purpose, all other "parallel" d-transitions where M_1 moves from state 3 to state 2 (denoted by $T_{d,3,2}$) are investigated to check if there is a common modification factor for all transitions (algorithm line 38). Both the above mentioned transitions stem from the same transition in M_1 which is $(3) \xrightarrow{d,1} (2)$. Since the modification factor f is the same for both transitions, it is clear that local model repair in M_1 is possible, so the algorithm sets the rate of transition $(3) \xrightarrow{d,1} (2)$ in M_1 to the value $1 \cdot f$.

Impossibility of Model Repair of Non-Synchronising Transitions

We now study a similar case as the previous one, but with different modification factors. Assume that the following d-transitions need to be changed:

$$(1,1) \xrightarrow{d,1 \cdot f_1} (2,1) \qquad (1,2) \xrightarrow{d,1 \cdot f_2} (2,2) \qquad (1,3) \xrightarrow{d,1 \cdot f_3} (2,3)$$

where $f_1 \neq f_2$ or $f_1 \neq f_3$. Action d is a non-synchronising action and it is obvious that local model repair is not possible, since condition in line 38 of the algorithm is not satisfied.

According to the condition in line 57 of the algorithm, model repair is impossible, since the non-synchronising action d is present in M_1 and M_2 and state $(1,3)$ in the flat model (which is a reachable state) has two outgoing d-transitions, one in the M_1-dimension and one in the M_2-dimension (the same is true for state $(3,3)$). The algorithm would stop at this point, as it should. If the algorithm went ahead and made action d into a synchronising action, then two spurious transitions would be created: one from state $(1,3)$ to state $(2,2)$, and one from $(3,3)$ to $(2,2)$. So making d into a synchronising action is not an option here.

Successful Model Repair of Non-synchronising Transitions

Assume that the following c-transitions need to be modified, where action c is not a synchronising action and $f_1, f_2 \neq 1$:

$$(1,1) \xrightarrow{c,1 \cdot f_1} (1,2) \qquad (1,2) \xrightarrow{c,1 \cdot f_2} (1,3)$$

The difference between this case and the former case is that there is no reachable state in the flat model (Fig. 4) with two outgoing c-transitions stemming from M_1 and M_2, so the impossibility condition of line 57 of the algorithm is not satisfied.

It is clear that local model repair is not possible, since the two transitions $(1,1) \xrightarrow{c,f_1} (1,2)$ and $(2,1) \xrightarrow{c,1} (2,2)$ are contradicting for $f_1 \neq 1$. Therefore according to the algorithm, action c is added to the synchronising set and we need to consider all reachable c-transitions:

$$(1,1) \xrightarrow{c,1 \cdot f_1} (1,2) \implies x_{11} \cdot y_{12} = f_1$$
$$(2,1) \xrightarrow{c,1} (2,2) \implies x_{22} \cdot y_{12} = 1$$
$$(1,2) \xrightarrow{c,1 \cdot f_2} (1,3) \implies x_{11} \cdot y_{23} = f_2$$
$$(2,2) \xrightarrow{c,1} (2,3) \implies x_{22} \cdot y_{23} = 1$$
$$(3,2) \xrightarrow{c,1} (3,3) \implies x_{33} \cdot y_{23} = 1$$

The necessary condition for this system of equations to have a solution is $\frac{y_{12}}{y_{23}} = \frac{f_1}{f_2} = \frac{1}{1}$ which implies $f_1 = f_2$. So only if this condition is satisfied, lifting is possible. One unknown variable can be chosen freely, say $x_{11} = 1$, then the other unknowns are determined:

$$x_{22} = x_{33} = 1/f_1$$
$$y_{12} = y_{23} = f_1$$

Figure 6 shows the modified processes M_1' and M_2', with only c-transitions drawn.

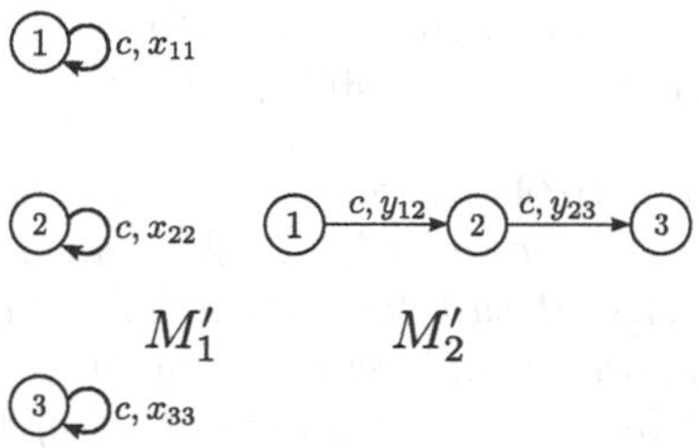

Fig. 6. Processes M_1' and M_2' (only c-transitions shown)

4   Application to SPA Models with Product Form

In this section, we identify a class of models for which the algorithm from Sect. 3 is guaranteed to always find a solution. In [14], a class of PEPA models is defined, based on Boucherie's framework [17] of Markov processes competing over resources, for which it is shown that the equilibrium probability distribution is of product form. These SPA models consist of a set of cyclic processes and a set of mutually independent resources

$$Sys = (M_1 \| \ldots \| M_K) \|_L (R_1 \| \ldots \| R_M)$$

There is no direct interaction among processes M_k ($k = 1, \ldots, K$), but indirect interaction because of the mutually exclusive use of the resources R_m ($m = 1, \ldots, M$). Apart from the interaction with the processes, the resources must not have any internal behaviour, thus the resources are redundant at the state level. "Redundant" means that the current state of any of the resources can be inferred from the states of the K processes.

The original Boucherie framework of [17] requires a strong blocking condition, which means that when a process occupies a certain resource, all other processes competing over the same resource are fully blocked and not allowed to move at all. But in [14], instead of the strong blocking condition, there is a strong restriction on components, based on the notion of so-called *guarding* and *returning* resources. A resource is *guarding* with regard to a sequential component if all paths (which are actually cycles) starting from the initial state of the component and returning to the initial state, either cooperate with the resource on the first action of the cycle or are completely independent of the resource actions during the whole cycle. Similarly, a resource is *returning* with regard to a sequential component if all paths (cycles) starting from the initial state and returning to the initial state, either cooperate with the resource on the last action of the cycle or are completely independent of the resource actions during the whole cycle. For the formal definition of *guarding resource* and *returing resource* the reader is referred to [14].

We now study what happens when we apply our lifting algorithm from Sect. 3 to SPA product form models as described in [14]. As mentioned, resources are redundant at the state level, so their state is implicit and does not need to be recorded in the state descriptor of the combined model. The following theorem provides sufficient conditions for successful lifting of model repair information.

Theorem 1. *Let Sys be a SPA product form model as described in [14], i.e.* $Sys = (M_1 \parallel \ldots \parallel M_K) \parallel_L R$, *where* $M_1, \ldots, M_K$ *are cyclic sequential components and R is the independent parallel composition of distinct simple resource components which are guarding and returning with respect to each* M_k ($k = 1, \ldots, K$) *and redundant in the state representation of the model. Let* T_{mod} *be the subset of transitions of the low-level model of Sys whose rates are to be multiplied by given factors. Lifting this model repair information to the specification level by applying the algorithm from Sect. 3 will be successful if:*

1. *all local actions within* M_k *(i.e. all actions of* $Act(M_k) \cap \overline{L}$*) are pairwise distinct (for all* $k = 1, \ldots, K$*)*
2. *the local actions of any two components are disjoint, i.e.*
   $Act(M_k) \cap Act(M_l) \cap \overline{L} = \emptyset$ *(for all* $k, l = 1, \ldots, K$*)*
3. *the rates of the synchronising actions are not to be modified, i.e.*
   $Act(T_{mod}) \cap L = \emptyset$

Note that in this Product Form framework there is no synchronisation among components, so Case (1) of the algorithm never occurs (all transitions in the combined model are just along one dimension, with exactly one process changing its state). Model repair will take place by either local repair inside one of the components M_k, or by inserting self-loops (for context-dependent control of the rates) and making the components synchronising over some action set $\Sigma_s \subseteq Act(T_{mod})$. The resulting repaired model is $(M_1' \parallel_{\Sigma_s} \ldots \parallel_{\Sigma_s} M_k') \parallel_L R$ where the M_k' are the modified components. We now give a proof sketch for the theorem.

Proof. For simplicity, the proof is carried out for the special case of $K = 2$ components, thus the system can be written as $Sys = (M_1 \parallel M_2) \parallel_L R$. The conditions in Theorem 1 indicate that any action $c \in Act(T_{mod})$ only exists in one of the components M_1 or M_2, and in this component there is only one c-transition. Assume that this c-transition is in M_1 and there are N reachable states in M_2, as shown in Fig. 7:

Then there exist (at most) N c-transitions in the flat model (with f_n, $n = 1, \ldots, N$, being the associated modification factors). Now either the system can be repaired by local repair of M_1, or we need to solve the following system of at most N equations (there might be fewer than N c-transitions if some combined

Fig. 7. Processes M_1 and M_2

states are unreachable):

$$(a_i, b_1) \xrightarrow{c,1 \cdot f_1} (a_j, b_1) \qquad x_{ij} \cdot y_{11} = f_1$$
$$(a_i, b_2) \xrightarrow{c,1 \cdot f_2} (a_j, b_2) \qquad x_{ij} \cdot y_{22} = f_2$$
$$\vdots \qquad\qquad \vdots$$
$$(a_i, b_N) \xrightarrow{c,1 \cdot f_N} (a_j, b_N) \qquad x_{ij} \cdot y_{NN} = f_N$$

For arbitrary values of the multiplication factors $f_1, \ldots, f_N$, this system of equations always has a solution. One solution is $x_{ij} = 1$ and $y_{nn} = f_n$ for all $1 \leq n \leq N$. □

5   Summary and Future Work

In this paper, we have presented an algorithm which lifts model repair information, given in the form of transition rate modification factors, from a flat low-level CTMC to the associated high-level compositional model. The algorithm modifies a subset of the model components' transition rates, and it may also change the interaction between the components by adding actions to the synchronisation set. While such a solution to the lifting problem does not always exist, the algorithm is guaranteed to find a valid solution if it exists. For a special class of SPA product form models, we have shown that lifting is always possible.

In future work, we are planning to elaborate on the extension of the lifting algorithm to more than two processes. We are also planning to work on optimisations of the algorithm, such as splitting a large system of nonlinear equations, as created by the algorithm, into several smaller, independent systems of equations, whenever this is possible. There is also the question whether additional measures, apart from local rate modifications and augmenting the synchronisation set, could open up further opportunities for lifting. The long-term goal is to develop a truly compositional model repair approach, which – as opposed to the lifting approach presented here – would work directly at the level of the high-level compositional model specification.

Acknowledgement. The authors would like to thank Alexander Gouberman for critical comments on the manuscript.

References

1. Hillston, J.: A Compositional Approach to Performance Modelling. Cambridge University Press, Cambridge (1996)

2. Bernardo, M., Gorrieri, R.: A tutorial on EMPA: a theory of concurrent processes with nondeterminism, priorities, probabilities and time. Theoret. Comput. Sci. **202**(1), 1–54 (1998)
3. Kuntz, M., Siegle, M., Werner, E.: Symbolic performance and dependability evaluation with the Tool CASPA. In: Núñez, M., Maamar, Z., Pelayo, F.L., Pousttchi, K., Rubio, F. (eds.) FORTE 2004. LNCS, vol. 3236, pp. 293–307. Springer, Heidelberg (2004). https://doi.org/10.1007/978-3-540-30233-9_22
4. Kwiatkowska, M., Norman, G., Parker, D.: PRISM 4.0: verification of probabilistic real-time systems. In: Gopalakrishnan, G., Qadeer, S. (eds.) CAV 2011. LNCS, vol. 6806, pp. 585–591. Springer, Heidelberg (2011). https://doi.org/10.1007/978-3-642-22110-1_47
5. Dehnert, C., Junges, S., Katoen, J.-P., Volk, M.: A **Storm** is coming: a modern probabilistic model checker. In: Majumdar, R., Kunčak, V. (eds.) CAV 2017. LNCS, vol. 10427, pp. 592–600. Springer, Cham (2017). https://doi.org/10.1007/978-3-319-63390-9_31
6. Bartocci, E., Grosu, R., Katsaros, P., Ramakrishnan, C.R., Smolka, S.A.: Model repair for probabilistic systems. In: Abdulla, P.A., Leino, K.R.M. (eds.) TACAS 2011. LNCS, vol. 6605, pp. 326–340. Springer, Heidelberg (2011). https://doi.org/10.1007/978-3-642-19835-9_30
7. Chen, T., Hahn, E.M., Han, T., Kwiatkowska, M., Qu, H., Zhang, L.: Model repair for Markov decision processes. In: Proceedings of the 7th International Symposium Theoretical Aspects of Software Engineering (TASE), IEEE CS Press, pp. 85–92 (2013)
8. Pathak, S., Ábrahám, E., Jansen, N., Tacchella, A., Katoen, J.-P.: A greedy approach for the efficient repair of stochastic models. In: Havelund, K., Holzmann, G., Joshi, R. (eds.) NFM 2015. LNCS, vol. 9058, pp. 295–309. Springer, Cham (2015). https://doi.org/10.1007/978-3-319-17524-9_21
9. Tati, B., Siegle, M.: Parameter and controller synthesis for Markov chains with actions and state labels. In: André, É., Frehse G., (eds.) 2nd International Workshop on Synthesis of Complex Parameters (SynCoP 2015), vol. 44 of OpenAccess Series in Informatics (OASIcs), Dagstuhl, Germany, pp. 63–76 (2015)
10. Baier, C., Haverkort, B., Hermanns, H., Katoen, J.-P.: Model-checking algorithms for continuous-time Markov chains. IEEE Trans. Softw. Eng. **29**(6), 524–541 (2003)
11. Baier, C., Cloth, L., Haverkort, B., Kuntz, M., Siegle, M.: Model checking Markov chains with actions and state labels. IEEE Trans. Softw. Eng. **33**(4), 209–224 (2007)
12. Tati, B., Siegle, M.: Rate reduction for state-labelled Markov chains with upper time-bounded CSL requirements. In: Brihaye, T., et al. (eds.) Proceedings of the Cassting Workshop on Games for the Synthesis of Complex Systems and 3rd International Workshop on Synthesis of Complex Parameters, Open Publishing Association, Electronic Proceedings in Theoretical Computer Science, vol. 220, pp. 77–89 (2016)
13. Tati, B.: Quantitative model repair of stochastic systems. Ph.D. thesis, Department of Computer Science, Bundeswehr University, Munich (2018)
14. Hillston, J., Thomas, N.: Product form solution for a class of PEPA models. Perform. Eval. **35**(3), 171–192 (1999)
15. Hillston, J.: The nature of synchronisation. In: Herzog, U., Rettelbach, M., (eds.) Proceedings of the 2nd Workshop on Process Algebras and Performance Modelling, Arbeitsberichte des IMMD 27(4), Universität Erlangen-Nürnberg, Regensberg/Erlangen, pp. 51–70 (1994)

16. Gouberman, A., Siegle, M., Tati, B.: Markov chains with perturbed rates to absorption: theory and application to model repair. Perform. Eval. **130**, 32–50 (2019)
17. Boucherie, R.J.: A characterization of independence for competing Markov chains with applications to stochastic Petri nets. IEEE Trans. Softw. Eng. **20**(7), 536–544 (1994)

An Efficient Brute Force Approach to Fit Finite Mixture Distributions

Falko Bause[(✉)]

LS Informatik IV, Department of Computer Science, TU Dortmund,
44221 Dortmund, Germany
falko.bause@cs.tu-dortmund.de

Abstract. This paper presents a brute force approach to fit finite mixtures of distributions considering the empirical probability density and cumulative distribution functions as well as the empirical moments. The fitting problem is solved using a non-negative least squares method determining a mixture from a larger set of distributions.

The approach is experimentally validated for finite mixtures of Erlang distributions. The results show that a feasible number of component distributions, which accurately fit to the empirical data, is obtained within a short CPU time.

Keywords: Mixture distributions · Hyper-Erlang distributions · Non-negative least squares · Farey sequences

1 Introduction

Mixture distributions are a well explored model type for the description of statistically varying events. In this paper, we focus on the fitting of continuous univariate finite mixture distributions and assume that all probability density functions and moments do exist. Mixture distributions are usually defined by a set of $G, G \in \mathbb{N}$, component distributions specified by their probability density functions (PDFs) $f_i(x|\boldsymbol{\theta}_i)$ with $\boldsymbol{\theta}_i \in \mathbb{R}^{m_i}, m_i \in \mathbb{N}$, denoting the component-specific parameters and mixing probabilities $\pi_i \in [0, 1], i = 1, \ldots, G$ satisfying $\sum_{i=1}^{G} \pi_i = 1$ [14]. The PDF of the mixture distribution is defined by

$$f(x|(\boldsymbol{\pi}, \boldsymbol{\theta})) = \sum_{i=1}^{G} \pi_i f_i(x|\boldsymbol{\theta}_i) \tag{1}$$

with $\boldsymbol{\theta} = (\boldsymbol{\theta}_1, \ldots, \boldsymbol{\theta}_G)$ the vector containing all parameters and $\boldsymbol{\pi} = (\pi_1, \ldots, \pi_G)$. Additionally, the cumulative distribution function (CDF) F and the moments $E[X^j]$ are given by a convex combination of the components' counterparts:

$$F(x|(\boldsymbol{\pi}, \boldsymbol{\theta})) = \sum_{i=1}^{G} \pi_i F_i(x|\boldsymbol{\theta}_i) \tag{2}$$

© Springer Nature Switzerland AG 2020
H. Hermanns (Ed.): MMB 2020, LNCS 12040, pp. 208–224, 2020.
https://doi.org/10.1007/978-3-030-43024-5_13

$$E[X^j|(\boldsymbol{\pi}, \boldsymbol{\theta})] = \sum_{i=1}^{G} \pi_i E[X_i^j|\boldsymbol{\theta}_i], \quad j \in \mathbb{N} \tag{3}$$

where X and X_i denote the random variables with CDFs F and F_i, respectively.

For performance modeling phase-type distributions (PHDs, [24,25]) are popular, since they allow analytical analysis approaches. Different from Eq. (1) general PHDs are usually specified in a more compact notation, since component parameters might be dependent. Common subclasses of PHDs are mixtures of exponential (hyper-exponential) and mixtures of Erlang (hyper-Erlang) distributions, especially since hyper-Erlang distributions can approximate any PDF of a nonnegative random variable [12]. In practice, applicability of mixture distributions depends on efficient fitting procedures which construct a mixture distribution approximating an empirical distribution given by trace data $T = (t_1, \ldots, t_n), t_i \in \mathbb{R}$. There exists a vast number of literature on fitting mixture distributions, see, e.g., [9,15,33] for an overview. In the following only a sketch is presented emphasizing those from a Markovian setting being relevant here.

Trace based fitting methods use T and try to determine $(\boldsymbol{\pi}, \boldsymbol{\theta})$ which maximizes the likelihood or equivalently the log-likelihood $\sum_{i=1}^{n} \log(f(t_i|(\boldsymbol{\pi}, \boldsymbol{\theta})))$. Corresponding fitting procedures are commonly based on expectation maximization (EM) algorithms [2,27], some of them on the basis of sub-classes of PHDs, as, e.g., hyper-exponential [22] or hyper-Erlang distributions [32]. EM based methods often become inefficient for large traces, but there are attempts to overcome this problem, e.g., by aggregating the trace [28]. A different approach applicable to large traces is presented in [29,30], where the user identifies peaks of the empirical PDF being the basis for a cluster analysis of the trace. The cluster sizes determine parameter $\boldsymbol{\pi}$ and component Erlang distributions are fitted on the basis of the clustered data. Since being based on Eq. (1) trace based fitting methods usually fit the empirical PDF fairly precise, but have difficulties to approximate the empirical moments.

Moment matching methods are based on Eq. (3) and the empirical moments. Some approaches consider specific structures of PHDs to match a finite set of moments trying to cope with possible non-unique representations of the same distribution, but suffer from the problem that only a restricted set of values are feasible moments, which makes fitting difficult [5,19]. Other approaches use more flexible structures and some of them consider hyper-Erlang distributions (or variants), since they can match any set of moments of a distribution [18,21]. [8] considers acyclic PHDs with n states (being characterized by $(2n-1)$ feasible moments [31]) and iteratively specifies sequences $\boldsymbol{\pi}^{(i)}$ and $\boldsymbol{\theta}^{(i)}$, where $\boldsymbol{\pi}^{(i+1)}$ is determined solving a constrained non-negative least squares (NNLS) problem for given $\boldsymbol{\theta}^{(i)}$. $\boldsymbol{\theta}^{(i+1)}$ is computed by standard polynomial optimization techniques for given $\boldsymbol{\pi}^{(i+1)}$ to obtain the parameter setting for the next iteration. Hardly surprising, being based on Eq. (3) moment matching methods have difficulties to approximate the empirical PDF/CDF.

The approach presented in this paper heads towards fitting of mixture distributions approximating the empirical PDF/CDF as well as the empirical moments and profits from the existence of efficient algorithms for solving NNLS problems. The main idea is partly along the lines of [8], for given $\boldsymbol{\theta}$ all Eqs. (1)–(3) can be used to formulate the fitting problem as a constrained NNLS problem. The main problem is to find an appropriate setting for $\boldsymbol{\theta}$. In this paper, a method is proposed to construct a possibly large parameter vector $\tilde{\boldsymbol{\theta}}$ such that the solution $\tilde{\boldsymbol{\pi}}$ of the NNLS problem gives a distribution $f(x|(\tilde{\boldsymbol{\pi}}, \tilde{\boldsymbol{\theta}}))$ approximating the empirical PDF/CDF and moments. For construction, values from Farey sequences are used, which are transformed to values possibly conforming with the empirical trace data. Experiment results for mixtures of Erlang distributions show that most of the entries of $\tilde{\boldsymbol{\pi}}$ are almost vanishing and can be neglected giving a mixture distribution with a moderate number of components.

The next section presents the main idea behind the brute force approach and in Sect. 3 its adaption to the fitting of hyper-Erlang distributions is described. Section 4 shows results from experiments followed by an extension of the approach presented in Sect. 5.

2   A General Brute Force Approach

In the following, we assume that (empirical) PDF f_e, CDF F_e and (finite) moments m_e^j of order $j = 1, \ldots, K, K \in \mathbb{N}$, are given or can be derived from a given trace. For notational convenience all component distributions are assumed to belong to the same known family (thus $\boldsymbol{\theta}_i \in \mathbb{R}^m, \forall i$) although the approach can be easily extended to heterogeneous mixtures. The main idea is to define an appropriate set $\tilde{S}$ (of size $\tilde{G} \in \mathbb{N}$) of component distributions with parameter vector $\tilde{\boldsymbol{\theta}} = (\tilde{\boldsymbol{\theta}}_1, \ldots, \tilde{\boldsymbol{\theta}}_{\tilde{G}})$ and to determine mixing probabilities $\tilde{\boldsymbol{\pi}}$ by solving an appropriate NNLS problem such that the resultant mixture distribution approximates f_e, F_e and m_e^j.

Obviously, constructing such a set needs to be done systematically in order to promise better approximation results with increasing set size $\tilde{G}$. First a sequence of basic value sets $\mathcal{F}_1 \subset \mathcal{F}_2 \subset \mathcal{F}_3 \subset \ldots$ with elements from $[0, 1]$ is defined which satisfy a denseness property within the unit interval. Then the elements of some set $\mathcal{F}_i$ are transformed by one or more transformation functions $TF_{(\cdot, j)}$ defined for the j-th component parameter. E.g., in Sect. 3, components with Erlang distributions are considered so that here two component parameters μ, k exist implying $j \in \{1, 2\}$. The transformed values are then taken to specify the component distributions of set $\tilde{S}$ by using all combinations of the component parameter values. In the following this construction process is described in more detail.

2.1   Farey Sequences as a Basic Value Set

As a basic value set Farey sequences, also known as Farey series [16] are utilized. A Farey series $\mathcal{F}_n$ is the increasing sequence of irreducible fractions in $[0, 1]$ with denominators not exceeding n. In the following, we will define Farey sequences as sets, since the order is irrelevant for our approach.

Definition 1 (Farey sequence (cf. [16])). *The Farey sequence $\mathcal{F}_n, n \in \mathbb{N}$, is defined as*

$$\mathcal{F}_n = \left\{ \frac{p}{q} \;\middle|\; p \in \mathbb{N}_0, q \in \mathbb{N} : 0 \leq p \leq q \leq n \;\; with \;\; gcd(p,q) = 1 \right\}$$

where $gcd(p,q)$ is the greatest common divisor of p and q.

The elements of a Farey sequence are called Farey numbers and the first Farey sequences are

$$\mathcal{F}_1 = \left\{ \frac{0}{1}, \frac{1}{1} \right\}, \mathcal{F}_2 = \left\{ \frac{0}{1}, \frac{1}{2}, \frac{1}{1} \right\}, \mathcal{F}_3 = \left\{ \frac{0}{1}, \frac{1}{3}, \frac{1}{2}, \frac{2}{3}, \frac{1}{1} \right\}, \mathcal{F}_4 = \left\{ \frac{0}{1}, \frac{1}{4}, \frac{1}{3}, \frac{1}{2}, \frac{2}{3}, \frac{3}{4}, \frac{1}{1} \right\}$$

illustrating the following properties of Farey sequences.

Theorem 1 ((cf. [16])). *Let $\frac{p}{q}, \frac{p'}{q'} \in \mathcal{F}_n$ be two consecutive elements of $\mathcal{F}_n$, i.e. $\forall x \in \mathbb{R} : \frac{p}{q} < x < \frac{p'}{q'} \Rightarrow x \notin \mathcal{F}_n$ then*

(i) $qp' - pq' = 1$ and $q + q' > n$

(ii) $\frac{p'}{q'} - \frac{p}{q} = \frac{1}{qq'}$

(iii) $\mathcal{F}_n \subset \mathcal{F}_{n+1}, \quad \forall n \in \mathbb{N}$

(iv) Approximate cardinality of Farey sequences: $|\mathcal{F}_n| \approx \dfrac{3n^2}{\pi^2}$

where $\pi \approx 3.14$ is here the transcendental number.

Farey sequences have some favorable properties which support the design of a fitting procedure. Properties (i) + (ii) show that all elements of $[0,1]$ can be approximated arbitrarily close selecting an appropriate $n \in \mathbb{N}$ [16]. Thus, theoretically Farey numbers can be used to approximate all elements of the unknown parameter vector θ by means of appropriate transformations. Property (iii) is of decisive importance. It is the basis to ensure that an increasing effort, by using more Farey numbers ("$n \to n + 1$") will not deteriorate fitting results. Finally, property (iv) gives hope that this increase might still lead to problem instances of manageable size.

2.2   Transformation of Basic Value Set

Since Farey numbers are inside the interval $[0,1]$ they can not be used directly for an approximation of a single component parameter $\theta \in \mathbb{R}$ and have to be transformed accordingly. Generally, one can distinguish between the following two possibilities. A finite interval $[a,b], a, b \in \mathbb{R}, a < b$, might be assumed to contain parameter values of one or several components or due to the lack of information only an infinite interval can be supposed. In the first case, linear function $a + (b-a)x$ maps Farey numbers of $[0,1]$ to $[a,b]$. For an infinite interval

$[\alpha, \infty], \alpha \in \mathbb{R}, \alpha \geq 0$ we use a stereographic projection of the two-dimensional unit sphere mapping a point $(x_1, x_2), x_1^2 + x_2^2 = 1$, to $(x_1, x_1/(1 - x_2))$ giving a mapping of the interval $[0, 1]$ to $[\alpha, \infty]$ by

$$y = \left(\frac{x}{1 - \sqrt{1 - x^2}} - 1 + \alpha \right), \text{ if } x > 0 \quad \text{and } y = \alpha, \text{ if } x = 0 \quad (4)$$

If useful, the values can be further transformed (stretched or compressed) by an exponential transformation $z = \exp(\beta y) - \exp(\beta \alpha) + \alpha$ with parameter $\beta \in \mathbb{R}, \beta > 0$ to ensure that also for small n the transformed values of basic value set $\mathcal{F}_n$ result in component definitions, such that Eqs. (1)–(3) might be fulfillable. Note that all equations specify convex combinations so that, e.g. considering Eq. (1), for all allowed $x \in \mathbb{R}$, components i, j have to exist in the mixture with $f(x|(\boldsymbol{\pi}, \boldsymbol{\theta})) \leq f_i(x|\boldsymbol{\theta}_i)$ and $f(x|(\boldsymbol{\pi}, \boldsymbol{\theta})) \geq f_j(x|\boldsymbol{\theta}_j)$. The same holds for Eqs. (2)–(3).

Similar transformations can be specified for co-domains $[-\infty, -\alpha]$ or $[-\infty, \infty]$ with $-y$ or by applying linear function $(2x - 1)$ and Eq. (4) in succession. If $\theta \in \mathbb{N}$, rounded values can be used. Generally, a transformation function $TF_{(I,j)}$ for interval I and the j-th parameter can be defined arbitrarily, but has to ensure that for all possible allowed values θ of the assumed finite or infinite interval I one has $\forall \epsilon > 0 : \exists n \in \mathbb{N}, x \in \mathcal{F}_n : |TF_{(I,j)}(x) - \theta| < \epsilon$, so that "denseness" of Farey sequences carries over to the range of transformed values.

For the definition of appropriate finite intervals one can exploit characteristics of the trace. E.g., the minimum and maximum value of a trace might give a very rough interval for an estimation of the components expected values. Narrower intervals might be obtained from empirical quantile values, which are, e.g., used in Sects. 3 and 4.

Parameter values of several mixture components $\tilde{\boldsymbol{\theta}}_i$ can now be obtained vector componentwise from Farey sequences possibly of different sizes, the assumed finite or infinite intervals and the corresponding transformation functions. For simplicity, we assume that a single Farey sequence $\mathcal{F}_{n_j}, n_j \in \mathbb{N}$, is used for the j-th component parameter. Let $I_{i,j}, i = 1, \ldots, k_j, j = 1, \ldots, m$ denote the i-th interval for the j-th parameter, where $k_j \in \mathbb{N}$ denotes the number of intervals defined for the j-th parameter. Note that all component distributions are assumed to belong to the same family. Then, a set of transformed values for the j-th parameter is given by $V_j = \{TF_{(I_{i,j},j)}(x)|i = 1, \ldots, k_j, x \in \mathcal{F}_{n_j}\}$ and set $\tilde{S}$ is composed from component definitions where all combinations are taken into account $V_{\tilde{S}} = \{(\tilde{\theta}_1, \ldots, \tilde{\theta}_m)|\tilde{\theta}_j \in V_j, j = 1, \ldots, m\}$. Since the order of mixture components is irrelevant for the approach presented here, an arbitrary vectorization of all elements of $V_{\tilde{S}}$ can be used to define $\tilde{\boldsymbol{\theta}}$.

2.3 Non-Negative Least Squares Problem Definition

With given components a NNLS problem can be specified as follows. Assume that empirical PDF f_e, CDF F_e and a finite number of moments $m_e^j, j \in \mathbb{N}$, are given or can be derived from a given trace. With $c, p \in \mathbb{N}$, let $P_{PDF} = \{x_1, \ldots, x_p\}, x_i \in \mathbb{R}$, be a finite set such that for all $x_i \in P_{PDF}$ $f_e(x_i), \tilde{f}(x_i|\cdot)^1$ are defined and let $P_{CDF} = \{x_1, \ldots, x_c\}, x_i \in \mathbb{R}$, be a finite set such that for all $x_i \in P_{CDF}$ $F_e(x_i), \tilde{F}(x_i|\cdot)$ are defined. Considering a finite set of K moments and Eqs. (1)–(2) at $x \in P_{PDF}$ and $x \in P_{CDF}$ respectively, results in a finite set of equations, such that the fitting problem can be formulated as a constrained NNLS problem for which very efficient algorithms exist being able to solve large problem instances [23]. Since numerical values, especially of the moments, might differ orders of magnitude, it is common to introduce appropriate weights, here $\gamma_{PDF}, \gamma_{CDF}, \gamma_j, j = 1, \ldots, K$, with $\gamma_* \in \mathbb{R}$. Defining with $i = 1, \ldots, \tilde{G}$

$$A = \gamma_{PDF}\left(\tilde{f}_i(x_j|\theta_i)\right), \qquad a = \gamma_{PDF}\left(f_e(x_j)\right), \qquad x_j \in P_{PDF}$$

$$B = \gamma_{CDF}\left(\tilde{F}_i(x_j|\theta_i)\right), \qquad b = \gamma_{CDF}\left(F_e(x_j)\right), \qquad x_j \in P_{CDF}$$

$$C = \left(\gamma_j E[\tilde{X}_i^j|\theta_i]\right), \qquad c = \left(\gamma_j m_e^j\right), \qquad j = 1, \ldots, K.$$

$$D = (A|B|C), \qquad d = (a|b|c) \qquad\qquad\qquad (5)$$

the NNLS problem is $\min_{\pi} \|d - \pi D\|_2^2$ subject to $\sum_{i=1}^{\tilde{G}} \pi_i = 1, \pi_i \geq 0$.

The weights γ_* can be used to control the impact of PDF, CDF and moments within the fitting process. Defining e.g., as in Sect. 4, weights γ_* such that $\sum_j a_j = \sum_j b_j = \sum_j c_j$ results in a similar contribution of the PDF, CDF and moments within the NNLS problem definition.

3   Fitting Finite Mixtures of Erlang Distributions

In the following, the approach of Sect. 2 is applied to mixtures of Erlang distributions with PDF, CDF and moments of an Erlang distribution given by

$$f(x|(\mu, k)) = \left(\frac{k}{\mu}\right)^k \frac{x^{k-1}}{(k-1)!} \exp\left(-\frac{k}{\mu}x\right)$$

$$F(x|(\mu, k)) = 1 - \exp\left(-\frac{k}{\mu}x\right) \sum_{r=0}^{k-1} \frac{(kx)^r}{\mu^r r!}$$

$$E[X^j|(\mu, k)] = \frac{(k+j-1)!}{(k-1)!}\left(\frac{\mu}{k}\right)^j$$

where exp denotes the exponential function, $\mu \in \mathbb{R}^+$ is the expected value and $k \geq 1, k \in \mathbb{N}$, denotes the number of phases. Common definitions of an Erlang distribution use a parameter $\lambda = k/\mu$, here the expected value is used to make the fitting approach directly applicable.

Obviously, the first parameter is a candidate for the definition of transformation functions based on finite intervals, since it seems reasonable to assume,

---

^{1} $g(x|\cdot)$ denotes $g(x|(\pi, \theta))$ for arbitrary parameters (π, θ).

e.g., that the expected values of all component distributions might be bounded by the minimum and maximum values T_{min}, T_{max} of the trace, although this is of course theoretically not guaranteed. As mentioned, empirical quantiles $q_e(r)$ of order r can be used here for the definition of a set of contiguous intervals, assuming that the expected values of some components might be covered by an interval. For all later experiments 10 quantile values $q_e(i/11), i = 1, \ldots, 10$ and T_{min}, T_{max} have been used to define a set of intervals. If the minimum/maximum of the quantile values and the minimum/maximum of the trace differ orders of magnitude, i.e., if $(q_e(1/11)/T_{min}) > 10$ or $(T_{max}/q_e(10/11)) > 10$ larger finite intervals might occur. Additional quantile values of orders $1/10^z$ and $(10^z - 1)/10^z, z \in \mathbb{N}$, give narrower intervals. In experiments these additional quantile values have been used, increasing $z \in \mathbb{N}$ until the mentioned quantities do not differ orders of magnitude. Large differences might occur if the trace contains outliers or if the empirical skewness is significant.

The second parameter of the Erlang distributions is a candidate for the definition of an infinite interval and corresponding transformation function, since it seems difficult to set up one or several reasonable finite intervals. Some information can be obtained to support fitting. For $k \to \infty$ an Erlang distribution tends toward a normal distribution with expected value μ and variance $\sigma^2 = \mu^2/k$. Since the maximum of the PDF of a normal distribution is at $x = \mu$ with $f(\mu) = 1/\sqrt{2\pi\sigma^2}$, $(\pi \approx 3.14)$, the number of phases of one of the component distributions has to be at least $k^* = 2\pi \cdot \max_x\{(xf_e(x))^2\}$. This fact can be used to define an appropriate transformation onto the infinite interval $[1, \infty]$ followed by rounding the resultant values. For experiments $\beta > 0$ has been determined iteratively, such that the maximum of the set of transformed values of a fixed set size ($|V_2| = 30$ in all experiments) exceeds k^* significantly ($100 \cdot k^*$ in all experiments) and β has been kept fixed for all experiments with the same trace, so that property (iii) of Theorem 1 in essence also holds for the transformed values. Since rounded values are used, a strict $\subset$ relation might not always hold and even large Farey sequences might result in relatively small value sets after transformation and rounding.

4 Experimental Results

The brute force approach has been implemented in MATLAB (release R2017b). For experiments several synthetically generated traces and two real traces have been used and reported CPU times are from runs on a computer using a single core of an E5-2699 processor with 64 GB RAM. Results are compared with those from the tools G-FIT [32] and MomFit [8]. G-FIT uses an EM algorithm to find the maximum likelihood estimates and MomFit is designed to fit an acyclic PHD to the empirical moments. G-FIT's parameters have been set to a maximum of 20 states and to aggregate the trace [28]. The brute force approach of Sects. 2 and 3 is named *shotgun* in corresponding figures.

The Freedman-Diaconis rule [13] has been used for the representation of the empirical PDF defining the width of the histogram bins by $2(Q_3 - Q_1)/\sqrt[3]{n}$

with Q_i denoting the i-th quartile and n being the number of trace elements. The set P_{PDF} is formed by the midpoints of the histogram bins. The size of set P_{CDF} is a user input giving equidistant points $x_j \in [T_{min}, T_{max}]$. In all experiments $|P_{CDF}|$ has been set such that the resultant NNLS problems are not underdetermined. $K = 10$ moments have been used for fitting and weights γ_* have been set such that $\sum_{x_j \in P_{PDF}} \gamma_{PDF} f_e(x_j) = \sum_{x_j \in P_{CDF}} \gamma_{CDF} F_e(x_j) = 1$. Likewise, the weights for the moments have been defined by $\gamma_j = \frac{2(K+1-j)}{K(K+1)m_e^j}$, $j = 1, \ldots, K$, emphasizing lower order moments, however giving $\sum_{j=1}^{K} \gamma_j m_e^j = 1$ as well. Irrelevant components ($\pi_i \leq 10^{-12}$) have been deleted from the results. The ProFiDo toolset [3] has been used for plots, generating traces from the fitted distributions, if necessary.

First, fitting of a triangular distribution is discussed. Figure 1 shows several results for different sets of components with set size $\tilde{G}$ giving the number of variables for the NNLS problem (#Vars). Figure 1(b) depicts the first moments of the fitted distribution relative to the empirical moments of the trace. Note that a few more higher order moments are shown than having been utilized for fitting. The table of Fig. 1(c) presents corresponding numerical values, amongst the log-likelihood, the relative error of the 10-th moment is given, since in all experiments this moment shows the largest relative error compared to lower order moments. Column #Comp gives the number of resultant components and column #States shows the sum of the phases of all Erlang branches. The last part presents concrete fitting results for $\tilde{G} = 132$ and 240. Not surprisingly, tiny NNLS problem instances give bad results, but a bit unexpectedly, even relatively small instances lead to satisfactory fitting results. The results show that PDF, CDF and the requested moments are fitted accurately, but at the price of Erlang distributions with a large number of phases. An additional interesting effect, which is also exhibited in other experiments, is the significantly reduced number of resultant components compared to the initial size of set $\tilde{S}$.

Another synthetically generated trace is from a mixture of three Beta distributions ("Beta3") with PDF $\frac{1}{5} f_B(x|(1, 30)) + \frac{3}{5} f_B(x|(10, 10)) + \frac{1}{5} f_B(x|(25, 1))$ where $f_B(x|(\alpha, \beta))$ is the PDF of a Beta distribution with shape parameters $\alpha, \beta \in \mathbb{R}^+$. Figures 2(a) and (b) show corresponding fitting results. Illustration of the CDF is omitted here and in the following experiment results, since corresponding curves are quite close. Figure 2(a) shows that the right part of the distribution is not fitted exactly. Experiments with larger sets of components showed slightly better fittings. Since the PDFs of PHDs and thus hyper-Erlang distributions exhibit an exponential decay [26] exact fits cannot be expected in practice.

In addition, three traces have been selected which were also used for fitting with G-FIT [32]: traces from a uniform distribution on interval $[0.5, 1.5]$ ("Uniform") and traces from a Shifted Exponential and a Matrix Exponential Distribution [6]. Corresponding results are shown in Fig. 2 and numerical results are presented in Table 1, which extends the table of Fig. 1(c) by a few columns: The first two of them denote the name as well as the length of the trace and the tool used, the last column gives the CPU time in seconds needed for fitting.

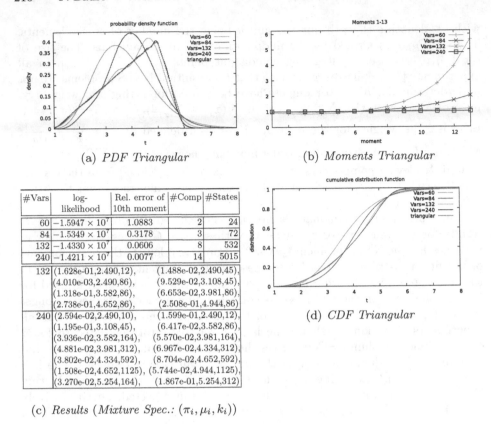

(a) *PDF Triangular*

(b) *Moments Triangular*

#Vars	log-likelihood	Rel. error of 10th moment	#Comp	#States
60	-1.5947×10^7	1.0883	2	24
84	-1.5349×10^7	0.3178	3	72
132	-1.4330×10^7	0.0606	8	532
240	-1.4211×10^7	0.0077	14	5015
132	(1.628e-01,2.490,12),	(1.488e-02,2.490,45),		
	(4.010e-03,2.490,86),	(9.529e-02,3.108,45),		
	(1.318e-01,3.582,86),	(6.653e-02,3.981,86),		
	(2.738e-01,4.652,86),	(2.508e-01,4.944,86)		
240	(2.594e-02,2.490,10),	(1.599e-01,2.490,12),		
	(1.195e-01,3.108,45),	(6.417e-02,3.582,86),		
	(3.936e-02,3.582,164),	(5.570e-02,3.981,164),		
	(4.881e-02,3.981,312),	(6.967e-02,4.334,312),		
	(3.802e-02,4.334,592),	(8.704e-02,4.652,592),		
	(1.508e-02,4.652,1125),	(5.744e-02,4.944,1125),		
	(3.270e-02,5.254,164),	(1.867e-01,5.254,312)		

(d) *CDF Triangular*

(c) *Results (Mixture Spec.:* (π_i, μ_i, k_i)*)*

Fig. 1. Fitting results for a trace from a triangular distribution

Since the fitting time of MomFit was more than 130 s in all cases, we give figures depicting the first moments of the fitted distributions relative to the empirical moments of the trace and present numerical results for G-FIT only. For the fitting of all three traces accurate fitting results have been received in short CPU time. Table 1 shows that CPU times increase with larger traces. Most of the fitting time is used for the determination of the empirical PDF and CDF and thus for the specification of the NNLS problem. Solving the NNLS problem usually takes only a few seconds down to less than a second.

Also a larger trace from a heavy tailed Pareto-II distribution (cf. [17,32]) has been selected for fitting. [32] used a smaller trace with 10^4 elements. Figure 3 shows results for different sets of components initially used for fitting. Since the first 10 quantile values significantly differ from T_{min}, T_{max} fitting of this trace greatly benefits from additional quantile values used for the definition of finite intervals. Table 1 shows that G-FIT obtained a higher log-likelihood value, but did not match the moments accurately, see Fig. 3. Figure 3(d) shows results for the first 15 moments. Note that only 10 moments have been used for fitting. Plots have been generated from traces of the fitted mixture distributions and

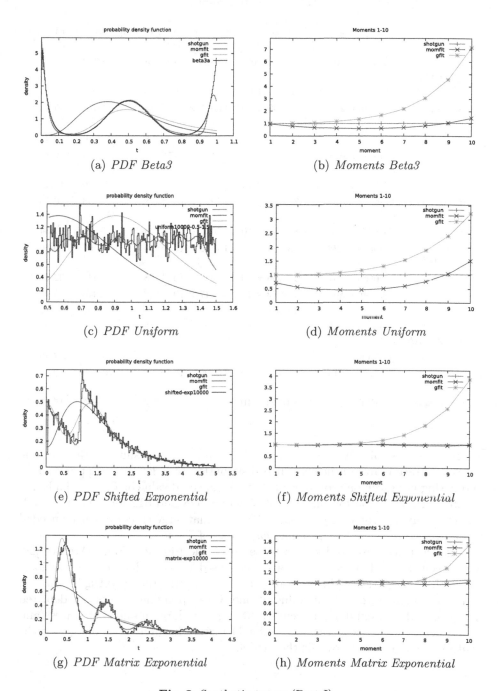

(a) *PDF Beta3*

(b) *Moments Beta3*

(c) *PDF Uniform*

(d) *Moments Uniform*

(e) *PDF Shifted Exponential*

(f) *Moments Shifted Exponential*

(g) *PDF Matrix Exponential*

(h) *Moments Matrix Exponential*

Fig. 2. Synthetic traces (Part I)

Table 1. Fitting results

Trace (Length)	Tool	#Vars	Log-likelihood	Rel. error of 10th moment	#Comp	#States	Fitting time (s)
Beta3 (5.0×10^6)	Shotgun	400	1.9807×10^6	5.8253×10^{-2}	14	6392	15.32
	G-FIT		6.1510×10^5		3	20	8.34
Uniform (1.0×10^4)	Shotgun	240	-5.2868×10^2	3.0065×10^{-2}	14	10030	0.70
	G-FIT		-1.8276×10^3		9	20	4.24
Shifted Exp. (1.0×10^4)	Shotgun	352	-1.3047×10^4	7.7144×10^{-3}	21	1825	0.79
	G-FIT		-1.3179×10^4		5	20	10.44
Matrix Exp. (1.0×10^4)	Shotgun	333	-7.7801×10^3	4.1290×10^{-2}	28	3153	0.75
	G-FIT		-8.7481×10^3		4	20	7.34
Pareto (1.0×10^7)	Shotgun	428	-2.0084×10^7	4.7756×10^{-1}	24	691	19.50
	Shotgun	667	-1.9966×10^7	1.1212×10^{-1}	28	1648	22.48
	Shotgun	864	-1.9872×10^7	3.9117×10^{-2}	28	2045	27.95
	G-FIT		-1.9831×10^7		6	20	11.12
LBL3 ($\approx 1.79 \times 10^6$)	Shotgun	275	-1.5995×10^6	3.5725×10^{-2}	15	283	3.35
	G-FIT		-1.634×10^6		5	20	17.14
pAug (1.0×10^6)	Shotgun	314	-7.9409×10^5	4.2109×10^{-2}	27	12845	2.53
	G-FIT		-8.0743×10^5		4	20	15.68

are here not completely conforming with the numerical results of Table 1. The "Pareto" trace is from a heavy tailed distribution (e.g. kurtosis is approx. 10^6) and fitting has given one component with an expected value of T_{max} and a larger number of phases (55 for the case of #Vars = 428 and 512 for #Vars = 864), but with mixing probability less than 10^{-7}, so that large traces might be needed to be in accordance with the numerical values of Table 1.

As real traces two well-known traces from the Internet Traffic Archive [20] have been selected, which also have been used in several other publications: the LBL-TCP-3 trace ("*LBL3*") and the BC-pAug89 trace ("*pAug*"), with all values normalized to a mean value of one. Corresponding results are depicted in Fig. 4 and also exhibit an accurate fitting. The large number of states (and components) for trace pAug (see Table 1) reveal the immanent danger of the brute force approach to overfit the model.

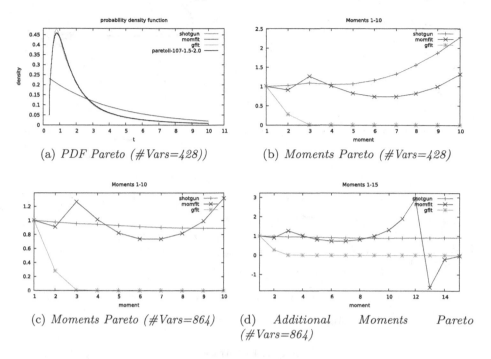

(a) *PDF Pareto (#Vars=428))*   (b) *Moments Pareto (#Vars=428)*

(c) *Moments Pareto (#Vars=864)*   (d)   *Additional   Moments   Pareto (#Vars=864)*

Fig. 3. Synthetic traces (Part II)

5 Extending the Approach

The presented approach fits mixture distributions to data taking account of the PDF/CDF and moments. Also other criteria can be considered as long as they can be encoded into the NNLS problem definition. Typical criteria might be those which help to reduce the risk of overfitting, as, e.g., the Akaike information criterion [1]. In the following, the model size is considered.

For mixtures of Erlang distributions the number of states might be an appropriate indicator for the overall size of the mixture distribution. Consequently, penalizing those Erlang distributions with several phases might reduce the model size. Extending Eq. (5) by an additional penalty factor $p_f \in \mathbb{R}_0^+$ and column vector $\boldsymbol{p} = \left(p_f \left(1 + k_i / \left(\sum_{j=1}^{\tilde{G}} k_j \right) \right) \right)$ gives $\boldsymbol{D} = (\boldsymbol{A}|\boldsymbol{B}|\boldsymbol{C}|\boldsymbol{p})$, $\boldsymbol{d} = (\boldsymbol{a}|\boldsymbol{b}|\boldsymbol{c}|p_f)$.

Like the weights γ_*, factor p_f controls the impact state penalization has within the fitting process. E.g., setting $p_f = 1$ gives the same weight to this criterion as given to other parts of vector $\boldsymbol{d}$.

For additional experiments a trace from a hyper-Erlang distribution with 2 components and 3 states has been selected using an initial set of 215 Erlang distributions. Again 10 moments have been used for fitting and other parameters have been set as described in Sect. 4. Fitting with no penalty factor results in a mixture of 20 components and 222 states. G-FIT determines a mixture with 15 components and 20 states, whereas MomFit fits an acyclic PHD of order

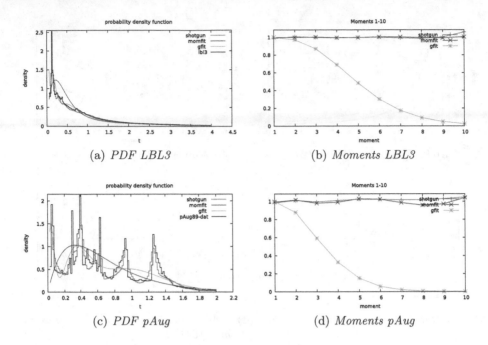

(a) *PDF LBL3*

(b) *Moments LBL3*

(c) *PDF pAug*

(d) *Moments pAug*

Fig. 4. Real traces

5. Introducing a penalty factor $p_f = 10$ reduces the number of components as well as the number of states without worsening the fitting accuracy significantly (see. Fig. 5[2]) giving a hyper-Erlang distribution with 4 components and 8 states.

Figure 6 shows the results from fitting the trace of the uniform distribution presented in Sect. 4 with penalty factor $p_f = 10$. In this case, the size of the

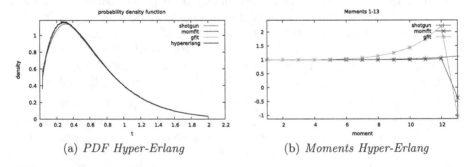

(a) *PDF Hyper-Erlang*

(b) *Moments Hyper-Erlang*

Fig. 5. Hyper-Erlang distribution $\left(\boldsymbol{\pi} = (1/\pi^2, 1 - 1/\pi^2), \boldsymbol{\theta} = ((1/e, 1), (2/\pi, 2))\right)$ fitting result: $(\boldsymbol{\pi}' = (1.19e{-}01, 7.12e{-}01, 9.9e{-}02, 7.0e{-}02), \boldsymbol{\theta}' = ((3.51e{-}01, 1), (6.09e{-}01, 2), (7.01e{-}01, 2), (8.80e{-}01, 3)))$

---

[2] π, e the transcendental numbers.

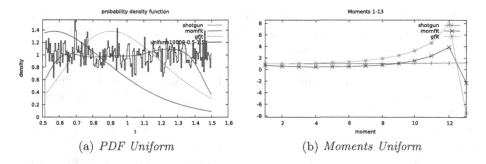

(a) *PDF Uniform*   (b) *Moments Uniform*

Fig. 6. Fitting of uniform distribution with penalty factor $p_f = 10$. Fitting result: $(\pi' = (1.47\mathrm{e}{-}01, 4.88\mathrm{e}{-}04, 3.10\mathrm{e}{-}01, 2.47\mathrm{e}{-}01, 2.32\mathrm{e}{-}01, 1.26\mathrm{e}{-}02, 5.14\mathrm{e}{-}02)$, $\theta' = ((6.09\mathrm{e}{-}01, 33), (6.09\mathrm{e}{-}01, 45), (8.24\mathrm{e}{-}01, 17), (1.05, 33), (1.28, 86), (1.39, 164), (1.39, 312)))$

fitted distribution has been reduced significantly from 10030 states to 690 states still giving good fitting results.

6   Conclusions

This paper has presented a general brute force approach to fit finite mixture distributions taking the PDF/CDF as well as the moments into account. Since "dense" Farey sequences are used, the fitting approach is designed to approximate unknown parameter values arbitrarily close, provided transformation functions and intervals are suitably defined. Experiments have shown that only a small number of values is necessary and that the number of components resulting from solving the NNLS problem is also relatively small. An additional advantage of the approach is that no assumption on the number of resultant components is needed for fitting.

Experiments with hyper-Erlang distributions have given very accurate results in reasonable CPU times, but also indicate an immanent danger of overfitting as the resultant hyper-Erlang distributions tend to increase in size. In case of fitting mixture distributions to empirical data accurate fits might be problematic. E.g., estimating higher order moments is unreliable even for large traces [8], also the specification of the empirical PDF (and set P_{PDF}) is crucial. Apart from this aspect, hyper-Erlang distributions with a large number of phases might not be avoidable, since it is known that mixtures of fixed delays and Erlang distributions are necessary to approximate general positive distributions arbitrarily close [11]. As shown, the approach can be extended, so that the number of phases might be reduced still giving accurate results. However, concise representations are not always desirable. E.g., if also correlation structures need to be considered, some methods apply (similarity) transformations [10,31] to obtain a suitable, often enlarged representation of the distribution for further fitting steps (cf. [4,7]).

The brute force approach has been implemented for fitting mixtures of Erlang distributions and the method is easily adaptable to families of distributions with similar parameter definitions where component specifications are independent of each other, as, e.g., mixtures of normal distributions. For other types of mixtures an adaption needs more research. E.g., phase-type distributions (PHDs) can be represented as mixture distributions, but the parameters of the individual components are usually dependent, making the definition of set $\tilde{S}$ not that easy. Even when considering sub-classes of PHDs, as e.g. acyclic PHDs, the definition of set $\tilde{S}$ might still offer multiple options, so that it is not directly evident how information on trace data can be used for the definition of appropriate finite intervals for component parameters. Similar to some other fitting methods for PHDs, a possible approach might be to consider also here specific finite PHD structures.

References

1. Akaike, H.: A new look at the statistical model identification. IEEE Trans. Autom. Control **19**(6), 716–723 (1974)
2. Asmussen, S., Nerman, O., Olsson, M.: Fitting phase-type distributions via the EM algorithm. Scand. J. Stat. **23**(4), 419–441 (1996)
3. Bause, F., Buchholz, P., Kriege, J.: ProFiDo - the processes fitting toolkit Dortmund. In: Proceedings of the 7th International Conference on Quantitative Evaluation of SysTems (QEST 2010), pp. 87–96. IEEE Computer Society (2010)
4. Bause, F., Horvath, G.: Fitting Markovian arrival processes by incorporating correlation into phase type renewal processes. In: Proceedings of the 2010 Seventh International Conference on the Quantitative Evaluation of Systems, QEST 2010, pp. 97–106. IEEE Computer Society, Washington, DC, USA (2010)
5. Bobbio, A., Horváth, A., Telek, M.: Matching three moments with minimal acyclic phase type distributions. Stoch. Models **21**(2–3), 303–326 (2005)
6. Bobbio, A., Telek, M.: A benchmark for PH estimation algorithms: results for acyclic-PH. Commun. Stat. Stoch. Models **10**(3), 661–677 (1994)
7. Buchholz, P., Felko, I., Kriege, J.: Transformation of acyclic phase type distributions for correlation fitting. In: Dudin, A., De Turck, K. (eds.) ASMTA 2013. LNCS, vol. 7984, pp. 96–111. Springer, Heidelberg (2013). https://doi.org/10.1007/978-3-642-39408-9_8
8. Buchholz, P., Kriege, J.: A heuristic approach for fitting MAPs to moments and joint moments. In: Proceedings of the 6th International Conference on Quantitative Evaluation of SysTems (QEST 2009), pp. 53–62. IEEE Computer Society, Los Alamitos, CA, USA, (2009)
9. Buchholz, P., Kriege, J., Felko, I.: Input Modeling with Phase-Type Distributions and Markov Models - Theory and Applications. SpringerBriefs in Mathematics. Springer, Heidelberg (2014). https://doi.org/10.1007/978-3-319-06674-5
10. Buchholz, P., Telek, M.: Stochastic Petri nets with matrix exponentially distributed firing times. Perform. Eval. **67**(12), 1373–1385 (2010)
11. David, A., Larry, S.: The least variable phase type distribution is Erlang. Commun. Stat. Stoch. Models **3**(3), 467–473 (1987)
12. Fang, Y.: Hyper-Erlang distribution model and its applications in wireless mobile networks. Wirel. Netw. **7**, 211–219 (2001)
13. Freedman, D., Diaconis, P.: On the histogram as a density estimator: L_2 theory. Zeitschrift für Wahrscheinlichkeitstheorie und Verwandte Gebiete **57**(4), 453–476 (1981)

14. Frühwirth-Schnatter, S.: Finite Mixture and Markov Switching Models. Springer Series in Statistics. Springer, New York (2006). https://doi.org/10.1007/978-0-387-35768-3

15. Frühwirth-Schnatter, S., Celeux, G., Robert, C.: Handbook of Mixture Analysis. Chapman & Hall/CRC Handbooks of Modern Statistical Methods. CRC Press, Taylor & Francis Group, Boca Raton (2019)

16. Hardy, G., Wright, E.: An Introduction to the Theory of Numbers, 5th edn. Oxford Science Publications. Clarendon Press, Oxford (1979)

17. Horváth, A., Telek, M.: Markovian modeling of real data traffic: heuristic phase type and MAP fitting of heavy tailed and fractal like samples. In: Calzarossa, M.C., Tucci, S. (eds.) Performance 2002. LNCS, vol. 2459, pp. 405–434. Springer, Heidelberg (2002). https://doi.org/10.1007/3-540-45798-4_17

18. Horváth, G.: Moment matching-based distribution fitting with generalized hyper-Erlang distributions. In: Dudin, A., De Turck, K. (eds.) ASMTA 2013. LNCS, vol. 7984, pp. 232–246. Springer, Heidelberg (2013). https://doi.org/10.1007/978-3-642-39408-9_17

19. Horváth, G., Telek, M.: On the canonical representation of phase type distributions. Perform. Eval. **66**(8), 396–409 (2009). Selected Papers of the Fourth European Performance Engineering Workshop (EPEW) 2007 in Berlin

20. Internet Traffic Archive. ftp://ita.ee.lbl.gov/html/traces.html. Accessed: 13 Nov 2019

21. Johnson, M.A., Taaffe, M.R.: Matching moments to phase distributions: mixtures of Erlang distributions of common order. Commun. Stat. Stoch. Models **5**(4), 711–743 (1989)

22. Khayari, R.E.A., Sadre, R., Haverkort, B.R.: Fitting world-wide web request traces with the EM-algorithm. Perform. Eval. **52**(2–3), 175–191 (2003)

23. Lawson, C., Hanson, R.: Solving Least Squares Problems. Society for Industrial and Applied Mathematics. SIAM, New Delhi (1995)

24. Neuts, M.: A versatile Markovian point process. J. Appl. Probab. **16**(4), 764–779 (1979)

25. Neuts, M.: Matrix-Geometric Solutions in Stochastic Models: An Algorithmic Approach. Johns Hopkins Series in the Mathematical Sciences. Johns Hopkins University Press, Baltimore (1981)

26. O'Cinneide, C.A.: Phase-type distributions: open problems and a few properties. Commun. Stat. Stoch. Models **15**(4), 731–757 (1999)

27. Okamura, H., Dohi, T., Trivedi, K.S.: A refined EM algorithm for PH distributions. Perform. Eval. **68**(10), 938–954 (2011)

28. Panchenko, A., Thümmler, A.: Efficient phase-type fitting with aggregated traffic traces. Perform. Eval. **64**(7–8), 629–645 (2007)

29. Reinecke, P., Krauß, T., Wolter, K.: Cluster-based fitting of phase-type distributions to empirical data. Comput. Math. Appl. Theory Pract. Stoch. Model. **64**(12), 3840–3851 (2012)

30. Reinecke, P., Krauß, T., Wolter, K.: Phase-type fitting using HyperStar. In: Balsamo, M.S., Knottenbelt, W.J., Marin, A. (eds.) EPEW 2013. LNCS, vol. 8168, pp. 164–175. Springer, Heidelberg (2013). https://doi.org/10.1007/978-3-642-40725-3_13

31. Telek, M., Horvath, G.: A minimal representation of Markov arrival processes and a moments matching method. Perform. Eval. **64**(9–12), 1153–1168 (2007)

32. Thümmler, A., Buchholz, P., Telek, M.: A novel approach for fitting probability distributions to real trace data with the EM algorithm. In: Proceedings of the International Conference on Dependable Systems and Networks, DSN 2005, pp. 712–721, June 2005 (2005)
33. Titterington, D.M., Smith, A.F.M., Makov, U.E.: Statistical Analysis of Finite Mixture Distributions. Wiley, Hoboken (1985)

Freight Train Scheduling
in Railway Systems

Rebecca Haehn$^{(\boxtimes)}$, Erika Ábrahám, and Nils Nießen

RWTH Aachen University, Aachen, Germany
`haehn@cs.rwth-aachen.de`

Abstract. Passenger train timetables in Europe are often periodical and predetermined for longer periods of time to facilitate the planning of travel. Freight train schedules, however, depend on the actual demand. Therefore it is a common problem in railway systems to schedule additional freight train requests, under consideration of a given timetable for passenger trains. In this paper, we present a model for railway systems that allows us to solve this scheduling problem as a constrained time-dependent shortest path problem. We adapt and implement an algorithm to solve this type of problems, examine our results, and discuss possible modifications and extensions to this approach.

1 Introduction

Over the last years the amount of *rail freight transport* continuously increased [17]. This development has several positive aspects. Rail transport is safer than transporting goods by trucks, and contributes to the reduction of traffic jams on highways. Additionally, at least for large amounts of freight and long distances, rail transport is better for the environment and cheaper than transport via trucks [7].

Since changes in the railway infrastructure are expensive and take a long time, in order to support this development, it is necessary to optimize the exploitation of the network capacity such that as many passenger and freight trains as possible should be able to use the infrastructure, while meeting certain other criteria. For example, it is absolutely necessary to fulfil safety requirements, like minimum distances between trains.

Passengers want to know their travel routes and times in advance and prefer to travel without disruptions. Therefore the passenger train *timetable* is usually periodical and fixes all passenger train routes and arrival and departure times at the visited stations. Also some freight trains operate regularly and follow a fixed schedule, which might be also included in those periodical timetables.

In contrast, companies sometimes request the dispatch of freight trains with fixed start and destination locations but without a fixed route. Due to passengers relying on the timely execution of the periodically scheduled train rides, it is

This research is funded by the Research Training Group UnRAVeL (RTG 2236).

H. Hermanns (Ed.): MMB 2020, LNCS 12040, pp. 225–241, 2020.
https://doi.org/10.1007/978-3-030-43024-5_14

desirable that the additional train's schedule is *feasible*, meaning that it does not disturb the existing timetable. Naturally, under the feasible routes there is a preference for short and direct routes, but there are further important aspects such as robustness under possible delays and low delay propagation. In practice, this problem is typically solved by human decision makers, but manual methods reach their limits at some point and can not always guarantee optimality. To offer computer-aided support, in this paper we assume a fixed timetable and develop an automated solution to the *train timetabling problem*, which is the problem of finding a feasible schedule for an additional freight train.

Though there are numerous techniques for different train routing and scheduling problems, the specific problem that we address received less attention. In [2] the authors proposed to model the problem as a job-shop scheduling problem and to use a meta-heuristic scheduling technique. However, they assume fixed paths for the requested trains for which they compute temporal schedules. Another approach [3,4] assumes ideal routes as well as timing as input, and searches for solutions as close as possible to the ideal ones using integer linear programming.

Recently, a mixed-integer non-linear programming formulation has been proposed [1] that does not assume any fixed or ideal routes or schedules; however, this approach comes with a limited precision because it requires the division of the considered time window into intervals and aggregates infrastructure usage over those time intervals.

All the above-mentioned works either assume fixed routes or ideal schedules for the requested freight trains or they offer limited precision. Furthermore, they consider capacity restrictions for tracks between *operation control posts* (*OCP*), which are the stations, junctions and all infrastructure elements where trains can change directions, but *no capacity restrictions for the OCPs*. Our aim is to find *optimal* solutions to the problem *without* any input route and using *more precise* models.

Another approach, presented in [20], first computes many short sub-paths that are then combined to construct feasible shortest paths. However, this method is not applicable to our problem because it is applied during the passenger timetable computation but we assume a fixed timetable for them. Another related approach [6] uses discrete time, so the more precise the time is modeled the worse the running time gets. More recently, several papers about resource-constrained shortest path problems have been published [9,16,18]. In [10,15] time-dependent travel times (edge weights) have been included. But these algorithms are also not suitable for our application, because they can only model a single time-window interval for each vertex within which it may be visited, whereas our application requires several intervals.

The only work we are aware of that considers both OCP-connecting as well as OCP-internal time-dependent restrictions supporting multiple time windows in continuous time, goes back to Halpern and Priess [12,13]. They solved a related shortest/fastest path problem in graphs with time-dependent vertex and edge capacities, and already mentioned potential railway applications for single-track lanes. However, our application domain has some requirements that are not considered in [12,13]: for example the algorithm in [12,13] (called Halpern-Priess algorithm in the following) allows feasible paths in a graph to visit a vertex even if there is no free capacity left, as long as the path does not reside in the vertex but leaves it immediately. However, in our application passing a train station is obviously not possible if all tracks are occupied by other trains. Another application-specific issue is that we prefer schedules without waiting at the OCPs and without moving from one OCP to another one and directly back. Also loops are not acceptable in reality.

The main contribution of this paper is an algorithm for solving real-world train timetabling problems without fixed routes or ideal timetables for the train to be scheduled, and under additional application-specific requirements. To the best of our knowledge, none of the currently existing algorithms is able to solve this problem without further modification. We modeled the railway infrastructure and timetable as a time-constrained graph and developed an adaption of the Halpern-Priess algorithm to satisfy the requirements of the considered application. Then we implemented the approach and evaluated our method using existing German railway network topologies and timetables. Thus this work can be seen as an application paper with some novel theoretical aspects.

This paper begins with a description of the model of the railway system that we use in Sect. 2. We then proceed with a formal definition of the problem we are dealing with and explain our solution approach in Sect. 3. The detailed experimental evaluation of these algorithms is presented in Sect. 4. Finally, we conclude the paper and briefly discuss future work in Sect. 5.

2   Modeling

We use $\mathbb{R}$ and $\mathbb{N}$ for the set of all real resp. natural ($0 \notin \mathbb{N}$) numbers, and use lower indices for restrictions, e.g. $\mathbb{R}_{>0}$ denotes the set of all positive real numbers. By $\mathcal{I}$ we denote the set of all bounded and closed intervals from $\mathbb{R}_{\geq 0}$, and by $\mathcal{P}(A)$ the set of all subsets of A.

Railway System. A *railway system* is a directed graph $G = (V, E)$ with a set of vertices V and a set of edges $E \subseteq V \times V$ without self-loops, i.e. $v \neq u$ for all $(u, v) \in E$. The vertices model the OCPs, whereas a directed edge from one vertex to another models that there exists at least one *track* connecting the respective OCPs that can be used in the corresponding direction; for each vertex $u \in V$ we define the vertices (OCPs) to which a train can move on from u as $successor(u) = \{v \in V | (u, v) \in E\}$. If two OCPs are connected by several parallel tracks in the same direction, we model all those tracks by a single edge and annotate the edge by the number of parallel tracks as described in the paragraph below. While the topology is quite detailed, we tolerate imprecision in the overall model. For example we assume that all tracks represented by one vertex or one edge are equivalent in the sense that they could replace each other. We also model bi-directional tracks (which can be used in both directions) like two tracks, one in each direction, thereby over-approximating the available capacity. Furthermore, we neglect whether halting is not intended in some OCPs. Nevertheless, we expect the model to reflect the real conditions to a sufficient extent.

We model the *number of parallel tracks* by the function $\#tracks : (V \cup E) \to \mathbb{N}$. For vertices $v \in V$, $\#tracks(v)$ is the number of halting points at the given OCP. For edges $e \in E$, $\#tracks(e)$ is the number of parallel tracks available in the given direction from the source to the target OCP.

Track lengths are modeled by the function $len : (V \cup E) \to \mathbb{R}_{\geq 0}$, specifying distances in kilometres, where in this work we set $len(v) = 0$ for $v \in V$ and $len(e) > 0$ for $e \in E$.

For the problems we consider we assume a fixed day on which a freight train should be scheduled, but it is straightforward to adapt the approach to over-night or multiple-days cases. We use continuous dense *time* to model a day in the unit of a minute, starting with zero at 00:00 o'clock; we also write $hh : mm$ with the meaning $hh \cdot 60 + mm$. We annotate edges by approximate *travel durations* (in minutes) for a freight train using the function $dur : E \to \mathbb{R}_{>0}$. This travel time is estimated under the assumption that the freight train is driving with a constant speed of $100\,km/h$, i.e., $dur(e) = (len(e)/100) * 60$.

Timetable. A (finite) *path* in a given graph $G = (V, E)$ of a railway system is a finite sequence $\pi = (v_1, v_2, \ldots, v_k)$ of vertices $v_i \in V$ for $i \in \{1, \ldots, k\}$ with $(v_i, v_{i+1}) \in E$ for $i \in \{1, \ldots, k-1\}$. We define the *length* of π as $len(\pi) = \sum_{i=1}^{k-1} len((v_i, v_{i+1}))$.

A *timed path* $\pi_t = (v_1(a_1 \mapsto d_1), \ldots, v_k(a_k \mapsto d_k))$ in G is a path $\pi = (v_1, \ldots, v_k)$ in G annotated with arrival times a_i and departure times d_i such that $00:00 \leq a_i \leq d_i < 24:00$ for all $i \in \{1, \ldots, k\}$ and $a_{i+1} = d_i + dur((v_i, v_{i+1}))$ for $i \in \{1, \ldots, k-1\}$. For a given timed path π_t we define its *duration* by $dur(\pi_t) = a_k - a_1$, *waiting time* by $wait(\pi_t) = \sum_{i=1}^{k-1} d_i - a_i$, as well as *length* by $len(\pi_t) = len(\pi)$. In a_1 we encode the time at which the train is available to start from its source, which can be less than the actual starting time d_1. Similarly, a_k is the actual arrival time at the destination, whereas we use d_k to express how long a train resides there (in timetables) or to store a deadline for the arrival (when scheduling a new train).

For a given railway system G, a *timetable* is a finite set $\{\pi_t^1, \ldots, \pi_t^n\}$ of timed paths in G. Informally, a timetable schedules a certain number n of train rides on a given day by specifying for each train its route by the list of visited OCPs, and the times at which it arrives at and departs from each of them. We assume that the timetable is fixed and should not be modified, therefore the individual trains are not of interest for us, but rather the remaining availability of the railway network. We further assume the timetable to be *feasible*, i.e., each network element $x \in V \cup E$ is used at all times by at most $\#tracks(x)$ trains.

To model usage by timetable trains, we store for each vertex and each edge a set of intervals: For each OCP and each train that visits it we add to the corresponding vertex the time interval when the train resides at the OCP, i.e. the interval from the train's arrival time at to its departure time from the OCP, annotated with the train's identity. We also take some safety distances [19] into account by enlarging these usage intervals by two minutes in both directions:

$$used(v) = \{[a - 2, d + 2]_i \mid i \in \{1, \ldots, n\} \wedge \pi_t^i = (\ldots, v(a \mapsto d), \ldots)\}$$

Thereby we assume in the timetable meaningful departure times also for the destinations of trains (last vertices in timed paths) to indicate how long a train occupies a track there.

For edges $e = (u, v)$ we add the interval from the departure time at the start vertex u to the arrival time at the target vertex v:

$$used((u, v)) = \{[d - 2, a + 2]_i \mid i \in \{1, \ldots, n\} \wedge$$
$$\pi_t^i = (\ldots, u(a' \mapsto d), v(a \mapsto d'), \ldots)\}$$

Thus the set of all time intervals at a vertex or edge describes the total usage of the entities by all trains scheduled in the timetable for the considered day.

For a given vertex or edge $x \in V \cup E$ with $\#tracks(x)$ parallel tracks, its remaining *availability* is approximated as the union of all time intervals during which less than $\#tracks(x)$ trains occupy the infrastructure element. We refer to this set of availability intervals as $avail(x)$. Formally, we define $I = \{t_1, \ldots, t_m\}$ to be the increasingly ordered set of $t_1 = 00 : 00$, $t_m = 24 : 00$ and all endpoints of the time intervals in $used(x)$ that are between $00 : 00$ and $24 : 00$ (note that through the enlarging of occupations by $2\,\mathrm{min}$ we can get interval endpoints outside of the considered day). Note furthermore that since I is ordered and contains all endpoints of all intervals in $used(x)$ (on the given day), we have for each $i \in \{1, \ldots, m - 1\}$ and each $[l, u]_j \in used(x)$ either $[t_i, t_{i+1}] \subseteq [l, u]$ or $(t_i, t_{i+1}) \cap [l, u] = \emptyset$. Thus $avail(x)$ for $x \in V \cup E$ can be computed as follows:

$$avail(x) = \cup_{i \in \{1, \ldots, m-1\} \wedge \mid \{[l,u]_j \in used(x) \mid [t_i, t_{i+1}] \subseteq [l,u]\} \mid < \#tracks(x)} [t_i, t_{i+1}]$$

In the following we assume for each $x \in V \cup E$ that $avail(x) \subseteq I$ is stored as a set of maximal intervals, i.e., such that $[t_1, t_2] \cap [t_1', t_2'] = \emptyset$ for each $[t_1, t_2], [t_1', t_2'] \in avail(x)$. We call a timed path $\pi_t = (v_1(a_1 \mapsto d_1), \ldots, v_k(a_k \mapsto d_k))$ *feasible* (for the given timetable) iff

$$(\forall i \in \{1, \ldots, k\}. \ [a_i, d_i] \subseteq avail(v_i)) \wedge$$
$$(\forall i \in \{1, \ldots, k - 1\}. \ [d_i, a_{i+1}] \subseteq avail((v_i, v_{i+1})))$$

3 The Time-Dependent Shortest Path Problem

Given a graph model $G = (V, E)$ for a railway system as described in the previous section, we can now deal with the main topic of this paper, which is scheduling an additional freight train. In the following we assume that a specific additional train is requested with desired source and destination vertices $v_s, v_d \in V$ and a preferred departure time t_{start}. For this input we want to compute a feasible timed path in the graph, i.e. a timed path, such that the departure time from the source vertex is at least t_{start}, and such that it does not disturb the timetable.

Let Π^t denote all timed paths from v_s to v_d in G. Depending on whether we want to minimize the distance or the duration, we aim at finding a shortest or fastest feasible timed path for the considered train. A *shortest* timed path from v_s to v_d in G is a timed path $\pi_t \in \Pi^t$ with $len(\pi_t) \leq len(\pi_t')$ for all $\pi_t' \in \Pi^t$.

Algorithm 1. Dijkstra's algorithm

1: **procedure** DIJKSTRA($G = (V, E)$, $dur : E \to \mathbb{R}_{>0}$, $v_s, v_d \in V$)
2:     $dist[v_s] \leftarrow 0$; $pred[v_s] \leftarrow null$; $Q \leftarrow V$;
3:     **for each** $v \in V \setminus \{v_s\}$ **do**
4:         $dist[v] \leftarrow \infty$; $pred[v] \leftarrow null$;
5:     **while** $d \in Q$ **do**
6:         $u \leftarrow argmin_{v \in Q} dist[v]$;
7:         $Q \leftarrow Q \setminus \{u\}$;
8:         **for each** $v \in successor(u) \cap Q$ **do**
9:             **if** $dist[v] > dist[u] + dur((u, v))$ **then**
10:                $dist[v] \leftarrow dist[u] + dur((u, v))$;
11:                $pred[v] \leftarrow u$;

In order to take the requested departure time into account, we search for a shortest/fastest timed path with $a_1 \geq t_{start}$. A *fastest* timed path is a timed path $\pi_t = (v_1(a_1 \mapsto d_1), \ldots) \in \Pi^t$ that satisfies $a_1 \geq t_{start}$ and $dur(\pi_t) \leq dur(\pi_t')$ for all $\pi_t' = (v_1(a_1' \mapsto d_1'), \ldots) \in \Pi^t$ with $a_1' \geq t_{start}$. Note that fastest paths do not necessarily spend the shortest time between leaving the source and entering the destination, but *from t_{start} till entering the destination*; therefore, in the literature they are also called *earliest arriving* paths.

3.1 Dijkstra's Algorithm

Probably the first algorithm that comes to mind in relation to shortest path problems is *Dijkstra's algorithm* [8], shown in Algorithm 1. When we define the weight of each edge (u, v) to be the track length $len((u, v))$, the result of this algorithm would be a shortest path $\pi = (v_1, \ldots, v_k)$ from v_s to v_d with $v_k = v_d$ and $v_i = pred[v_{i+1}]$ for $i \in \{1, \ldots, k - 1\}$.

Since we assume a constant speed for the additional freight train when computing the travel times, any timed path with waiting time 0 that is shortest with respect to the path length is also a fastest path. Therefore in the following we are using the travel times as edge weights consistently. However, without considering the given timetable, the result is most likely *infeasible*.

Nevertheless, Dijkstra's algorithm is suitable to determine a lower bound for the path length and duration of any feasible solution. It also has the advantage that it is quite fast (shortest/fastest path can be computed in polynomial time).

3.2 Edge Restrictions

A fastest path computed with Algorithm 1 is not necessarily feasible, because some infrastructure components might be unavailable at the time the train would use them optimally, due to another train that is part of the timetable. The unavailability of tracks that connect OCPs (modeled by edges) is discussed in the following, and the unavailability of the OCPs themselves (modeled by vertices) in Sect. 3.3.

Let $\pi = (v_1, \ldots, v_k)$ be a shortest path and let $\pi_t = (v_1(a_1 \mapsto d_1), \ldots, v_k(a_k \mapsto d_k))$ be the timed path that annotates π with the earliest possible arrival and departure times without waiting, i.e., $a_i = d_i = t_{start} + \sum_{j=1}^{i-1} dur((v_j, v_{j+1}))$ for all $i \in \{1, \ldots, k\}$. Unavailability of an edge means that there exists some $i \in \{1, \ldots, k-1\}$, for which $[d_i, a_{i+1}] \not\subseteq avail((v_i, v_{i+1}))$. In that case the fastest way to reach the destination might be to make a detour or to wait at some vertex and use the edge later when it is available again.

Consider the example railway system on the right, where the numbers on the edges e denote $dur(e)$. Assume furthermore the starting time $t_{start} = 0$, source vertex v_s and destination vertex v_d. A shortest path between v_s and v_d is $\pi = (v_s, v_1, v_d)$. Without waiting, this is also the route of the fastest path $\pi_t = (v_s(0 \mapsto 0), v_1(1 \mapsto 1), v_s(2 \mapsto 2))$ with duration $dur(\pi_t) = 2$. But in case the availability from (v_1, v_d) is restricted to $avail((v_1, v_d)) = [2, 5]$, while $avail((u, v)) = [0, 5]$ for all other edges $(u, v) \in E \setminus \{(v_1, v_d)\}$, this timed path is infeasible because $[1, 2] \not\subseteq [2, 5]$. The fastest path under consideration of the edge restrictions is therefore $\pi_t' = (v_s(0 \mapsto 0), v_1(1 \mapsto 2), v_d(3 \mapsto 3))$, waiting one time unit in v_1 and thus having the duration $dur(\pi_t') = 3$.

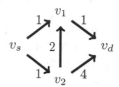

For this scenario, where we consider edge restrictions but allow unrestricted waiting in vertices, we can still use Dijkstra's algorithm if we modify the edge weights and use *time-dependent* weights. Instead of $dur(e)$ we now have to use

$$dur^*(e, t) = wait(e, t) + dur(e)$$
$$wait(e, t) = min\{t' - t \mid t' \geq t \wedge [t', t' + dur(e)] \subseteq avail(e)\},$$

where $wait(e, t)$ is the minimal waiting time at u till the next time point when $e = (u, v)$ is available for at least $dur(e)$ time units (minutes).

Our modified version of Dijkstra's algorithm to compute fastest paths under consideration of time-dependent edge availabilities differs from Algorithm 1 in two ways. Firstly, $dur : E \to \mathbb{R}_{>0}$ is replaced by $dur^* : E \times \mathbb{R}_{>0} \to \mathbb{R}_{>0}$. Therefore in lines 9 and 10 the distances are updated using the time-dependent edge weights $dur^*((u, v), dist[u])$ instead of $dur((u, v))$. Secondly, the starting time $t_{start} \in \mathbb{R}_{\geq 0}$ is used to initialize $dist[v_s]$.

The resulting fastest path is $\pi = (v_1, \ldots, v_k)$ with $v_k = v_d$ and $v_i = pred[v_{i+1}]$ for $i \in [1, k-1]$. To get the corresponding timing information, we generate the timed path $\pi_t = (v_1(a_1 \mapsto d_1), \ldots, v_k(a_k \mapsto d_k))$, where the arrival times are $a_i = dist[v_i]$, and the departure times are computed including waiting times as $d_i = a_{i+1} - dur((v_i, v_{i+1}))$ for $i \in \{1, \ldots, k-1\}$ and $d_k = a_k$.

The reason why we can still use Dijkstra's algorithm to compute such time-dependent shortest paths is that the modified edge weights fulfil the first-in-first-out (FIFO) property [5,14]. The FIFO property means that for all time values t, t' and for all $e \in E$ holds that $t \leq t' \Rightarrow t + dur^*(e, t) \leq t' + dur^*(e, t')$.

3.3   Vertex Restrictions

Additionally to the edge restrictions, the vertices might neither be available at all times. Considering also vertex availability the problem becomes more difficult, because the FIFO property is no longer given. Consider again our previous network example with edge restrictions. If we introduce additional vertex restrictions $avail(v_1) = [0, 1] \cup [3, 8]$ and $avail(v) = [0, 8]$ for all $v \in V \setminus \{v_1\}$, then the path π'_t is no longer feasible because $[1, 2] \not\subseteq avail(v_1)$, i.e. the train cannot reside at v_1 for the planned time. We can reach v_d from vertex v_1 at the later arrival time 4 along the timed path $\pi''_t = (v_s(0 \mapsto 0), v_2(1 \mapsto 1), v_1(3 \mapsto 3), v_d(4 \mapsto 4))$, $dur(\pi''_t) = 4$, which makes a detour via v_2, or waiting in v_s via $\pi'''_t = (v_s(0 \mapsto 2), v_1(3 \mapsto 3), v_d(4 \mapsto 4))$, $dur(\pi'''_t) = 4$.

In this scenario it is no longer possible to use Dijkstra's algorithm without further, more extensive modifications since it is not sufficient to examine every vertex just once. When we consider both edge and vertex restrictions, for a *feasible* fastest timed path $\pi_t = (v_1(a_1 \mapsto d_1), \ldots, v_k(a_k \mapsto d_k))$, not only $[d_i, a_{i+1}] \subseteq avail((v_i, v_{i+1}))$ for each $i \in \{1, \ldots, k - 1\}$ has to hold, but also $[a_i, d_i] \subseteq avail(v_i)$ for each $i \in \{1, \ldots, k\}$.

Problems with such combined vertex-edge-restrictions were discussed in 1974 by Halpern and Priess [12,13]. Their algorithm solves the fastest feasible path problem with time-dependent edge and vertex restrictions, but they allow passing a vertex without waiting there even at time points when no resources are available. They already mention potential railway applications, but very briefly and for single-track lanes only.

We can exploit the above algorithm, however, our application has some special characteristics that require adaptations. Firstly, as mentioned above, the Halpern-Priess algorithm considers timed paths that visit a vertex at a time point when all capacities are used feasible as long as no time passes in that vertex. Furthermore, stopping freight trains has several disadvantages, therefore we prefer fastest feasible paths *without waiting times in vertices*, i.e., paths of the form $\pi_t = (v_1(a_1 \mapsto d_1), \ldots, v_k(a_k \mapsto d_k))$ with $a_i = d_i$ for each $i \in \{1, \ldots, k-1\}$. We adapt the Halpern-Priess algorithm to satisfy these requirements.

Our method formalized in the Algorithms 2, 3 and 4 works as follows. Consider as before start and destination vertices $v_s, v_d \in V$ and earliest departure time t_{start} from v_s. We assume that v_s is available at t_{start}, i.e. there exists an interval $[t_1, t_2] \in avail(v_s)$ with $t_1 \leq t_{start} \leq t_2$. If this is not the case but there exists $[t_1, t_2] \in avail(v_s)$ with $t_1 > t_{start}$ then we re-set t_{start} to the smallest such t_1 before calling the algorithm; otherwise the routing is not possible.

This algorithm is iterative, considering in each iteration a certain vertex and its outgoing edges. The main difference to Dijkstra's algorithm is that we cannot avoid processing a vertex several times. However, we can assure termination after a finite number of iterations by considering possible *time intervals* for movements, instead of considering only their earliest possible time points.

In the main Algorithm 2, the set Q stores vertices u that have been already detected to be reachable via a feasible timed path from v_s, but for which we still need to consider successors on the way to v_d; initially Q contains only the source

---

Algorithm 2. The Halpern-Priess algorithm

1: **procedure** REACHABILITY($G = (V, E)$, $dur : E \to \mathbb{R}_{>0}$, $avail : V \cup E \to \mathcal{P}(\mathcal{I})$,
   $v_s, v_d \in V$, $t_{start} \in \mathbb{R}_{\geq 0}$)
2:     $Q \leftarrow \{v_s\}$; $u \leftarrow v_s$; $A[v_s] \leftarrow \{[t_{start}, t_{start}]\}$; $D[v_s] \leftarrow \emptyset$;
3:     **for each** $v \in V \setminus \{v_s\}$ **do**
4:         $A[v] \leftarrow \emptyset$; $D[v] \leftarrow \emptyset$;
5:     **while** $Q \neq \emptyset \,\wedge\, u \neq v_d$ **do**
6:         $Q \leftarrow Q \setminus \{u\}$;
7:         $D_{new} \leftarrow$ DEPARTURES($G, u, A[u]$, $avail$) $\setminus D[u]$;
8:         $D[u] \leftarrow D[u] \cup D_{new}$; $A[u] \leftarrow \emptyset$;
9:         **for each** $v \in successor(u)$ **do**
10:            $A[v] \leftarrow (A[v] \cup$ ARRIVALS($G, u, v, D_{new}, dur, avail$)$) \setminus D[v]$;
11:            **if** $A[v] \neq \emptyset$ **then**
12:                $Q \leftarrow Q \cup \{v\}$;
13:        **if** $Q \neq \emptyset$ **then**
14:            $u \leftarrow argmin_{v \in Q} \; inf\{t \mid [t, t'] \in A[v]\}$;

Algorithm 3. Departures

1: **procedure** DEPARTURES($G = (V, E)$, $u \in V$, $A_u \subseteq \mathcal{I}$, $avail : (V \cup E) \to \mathcal{P}(\mathcal{I})$)
2:     $D_u \leftarrow \emptyset$;
3:     **for each** $[t_1, t_2] \in A_u$ **do**
4:         find $I = [t_1', t_2'] \in avail(u)$ with $t_1 \in I$;
5:         $D_u \leftarrow D_u \cup \{[t_1, t_2']\}$;
6:     **return** D_u;

---

vertex v_s. When we computed those successors for a vertex $u \in Q$, we remove u from Q. Though each vertex can be added to Q and processed this way several times, the paths that we consider increase in duration; especially, the fastest feasible path from v_s to u is found by the very first processing. Therefore, the algorithm terminates when it would be the turn of v_d to be processed.

When processing a vertex $u \in Q$, we need to check extensions of a set of feasible timed paths arriving at u, whose arrival times at u are collected as a finite set of intervals $A[u]$. In each iteration, the vertex $u \in Q$ with the earliest possible arrival time in $A[u]$ is chosen to be considered next (line 14). For those arrival times in $A[u]$, all possible departure times D_{new} are computed that have not been considered yet for successor computations (line 7). The departure time computation basically extends the arrival intervals by waiting as long as the availability of the vertex allows it (see Algorithm 3).

Then for these departure times D_{new} at u, all possible arrival times are computed for each successor v of the vertex (lines 9–10). The main difference between the Halpern-Priess algorithm and our algorithm is in the method ARRIVALS (Algorithm 4). For each time interval $[t_1, t_2]$ during which we could depart from u (line 3), we first compute the set of intervals M_1 during which we could travel to v when starting from u within $[t_1, t_2]$, i.e. during which the availability of the edge is given (line 4). From the resulting intervals we select those with size at least the travelling duration of the edge (line 5). From those we extract the

---

Algorithm 4. Arrivals

1: **procedure** ARRIVALS($G = (V, E)$, $u \in V$, $v \in V$, $D_u \subseteq \mathcal{I}$, $dur : E \rightarrow \mathbb{R}_{>0}$,
   $avail : V \cup E \rightarrow \mathcal{P}(\mathcal{I})$)
2:     $A \leftarrow \emptyset$;
3:     **for each** $[t_1, t_2] \in D_u$ **do**
4:         $M_1 \leftarrow \{[t_1, t_2 + dur(u, v)] \cap I \mid I \in avail((u, v))\}$;
5:         $M_2 \leftarrow \{I \mid I \in M_1 \wedge |I| \geq dur((u, v))\}$;
6:         $M_3 \leftarrow \{[t_1' + dur((u, v)), t_2'] \mid [t_1', t_2'] \in M_2\}$;
7:         $A \leftarrow A \cup \{I \cap I_v \mid I \in M_3 \wedge I_v \in avail(v) \wedge I \cap I_v \neq \emptyset\}$;
8:     **return** A;

---

possible arrival times at v (line 6). To exclude passing a vertex at a time point
when it has no free capacities, we cut the intervals of possible arrival times at a
vertex v with $avail(v)$ (line 7). This way we only consider arrival and departure
times at which the vertex is actually available. After these vertex successors are
computed, Q is updated and the next vertex is chosen.

To additionally prevent trains from waiting at OCPs, we could replace line
7 in Algorithm 2 by $D_{new} \leftarrow A[u] \setminus D[u]$. To prevent moving forth and back
between two OCPs, we could annotate the arrival time intervals with their source
and exclude direct successor computations for that source. However, we did not
experiment with these options for reasons explained in Sect. 4.

We do not prove correctness and completeness here, but refer to the proof
in [12] that can be easily adapted to the modified algorithm, because we only
restrict successor arrival intervals compared to the original algorithm.

So far we have computed only the reachable time intervals, but not the fastest
feasible timed paths themselves. In [13] the authors also described how a fastest
feasible timed path can be computed backwards, based on these. However, only
conditions the predecessors have to fulfil are mentioned, no constructive way
to compute them. Since we are mainly interested in the paths themselves, we
additionally store for each arrival time interval its predecessors, which are tuples
containing a vertex and a time interval from which the respective time interval
can be reached. More concretely, we annotate each arrival interval $I \cap I_v$ that
is added to A in line 7 of Algorithm 4 for some $I = [t_1' + dur((u, v)), t_2'] \in M_3$
with the information that its predecessor was u and it departed from u within
$[t_1', t_2' - dur((u, v))]$. This enables us to compute suitable paths backwards in the
style of Dijkstra's algorithm, and similar to the path search approach in [11].
There essentially the same procedure is used to find shortest paths for robots
in an environment that contains moving obstacles. The main difference is that
they do not consider all possible arrival time intervals at a vertex at once, but
only the earliest one. It should be noted that the optimal route for this problem
might contain cycles. We get back to this in the following Sect. 4.

4   Experimental Results

The above explained algorithms were implemented in C++. In the implementation we use doubles to imprecisely represent time points. For our experiments

Table 1. Railway network properties and results for Dijkstra's original algorithm

Network	$|V|$	$|E|$	$|T|$	Running time (in secs)	Path duration (in hh:mm)	Path length (in km)	Path vertices
N	2632	6281	7964	0.0467	00:19	31.36	26
N_M	4514	11120	16329	0.1220	01:04	106.59	93
N_SO	4878	11100	8503	0.0735	01:00	100.70	68
W_M_SW	6356	15603	17268	0.1660	01:28	146.82	87
D	15456	36174	27972	0.3044	05:07	511.33	338

we used a computer with a 1.80 GHz × 8 Intel Core i7 CPU and 16 GB of RAM. First we discuss the resulting paths for the different algorithms, then we take a look at computational efficiency.

Five topologically different real-world railway networks were used to test the algorithms. These networks have been generated from confidential infrastructure data in XML form, provided by DB Netz AG (German Railways). For each of them an example timetable for a working day was given. Table 1 shows some properties of the networks: the second resp. third column lists the number of vertices resp. edges, and the fourth column the number of trains contained in the corresponding timetable. However, the latter information gives only a rough idea about the utilization, since the train lines contain highly varying numbers of OCPs. To the best of our knowledge, there is no measure for the utilization of a railway network, only for individual infrastructure elements [19].

For each network, different pairs of vertices between which the additional trains were supposed to be scheduled were chosen from typical real-world cases. Unfortunately, a direct comparison to the currently applied approach is not possible for reasons of confidentiality. To examine the influence of the given timetable, we used several different departure time requests for the additional trains, evenly distributed over a 24 h time window. This way the impact of different levels of infrastructure utilization can be examined, since the periodical timetable varies over the day.

For comparison the shortest paths between the chosen pairs of vertices were computed, without considering any restrictions, using Algorithm 1. The running times and results for one vertex pair in each graph can be found in the columns 5–8 of Table 1. The algorithm's running times are fairly short and as expected depend on the length of the paths, respectively the number of vertices and edges to be considered. For the resulting paths three properties are measured: length (in km), travel duration (rounded to $hh:mm$) and the number of vertices they contain. Since these paths do not contain any waiting times and we assumed constant speed for computing the travel time here the shortest are also the fastest paths.

This is no longer the case for the results of the other two algorithms, since both allow waiting at the vertices. Therefore we evaluate duration and length separately. By duration we mean here the difference between the arrival time at the destination and the requested departure time, which is the sum of driving

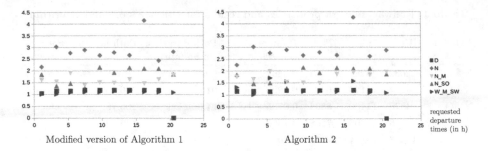

Fig. 1. Factors by which the path durations are slower than the unconstrained results

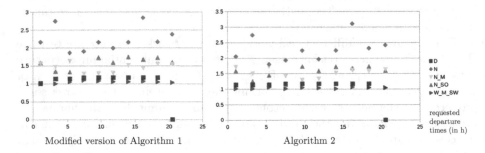

Fig. 2. Factors by which the path distances are longer than the unrestricted results

and waiting times. Both algorithms compute the fastest feasible timed path for a requested departure time, so the paths' duration (not length) is optimized. To compute optimal paths with respect to other criteria, like the length or the number of stops, requires a different algorithm and is not part of this paper.

In Fig. 1 we show the factors by which the duration of resulting paths increased compared to the unrestricted case shown in Table 1. On the left side the results of the modified Dijkstra algorithm are presented, on the right side those for the adapted Halpern-Priess algorithm. For the sake of clarity we only show the results for one example start-target vertex pair for each graph. The maximum factor by which a feasible path was slower than the unconstrained fastest path is 5.23 for both algorithms. Since the feasibility of the paths computed under consideration of only edge restrictions can not be guaranteed, those are sometimes faster, e.g. the W_M_SW example for start times 05:25 and 16:15. However, if they are that also means they are infeasible under consideration of additional vertex restrictions.

In the largest graph no path that arrives at the destination before 24:00 could be found for the latest requested departure time. This is due to the fact that we currently only consider exactly one day and even the unconstrained fastest path takes too long to still arrive at the same day, for this departure time. The planning horizon could be extended to the next day, but this would require some modifications in the implementation.

The corresponding lengths of the results are evaluated in Fig. 2. There the maximum factor for both algorithms is 3.37. The differences to the unrestricted results are smaller than for the duration, since the increased duration is additionally due to waiting times. It should also be noted, that since we optimize the duration there are some paths, which only consider edge restrictions, that are longer in distance than the respective paths considering also vertex restrictions.

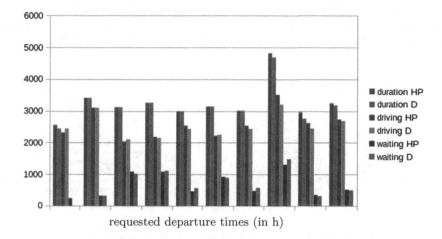

requested departure times (in h)

Fig. 3. Durations of the paths computed by the modified version of Algorithm 1 (D) and Algorithm 2 (HP) for example N

We show exemplarily for network N the direct comparison of the two different results in Fig. 3. There we also illustrate the waiting time shares. For this example they are relatively high, up to 34% of the overall duration. Furthermore we observe here as well that the two results differ in both waiting time and length.

Overall there are some paths that are acceptably fast; in practice, acceptable means up to about 1.5 times longer duration than the unconstrained fastest path. In general, the results are highly dependent on the timetable, which leads to some uneconomically slow paths. Another problem with those results is that it is not economical for freight trains to stop too often. 30% of the results contain stops at more than 10% of their vertices. Some of the paths even contain stops at up to 50% of their vertices. This could also lead to the paths being infeasible, since our model assumes constant speed, which breaking and accelerating freight trains clearly do not have.

So in further adjustments to the algorithms the number of vertices where waiting is allowed or the total waiting time could be restricted. However, this might prevent the algorithm from finding any solution at all and would certainly lead to even slower results. When waiting is completely forbidden the algorithm does not terminate within 10 min, which is approximately twice as long as the worst case running time with waiting. This is probably due to the algorithm exploiting the graph in all directions, without ever reaching the destination, and finding loops containing less utilized infrastructure elements. This might be avoided or at least restricted by selecting the next vertices under consideration of the minimal distances to the target vertex computed by Dijkstra's algorithm.

One further concern about Algorithm 2 is that it does not explicitly exclude cycles. In railway systems paths that contain cycles are in principle considered uneconomical. However, only 13 of the 270 computed paths contain one. These could be avoided by slightly changing the requested starting time or modifying the path computation based on the reachable intervals. Since this is rare we did not deem it necessary make such changes. We can always check whether the resulting paths contain cycles and in that case recompute individual paths.

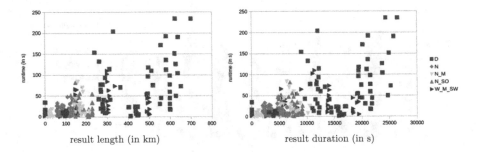

Fig. 4. Running times of the reachability computations

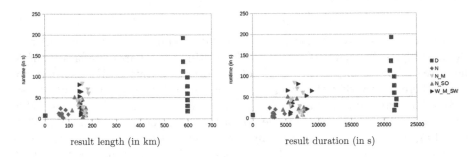

Fig. 5. Running times of the reachability computations for the detailed examples

Next we examine the algorithms' running times. The modified version of Dijkstra's algorithm has relatively constant running times of less than a second for the different requested starting times, it seems to depend mostly on the network topology. This was expected from Dijkstra's algorithm, whose computational effort is not so strongly effected by the time-dependent edge availabilities. Also, the fact that this algorithm is a lot faster than the Halpern-Priess algorithm was expected since it does not have to consider vertices multiple times.

For the Halpern-Priess algorithm a more detailed evaluation of the running times is reasonable. We consider the running times for the reachability and the

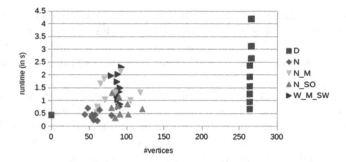

Fig. 6. Running times of the path computations for the detailed examples

following path computation separately, starting with the former. In Fig. 4 we plotted the running times of the reachability computation depending on the result's length on the left side, while the dependence on the result's duration is shown on the right side. The values for the different graphs have different colours. In both figures no strong correlation between the values can be witnessed. There is some trend to faster running times for results with long path length, which is probably caused by the given schedule. If the network is already highly utilized there are probably less possible paths left in the network, which means that the algorithm has to compute less intervals than for a lighter schedule. Also the resulting paths tend to be longer, respectively slower, paths. The running times for the five examples previously used in the Figs. 1 and 2, are also shown in Fig. 5. There is some correlation visible, but the running times also highly depend on the given passenger train timetable. For example the results for network D only vary slightly in length and duration while the running times differ between 20 and nearly 200 s.

The running times of the path computations based on the reachability results can be found in Fig. 6 for the five examples used in Fig. 5. Due to the fact that we explicitly store the predecessors of the individual intervals, we expect the running time to depend mainly on the number of intervals for which the predecessors have to be looked up, i.e. higher running times for a higher number of vertices in the result. However, this does not seem to be the only impact on the running time. Another factor could be the time needed to find the respective intervals. Depending on the timetable the number of reachable intervals for each vertex varies and for a higher number of intervals finding the one used in the final result takes longer. This could explain why there is no clear upwards trend.

5   Conclusion

The above experimental results demonstrate that our algorithm for solving the train timetabling problem is sufficiently fast to solve real-world problems and offers a promising automated alternative to manual solutions. To further increase practical usefulness, we plan to improve the accuracy of our models by a more realistic approximation of the vertex capacities, improving the availability computation by taking more specific minimum headway times and the varying lengths of the edges into consideration, as well as the fact that some tracks are used in both directions. Another possibility would be to further abstract from the real network by removing or combining vertices that offer no possibility for passing or alternative routes.

Currently we work on a satisfiability modulo theories encoding for comparison, but we do not expect better performance due to the combinatorial difficulty of the problem. We could also check the result of the modified version of Algorithm 1 for feasibility and modify it if needed since the results of both algorithms are somewhat similar and this one is much faster. Another advantage would be that the results definitely do not contain cycles, though they would not necessarily be optimal. In order to compute acceptably fast paths that are optimal according to other criteria Algorithm 2 could be modified.

Last but not least, we are also investigating the simultaneous scheduling of multiple additional trains, and consider aspects of robustness in the presence of delays.

References

1. Borndörfer, R., Fügenschuh, A., Klug, T., Schang, T., Schlechte, T., Schülldorf, H.: The freight train routing problem. Technical Report 13-36, ZIB (2013)
2. Burdett, R., Kozan, E.: Techniques for inserting additional trains into existing timetables. Transp. Res. Part B Methodol. **43**(8), 821–836 (2009)
3. Cacchiani, V., Caprara, A., Toth, P.: A column generation approach to train timetabling on a corridor. 4OR **6**(2), 125–142 (2008). https://doi.org/10.1007/s10288-007-0037-5
4. Cacchiani, V., Caprara, A., Toth, P.: Scheduling extra freight trains on railway networks. Transp. Res. Part B Methodol. **44**(2), 215–231 (2010)
5. Chabini, I.: Discrete dynamic shortest path problems in transportation applications: Complexity and algorithms with optimal run time. Transp. Res. Rec. **1645**(1), 170–175 (1998)
6. Dean, B.C.: Algorithms for minimum-cost paths in time-dependent networks with waiting policies. Networks **44**, 41–46 (2004)
7. Deutsche Bahn, A.G.: Energy efficiency increased. https://ib.deutschebahn.com/ib2016/en/group-management-report/group-performance-environmental-dimension/progress-in-climate-protection/energy-efficiency-increased/. Accessed 13 Nov 2019
8. Dijkstra, E.W.: A note on two problems in connexion with graphs. Numerische Mathematik **1**(1), 269–271 (1959)
9. El-Sherbeny, N.: The algorithm of the time-dependent shortest path problem with time windows. Appl. Math. **5**(17), 2764–2770 (2014)
10. El-Sherbeny, N.: The dynamic sortest path problems of minimum cost length time windows and time-varying costs. Int. J. Sci. Innov. Math. Res. **3**(3), 47–55 (2015)
11. Fujimura, K.: Time-minimum routes in time-dependent networks. IEEE Trans. Rob. Autom. **11**(3), 343–351 (1995)
12. Halpern, J.: Shortest route with time dependent length of edges and limited delay possibilities in nodes. Zeitschrift für Oper. Res. **21**(3), 117–124 (1977)

13. Halpern, J., Priess, I.: Shortest path with time constraints on movement and parking. Networks **4**(3), 241–253 (1974)
14. Orda, A., Rom, R.: Shortest-path and minimum-delay algorithms in networks with time-dependent edge-length. J. ACM **37**(3), 607–625 (1990)
15. Orda, A., Rom, R.: Minimum weight paths in time-dependent networks. Networks **21**(3), 295–319 (1991)
16. Pugliese, L.D.P., Guerriero, F.: A survey of resource constrained shortest path problems: Exact solution approaches. Networks **62**(3), 183–200 (2013)
17. Statistisches Bundesamt: Beförderungsmenge und Beförderungsleistung nach Verkehrsträgern (in German). https://www.destatis.de/DE/Themen/Branchen-Unternehmen/Transport-Verkehr/Gueterverkehr/Tabellen/gueterbefoerderung-lr.html. Accessed 24 June 2019
18. Thomas, B.W., Calogiuri, T., Hewitt, M.: An exact bidirectional A* approach for solving resource-constrained shortest path problems. Networks **73**(2), 187–205 (2019)
19. Union Internationale des Chemins de fer: UIC Code 406, Capacity (2004)
20. Weiß, R., Opitz, J., Nachtigall, K.: A novel approach to strategic planning of rail freight transport. In: Helber, S., et al. (eds.) Operations Research Proceedings 2012. ORP, pp. 463–468. Springer, Cham (2014). https://doi.org/10.1007/978-3-319-00795-3_69

A Tool for Requirements Analysis of Safety-Critical Cyber-Physical Systems

Freek van den Berg[1]($\boxtimes$) and Boudewijn R. Haverkort[2]($\boxtimes$)

[1] Eindhoven University of Technology, Groene Loper 3,
5612 AE Eindhoven, The Netherlands
f.g.b.v.d.berg@tue.nl
[2] Tilburg University, Warandelaan 2, 5037AB Tilburg, The Netherlands
B.R.H.M.Haverkort@tilburguniversity.edu

Abstract. One of the key challenges in the design of a Safety-Critical Cyber-Physical Systems is Requirements Analysis. Current Requirements Analysis approaches range from informal, human-centered ones that are hard to automate, to formal approaches that often lack freedom of expression. Furthermore, most approaches are general-purpose and do not focus on a particular domain, which makes identifying the specific requirements of a given domain less trivial.

To overcome these challenges, this paper presents aDSL, a Domain-Specific Language and toolset for Requirement Analysis of Safety-Critical Cyber-Physical Systems. The approach comprises a mixture of informal and formal elements to enable both automation and freedom of expression; a number of stakeholders introduce and negotiate about their requirements. The aDSL language is used to precisely, concisely and unambiguously describe all such requirements. We have validated aDSL, using simulation techniques and actors that represent the stakeholders, on a case in the agro-machines domain. The proposed approach allows the discovery of requirements in a semi-automatic way.

Keywords: Safety-Critical Cyber-Physical System · Requirement analysis · System designer · Domain-Specific Language · Stakeholders · Negotiation

1 Introduction

A Cyber-Physical System (CPS) is a real-time feedback system that is controlled and monitored by computer-based algorithms. A CPS integrates [1] embedded systems, human users, networks [2], and concurrent physical systems [1,3]. Designing and constructing a CPS requires expertise from many disciplines, including signal processing [2], control engineering [2], computer engineering,

The work in this paper was initiated using a 4TU.NIRICT grant involving a cooperation between University of Twente and Wageningen University & Research.

H. Hermanns (Ed.): MMB 2020, LNCS 12040, pp. 242–258, 2020.
https://doi.org/10.1007/978-3-030-43024-5_15

software engineering and programming, electronics, and mechanical engineering [2]. CPSs are common in safety-critical domains, such as aerospace, civil infrastructure, automotive, energy and agriculture. A Safety-Critical CPS (SC-CPS, [4]) is defined as a CPS that is designed to be fail-safe for safety purposes [5]. Malfunction of a SC-CPS may lead to: death or serious injury to people, loss or damage to equipment or property or environmental harm. Hence, system engineering for SC-CPSs is very challenging because there is no room for error. One of the key activities in the design of these SC-CPSs is the Requirements Engineering process.

Requirements Engineering is mainly concerned with defining the requirements [6] and typically comprises the following five subsequent phases: (i) **system modeling**: generate a system model to test the requirements on; (ii) **requirements elicitation**: research and discover the premature system requirements; (iii) **requirements analysis**: make the requirements clear, complete, consistent and unambiguous; (iv) **requirements specification**: document requirements in a formal artifact; and (v) **requirements validation**: check whether the documented requirements meet the needs of the stakeholders. Requirements evolve and mature as they go through the different Requirements Engineering activities. Pohl proposes a 3D-model [7] for the maturity of a requirement: (i) representation: from informal to formal, (ii) specification: from opaque to complete; and, (iii) from personal to common view; requirements tend to be informal, opaque and person during the elicitation phase, and formal, complete and common during the specification phase.

In this paper, we will primarily focus on the second phase of Requirements Engineering, that is, requirement analysis (RA). Current RA processes range from informal, human-centered to formal approaches. Informal approaches, often driven by Unified Modelling Langage (UML, [8]), tend to include natural language-based documents, e.g., use cases [9], user stories, and process specifications. The use of natural language provides a great freedom of expression, but is hard to formalize when parts of the RA process need to be automated. On the other hand, formal approaches aim to deliver artefacts that are unambiguous and ready for automatic processing. However, their freedom of expression is restricted to their grammar, making it hard for the stakeholders to freely express what they mean. Moreover, the grammar of the language is likely to differ from the language they are accustomed to.

Although RA has been an important activity in current system engineering life-cycle processes for quite some time, current approaches are usually general-purpose and do not focus on a particular domain. Due to this general purpose nature, identifying the specific requirements of the given domain is more challenging. Particularly, SC-CPSs require a dedicated approach that is easy to use and tailored to its domain [4]. A Domain Specific Language (DSL), i.e., a computer language specialized to a particular application domain, enables such a dedicated approach. Hence, a DSL tends to be less comprehensive, much more expressive in the domain, and exhibits less redundancy than general-purpose languages. Therefore, solutions can be expressed and validated at the level of abstraction of the problem domain. On the downside, designing, implementing, maintaining and learning a DSL involves costs. DSLs are supported by tools such as JetBrains MPS, which is a DSL tool[1], and Xtext, an open-source software framework for developing DSLs[2]. For instance, iDSL [10–12], on which aDSL is inspired, has been constructed using Xtext and provides a DSL and toolset for performance evaluation of service-oriented systems.

To meet the aforementioned challenges, this paper proposes aDSL, a DSL and toolset for RA of SC-CPS. The aDSL approach is a mixture of informal and formal approaches to obtain the best of both worlds, i.e., the freedom of expression of informal methods and the ability to automate of formal methods. aDSL enables the system designer and other stakeholders to precisely describe the requirements of a SC-CPS, after which the aDSL toolset takes care of the RA task in a semi-automated manner. The aDSL language and toolset have been evaluated using a case study on agro-machines [13] for validation.

Outline. This paper's remainder is organized as follows. Section 2 introduces a generic algorithm for Requirements Analysis. Section 3 formalizes this approach using an illustrative case study. Section 4 present an implementation. In Sect. 5, the algorithm of Sect. 4 is validated. Section 6 concludes the paper.

2   A Generic Algorithm for Requirement Analysis

This section introduces an algorithm for RA, which we will apply to a CPS. The UML sequence diagram[3] of Fig. 1 displays the subsequent steps and iterations of the algorithm, will be implemented in Sect. 4. It can be observed that Fig. 1 logically combines all RE activities as presented in the introduction, as follows.

1. The input of the generic algorithm is a system model with a formal system description and requirements (cf. Sect. 1, RE step (i)). This model will be implemented in Sect. 3.
2. Requirements elicitation is simulated using two subsequent steps, viz., retrieving the initial requirements from the system model, followed by transforming them into many premature requirements (cf. Sect. 1, RE step (ii)).
3. Requirements analysis (cf. Sect. 1, RE step (iii)) comprises some iterations. In each iteration, two requirements are selected to be merged into one requirement. Typically, these requirements are similar. To this end, the two actors that represent the stakeholders that own these requirements negotiate about these requirements, yielding a new requirement that summarizes the two original requirements. One of the actors becomes the new requirement owner and both original requirements are removed. By the fact that we use a formal language, we consider requirements specification (cf. Sect. 1, RE step (iv)) to be taken care of automatically.

---

[1] JetBrains MPS https://www.jetbrains.com/.

[2] Xtext - Language Engineering Made Easy https://eclipse.org/.

[3] Figures 1 and 2 have been constructed using PlantUML: https://plantuml.com/.

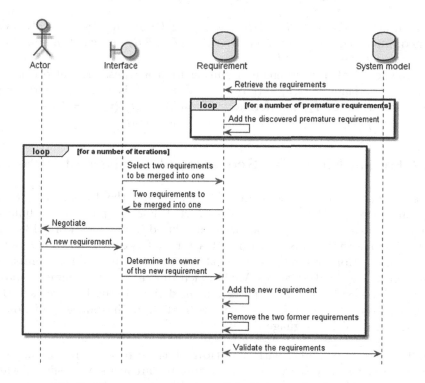

Fig. 1. The sequence diagram of the RA pseudo-algorithm.

4. Requirement validation (cf. Sect. 1, RE step (v)) ensures that the requirements meet stakeholders's needs and that the algorithm as presented in this paper is valid. As a consequence, the requirements generated by the algorithm and the initial requirements need to be similar.

We formalize the algorithm to reduce ambiguity and complexity, using the following notation.

1. Time $T : \{0, 1, 2, \ldots, m\}$ is discrete, where m is the number of iterations.
2. System model SM is constant for all time units $t \in T$. Hence, time is only used and relevant for the time it takes to run the algorithm.
3. System model SM encompasses n formal requirements $FR = \{r_1, r_2, \ldots, r_n\}$
4. A requirement $r \in FR$ has exactly one owner $o \in O$. Hence, $Owner : RF \rightarrow O$ is defined, where $Owner$ is the function that maps requirements to owners.
5. During elicitation, formal requirements $r_1, r_2, \ldots, r_n \in FR$ transform into premature requirements $r'_1, r'_2, \ldots, r'_o \in PR$, with o premature requirements.
6. A timed requirement $Rt : T \times FR$ describes a requirement $r \in FR$ achieved at $t \in T$.
7. All premature requirements are initiated at $t = 0$. Therefore, timed requirements $(0, r'_1), (0, r'_2), \ldots, (0, r'_o)$ exist; put formally: $Tir = \{(0, pr) \,|\, pr \in PR\}$, with PR the set of premature requirements.

8. A transaction $Trans : (T \times FR)^2 \to (T \times FR)$ at time $t \in T$ involves two timed, input requirements (t, r_1), $(t, r_2) \in (T \times FR)$ and yields a new timed requirement $(t + 1, r') \in (T \times FR)$.

9. The owner O of a requirement resulting from a transaction involving two timed requirements (t, r_1), $(t, r_2) \in (T \times FR)$ is either the owner of requirement r_1 or r_2; put formally: $Trans((t, r_1, t), (r_2)) = (t + 1, r') \to (Owner(r') = Owner(r_1) \bigvee Owner(r') = Owner(r_2))$.

3   A Formal Model for Requirement Analysis of CPSs

In this section, we present the model of aDSL, which is the domain-specific language and toolset for CPSs we have constructed. For this purpose, we built on an illustrating case study that has been introduced in previous work [13]. This case study concerns a CPS, which is a tractor that is connected to one out of several trailers. Moreover, a tractor can have different engines and transmissions, yielding many design alternatives. We have left this case study as intact as possible; the CPS, its subsystems, its parts and the design alternatives are as in [13]. To add support for Requirements Analysis to aDSL, we introduce the following three additions to the language:

1. aDSL has been extended with a **notion of time** to allow requirements to evolve over time. Initially, only premature requirements are defined, which evolve into mature requirements via a mechanism in which stakeholders that own an requirement *negotiate*. This mechanism enables the system designer and stakeholders to discover the requirements in a systematic, yet creative manner. In the aDSL language, the notion of time can been observed in the RA measure (cf. Table 1e), viz., the measure contains a parameter iterations that specifies the time the algorithm runs.

2. The formal requirements of the aDSL instance transform into **premature requirements** via reverse engineering, which are more informal, opaque and personal (to be implemented in Sect. 4). In the aDSL language, the conversion from formal requirements into premature ones is not visible because the toolset uses a fixed strategy.

3. A measure for RA has been added to aDSL to **configure experiments**. An experiment involves a number of iterations in which stakeholders with certain behavior, represented by automated actors, negotiate about requirements and the way these requirements are selected. A so-called experiment space can then be used to conveniently define many different instances of this measure. The RA measure and corresponding experiment space of the case study are introduced Table 1e

At its highest level of hierarchy, an aDSL instance comprises five so-called sections[4], as follows.

---

[4] The underlying aDSL grammar can be downloaded from https://www.utwente.nl/en/eemcs/adsl/appendices/appendix-online.pdf.

Table 1. The aDSL instance of the case study

(a) System

```
Section system
  Top-level System TractorTrailorCombination
  AbstractSystem Tractor tractor
  DesAlt(trailor)
  { chiselPlow AbstractPart TrailorChiselPlow tCPlow }
  { trailortiller AbstractPart TrailorTiller tTiller }
  { chaserbin AbstractPart ChaserBin chaserBin }
  { notrailor Part NoTrailor OperationSpace (load [0 0]
                      activity {none} ) }
System tractor
  AbstractSystem Transmission trans   AbstractSystem Fuel fuel

System trans
  DesAlt ( transmission )
  { unsynchronized AtomicSystem transUnsynchronized
    OperationSpace ( driverSkills { advanced moderate easy }
      continousOperation { no } gears [ 1 24 ] ) }
  { doubleClutch AtomicSystem transDoubleClutch OperationSpace
    ( driverSkills { moderate easy } gears [ 1 24 ] ) }
  { CVT AtomicSystem transCVT OperationSpace ( driverSkills
            { easy } efficiency { frictionLoss } gears [ 1 1000 ] ) }
System fuel
  DesAlt ( engineFuel )
  { steam AtomicSystem fuelSteam
    OperationSpace ( pollution [5 10] speed [0 30] ) }
  { diesel AtomicSystem fuelDiesel OperationSpace ( pollution [4 8]
fuelConsumption [3 5] speed [0 40] price {medium high} ) }
  { gasoline AtomicSystem fuelGasoline OperationSpace
    ( pollution [2 5] fuelConsumption [4 10] speed [0 50]
    price { medium high } ) }
  { electric AtomicSystem fuelElectric OperationSpace ( pollution[0 4]
    fuelConsumption[8 12] speed[0 55] price{high})}
```

(b) Part

```
Section part
  Part tCPlow OperationSpace
    ( speed [0 25] agility { low veryLow } activity { plow } )
  Part tTiller OperationSpace
    ( speed [0 25] agility { low veryLow } activity { till } )
  Part chaserBin OperationSpace
    ( speed [0 15] agility { veryLow } activity { harvest } )
```

Table 1. (continued)

(c) Requirement

```
Section requirement
  Requirement RA1 minimum OperationSpace (speed [5 15]
      fuelConsumption [8 10] price medium gears [1 30])
    maximum OperationSpace (speed [0 45] fuelConsumption [0 20] price
      { low medium high } driverSkills { easy } pollution [0 6])
  Requirement RA2 minimum OperationSpace (speed [7 12]
      fuelConsumption [4 7] price medium gears [4 24])
    maximum OperationSpace (speed [0 35] fuelConsumption [0 15]
      driverSkills easy pollution [4 8])
```

(d) Design space

```
Section design space
  DesignSpace ( transmission {unsynchronized doubleClutch CVT}
    trailor {chiselPlow trailortiller chaserbin notrailor}
    engineFuel { steam diesel gasoline electric } )
```

(e) Measure

```
Section measure
  Measurement RAnalysis simulation has 12 iterations 10 runs, actors
    have distribution espace (actorIntersection) intersection
    espace (actorConjunction) conjunction espace (actorCompromise)
    compromise espace (actorCoerce) coerce, requirements are selected
    using espace (selectReq) entropy (2-espace(selectReq)) jaccard,
    requirement owner is selected using espace (selectOwner) entropy
    (2-espace (selectOwner)) jaccard
  ExperimentSpace ( actorIntersection {0 1 2} actorConjunction
    {0 1 2} actorCompromise {0 1 2} actorCoerce {0 1 2}
    selectReq {0 1 2} selectOwner {0 1 2} )
```

Section system comprises one **top-level system**, i.e., the CPS under study, and its subsystems. The CPS and subsystems have a name and operation space (to be explained later). At a lower level, a system comprises one or more so-called SystemOrParts, i.e., either a **system**, **part**, **systemID** or **partID**.

Case Study. Table 1a contains the aDSL system instance. The top-level system "TractorTrailorCombination" comprises a "Tractor" (of type tractor) and a selection out of four possible trailors, which is expressed using the Design Alternative (DesAlt) construct in aDSL. In turn, a "Tractor" consists of a "Transmission", a DesAlt construct with three options, and a "Fuel" kind, a DesAlt construct with four options.

Section part encompasses zero or more parts. On top of that, a system and a part have an **operation space**, which represents a number of operational modes.

An operation space consist of zero or more dimensions. A dimension is either a bounded integer range or a finite set of elements.

Case Study. Table 1b shows parts "tCPlow", "tTiller" and "chaserBin", and their operation spaces. E.g., "chaserBin" has an operation space with dimensions "speed" (range: $[0:15]$), "agility" (value: veryLow) and "activity" (value: harvest).

Section requirement contains **requirements** that limit the valid operation spaces of a CPS. For this purpose, a requirement is defined using a minimum and maximum operation space. An ordering on operation spaces is then used to determine if the operation spaces of each system and part of a CPS meet a requirement, as follows. Let $O1$ and $O2$ be operation spaces, represented as sets of dimension and value pairs. Then $O1$ is at most $O2$ (denoted with the usual "$\leq$" operator) when $O1$ comprises dimension d, either $O2$ does not comprise dimension d or dimension d of $O2$ contains at least all values of dimension d of $O1$; put formally:

$$O1 \leq O2 \rightarrow \begin{cases} (d:v) \in O1 \rightarrow \not\exists x (d:x) \in O2 \\ (d:x) \in O1 \rightarrow (d:x) \in O2 \end{cases}$$

Hence, only common dimensions are considered for comparison. Note that previous work [13] discusses this ordering of operation spaces more extensively.

Case Study. Table 1c conveys two requirements, which are a combination of the requirements of previous work [13]. They transform into premature requirements as part of the implementation to be introduced in Sect. 4.

Section measure comprises measure "RAnalysis" to enable the experiments for requirements analysis. An experiment is initialized using twelve parameters, e.g., to define the actor behavior and the way requirements are selected, as carefully explained next in the case study. To conveniently define many instances of this measure, aDSL has also been equipped with a so-called experiment space. An experiment space comprises $K \in \mathbb{N}^+$ dimensions that each have a number of values. The K^{ary} Cartesian product of these dimensions form the set of experiment instances. We use a so-called espace construct with twelve parameters in order to vary all parameters of the experiment.

Case Study. Table 1e contains Measure "RAnalysis". It is initialized with a constant number of 12 iterations and 10 simulation runs in this case. The remaining ten parameters contain espace constructs that refer to ExperimentSpace dimensions. We define experiment space $\hat{E}$, which comprises the set of experiments E that have different parameters, as follows:

$$\hat{E} = \{E(12, 10, \qquad \text{\#the number of iterations (12) and runs (10).}$$

$$ac_1, ac_2, ac_3, ac_4, \qquad \text{\# the relative probabilities of actor}$$

$$\text{intersection}(ac_1), \text{conjunction } (ac_2),$$

$$\text{compromise } (ac_3) \text{and coercion } (ac_4).$$

$$rs_1, rs_2, \qquad \text{\# the relative probabilities of using Entropy } (rs_1)$$

$$\text{and Jaccard } (rs_2) \text{ for requirement selection.}$$

$$os_1, os_2) \mid \qquad \text{\#the relative probabilities of using Entropy } (os_1)$$

$$\text{and Jaccard}(os_2) \text{ for requirement owner selection.}$$

$$ac_1 + ac_2 + ac_3 + ac_4 > 0 \quad \text{\# at least one relative actor probability is not zero.}$$

$$rs_1 + rs_2 = 2 \qquad \text{\# the req. sel. rel. probs. are (2,0), (1,1) or (0,2).}$$

$$os_1 + os_2 = 2 \quad \text{\# the owner sel. rel. probs. are (2,0), (1,1) or (0,2).}$$

$$ac_1, ac_2, ac_3.ac_4, rs_1, rs_2, os_1, os_2 \in \{0, 1, 2\}\} \quad \text{\#the 10 parameters are 0, 1 or 2.}$$

$$(1)$$

Section design space contains a **design space** with n dimensions. The n^{ary} Cartesian product of the n dimensions is then set of design alternatives. On top of that, DesAlt refers to a dimension, and maps each dimension value to a SystemOrPart.

Case Study. Table 1d contains three dimensions, viz., "transmission", "trailer and "engineFuel". Combined, they yield $3 \times 4 \times 4 = 48$ design alternatives. The aDSL system (see Table 1a) contains three DesAlts, which are so-called variation points. That is, for each design alternative they are evaluated differently.

4 An Implemented Algorithm for RA of SC-CPS

In Sect. 2, a generic algorithm was presented for RA of CPSs (as depicted in Fig. 1). In this section, we implement this algorithm to make it executable[5]. To this end, the following individual parts are implemented as graphically depicted in Fig. 2: (i) capturing the premature requirements (cf. Sect. 4.1); (ii) evolution of the requirements (cf. Sect. 4.2); and, (iii) validation of the requirements (cf. Sect. 4.3). For precision, step (ii) is executed for 10 simulation runs as defined in Section Measure (see Table 1e).

4.1 Capturing the Premature Requirements

Capturing the requirements corresponds to system elicitation (cf. Sect. 1, RE step (ii)). In practice, this is a non-trivial, labor-intensive step which involves interviews, questionnaires, user observations, workshops, etc. Therefore, we simulate it using a reverse engineering step instead, as follows. We split the formal

---

[5] The work in this paper has been implemented using Xtext for DSLs and Xtend.

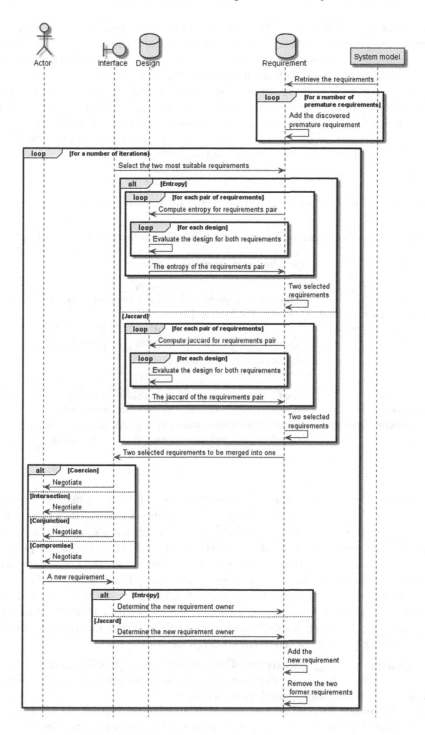

Fig. 2. The sequence diagram of the RA implemented-algorithm.

requirements (cf. Table 1c) of the system model into many smaller premature requirements. These premature requirements should then lead to the formal requirements again after executing the algorithm, which validates the approach (see Fig. 2). Premature requirements are generated, as follows.

Let $(o_{min}, o_{max}) = r$ represent formal requirement r with minimum operation space o_{min} and maximum operation space o_{max}. Then each premature requirement $pr \in PR$ derived from r has a minimum operation space o'_{min} and maximum operation space o'_{max}, where o'_{min} is o_{min} reduced by one element and o'_{max} is o_{max} reduced by one element; put formally:

$$R = \{(o'_{min}, o'_{max}) | o'_{min} = o_{min} \setminus e_i, e_i \in o_{min}, o'_{max} = o_{max} \setminus e_j, e_j \in o_{max}\} \quad (2)$$

where R is the set of generated requirements for requirement $(o_{min}, o_{max}) = r$

Table 2. The generation of premature requirements from requirement RA2

(a) Minimum operation spaces

i	e_i	$o_{min} \setminus e_i$
1	speed [7 12]	(fuelConsumption [4 7] price { medium } gears [4 24])
2	fuelConsumption [4 7]	(speed [7 12] price { medium } gears [4 24])
3	price { medium }	(speed [7 12] fuelConsumption [4 7] gears [4 24])
4	gears [4 24]	(speed [7 12] fuelConsumption [4 7] price { gears })

(b) Maximum operation spaces

j	e_j	$o_{max} \setminus e_i$
1	speed [0 35]	(fuelConsumption [0 15] driverSkills {easy} pollution [4 8])
2	fuelConsumption [0 15]	(speed [0 35] driverSkills {easy} pollution [4 8])
3	driverSkills {easy}	(speed [0 35] fuelConsumption [0 15] pollution [4 8])
4	pollution [4 8]	(speed [0 35] fuelConsumption [0 15] driverSkills {easy})

Case Study. We generate the premature requirements for formal requirement RA2 (see Table 1c), as follows. First, we compute the elements of operation spaces o'_{min} and o'_{max} (as shown in Table 2), which are the elements of o_{min} and o_{max} with one element omitted, respectively. Second, the operation spaces of the generated premature requirements are the Cartesian product of the resulting minimum (cf. Table 2a, third column) and maximum (cf. Table 2b, third column) operation spaces. Hence, formal requirement RA2 yields $4 \times 4 = 16$ premature requirements, where $R_{i,j}$ is the requirement with the ith and j^{th} element omitted with $i, j \in \{1, 2, 3, 4\}$ (cf. Table 2a and b, first column). For illustration, the first ($R_{1,1}$) and last premature requirement ($R_{4,4}$) are:

– **Requirement $R_{1,1}$ minimum OperationSpace** (fuelConsumption [4 7] price { medium } gears [4 24]) **maximum OperationSpace** (fuelConsumption [0 15] driverSkills {easy} pollution [4 8])
– **Requirement $R_{4,4}$ minimum OperationSpace** (speed [7 12] fuelConsumption [4 7] price { gears } **maximum OperationSpace** (speed [0 35] fuelConsumption [0 15] driverSkills {easy})

4.2   Evolution of the Requirements

The evolution of the requirements takes place in iterations of the following three steps (as in Figs. 1 and 2): (i) selecting requirements to evolve; (ii) stakeholders negotiating about requirements resulting in new requirements; and, (iii) select an owner for the requirement.

(i) Selecting two requirements to evolve occurs on the basis of their similarity, viz., when two requirements are similar, one of them is likely to be obsolete. aDSL provides two similarity measures to determine which two requirements are most similar, viz., Entropy and Jaccard. Each iteration, the measure Entropy is selected with probability $\frac{Rs_1}{Rs_1+Rs_2}$ and measure Jaccard with $\frac{Rs_2}{Rs_1+Rs_2}$ (cf. Eq. 2 and Table 1e). Let $R_1, R_2, \ldots, R_n$ be n requirements from which we would like to select the two most similar requirements. To this end, we evaluate all requirements for all n designs $D_1, D_2, \ldots, D_n$. Consequently, $M(d, r) = \top$ when design d meets requirement r, and $M(d, r) = \bot$ when it does not.

Next, we focus on pairs of requirements R_i and R_j. Hence, a design can be evaluated in four ways, viz., $M(d, R_i) = \bot$ or $\top$, and simultaneously $M(d, R_j) = \bot$ or $\top$. We then count all these four options individually, as follows:

$$k_{i,j} = \sum_{n=1}^{|D|} \mathbb{I}\{ \mid M(d_n, R_i) = i, M(d_n, R_j) = j \mid \} \tag{3}$$

where $k_{i,j}$ is the number of designs that yield i for R_1 and j for R_2, $i, j \in \{\bot, \top\}$, $\mathbb{I}(\top) = 1$ and $\mathbb{I}(\bot) = 0$, $|D|$ the number of designs, d_n the nth design, and R_1, R_2 the compared requirements. Also, $l_{i,j} = k_{i,j} / |D|$ is a relative version of $k_{i,j}$. Now, we compute Entropy and Jaccard for selecting requirements, as follows.

1. Entropy [14]: the expected amount of information. A higher outcome corresponds to less similarity. It is defined as:

$$E(r_1, r_2) = -\sum_{i=0}^{1}\sum_{j=0}^{1} l_{i,j} \cdot \log(l_{i,j}) \tag{4}$$

where we assume that $0 \cdot \log(0) = 0$, since $\lim_{n \to 0}(n \cdot log(n)) = 0$.
2. Jaccard [15]: originally used for the similarity of two sets. A higher outcome corresponds to a higher similarity. It is defined as:

$$J(r_1, r_2) = \frac{k_{1,1}}{k_{1,1} + k_{0,1} + k_{1,0}} \tag{5}$$

(ii) Stakeholders Negotiate About the Requirements They Own. Two stakeholders negotiate about the requirement they each own, i.e., R_1 and R_2, and come up with one new requirement, i.e., R_{new} that replaces the two previous requirements. In reality, this transformation is performed by two humans, actors or stakeholders. To be able to conduct many experiments (see Sect. 5 for the results), we simulate human actors using a combination of four actor implementations. In each iteration, they are selected with probabilities $\frac{Ac_n}{Ac_1 + Ac_2 + Ac_3 + Ac_4}$ (cf. Eq. 3 and Table 1e), where $n \in \{1, 2, 3, 4\}$ is the option number. The implementations are defined as follows.

1. **Intersection**: requirement R_{new} is satisfied iff the operation spaces of both requirements R_1 and R_2 are satisfied; put formally:

$$R_{new}^{min} = \{(d, x \cup y) \mid (d, x) \in R_1^{min}, (d, y) \in R_2^{min}\},$$
$$R_{new}^{max} = \{(d, x \cap y) \mid (d, x) \in R_1^{max}, (d, y) \in R_2^{max}\}. \tag{6}$$

   where d is an operation space dimension, and x and y operation space values.
2. **Conjunction**: requirement R_{new} is satisfied iff the operation spaces of at least one requirement are satisfied; put formally:

$$R_{new}^{min} = \{(d, x \cap y) \mid (d, x) \in R_1^{min}, (d, y) \in R_2^{min}\},$$
$$R_{new}^{max} = \{(d, x \cup y) \mid (d, x) \in R_1^{max}, (d, y) \in R_2^{max}\}. \tag{7}$$

3. **Compromise**: the operation spaces of requirement R_{new} contain dimensions from either R_1 or R_2. When a dimension appears in only one operation space of R_1 or R_2, it is automatically added to the operation space of R_{new}. When a dimension appears in both operation spaces, a coinflip[6] is used; put formally:

$$((d, x) \in R_1^{min} \wedge rnd_{bool} == \top) \rightarrow (d, x) \in R_{new}^{min}$$
$$((d, y) \in R_2^{min} \wedge rnd_{bool} == \bot) \rightarrow (d, y) \in R_{new}^{min} \tag{8}$$

   where rnd_{bool} is a random boolean generator that draws from $\{\top, \bot\}$. R_{new}^{max} is determined analogously. For conciseness, we have omitted the equations in which a dimension appears in one of the operation spaces of R_1 or R_2.
4. **Coercion**: one actor overrules the other, e.g., by having more power in a business. Hence, either R_1 or R_2 gets selected via a coinflip; put formally:

$$R_{new} = \begin{cases} R_1 & \text{if } rnd_{bool} == \top, \\ R_2 & \text{if } rnd_{bool} == \bot. \end{cases} \tag{9}$$

The operation spaces of R_1 and R_2 in Eqs. (6) and (7) are assumed to have the same dimensions, which might not always be the case. To compensate for this, $(d, x \cup y)$ is replaced by either (d, x) (or (d, y)) when dimension d is missing in one of the operation spaces in (6) and (7). Also, $(d, x \cap y)$ is replaced by $(d, \emptyset)$ when dimension d is not present in one of the operation spaces in (6) and (7).

---

[6] All random numbers used have been uniquely generated for this paper using https://www.random.org/.

(iii) Selecting an Owner for the New Requirement. The owner of the new requirement R_{new} is the owner of one of the former requirements (R_1 or R_2), viz., the one that is most similar to the new requirement. Entropy and Jaccard (as introduced in Eqs. 4 and 5) are used here for each iteration, with probabilities $\frac{Os_1}{Os_1+Os_2}$ and $\frac{Os_2}{Os_1+Os_2}$ (cf. (1) and Table 1e), respectively. The owner of R_{new} is R_1 when the distance between R_1 and R_{new} is smaller than the distance between R_2 and R_{new}, and R_2 otherwise.

4.3   Validation of the Requirements

We compare the generated requirements with the orginal formal system requirements (see Table 1c). For this purpose, we compute the relative number of satisfied requirements for each design, as follows:

$$RS_s(d) = \sum_{i=1}^{|R_s|} \mathbb{I}\left(M(d, r_i)\right) \tag{10}$$

where $RS_s(d) \in [0 : 1]$ is the relative amount of satisfied requirements for design d, $|R_s|$ the number of requirements in collection s, r_i the ith requirement, $\mathbb{I}(\top) = 1$ and $\mathbb{I}(\bot) = 0$. Following this, RS is used to compute the relative number of satisfied designs for the initial system requirements (RS_{init}) and the generated requirements (RS_{gen}). We compare them as follows.

$$V(RS_{init}, RS_{gen}) = \sqrt{\sum_{i=1}^{|D|}(RS_{init}(d_i) - RS_{gen}(d_i))^2}, \tag{11}$$

where $V \in [0 : 1]$ is the so-called *validity* degree (lower is better), RS_{init} and RS_{gen} are the relative number of satisfied requirements (of (10)), and d_i is the ith design.

Finally, we define two ways to compare the outcomes of experiments. First, we compare outcomes of experiments on the best average value, as follows.

$$V_{average} = \frac{\sum_{i=1}^{n} V(RS_{init}, RS_{gen})_i}{n} \tag{12}$$

where n is the number of experiments and $V(RS_{init}, RS_{gen})_i$ the outcome for the $i^t h$ experiment. Second, we compare outcomes of experiments on the best incidental value as:

$$V_{max} = \min_{i \in \{1..n\}} V(RS_{init}, RS_{gen})_i \tag{13}$$

where n is the number of experiments and $V(RS_{init}, RS_{gen})_i$ is the outcome for the ith experiment.

5   Experimental Results

We validate our approach by executing the case study of Table 1 in aDSL; aDSL executes the algorithm of Fig. 2 for each experiment of (2). Each experiment is simulated 10 times for more reliable results and contains 12 iterations in which stakeholders negotiate. At the end of each experiment, a validity degree is computed according to (11) to compare experiments. Table 3 shows the experiments that score best on average and incidentally, as follows.

Experiments that score **best on average** (see Table 3a and (12)) yield the lowest average score for V on 10 simulation runs. The six highest ranked experiments rely completely on compromise (ac_3) as the actor negotiation strategy,

Table 3. Experiments that score best

(a) on average.

Rank	Experiment								Average ± 95%CI
	ac_1	ac_2	ac_3	ac_4	rs_1	rs_2	os_1	os_2	
1	0	0	1	0	1	1	1	1	0.371 ± 0.076
2	0	0	1	0	0	2	2	0	0.374 ± 0.021
3	0	0	1	0	2	0	2	0	0.374 ± 0.021
4	0	0	1	0	1	1	2	0	0.376 ± 0.022
5	0	0	1	0	2	0	1	1	0.396 ± 0.062
6	0	0	1	0	0	2	1	1	0.408 ± 0.104
7	1	0	2	0	2	0	2	0	0.411 ± 0.068
8	1	0	2	0	0	2	2	0	0.416 ± 0.09
9	1	0	1	0	0	2	2	0	0.421 ± 0.055
10	1	0	2	0	1	1	2	0	0.423 ± 0.067

(b) incidentally.

Rank	Experiment								Minimum run
	ac_1	ac_2	ac_3	ac_4	rs_1	rs_2	os_1	os_2	
1	0	0	2	1	2	0	1	1	0.346
2	2	2	1	0	0	2	1	1	0.349
3	0	0	1	0	1	1	1	1	0.354
4	0	0	1	0	0	2	1	1	0.354
5	0	0	2	1	1	1	1	1	0.354
6	2	0	1	0	0	2	1	1	0.354
7	2	0	2	1	0	2	1	1	0.354
8	1	0	1	1	0	2	1	1	0.354
9	2	0	1	0	2	0	1	1	0.356
10	1	0	2	2	0	2	1	1	0.356

Legend: The relative probability of actor intersection is ac_1, conjunction ac_2, compromise ac_3 and coercion ac_4. The relative probability of requirement selection with Entropy is rs_1 and with Jaccard rs_2. The relative probability of requirement owner selection with Entropy is os_1 and with Jaccard os_2.

whereas the remaining four are a combination of this compromise strategy with the intersection (ac_1) strategy. Presumably, the conjunction (ac_2) strategy generates many invalid requirements by permitting all combinations of the operations spaces of the two old requirements. Moreover, the coercion (ac_4) strategy appears aggressive and is very random by selecting one requirement and neglecting the other requirement completely. Furthermore, we deduce that selecting either the Entropy or Jaccard measure for selecting two requirements or assigning an owner to a new requirement appears to be not significant; experiments with similar actor negotiation strategies score high.

Experiments that score **best incidentally** (see Table 3b and (13)) yield a low score for V on at least one of the 10 simulation runs. Hence, they sometimes perform well but do not need to do this structurally. Again, experiments with an intersection (ac_1, 6 experiments in the list) and compromise (ac_3, all experiments in the list) actor negotiation strategy score high. On top of this, the coercion (ac_4, 5 experiments in the list) is noteworthy. Namely, making random decisions, e.g., as with the coercion strategy, in order to score well on one experiment.

Summarized, aDSL has shown to be able to automatically compute the validation scores for all experiments. This enables us to define an actor negotiation strategy and see how it performs. Four negotiation strategies have been tested of which "intersection" and "compromise" are most promising. Besides this, the "coercion" strategy scores well, albeit only incidentally. Using either the Entropy or Jaccard measure does not seems to make much difference.

6   Conclusion

Many cyber-physical systems are safety-critical, which implies that their malfunctioning may cause serious property damage or even injure people. Requirement analysis is one of the key activities in the design of SC-CPSs. Current RA approaches range from informal, hard to automate ones to formal ones that lack freedom of expression; furthermore, most approaches are general-purpose, while in case of a SC-CPS, an approach that is easy to use and tailored to the application domain at hand is called for.

In this paper, we have presented aDSL, a DSL and toolset for requirements analysis of safety-critical cyber-physical systems. The approach is a mixture of informal, human-centered and formal approaches to enable both automation and freedom of expression. It comprises an algorithm that automatically requests stakeholders to negotiate about similar requirements and replaces them with new ones, viz., when two requirements are similar, one might be obsolete.

In practice, our approach would require real humans for testing. Instead, we have defined actors that automatically simulate the negotiation behavior of the stakeholders, enabling large-scale and high-speed testing. Consequently, we have been able to conduct many experiments which slightly differ in actor behavior. As somehow expected, the resulting requirements are of better quality when the actors compromise opposed to them displaying coercive behavior. Humans actors can keep these findings in mind, while engaging in real negotiations. Besides this, aDSL could be used to develop and test new actor strategies.

References

1. Lee, E.A.: Cyber-physical systems-are computing foundations adequate. In: Position Paper for NSF Workshop On Cyber-Physical Systems: Research Motivation, Techniques and Roadmap, vol. 2 (2006)
2. Rajkumar, R.R., Lee, I., Sha, L., Stankovic, J.: Cyber-physical systems: the next computing revolution. In: Proceedings of the 47th Design Automation Conference, pp. 731–736. ACM (2010)
3. Khaitan, S.K., McCalley, J.D.: Design techniques and applications of cyberphysical systems: a survey. IEEE Syst. J. 9(2), 350–365 (2015)
4. Banerjee, A., Venkatasubramanian, K.K., Mukherjee, T., Gupta, S.K.: Ensuring safety, security, and sustainability of mission-critical cyber-physical systems. Proc. IEEE 100(1), 283–299 (2012)
5. Bowen, J.: The ethics of safety-critical systems. Commun. ACM 43(4), 91–97 (2000)
6. Kotonya, G., Sommerville, I.: Requirements Engineering: Processes and Techniques. Wiley Publishing, Hoboken (1998)
7. Pohl, K.: The three dimensions of requirements engineering. In: Rolland, C., Bodart, F., Cauvet, C. (eds.) CAiSE 1993. LNCS, vol. 685, pp. 275–292. Springer, Heidelberg (1993). https://doi.org/10.1007/3-540-56777-1_15
8. Fowler, M.: UML Distilled: A Brief Guide to the Standard Object Modeling Language. Addison-Wesley Professional, Boston (2004)
9. Adolph, S., Cockburn, A., Bramble, P.: Patterns for Effective Use Cases. Addison-Wesley Longman Publishing Co., Inc., Boston (2002)
10. van den Berg, F., Remke, A., Haverkort, B.R.: A domain specific language for performance evaluation of medical imaging systems. In: 5th Workshop on Medical Cyber-Physical Systems, Service OpenAccess Series in Informatics, vol. 36, pp. 80–93. Schloss Dagstuhl (2014)
11. van den Berg, F., Haverkort, B.R., Hooman, J.: iDSL: automated performance evaluation of service-oriented systems. In: Katoen, J.-P., Langerak, R., Rensink, A. (eds.) ModelEd, TestEd, TrustEd. LNCS, vol. 10500, pp. 214–236. Springer, Cham (2017). https://doi.org/10.1007/978-3-319-68270-9_11
12. van den Berg, F., Remke, A., Haverkort, B.R.: iDSL: automated performance prediction and analysis of medical imaging systems. In: Beltrán, M., Knottenbelt, W., Bradley, J. (eds.) EPEW 2015. LNCS, vol. 9272, pp. 227–242. Springer, Cham (2015). https://doi.org/10.1007/978-3-319-23267-6_15
13. van den Berg, F., Garousi, V., Tekinerdogan, B., Haverkort, B.R.: Designing cyber-physical systems with aDSL: a domain-specific language and tool support. In: 13th System of Systems Engineering Conference. IEEE (2018)
14. Gray, R.: Entropy and Information Theory. Springer, Heidelberg (2011). https://doi.org/10.1007/978-1-4419-7970-4
15. Niwattanakul, S., Singthongchai, J., Naenudorn, E., Wanapu, S.: Using of Jaccard coefficient for keywords similarity. In: Proceedings of the International MultiConference of Engineers and Computer Scientists, vol. 1, no. 6 (2013)

Automated Rare Event Simulation for Fault Tree Analysis via Minimal Cut Sets

Carlos E. Budde[1](✉)[iD] and Mariëlle Stoelinga[1,2][iD]

[1] Formal Methods and Tools, University of Twente, Enschede, The Netherlands
{c.e.budde,m.i.a.stoelinga}@utwente.nl
[2] Department of Software Science, Radboud University, Nijmegen, The Netherlands

Abstract. Monte Carlo simulation is a common technique to estimate dependability metrics for fault trees. A bottleneck in this technique is the number of samples needed, especially when the interesting events are rare and occur with low probability. Rare Event Simulation (RES) reduces the number of samples when analysing rare events. Importance splitting is a RES method that spawns more simulation runs from promising system states. How promising a state is, is indicated by an importance function, which concentrates the information that makes this method efficient. Importance functions are given by domain and RES experts. This hinders re-utilisation and involves decisions entailing potential human error. Focusing in (general) fault trees, in this paper we automatically derive importance functions based on the tree structure. For this we exploit a common fault tree concept, namely cut sets: the more elements from a cut set have failed, the higher the importance. We show that the cut-set-derived importance function is an easy-to-implement and simple concept, that can nonetheless compete against another (more involved) automatic importance function for RES.

Keywords: Minimal cut sets · Rare event simulation · Dynamic fault trees · Importance splitting · Fault tree analysis

1 Introduction

Classical Monte Carlo simulation (CMC) is a common technique to evaluate stochastic models. Its applications range from systems biology, climate models, and social interaction, to reliability analysis, performance evaluation, network security, and many more.

By taking a large number of random samples, CMC estimates the metric of interest, such as the average package loss in a network. While this technique is very flexible in the stochastic models it can handle, as well as the metrics it can analyse, it suffers from a major drawback: to get accurate estimates, a large

---

This work was partially funded by EU project 102112 (*SUCCESS*), and NS, ProRail, and NWO project 15474 (*SEQUOIA*).

H. Hermanns (Ed.): MMB 2020, LNCS 12040, pp. 259–277, 2020.
https://doi.org/10.1007/978-3-030-43024-5_16

number of samples is needed. This problem is exacerbated in case of rare events, i.e. events with low probability of occurrence.

Rare event simulation (RES [24]) is a scientific field dealing with simulation techniques that efficiently handle rare events. Various methods exist, including importance sampling [10, 21], importance splitting [1, 15], sequential Monte Carlo [6], etc. These methods typically tweak the probabilities in the systems, or the way samples are taken, to make the rare event less rare. The metric of interest is then also adjusted, to account for the changes in the simulations. However, RES also comes with a drawback: all these techniques depend on expert knowledge.

This paper presents a theory to deploy automatic RES for an important class of models, namely *fault trees* (FTs). Fault trees are a prominent model in reliability engineering, and are widely deployed in industry, by companies like Siemens, Honeywell, NASA and many others.

An FT is a graphical model that shows why a system fails, i.e. which failure modes and mechanisms exist that can cause a top-level system failure. Thus, the leaves of the tree model basic failures; while gates represent how basic failures propagate through the system. Static gates represent Boolean combinations of failures, such as AND and OR, while dynamic gates model dependability patters, such as spare components management and functional dependencies.

Typical metrics for FTs include system *reliability* (the probability that the system does not fail during its mission time) and *availability* (its average uptime).

Numerical analysis of fault trees is achievable for large models, but it is not feasible for fault trees that are complex, and model important features such as maintenance, interdependent interactions, or non-Markovian probability distributions. Such FT models are often analyzed using Monte Carlo simulation. Rare events are an issue here [29], since fault trees are typically used to model safety-critical systems (power plants, rockets) whose failure probability is low. Our technique for rare event simulation is based on importance splitting. The key idea is to generate more samples from a path that looks promising. More precisely, importance splitting relies on an *importance function* that assigns a higher *importance* (viz. weight) to more promising states in a trace. The main contribution of this paper is to assign to each fault tree an importance function that can be automatically derived from its structure, in a similar way to [3]. The goals is also to deploy functions with low computation overhead and low variability, so that the RES algorithms implemented from them hare highly-performant.

To achieve this, our importance functions is based on (minimal) cut sets. Cut sets are sets of basic events such that, if all elements in the cuts set fail, the tree fails—we note that cut sets are defined for static fault trees; we conservatively extend these to dynamic fault trees. Thus, the more elements in a cut set that have failed, the higher its importance. Since a fault tree usually has multiple cut sets, we take the maximum importance over all cut sets.

In fact, we propose several variants of this idea, where we also normalize the cut sets by their maximum weights, or prune them based on their cardinality or failure probability. Our experimental evaluation shows that our functions, tested on the standard HECS benchmark for FTA for a fixed simulation time budget, can produce estimates as accurate as more involved approaches that consider the whole structure of the tree [3]. Moreover, the RES algorithms deployed by our functions show the highest stability in our tests. These results are a first step; elaborate experimental evaluation are an important topic for future research.

Outline. After reviewing related work, in Sect. 2 we present the basic theoretical concepts needed to understand our contribution. In Sect. 3 we introduce an heuristic importance function for RES, that uses the minimal cut sets of the FTs. Section 4 compares our approach—empirically—to other ways of analysing DFTs. This work concludes in Sect. 5, where we draw lines for future research.

Related Work. Much effort in RES has been dedicated to study highly reliable systems, which includes fault trees [29,30]. When the fail/repair times follow non-Markovian distributions, importance splitting is a usual choice. As long as a full system failure can be broken down into several smaller components failures, an importance splitting method can be devised. Of course, its efficiency relies heavily on the choice of importance function. This choice is typically done ad hoc for the model under study [17,31]. For instance, [29] defined a "state variable" (an importance function for the RESTART algorithm: $S(t) = \max_i\{c_i(t)\}$) for a specific system. In essence, viewing the system as a fault tree, $S(t)$ counts the max number of failed components in any MCS. This was generalised in [30] using cut set analysis to define the importance function $\Phi(t) = cl - oc(t)$. Unlike $S(t)$, $\Phi(t)$ does not require all cut sets to have the same cardinality. However, both functions are hindered when the branches of the fault tree have different failure probabilities. In this work we propose to alleviate this issue via *cut set pruning* and *importance normalisation* [3]. Regarding automation, [4,5,12,13] are among the first to attempt a heuristic derivation of all parameters required to implement splitting. In essence, here we extended [2,4,5], using the cut sets of the fault tree in conjunction with the structural function derived in [3].

2   Theoretical Framework

2.1   Fault Trees

A fault tree '$\triangle$' is a directed acyclic graph that models how component failures propagate and eventually cause the full system to fail. The leaves are called *basic elements* (or basic events), and model the failure of elemental components. Other nodes called intermediate events are labelled with *gates*, and describe how combinations of lower failures propagate to upper levels. A full-system failure is called a *top level event* (TLE), and takes place when the root node of the tree fails.

In this work we consider the repairable dynamic fault trees (RFTs) presented in [8,19]. Thus, each basic element (BE) b is equipped with a failure distribution F_b that governs its failure probability as a function of time, and a repair distribution R_b that governs its repair time. Some BEs are used as spare components: these (SBEs) replace a primary component when it fails. The dormancy distribution D_b of an SBE b describes its failure while *dormant*, i.e. not in use. Only if b becomes active its failure distribution is given by F_b.

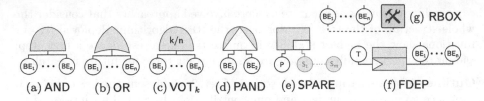

Fig. 1. Fault tree gates and the repair box [3]

RFTs have six types of gates. Their syntax is shown in Figs. 1a to f, and their meaning is as follows: the AND, OR, and VOT$_k$ gates fail if respectively all, one, or k of their m children fail. The latter is called the *voting* or k out of m gate. The *priority-and gate* (PAND) is an AND gate that only fails if its children fail from left to right (or simultaneously). SPARE gates have one *primary* child and one or more *spare* children: spares replace the primary when it fails. The FDEP gate has an input *trigger* and several *dependent events*: all dependent events become unavailable when the trigger fails. Figure 2a shows an RFT without repairs.

RFTs handle repairs by means of *repair boxes* (RBOX [22]). BEs and SBEs can be connected to an RBOX, which determines which basic element is repaired next according to a given policy. Note that the repair distribution (and thus, the time-to-repair of failed components) is an attribute of the basic element.

The semantics for (repairable) dynamic fault trees is given in terms of stochastic transition models, such as Markov automata, Petri nets, IOSA, etc. Following [19] we give semantics to RFT as Input/Output Stochastic Automata (IOSA), so that we can handle arbitrary probability distributions. Each state in the IOSA represents a system configuration, indicating which components are operational and which have failed. Transitions among states describe how the configuration changes when failures or repairs occur.

Dynamic fault trees may exhibit nondeterministic behaviour [7,14], for instance when two SPAREs have a single shared SBE: if all elements are failed, and the SBE is repaired first, the failure behaviour depends on which SPARE gets the SBE. Monte Carlo simulation cannot cope with nondeterminism. The theory from [8,19] overcomes this by imposing some mild syntactic conditions, to ensure that the IOSA semantics of an RFT is *weakly deterministic*. This means that all resolutions of nondeterministic choices lead to the same probability value. In particular (1) each BE must be connected to at most one SPARE gate, (2) BEs and SBEs connected to SPAREs are must not be connected to FDEPs, and (3) policies should be provided for RBOX and spare assignments. For full technical details the interested reader is referred to [19].

Fault Tree Analysis. An important goal in FTA is to compute relevant dependability metrics. A popular metrics is *system reliability*, which is the probability of observing no top level event before some mission time $T > 0$. This can be defined as $\mathrm{REL}_T = Prob\left(\forall_{t \in [0,T]} . X_t = 0\right)$, where X_t denotes the random variable that represents the state of the top event at time t, which takes the value 1 if there is a TLE, and 0 otherwise. System *unreliability* is $\mathrm{UNREL}_T = 1 - \mathrm{REL}_T$.

Minimal Cut Sets. Cut sets are a well known qualitative technique in FTA for static FTs. A *cut set* is a set of BEs whose joint failure will cause a TLE.

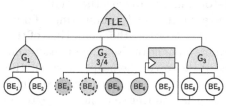

(a) An RFT without PANDs

Familiy	Minimal cut sets included
$\{\mathrm{MCS}_j\}$	$\{\mathrm{BE_1}\}$ $\{\mathrm{BE_2}\}$ $\{\mathrm{BE_7}\}$ $\{\mathrm{BE_8,BE_9}\}$ $\{\mathrm{BE_3,BE_4,BE_5}\}$ $\{\mathrm{BE_3,BE_5,BE_6}\}$ $\{\mathrm{BE_3,BE_4,BE_6}\}$ $\{\mathrm{BE_4,BE_5,BE_6}\}$
$\{\mathrm{MCS}_j\}_{<3}$	$\{\mathrm{BE_1}\}$ $\{\mathrm{BE_2}\}$ $\{\mathrm{BE_7}\}$ $\{\mathrm{BE_8,BE_9}\}$
$\{\mathrm{MCS}_j\}_{>\frac{1}{4}}$	$\{\mathrm{BE_2}\}$ $\{\mathrm{BE_3,BE_4,BE_5}\}$ $\{\mathrm{BE_3,BE_4,BE_6}\}$ $\{\mathrm{BE_3,BE_5,BE_6}\}$ $\{\mathrm{BE_4,BE_5,BE_6}\}$

(b) Minimal cut sets of Fig. 2a

Fig. 2. Fault trees & minimal cut sets

A *minimal cut set* (MCS) is a cut set of which no subset is a cut set. These concepts can be lifted to dynamic fault trees (and RFTs) in general, but this requires introducing an order to capture temporal dependencies, plus several other subtleties [14,25]. Nevertheless, RFTs as defined above rule out several issues raised by cut sets in DFTs, such as event simultaneity [14]. Furthermore, in this work we exclude order dependence by considering RFTs without PAND gates. This enables a conservative treatment of cut sets in RFTs, of which we give more details in Sect. 3.1.

For an illustration, Fig. 2b lists all minimal cut sets of the tree from Fig. 2a. We use the notation: $\{\mathrm{MCS}_j\}$ for the family of all minimal cut sets; $\{\mathrm{MCS}_j\}_{<N}$ for the subset of $\{\mathrm{MCS}_j\}$ that excludes cut sets with N or more BEs (called *pruning* of order N); $\{\mathrm{MCS}_j\}_{>\lambda}$ for the subset of $\{\mathrm{MCS}_j\}$ that excludes cut sets where the product of the failure rate of the BEs is $\leqslant \lambda \in \mathbb{R}_{>0}$. The latter is well defined iff all BEs and SBEs in the RFT have Markovian failure and dormancy distributions. To obtain $\{\mathrm{MCS}_j\}_{>\frac{1}{4}}$ in Fig. 2b, we make this the case with failure rates: $\frac{1}{4}$ for $\mathrm{BE_1}$ and $\mathrm{BE_7}$, $\frac{6}{20}$ for $\mathrm{BE_2}$, $\frac{2}{3}$ for $\{\mathrm{BE_i}\}_{i=3}^6$, and $\frac{1}{2}$ for $\mathrm{BE_8}$ and $\mathrm{BE_9}$.

Cut set pruning as in $\{\mathrm{MCS}_j\}_{<N}$ and $\{\mathrm{MCS}_j\}_{>\lambda}$ is a standard way to speed up FT analyses [28]. The goal is to ignore the most unlikely (and hard to compute) cut sets: pruning of order N assumes that the TLE will most likely occur by cut sets with less than N BEs; pruning by rate $\leqslant \lambda$ assumes that the TLE will occur first by cut sets where BEs have higher rates and thus fail faster. Choosing such N and λ to prune irrelevant MCS of a given tree depends on its structure and the BEs failure/dormancy/repair distributions.

2.2   Fault Tree Analysis via (Rare Event) Simulation

In this work, we analyse dependability metrics of RFTs using methods based on Monte Carlo simulation. This involves taking random samples from the (stochastic) IOSA model that underlies the RFT. More specifically, *Monte Carlo simulation* means the discrete-event simulation process used to generate failures and repairs of the (IOSA components that model the) BEs of the tree. As described in [3,16], this process begins at simulation time 0 when all basic elements are operational. The next failure time of all these BEs and SBEs is randomly sampled, according to their failure/dormancy distributions, and stored in a heap with the smallest time T_1 at the top. Then, simulation time advances until time T_1, simulating a failure of the corresponding component. As soon as this happens, the repair time of that component is sampled and stored in the events-time heap. Next, simulation time advances until the smallest next-event time at the top of the heap, T_2, simulating either another failure, or a repair of the broken component. This process continues until the predefined end-of-simulation time T. The resulting sequence of fail/repair events in times $T_1 < T_2 < \cdots < T_N < T$ is called a *simulation trace*. The mathematical definition of a compositional semantics for repairable DFTs that allows this approach is introduced in [20]; moreover, [3] formally defines simulation traces in such IOSA semantics.

A main advantage of this approach when compared to purely combinatorial analyses is the capability to deal with non-Markovian distributions. Sampling discrete (random) events is a straightforward and efficient process with today's scientific libraries and computer power. For instance, to estimate the unreliability of an RFT one can sample N independent traces from its IOSA semantics as described above. Then, an unbiased statistical estimator for $p = \text{UNREL}_T$ is the proportion of traces observing a TLE, $\hat{p}$ [16]. The statistical error of $\hat{p}$ can be quantified with two numbers δ and ε s.t. $\hat{p} \in [p - \varepsilon, p + \varepsilon]$ with probability at least δ. The interval $\hat{p} \pm \varepsilon$ is called a *confidence interval* (CI) with coefficient δ and precision 2ε. Such procedures scale linearly with the number of tree nodes and can handle non-Markovian failure and repair PDFs. However, they find a bottleneck to estimate *rare events*: i.e. if $p \approx 0$, then very few traces observe the TLE. Increasing the number of traces alleviates this problem, but even standard CI settings—where ε is relative to p—require sampling an unacceptable number of traces [23]. Rare event simulation techniques solve this specific problem.

RES techniques [23] increase the amount of traces that observe the rare event. In particular, *importance splitting* RES [17] is very flexible w.r.t. the probability distributions it can handle, which makes it a perfect candidate to analyse RFTs. Importance splitting can be efficiently deployed as long as the rare event γ can be described as a nested sequence of less-rare events $\gamma = \gamma_M \subsetneq \gamma_{M-1} \subsetneq \cdots \subsetneq \gamma_0$. This decomposition allows to study the conditional probabilities $p_k = Prob(\gamma_{k+1} \mid \gamma_k)$ separately, to then compute $p = Prob(\gamma) = \prod_{k=0}^{M-1} Prob(\gamma_{k+1} \mid \gamma_k)$. Moreover, importance splitting requires all conditional probabilities p_k to be much greater than p, so that estimating each p_k can be done efficiently with classical Monte Carlo (CMC).

For this, importance splitting defines the γ_k via an *importance function* $\mathcal{I} \colon S \to \mathbb{N}$, that assigns an *importance* to each state in the system. For us, a state $s \in S$ is a configuration of failed/operational BEs in a tree, where the state space S includes all possible combinations of BE failures. The higher the importance of a state s, the closer it is to the rare event γ_M. Event γ_k collects states with importance at least ℓ_k, for certain sequence of *threshold levels* $0 = \ell_0 < \ell_1 < \cdots < \ell_M$. Formally: $\gamma_k = \{s \in S \mid \mathcal{I}(s) \geqslant \ell_k\}$

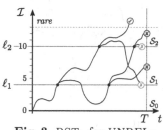

Fig. 3. RST$_2$ for UNREL$_T$

Importance splitting samples more (partial) traces from states with higher importance. Two well-known methods are Fixed Effort and RESTART. *Fixed Effort* [9] samples a predefined amount of traces in each region $S_k = \gamma_k \setminus \gamma_{k+1} = \{s \in S \mid \ell_{k+1} > \mathcal{I}(s) \geqslant \ell_k\}$. If the amount of sampled traces is the same in all regions, the *effort* $e \in \mathbb{N}$, we call this method FE$_e$. Thus, starting at γ_0, FE$_e$ first estimates the proportion of traces that reach γ_1: $p_0 = Prob(\gamma_1 \mid \gamma_0) = Prob(S_0)$. Next, from the states that reached γ_1 new traces are generated to estimate $p_1 = Prob(S_1)$, and so on until p_M. *RESTART* (RST [32,33]) is another algorithm that starts one trace in γ_0 and monitors the importance of the states visited. If the importance of the trace up-crosses threshold ℓ_1, the first state visited in S_1 is saved and the trace is cloned, aka *split*—see Fig. 3. This mechanism rewards traces that get closer to the rare event. Each clone then evolves independently, and if one up-crosses threshold ℓ_2 the splitting mechanism is repeated. Instead, if a state with importance below ℓ_1 is visited, the trace is *truncated*. This penalises traces that move away from the rare event. To avoid truncating all traces, the one that spawned the clones in region S_k can go below importance ℓ_k. To deploy an unbiased estimator for p, RESTART measures how much split was required to visit a rare state [32]. If the same amount of splitting is used throughout, we call this method RST$_e$, to mean that $e - 1$ clones are spawned when a simulation up-crosses a threshold ℓ_i.

3 RES Using Minimal Cut Sets

The effectiveness of importance splitting relies heavily on the choice of the importance function [17]. Traditionally, this function is given by domain and/or RES experts, requiring domain knowledge both in the application and in the simulation techniques. In this section we introduce a series of importance functions that can be automatically derived from systems described as fault trees.

3.1 MCS Re-writing of Trees

The initial observation is that a fault tree—without temporal requirements such as PAND gates—can be re-written as a disjunction of its minimal cut sets. This is a well-known fact: the key insight is that the structure of the resulting tree can be readily exploited to derive importance functions automatically.

More in detail, given a fault tree $\triangle$ one can build a tree $\triangle^*$ which is equivalent w.r.t. the MCS of $\triangle$. Essentially, $\triangle^*$ is a re-writing in disjunctive normal form (DNF) of the logical formula represented by $\triangle$. The TLE of $\triangle^*$ is an OR gate, the children of that OR are AND gates (or BEs), and the children of the ANDs are BEs. The first-level nodes of $\triangle^*$, i.e. the direct children of the OR, are the conjunctions of the DNF. If a conjunction has a single literal, the AND is omitted and the corresponding BE is a direct input of the OR. Thus, each AND (or first-level BE) in $\triangle^*$ stands for an MCS of $\triangle$.

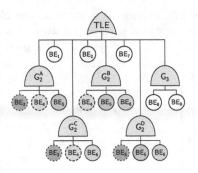

Fig. 4. MCS re-write of Fig. 2a

Figure 4 shows the result of applying this re-writing to the DFT from Fig. 2a. Although it is represented as a tree, note that the G_2^* gates in Fig. 4 share children: e.g. BE_4 and BE_5 are both children of G_2^A and G_2^B.

For general FTA the scope of this technique is limited. First and foremost, the set $\{MCS_j\}$ can be exponential in the size of the fault tree, e.g. when $\triangle$ has a conjunctive normal form structure. This is a general limitation of cut set analysis: in such cases the computation of all MCS can be very time/memory consuming, and pruning helps to alleviate the issue. Moreover, minimal cut sets are standard for the analysis of *static* fault trees. In *dynamic* fault trees, PAND gates introduce order dependencies that cannot be captured with MCS. Also, notions of simultaneity and causality of events must be considered to properly lift MCS for the general analysis of DFTs [14]. Note however that repairs do not affect MCS. Thus, in this work we consider the class of *repairable fault trees* (RFT) described in [20]—but excluding PAND gates.

In essence, RFTs are DFTs enriched with RBOX elements, where the propagation of events from children to parents is instantaneous. Potential sources of nondeterminism (e.g. an SBE claimed by two SPAREs) are proven weakly-deterministic, as long as the RFT adheres to the syntactic rules described in Sect. 2. Thus, SPARE gates are essentially ANDs. Moreover, FDEPs in RFTs are non-destructive: if a failed trigger is repaired, the BEs affected by the gate become *available* (not necessarily operational) once again [20]. This can be modelled with OR gates: in Fig. 2a, the FDEP and gate G_3 are equivalent to OR(BE_7, G_3). Therefore, an RFT without PANDs can be seen as a static fault tree whose BEs can be repaired. This means that the MCS re-write of an RFT as $\triangle^*$, gives a faithful description of the sources of top-level failures in the original tree $\triangle$.

To exploit this for the automation of RES analysis of fault trees, we combine this fact with the theory deployed in [3]. As explained in Sect. 2.2, the key ingredient to implement importance splitting is the importance function $\mathcal{I}$. [3] introduces a recursive construction for $\mathcal{I}$ based on the structure of the RFT $\triangle$, which begins from its BEs and ends in the top level gate. The essential contribution of the current work is to apply this same construction to the MCS re-write $\triangle^*$.

3.2   Importance Functions from Minimal Cut Sets

The compositional importance function of [3] is defined per gate (and BE) type. The key concept is that, in general, importance should reflect proximity to the rare event. For fault trees this means that *the importance of a gate should increase as the gate approaches its own failure*. Note that the type of a gate defines how, as its children fail, the gate approaches its own failure. This is used in [3] to define a local importance function for each gate, which assigns an importance to the gate based on its type and on the state of its children.

For instance, AND gates fail when all its children fail, so the importance of an AND should increase with the failure of every child. Thus, the local importance function of ANDs is a summation *of the importance* of its children. By the same argument, the importance of an OR is the max importance among its children. Basic events are the base case of this recursion: BEs and SBEs essentially have a binary state, failed or not,[1] which are assigned importance 1 and 0 resp.

In [3] this recursive construction starts from the leaves of the tree and ends in the top gate, thus deriving a function $\mathcal{I}_{\mathsf{FT}}$ that considers every single gate in the original FT $\triangle$. Instead, here we work on the MCS re-write $\triangle^*$, for which the three cases described above suffice. $\triangle^*$ consists of the top OR, potentially some ANDs, and the base BEs and SBEs: the importance function assigned to such tree is a max (OR) over the summation (ANDs) of every basic event in an MCS.

Table 1 gives the mathematical expression of this formula, which we denote $\mathcal{I}_{\mathsf{MCS}}$. Note that each AND of the MCS re-write $\triangle^*$ represents a minimal cut set of the original tree, viz. an element of $\{\mathrm{MCS}_j\}$. In the mathematical expressions of Table 1, BE_i stands for the elementary importance function described above, which takes the value 1 if the BE is failed and 0 otherwise.

We further consider pruned variants of $\mathcal{I}_{\mathsf{MCS}}$, that discard cut sets based on their cardinality ($\mathcal{I}_{\mathsf{MCS\text{-}P}}$) or, if BE failures are exponentially distributed, based on the product of the failure rates of the BEs in the cut set ($\mathcal{I}_{\mathsf{MCS\text{-}PR}}$). The only difference between these functions and $\mathcal{I}_{\mathsf{MCS}}$ is the range of the max, which reflects the pruning of some minimal cut sets.

Another concept introduced in [3] is *importance normalisation*. The intention is to level the importance values that a parent gate reads from its children. This has the following motivation: take a binary AND gate whose left child is an AND of 2 BEs, and whose right child is an AND of 6 BEs. The top AND fails iff both AND children fail. Thus, having *one* BE of the left AND fail, is just as important as having *three* BEs of the right AND fail, because in both cases one child of the top AND is half-failed. To achieve this, [3] divides the importance of the children of a gate by its maximum possible value—which corresponds to a failed child. In this way, the importance of a gate uses the "percentage of failure" of its children.

We also experiment with this concept: in Table 1, $\mathcal{I}_{\mathsf{MCS\text{-}N}}$ stands for the normalised version if $\mathcal{I}_{\mathsf{MCS}}$. Note that j_n is the number of children of an AND that represents an MCS in the original tree. The importance function of this AND is the summation if its children, all of which are BEs whose max importance is

---

[1] This is given more thorough semantics in [3] via an output function z_i.

Table 1. Importance functions for automatic RES in fault trees

Name	Expression	Description
$\mathcal{I}_{\mathsf{FT}}$	[3, Table 2]	Based on the full FT structure, this importance function considers all nodes recursively, defining local functions for BEs and moving up until the TLE
$\mathcal{I}_{\mathsf{MCS}}$	$\displaystyle\max_{\{\mathsf{BE}_1,\ldots,\mathsf{BE}_{j_n}\}\in\{\mathrm{MCS}_j\}}\left\{\sum_{i=1}^{j_n}\mathsf{BE}_i\right\}$	For each MCS of the tree, $\mathcal{I}_{\mathsf{MCS}}$ counts the number of BEs that have failed. The importance of the current state of the tree is the max among these counts
$\mathcal{I}_{\mathsf{MCS\text{-}P}}$	$\displaystyle\max_{\{\mathsf{BE}_1,\ldots,\mathsf{BE}_{j_n}\}\in\{\mathrm{MCS}_j\}_{<N}}\left\{\sum_{i=1}^{j_n}\mathsf{BE}_i\right\}$	$\mathcal{I}_{\mathsf{MCS\text{-}P}}$ operates similarly to function $\mathcal{I}_{\mathsf{MCS}}$ above, but here the max ranges over a *pruned* set of MCS, discarding cut sets with N or more BEs
$\mathcal{I}_{\mathsf{MCS\text{-}PR}}$	$\displaystyle\max_{\{\mathsf{BE}_1,\ldots,\mathsf{BE}_{j_n}\}\in\{\mathrm{MCS}_j\}_{>\lambda}}\left\{\sum_{i=1}^{j_n}\mathsf{BE}_i\right\}$	Similar to $\mathcal{I}_{\mathsf{MCS\text{-}P}}$ but using the failure *rates* for pruning, $\mathcal{I}_{\mathsf{MCS\text{-}PR}}$ considers only MCS where the product of the failure rate of all BEs is greater than λ
$\mathcal{I}_{\mathsf{MCS\text{-}N}}$	$\displaystyle\max_{\{\mathsf{BE}_1,\ldots,\mathsf{BE}_{j_n}\}\in\{\mathrm{MCS}_j\}}\left\{\mathrm{lcm}\cdot\sum_{i=1}^{j_n}\frac{\mathsf{BE}_i}{j_n}\right\}$	$\mathcal{I}_{\mathsf{MCS\text{-}N}}$ is a normalised version of $\mathcal{I}_{\mathsf{MCS}}$ (see *normalisation of the importance functions* in [3]) based on the number of BEs of each cut set in $\{\mathrm{MCS}_j\}$

- $\mathsf{BE}_i = 1$ if the i-th BE is in a failed state, and $\mathsf{BE}_i = 0$ otherwise.
- lcm is the least common multiple of the cardinality of every MCS in range.

1. By dividing this summation by its max possible value, j_n, we compute the percentage of failure of the AND. The scaling factor lcm ensures that the resulting value is an integer, as required by our tooling framework. Finally, although omitted in Table 1, we further define the functions $\mathcal{I}_{\mathsf{MCS\text{-}P\text{-}N}}$ and $\mathcal{I}_{\mathsf{MCS\text{-}PR\text{-}N}}$ as the normalised versions of the functions $\mathcal{I}_{\mathsf{MCS\text{-}P}}$ and $\mathcal{I}_{\mathsf{MCS\text{-}PR}}$.

Tool Automation. The theory described in this section is piggybacked in the tool chain of [3], where RFTs are input in an extended version of the Galileo textual format [26,27]. A Java converter builds its IOSA semantics following [20], as well as the compositional importance function of [3]. Model and function are then fed to the FIG tool, which implements various flavours of (importance splitting) RES. FIG output is a confidence interval that estimates the answer to a quantitative user query, such as system reliability for a given time horizon. Minimal cut sets, required to implement the importance functions in Table 1 other than $\mathcal{I}_{\mathsf{FT}}$, can be computed using the classical top-down algorithms; more efficient methods employ Binary Decision Diagrams [18, 25].

4   Empirical Evaluation

To assess the efficiency of our approach, we analyse the reliability of a classic benchmark in FTA: the Hypothetical Example Computer System (HECS [28]).

4.1   Case Study and Experimental Setting

We study a parameterised version of HECS deployed in [3]. The parameter p in HECS$_p$ determines the number of spare processors and parallel buses: HECS$_p$ features p spare processors (PS$_i$) and $2p$ buses (B$_j$). Moreover, the system analysed in [3] is repairable and defines one independent RBOX per subsystem (Memory, Interface, Bus, and Processor). Figure 5 shows HECS$_3$. The full DFT described in (extended) Galileo can be found in Appendix A.

Note that the repair times of BEs are given by PDFs with non-Markovian distributions, but their failure (and dormant-failure) times are all exponential. This allows us to experiment with the pruned importance functions $\mathcal{I}_{\mathsf{MCS\text{-}P}}$ and $\mathcal{I}_{\mathsf{MCS\text{-}PR}}$. Furthermore HECS has cold spares: the SBEs PS$_i$ must not fail while inactive. To encode this and analyse REL$_T$ in our tool chain, we select a dormant-failure time beyond T for the PS$_i$, e.g. the dormancy distribution Dirac($T + \varepsilon$).

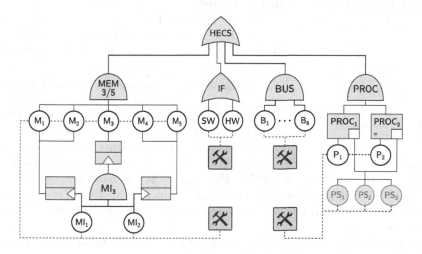

Fig. 5. Repairable DFT for the HECS$_3$ case study

As in [3] we estimate UNREL$_{1000}$, hereby called φ. We analyse the systems $\{\mathrm{HECS}_p\}_{p=3}^5$ to measure how, as p grows and the corresponding value of φ

decreases, RES analysis can yield increasingly narrower CIs for a fixed simulation time budget of 25 min. We also consider variants of HECS without repairs for which we estimate UNREL_{750}, hereby called ψ.

On the one hand we compare RES vs. CMC, and show that classical Monte Carlo simulation cannot yield useful results when $\varphi < 2.0 \times 10^{-6}$. On the other hand we compare the efficiency of the functions presented in Table 1. For this, on each model HECS_p and for different RES algorithms, we estimate φ, ψ with FIG running RES for 25 min. The best importance functions are those with which FIG can implement RES and produce the narrowest confidence intervals. Thus, the goal is to identify whether any importance function can consistently produce the narrowest CIs, with most RES algorithms, in all HECS_p models.

Importance functions $\mathcal{I}_{\text{MCS-P}}$ and $\mathcal{I}_{\text{MCS-PR}}$ (and their normalised versions) require a pruning criterion. We selected $N = 4$ for the former and $\lambda = 1 \times 18^{-18}$ for the latter. Thus, for all models, $\mathcal{I}_{\text{MCS-P}}$ discards the cut sets corresponding to the Bus and Processor subsystems. Instead, $\mathcal{I}_{\text{MCS-PR}}$ discards all cut sets corresponding to the Memory subsystem (with the sole exception of $\{\text{MI}_1, \text{MI}_2\}$) for HECS_3 and HECS_4. For HECS_5, $\mathcal{I}_{\text{MCS-PR}}$ also discards the cut set of Processors. All functions for HECS_3 are shown in Appendix B.

4.2 Results and Discussion

Figure 7 shows the results of our experiments on HECS without repairs, where we estimated $\psi = \text{UNREL}_{750}$. Figure 8 shows the results for HECS with repairs, where we estimated $\varphi = \text{UNREL}_{1000}$. We ran FIG on a computer with a CPU Intel® Xeon® E7-8890 v4 @ 2.20 GHz and 2 TB of RAM DDR4 @ 1866 MHz, running Linux x64 (Ubuntu, kernel 3.13.0-168).

Fig. 6. Color legend of bar plots

We use whisker-bar plots to show the width of the 95% CIs estimated for each instance. An *instance* is a combination of a RES algorithm, a model, and an importance function—e.g. $\text{FE}_{e=8}$, HECS_3, and $\mathcal{I}_{\text{MCS}}$—represented in Figs. 7 and 8 by one bar in one plot. Each instance was repeated 13 times. The height of a bar represents the resulting average CI width: achieved by that algorithm, in that model, via that importance function (we removed outliers using a Z-score$_{m=2}$ [11]). The whiskers on top of the bar represent the variance of these widths. The number at the base of a bar indicates how many out of the 13 repetitions of that instance yielded valid results—if no rare event is observed, FIG outputs the "null CI" $[0, 0]$ to indicate an invalid estimation.

We use the same colour of bar-instance to identify the importance functions across plots. The colour legend is shown in Fig. 6, where CMC stands for classical Monte Carlo (i.e. not an importance function), FT stands for the $\mathcal{I}_{\text{FT}}$ importance function from [3], MCS stands for $\mathcal{I}_{\text{MCS}}$ from Table 1, and so on. Therefore, to assess an importance function, we must see how each colour fared in the following orthogonal criteria: *bar height*, where shorter means narrower CIs and is thus better, *whisker length*, where shorter means less variance and is thus better, and *validity count*, where 13 is best and 0 (or absence of a bar) is worst.

Functions $\mathcal{I}_{\text{MCS-P}}$ and $\mathcal{I}_{\text{MCS-P-N}}$ are not shown in Figs. 7 and 8 because they only yielded null CIs. This was expected: the Processors cut set is a main cause of TLEs due to the failure rates involved—see Code 1 in Appendix A. Pruning that cut set makes importance insensitive to the relevant failures of the system. Thus, cloning and truncating simulation traces is a futile overhead, which makes RES fare even worse than CMC. This also explains why $\mathcal{I}_{\text{MCS-PR}}$ is competitive for HECS$_{3,4}$ but never for HECS$_5$, where it prunes the Processors cut sets.

Regarding CMC, Fig. 7 shows that RES does not pay off in general to estimate metrics like ψ when these are above 2×10^{-6}. This changes in Fig. 8, where CMC lost to almost every RES implementation for HECS$_4$, and for HECS$_5$ (where $\varphi \approx 3 \times 10^{-7}$) it could not produce CIs narrower than 3×10^{-6}, thus including 0.

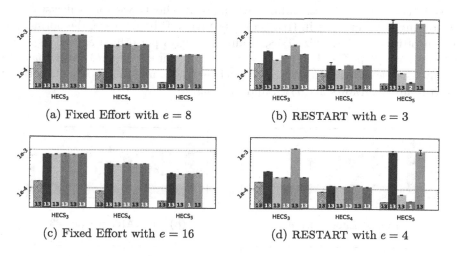

(a) Fixed Effort with $e = 8$ (b) RESTART with $e = 3$

(c) Fixed Effort with $e = 16$ (d) RESTART with $e = 4$

Fig. 7. CI precision for UNREL$_{750}$ of HECS without repairs: four RES algorithms

Going back to the results for HECS without repairs (Fig. 7) we see that CMC consistently outperforms RES. Here we estimated $\psi = \text{UNREL}_{750}$ instead of UNREL$_{1000}$. Our importance functions are oblivious to the simulation time, and therefore a smaller time horizon hinders importance splitting w.r.t. CMC. This is because simulation runs are cloned closer to the (truncating) time limit, incurring computation overhead that may yield no rare event observations. Automatic importance functions sensitive to simulation time are an interesting line of research: we addressed this again in the conclusions. On the other hand, our method performs best when operating with large time horizons, such that the rarity of UNREL$_T$ is only lightly influenced by T^2.

---

[2] This complements standard model checking, where time-bounded properties with large time bounds entail memory problems [25].

Also remarkable is the fact that $\mathcal{I}_{FT}$ and $\mathcal{I}_{MCS-N}$ performed very bad for RST_3 and RST_4 in $HECS_5$ without repairs—Figs. 7b and d. We repeated our experiments and the same behaviour was observed. For these two cases, it was found that the expression of the importance functions had large scaling factors (lcm in Table 1) due to importance normalisation, namely 210. For other functions this factor ranges from 2 to 30. We suspect that the variability of importance during RES resulted in over-splitting and truncation, to which RESTART is more sensitive than Fixed Effort. This is also observed (to a lesser degree) in $HECS_3$, where again $\mathcal{I}_{FT}$ and $\mathcal{I}_{MCS-N}$ have the largest scaling factor (30)—see Table 2.

Focusing now in Fig. 8 and to our surprise, we see that $\mathcal{I}_{MCS}$ fared quite well, many times even outperforming $\mathcal{I}_{FT}$—see e.g. Fig. 8b and d, in particular for $HECS_5$. We had expected that the absence of importance normalisation would unbalance importance computations, making RES implementations from $\mathcal{I}_{MCS}$ loose on performance, which was clearly not the case. This however could be a result that most system failures originate in the Processors subsystem, so considering other cut sets in HECS may not pay off. In any case, the normalised version of this function, viz. $\mathcal{I}_{MCS-N}$, almost always performed as well as $\mathcal{I}_{MCS}$, and similarly with $\mathcal{I}_{FT}$. For RFTs with several (three or more) MCS that can equally likely lead to a TLE, functions such as $\mathcal{I}_{MCS-N}$ and $\mathcal{I}_{FT}$ should outperform un-normalised variants like $\mathcal{I}_{MCS}$ and $\mathcal{I}_{MCS-PR}$.

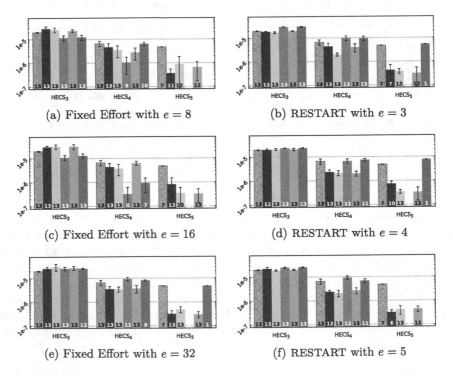

(a) Fixed Effort with $e = 8$

(b) RESTART with $e = 3$

(c) Fixed Effort with $e = 16$

(d) RESTART with $e = 4$

(e) Fixed Effort with $e = 32$

(f) RESTART with $e = 5$

Fig. 8. CI precision for $UNREL_{1000}$ of HECS with repairs: six RES algorithms

As mentioned in Sect. 1, $\mathcal{I}_{MCS}$ is equivalent to the importance function $\Phi(t)$ from [30], essentially counting the number of failed BEs in the MCS with the largest such number. A simpler approach would be to count the number of failed elements in the tree, i.e. disregarding cut sets. This function was named AC_1 in [5], and applied to a small tree representing a database system. There, the function AC_4 represents what we here call $\mathcal{I}_{MCS}$. Both functions AC_1 and AC_4 performed similarly, which was explained by the balanced nature of the RFT: the failure of any one branch (cut set) was similar to the rest. This was further corroborated in [2] with another system representing an oil-refinery pipeline.

A final insight is given by the near absence of valid results by $\mathcal{I}_{MCS-PR-N}$ for $HECS_5$, most likely due to its pruning of the Processors cut set. This suggests that cut set pruning is non-trivial for relatively complex repairable fault trees, even when the failure of all BEs is given in terms of exponential rates.

5   Conclusions

In this work we have defined importance functions for RES analysis of fault trees. These functions can be automatically derived from the tree structure, by re-writing the tree as a disjunction of its minimal cut sets. This can be applied to repairable dynamic fault trees without PAND gates, that are given semantics as IOSA. Our method exploits a simple concept, and yet we have demonstrated that it can outperform classical Monte Carlo analysis, and even compete against other automatically derived importance functions for RES analysis of RFTs.

Our empirical evaluation was sound yet arguably modest in size. HECS is a classical FTA benchmark that features several gates an heterogeneous sub-tree structures, but it remains a single case study. It is important to exercise our techniques in further systems, e.g. to determine whether mildly-balanced trees (where most MCS have roughly similar contributions to the TLE) makes a distinction between $\mathcal{I}_{MCS}$ and its normalised counterpart $\mathcal{I}_{MCS-N}$.

An interesting line of future research would be to weigh the cut sets based on their failure probability or failure rates. Moreover, the study of REL_{750} for HECS without repairs raised the issue of time-awareness for importance computation. If the rarity of the dependability metric is based on the shortness of the time horizon, our approach will most likely not perform well, since it is oblivious to this dimension. Penalising importance based on the remaining time may be a way to approach this issue.

A   Galileo of the $HECS_3$ DFT

```
1  toplevel "HECS";
2  "HECS" or "IF" "MEM" "BUS" "PROC";
3
4  "IF" or "SW" "HW";
5  "SW"  lambda=4.5e-12  EXT_repairPDF=uniform(28,56);
6  "HW"  lambda=1.0e-10  EXT_repairPDF=uniform(28,56);
7
```

```
 8  "MEM" 3of5 "M1" "M2" "M3" "M4" "M5";
 9  "MEM1" fdep "MI1" "M1" "M2";
10  "MEM2" fdep "MI2" "M4" "M5";
11  "MEM3" fdep "MI3" "M3";
12  "MI3" and "MI1" "MI2";
13  "MI2" lambda=5.0e-9  EXT_repairPDF=uniform(21,28);
14  "MI1" lambda=5.0e-9  EXT_repairPDF=uniform(21,28);
15  "M1"  lambda=6.0e-8  EXT_repairPDF=uniform(21,28);
16  "M2"  lambda=6.0e-8  EXT_repairPDF=uniform(21,28);
17  "M3"  lambda=6.0e-8  EXT_repairPDF=uniform(21,28);
18  "M4"  lambda=6.0e-8  EXT_repairPDF=uniform(21,28);
19  "M5"  lambda=6.0e-8  EXT_repairPDF=uniform(21,28);
20
21  "BUS" and "B1" "B2" "B3" "B4" "B5" "B6";
22  "B1"  lambda=8.7e-4  EXT_repairPDF=lognormal(4.45,0.24);
23  "B2"  lambda=8.7e-4  EXT_repairPDF=lognormal(4.45,0.24);
24  "B3"  lambda=8.7e-4  EXT_repairPDF=lognormal(4.45,0.24);
25  "B4"  lambda=8.7e-4  EXT_repairPDF=lognormal(4.45,0.24);
26  "B5"  lambda=8.7e-4  EXT_repairPDF=lognormal(4.45,0.24);
27  "B6"  lambda=8.7e-4  EXT_repairPDF=lognormal(4.45,0.24);
28
29  "PROC" and "PROC1" "PROC2";
30  "PROC1" wsp "P1" "PS1" "PS2" "PS3";
31  "PROC2" wsp "P2" "PS1" "PS2" "PS3";
32  "P1"  lambda=1.0e-3                    EXT_repairPDF=lognormal(4.45,0.24);
33  "P2"  lambda=1.0e-3                    EXT_repairPDF=lognormal(4.45,0.24);
34  "PS1" lambda=1.5e-3 EXT_dormPDF=dirac(1e4) EXT_repairPDF=lognormal(4.45,0.24);
35  "PS2" lambda=1.5e-3 EXT_dormPDF=dirac(1e4) EXT_repairPDF=lognormal(4.45,0.24);
36  "PS3" lambda=1.5e-3 EXT_dormPDF=dirac(1e4) EXT_repairPDF=lognormal(4.45,0.24);
37
38  "RB_I" repairbox_priority "HW" "SW";
39  "RB_M" repairbox_priority "MI1" "MI2" "M1" "M2" "M3" "M4" "M5";
40  "RB_B" repairbox_priority "B1" "B2" "B3" "B4" "B5" "B6";
41  "RB_P" repairbox_priority "P1" "P2" "PS1" "PS2" "PS3";
```

Code 1. Description of HECS$_3$ in (extended) Galileo

B   Importance Functions Used for HECS Experiments

In Table 2 we give the importance functions used in Sect. 4, for experimentation with the case study HECS$_3$, which are oblivious of repairs. The arithmetic expressions use the names of the IOSA modules that give semantics to the BEs of the DFT. For instance nodes SW, HW, MI1, and MI2, are all BEs. In the IOSA semantics these BEs correspond to modules named BE_0, BE_1, BE_3, and BE_8 resp. Since the $\{\text{MCS}_j\}$ family of HECS$_3$ includes $\{\text{SW}\}$, $\{\text{HW}\}$, and $\{\text{MI1}, \text{MI2}\}$, therefore in Table 2 the max of function $\mathcal{I}_{\mathsf{MCS}}$ ranges (among others) over the following three summations: BE_0, BE_1, and BE_3+BE_8.

We highlight that the importance function $\mathcal{I}_{\mathsf{FT}}$ from [3] is more complex, but not necessarily larger than the functions introduced in the current work. This is mainly a consequence of the VOT gate in the Memory subsystem, a 3of5, which yields 10 minimal cut sets. The FDEPs give even further TLE possibilities. Indeed, from the 21 minimal cut sets of HECS, 17 come from failure combinations in the Memory subsystem.

Table 2. Importance functions used for HECS$_3$

IFUN	Expression in terms of the IOSA semantic model

$\mathcal{I}_{\mathsf{FT}}$	`max(30*(max(BE_0,BE_1)),5*(summax(3,2*(max(BE_3,BE_4)),2*(max(BE_3,BE_6)),max(BE_3+`
	`BE_8,2*(BE_10)),2*(max(BE_8,BE_12)),2*(max(BE_8,BE_14)))),5*(BE_17+BE_18+BE_19+BE_20`
	`+BE_21+BE_22),3*(max(BE_24+BE_25+BE_29+BE_31,(5.0*(SPARE_26==9?1:0)))+max(BE_33+`
	`BE_25+BE_29+BE_31,(5.0*(SPARE_27==9?1:0)))));0;30`

$\mathcal{I}_{\mathsf{MCS}}$	`max(BE_0,BE_1,BE_4+BE_6+BE_10,BE_4+BE_6+BE_12,BE_4+BE_6+BE_14,BE_4+BE_10+BE_12,BE_4`
	`+BE_10+BE_14,BE_4+BE_12+BE_14,BE_6+BE_10+BE_12,BE_6+BE_10+BE_14,BE_6+BE_12+BE_14,`
	`BE_10+BE_12+BE_14,BE_3+BE_10,BE_3+BE_12,BE_3+BE_14,BE_8+BE_4,BE_8+BE_6,BE_8+BE_10,`
	`BE_3+BE_8,BE_24+BE_33+BE_25+BE_29+BE_31,BE_17+BE_18+BE_19+BE_20+BE_21+BE_22);0;6`

$\mathcal{I}_{\mathsf{MCS\text{-}PR}}$	`max(BE_0,BE_1,BE_3+BE_10,BE_3+BE_12,BE_3+BE_14,BE_8+BE_4,BE_8+BE_6,BE_8+BE_10,BE_3+` `BE_8,BE_24+BE_33+BE_25+BE_29+BE_31);0;5`

$\mathcal{I}_{\mathsf{MCS\text{-}N}}$	`max(30*(BE_0),30*(BE_1),10*(BE_4+BE_6+BE_10),10*(BE_4+BE_6+BE_12),10*(BE_4+BE_6+`
	`BE_14),10*(BE_4+BE_10+BE_12),10*(BE_4+BE_10+BE_14),10*(BE_4+BE_12+BE_14),10*(BE_6+`
	`BE_10+BE_12),10*(BE_6+BE_10+BE_14),10*(BE_6+BE_12+BE_14),10*(BE_10+BE_12+BE_14),15*(`
	`BE_3+BE_10),15*(BE_3+BE_12),15*(BE_3+BE_14),15*(BE_8+BE_4),15*(BE_8+BE_6),15*(BE_8+`
	`BE_10),15*(BE_3+BE_8),6*(BE_24+BE_33+BE_25+BE_29+BE_31),5*(BE_17+BE_18+BE_19+BE_20+`
	`BE_21+BE_22));0;30`

$\mathcal{I}_{\mathsf{MCS\text{-}PR\text{-}N}}$	`max(10*(BE_0),10*(BE_1),5*(BE_3+BE_10),5*(BE_3+BE_12),5*(BE_3+BE_14),5*(BE_8+BE_4),5` `*(BE_8+BE_6),5*(BE_8+BE_10),5*(BE_3+BE_8),2*(BE_24+BE_33+BE_25+BE_29+BE_31));0;10`

References

1. Bayes, A.J.: Statistical techniques for simulation models. Aust. Comput. J. **2**(4), 180–184 (1970)
2. Budde, C.E.: Automation of importance splitting techniques for rare event simulation. Ph.D. thesis, Universidad Nacional de Córdoba, Córdoba, Argentina (2017)
3. Budde, C.E., Biagi, M., Monti, R.E., D'Argenio, P.R., Stoelinga, M.: Rare event simulation for non-Markovian repairable fault trees. In: TACAS 2020 (to appear)
4. Budde, C.E., D'Argenio, P.R., Hermanns, H.: Rare event simulation with fully automated importance splitting. In: Beltrán, M., Knottenbelt, W., Bradley, J. (eds.) EPEW 2015. LNCS, vol. 9272, pp. 275–290. Springer, Cham (2015). https://doi.org/10.1007/978-3-319-23267-6_18
5. Budde, C.E., D'Argenio, P.R., Monti, R.E.: Compositional construction of importance functions in fully automated importance splitting. In: VALUETOOLS. ICST (2016). https://doi.org/10.4108/eai.25-10-2016.2266501
6. Cérou, F., Del Moral, P., Furon, T., Guyader, A.: Sequential Monte Carlo for rare event estimation. Stat. Comput. **22**(3), 795–808 (2012). https://doi.org/10.1007/s11222-011-9231-6
7. Crouzen, P., Boudali, H., Stoelinga, M.: Dynamic fault tree analysis using input/output interactive Markov chains. In: DSN 2007, pp. 708–717 (2007). https://doi.org/10.1109/DSN.2007.37
8. D'Argenio, P.R., Monti, R.E.: Input/output stochastic automata with urgency: confluence and weak determinism. In: Fischer, B., Uustalu, T. (eds.) ICTAC 2018. LNCS, vol. 11187, pp. 132–152. Springer, Cham (2018). https://doi.org/10.1007/978-3-030-02508-3_8
9. Garvels, M.J.J.: The splitting method in rare event simulation. Ph.D. thesis, University of Twente, Enschede, The Netherlands (2000)

10. Heidelberger, P.: Fast simulation of rare events in queueing and reliability models. ACM Trans. Model. Comput. Simul. **5**(1), 43–85 (1995). https://doi.org/10.1145/203091.203094
11. Iglewicz, B., Hoaglin, D.: How to Detect and Handle Outliers. ASQC Basic References in Quality Control. ASQC Quality Press, Milwaukee (1993)
12. Jegourel, C., Legay, A., Sedwards, S.: Importance splitting for statistical model checking rare properties. In: Sharygina, N., Veith, H. (eds.) CAV 2013. LNCS, vol. 8044, pp. 576–591. Springer, Heidelberg (2013). https://doi.org/10.1007/978-3-642-39799-8_38
13. Jégourel, C., Legay, A., Sedwards, S., Traonouez, L.M.: Distributed verification of rare properties using importance splitting observers. In: ECEASST, vol. 72 (2015). https://doi.org/10.14279/tuj.eceasst.72.1024
14. Junges, S., Guck, D., Katoen, J., Stoelinga, M.: Uncovering dynamic fault trees. In: DSN 2016, pp. 299–310. IEEE (2016). https://doi.org/10.1109/DSN.2016.35
15. Kahn, H., Harris, T.E.: Estimation of particle transmission by random sampling. Natl. Bur. Stand. Appl. Math. Ser. **12**, 27–30 (1951)
16. Law, A.M.: Simulation Modeling and Analysis. McGraw-Hill Education, New York (2014)
17. L'Ecuyer, P., Le Gland, F., Lezaud, P., Tuffin, B.: Splitting techniques. In: Rubino and Tuffin [24], pp. 39–61. https://doi.org/10.1002/9780470745403.ch3
18. Lee, W., Grosh, D., Tillman, F., Lie, C.: Fault tree analysis, methods, and applications–a review. IEEE Trans. Reliab. **R–34**(3), 194–203 (1985). https://doi.org/10.1109/TR.1985.5222114
19. Monti, R.E.: Stochastic automata for fault tolerant concurrent systems. Ph.D. thesis, Universidad Nacional de Córdoba, Argentina (2018)
20. Monti, R.E., D'Argenio, P.R., Budde, C.E.: A compositional semantics for repairable fault trees with general distributions. arXiv e-prints arXiv:1910.10507 (2019)
21. Nicola, V.F., Shahabuddin, P., Nakayama, M.K.: Techniques for fast simulation of models of highly dependable systems. IEEE Trans. Reliab. **50**(3), 246–264 (2001). https://doi.org/10.1109/24.974122
22. Raiteri, D., Iacono, M., Franceschinis, G., Vittorini, V.: Repairable fault tree for the automatic evaluation of repair policies. In: DSN 2004, pp. 659–668 (2004). https://doi.org/10.1109/DSN.2004.1311936
23. Rubino, G., Tuffin, B.: Introduction to rare event simulation. In: Rubino and Tuffin [24], pp. 1–13. https://doi.org/10.1002/9780470745403.ch1
24. Rubino, G., Tuffin, B. (eds.): Rare Event Simulation Using Monte Carlo Methods. Wiley, New York (2009). https://doi.org/10.1002/9780470745403
25. Ruijters, E., Stoelinga, M.: Fault tree analysis: a survey of the state-of-the-art in modeling, analysis and tools. Comput. Sci. Rev. **15–16**, 29–62 (2015). https://doi.org/10.1016/j.cosrev.2015.03.001
26. Sullivan, K., Dugan, J.: Galileo user's manual & design overview (1998). v2.1-alpha. https://www.cse.msu.edu/~cse870/Materials/FaultTolerant/manual-galileo.htm
27. Sullivan, K., Dugan, J., Coppit, D.: The Galileo fault tree analysis tool. In: 29th Annual International Symposium on Fault-Tolerant Computing (Cat. No. 99CB36352), pp. 232–235 (1999). https://doi.org/10.1109/FTCS.1999.781056
28. Vesely, W., Stamatelatos, M., Dugan, J., Fragola, J., Minarick, J., Railsback, J.: Fault tree handbook with aerospace applications. NASA Office of Safety and Mission Assurance, version 1.1 (2002)
29. Villén-Altamirano, J.: RESTART method for the case where rare events can occur in retrials from any threshold. Int. J. Electron. Commun. **52**, 183–189 (1998)

30. Villén-Altamirano, J.: Importance functions for RESTART simulation of highly-dependable systems. Simulation **83**(12), 821–828 (2007). https://doi.org/10.1177/0037549707081257
31. Villén-Altamirano, J.: RESTART vs splitting: a comparative study. Perform. Eval. **121–122**, 38–47 (2018). https://doi.org/10.1016/j.peva.2018.02.002
32. Villén-Altamirano, M., Martínez-Marrón, A., Gamo, J., Fernández-Cuesta, F.: Enhancement of the accelerated simulation method RESTART by considering multiple thresholds. In: Proceedings of the 14th International Teletraffic Congress. Teletraffic Science and Engineering, vol. 1, pp. 797–810. Elsevier (1994). https://doi.org/10.1016/B978-0-444-82031-0.50084-6
33. Villén-Altamirano, M., Villén-Altamirano, J.: RESTART: a method for accelerating rare event simulations. In: Queueing, Performance and Control in ATM (ITC-13), pp. 71–76. Elsevier (1991)

Author Index

Printed in the United States
By Bookmasters